June 20, 2013
Seattle, Washington, USA

**Association for
Computing Machinery**

Advancing Computing as a Science & Profession

ISMM '13

Proceedings of the ACM SIGPLAN
International Symposium on Memory Management

Sponsored by:
ACM SIGPLAN

Supported by:
IBM Research, Microsoft Research, and Oracle Labs

**Association for
Computing Machinery**

Advancing Computing as a Science & Profession

The Association for Computing Machinery
2 Penn Plaza, Suite 701
New York, New York 10121-0701

Notice to Past Authors of ACM-Published Articles
ACM intends to create a complete electronic archive of all articles and/or other material previously published by ACM. If you have written a work that has been previously published by ACM in any journal or conference proceedings prior to 1978, or any SIG Newsletter at any time, and you do NOT want this work to appear in the ACM Digital Library, please inform permissions@acm.org, stating the title of the work, the author(s), and where and when published.

ISBN: 978-1-4503-2100-6

Additional copies may be ordered prepaid from:

ACM Order Department
PO Box 30777
New York, NY 10087-0777, USA

Phone: 1-800-342-6626 (USA and Canada)
+1-212-626-0500 (Global)
Fax: +1-212-944-1318
E-mail: acmhelp@acm.org
Hours of Operation: 8:30 am – 4:30 pm ET

ACM Order Number: 565132

Printed in the USA

Welcome

It is with great pleasure that we welcome you to the ACM SIGPLAN 2013 International Symposium on Memory Management (ISMM'13). This year continues ISMM's tradition as the top venue for presenting research results on memory management.

The eleven papers appearing in these proceedings cover diverse and interesting aspects of memory management. A double-blind reviewing system was used, and the Program Committee met in person to facilitate thorough discussion of the papers. In addition to three reviews by Program Committee members, each paper received one review by a member of the External Review Committee, which increased the range and depth of reviewer expertise. Authors were provided an opportunity to submit rebuttal responses to initial reviews, which helped ensure that decisions were not based on faulty interpretations. Review Committee members were allowed to be authors of submitted papers. Program Committee members were allowed to submit papers, but such submissions are held to a higher standard; no such papers were submitted this year.

Putting together ISMM'13 was a community effort. First of all, we thank all of the authors who submitted papers to ISMM. The Program and Review Committees did an extraordinary job in a very short amount of time, and the Steering Committee provided valuable insight and guidance. ISMM was collocated with PLDI, and we thank the PLDI organizers for handling all local arrangements issues, and making the General Chair's job much easier. We thank Oracle, IBM Research, and Microsoft Research for generously providing financial support for ISMM, and allowing us to continue to subsidize student registration.

We hope that you will find the ISMM'13 program interesting and thought provoking and that the symposium will provide you with an opportunity to share ideas with other researchers and practitioners from institutions around the world.

Erez Petrank
ISMM'13 Program Chair
Technion
Haifa, Israel

Perry Cheng
ISMM'13 General Chair
IBM Research
Cambridge, MA, USA

Table of Contents

Keynote Address
Session Chair: Erez Petrank *(Technion)*

Session: Garbage Collection, Runtime, & Cache Management
Session Chair: Michael D. Bond *(Ohio State University)*

Session: Debugging & Benchmarking
Session Chair: Eliot B. Moss *(University of Massachusetts, Amherst)*

Session: Analysis, Design, & Tools
Session Chair: David L. Detlefs *(Google)*

ISMM 2013 Conference Organization

General Chair: Perry S. Cheng *(IBM Research, USA)*

Program Chair: Erez Petrank *(Technion, Israel)*

Publicity Chair: Jeremy Singer *(University of Glasgow, Scotland)*

Steering Committee: David F. Bacon *(IBM Research, USA)*
Hans Boehm *(HP Labs, USA)*
Perry S. Cheng *(IBM Research, USA)*
Hillel Kolodner *(IBM Research, Israel)*
Doug Lea *(SUNY Oswego, USA)*
Vechev Martin *(ETH, Switzerland)*
Kathryn McKinley *(Microsoft Research, USA)*
Erez Petrank *(Technion, Israel)*
Guy Steele *(Oracle Labs, USA)*
Jan Vitek *(Purdue University, USA)*

Program Committee: Mike Bond *(Ohio State University, USA)*
Dave Detlefs *(Google, USA)*
David Grove *(IBM Research, USA)*
Tim Harris *(Oracle Labs, UK)*
Mark Marron *(Microsoft Research, USA)*
Matthias Meyer *(University of Stuttgart, Germany)*
Onur Mutlu *(Carnegie Mellon University, USA)*
Michael Philippsen *(University of Erlangen-Nuremberg, Germany)*
Jennifer Sartor *(Ghent University, Belgium)*
Fridtjof Siebert *(Aicas, Germany)*
Guy Steele *(Oracle Labs, USA)*
Bjarne Steensgaard *(Microsoft, USA)*

External Review Committee: Elvira Albert *(Complutense University of Madrid, Spain)*
Daniel Frampton *(Microsoft, USA)*
Sam Guyer *(Tuft University, USA)*
Tony Hosking *(Purdue University, USA)*
Maria Jump *(King's College, USA)*
Simon Marlow *(Facebook, UK)*
Kathryn McKinley *(Microsoft Research and Univ. of Texas at Austin, USA)*
Eliot Moss *(University of Massachusetts, USA)*
Filip Pizlo *(Apple, USA)*
Kostis Sagonas *(Uppsala University and National Technical University of Athens, Sweden and Greece)*
Xipeng Shen *(MIT and College of William and Mary, USA)*
Dan Tsafrir *(Technion, Israel)*
Ronald Veldema *(University of Erlangen-Nuremberg, Germany)*

Additional reviewers: Chris Fallin

Samira Khan

Justin Meza

Vivek Seshadri

Lavanya Subramanian

Damiano Zanardini

ISMM 2013 Sponsors & Supporters

Sponsor:

Supporters:

IBM Research

Microsoft
Research

Oracle Labs

Safety-first Approach to Memory Consistency Models

Madanlal Musuvathi

Microsoft Research
madanm@microsoft.com

A *safe* programming language is one that protects its own abstractions [13]. Safe languages provide strong guarantees to programmers for all programs that are allowed to execute, obviating large classes of subtle and dangerous errors and cleanly separating a language's interface to programmers from its implementation details. Modern languages (and programmers) have embraced the compelling programmability benefits of safety despite the additional run-time overhead. Specifically, memory- and type-safe languages such as Java, C#, Python, and JavaScript protect the abstraction of memory as a collection of disjoint entities, each with a well-defined structure and set of operations based on its type.

Unfortunately, recent work [5, 11] to standardize concurrency semantics in mainstream programming languages is reversing this trend. While a significant improvement over prior informally-specified semantics, the current standards subvert fundamental programming language abstractions by exposing the complexities of compiler and hardware optimizations to the programmer. This makes it easy for programmers to shoot themselves in the foot in ways that are difficult to detect and correct. This is the case not only for "unsafe" languages like C and C++ but also for "safe" languages like Java.

Consider a simple Java program shown in Figure 1. One thread creates an object and publishes it to another thread by setting the `init` variable. Most programmers would expect statement D to correctly dereference the object allocated in statement A. This expectation is borne out of two programming abstractions that we usually take for granted when analyzing a program snippet: *program order*, which requires that instructions in a thread execute one after the other in the order they appear in the program text; and *shared memory*, which requires that memory behave as a map from addresses to values with each memory operation taking effect immediately. The memory model that preserves these two programming abstractions is formally known as *sequential consistency* (SC) [9].

But contrary to intuition, statement D can trigger a null-pointer exception. This is because mainstream languages like Java and C++ provide a weaker semantics known as *data-race-free-0* (DRF0) [5, 11]. A data race is a pair of concurrent accesses to a shared variable in which at least one of the two accesses is a write. The accesses to the `init` variable in Figure 1 is an example of a data race.

In the presence of such data races, DRF0 exposes compiler and hardware optimizations that reorder, remove, or add memory accesses to the programmer. For instance, a compiler optimization that reorders the two assignments by the first thread in Figure 1 can

```
T x = null;
boolean init = false;

// Thread 1          // Thread 2
A: x = new T();      C: if(init)
B: init = true;      D:   x.f++;
```

Figure 1. This Java program contains a null-dereference at D.

result in a null-pointer exception at D. To avoid this behavior, the programmer is required to annotate all data races with a `volatile` (`atomic` in C++) type specifier. For such *well-annotated* programs DRF0 guarantees SC by appropriately limiting optimizations on volatile variables.

However, simple annotation errors can result in counter-intuitive behavior like the null-dereference above, very much like simple programming errors breaking type safety in unsafe languages. In fact, this similarity is dangerously apt. Boehm [4] describes how unannotated data races can lead to arbitrary control flow under DRF0. An attacker, in theory, can exploit this vulnerability for heinous purposes. On one hand, such vulnerabilities are inherently nondeterministic and thus harder to exploit than classical memory-safety violations. On the other hand, it is not necessary to generate an adversarial input to compromise the system, simply stressing the system, say from within a browser sandbox, is sufficient.

Instead, this paper argues for a safety-first approach to memory models in which the SC abstraction is guaranteed for all programs, completely protecting the programmers from the inner workings of the compiler and the hardware. In this approach, all variables are treated as "volatiles" by default, i.e. potentially participating in a data race. The compiler and the hardware conservatively only perform SC-preserving optimizations on these variables. Additionally, the compiler (and possibly the hardware, at runtime) identifies data-race-free accesses in the program and performs all DRF0-compatible optimizations on these accesses without breaking the SC abstraction. Programmers can further aid the analysis through annotations, which are checked by the compiler for safety.

The safety and security benefits of this approach are obvious. Programmers do not have to understand the complex optimizations that the compiler and hardware might perform when reasoning about the correctness of their programs. For instance, they no longer have to insert fences to make their programs work.

But, what is the cost of providing the SC abstraction? To answer this question, let us classify memory accesses in a program into three kinds: (a) DRF-provable, accesses that the compiler can prove are data-race free (b) DRF-unprovable, accesses that are data-race

ISMM'13, June 20–21, 2013, Seattle, Washington, USA.
Copyright © 2013 ACM 978-1-4503-2100-6/13/06. . . $15.00

Categories and Subject Descriptors D.3.2 [*Programming Languages*]: Language Classifications—Concurrent, distributed, and parallel languages; D.3.4 [*Programming Languages*]: Processors—Optimization

Keywords memory models; sequential consistency; data races;

free, but the compiler is unable to prove them as such, (c) data races, which by our definition above include accesses used to implement shared-memory synchronization, such as locks. Both SC and DRF0 can aggressively optimize DRF-provable accesses while both have to equally limit their optimizations on data races. The difference in performance is from the missed opportunities in optimizing DRF-unprovable accesses in performance-critical parts of the program.

Recent work [12] has shown that most of the benefits of compiler optimizations come from optimizing thread-local accesses, such as operations on non-escaping stack variables and compiler-generated temporaries. For a large class of performance-intensive benchmarks (SPLASH-2 [14], PARSEC [3], and SPEC CINT2006, the integer component of SPEC CPU2006 [8]) the SC-preserving version of an industrial-grade compiler (LLVM [10]) is only 2% slower on average than the one with all optimizations enabled. Since thread-local accesses are easily DRF-provable, this result indicates that the compiler cost of the SC abstraction is already minimal.

The hardware cost is perhaps more troubling. Current hardware architectures require heavy handed mechanisms, such as fences, to disable hardware optimizations. Using such mechanisms for all DRF-unprovable accesses is not going to be efficient.

Fortunately, two recent trends will substantially alleviate this problem. First, in order to efficiently support DRF0 volatiles, hardware vendors are beginning to provide "synchronizing" instructions [1]. The hardware only performs SC-preserving optimizations on these subset of instructions. As the implementations of these instructions get more efficient over time, safe compilers can efficiently translate all DRF-unprovable accesses into these synchronizing instructions.

Second, language extensions [6, 7] that allow programmers to better express locking disciplines, ownership transfers, and noninterference, that at the same time are modularly checkable at compile time, will enable the compiler to statically prove a larger set of accesses as data-race-free. As these extensions get into mainstream programming languages [2], not only will concurrent programs become easier to understand and maintain, they will drastically reduce the number of DRF-unprovable accesses in a program.

Both these trends will reduce the cost of SC abstraction in the future to the point where the safety and security benefits will more than justify its marginal cost over DRF0.

Acknowledgments

This is joint work with Daniel Marino, Todd Millstein, Satish Narayanasamy, and Abhayendra Singh.

References

[1] ARMv8 instruction set overview. URL http://infocenter.arm.com/help/topic/com.arm.doc.genc010197a

[2] Annotating locking behavior. URL http://msdn.microsoft.com/en-us/library/hh916381.aspx.

[3] C. Bienia, S. Kumar, J. P. Singh, and K. Li. The PARSEC Benchmark Suite: Characterization and Architectural Implications. In *PACT '08*, pages 72–81. ACM, 2008.

[4] H. J. Boehm. Simple thread semantics require race detection. In *FIT session at PLDI*, 2009.

[5] H. J. Boehm and S. V. Adve. Foundations of the C++ Concurrency Memory Model. In *PLDI '08*, pages 68–78, 2008.

[6] C. Flanagan and S. N. Freund. Type-Based Race Detection for Java. In *PLDI '00*, pages 219–232, 2000.

[7] C. S. Gordon, M. J. Parkinson, J. Parsons, A. Bromfield, and J. Duffy. Uniqueness and reference immutability for safe parallelism. In *OOPSLA '12*, pages 21–40, 2012.

[8] J. L. Henning. SPEC CPU2006 benchmark descriptions. *SIGARCH Computer Architecture News*, 34:1–17, September 2006. ISSN 0163-5964.

[9] L. Lamport. How to Make a Multiprocessor Computer that Correctly Executes Multiprocess Programs. *IEEE Computer*, 28(9):690–691, Sept. 1979.

[10] C. Lattner and V. Adve. LLVM: A Compilation Framework for Lifelong Program Analysis & Transformation. In *CGO '04*, pages 75–88, 2004.

[11] J. Manson, W. Pugh, and S. V. Adve. The Java Memory Model. In *POPL '05*, pages 378–391, 2005.

[12] D. Marino, A. Singh, T. Millstein, M. Musuvathi, and S. Narayanasamy. A Case for an SC-Preserving Compiler. In *PLDI '11*, pages 199–210, 2011.

[13] B. C. Pierce. *Types and programming languages*. MIT press, 2002.

[14] S. C. Woo, M. Ohara, E. Torrie, J. P. Singh, and A. Gupta. The SPLASH-2 Programs: Characterization and Methodological Considerations. In *ISCA '95*, pages 24–36. ACM, 1995.

Towards Hinted Collection *

Annotations for Decreasing Garbage Collector Pause Times

Philip Reames

University of California, Berkeley
reames@cs.berkeley.edu

George Necula

University of California, Berkeley
necula@cs.berkeley.edu

Abstract

Garbage collection is widely used and has largely been a boon for programmer productivity. However, traditional garbage collection is approaching both practical and theoretical performance limits. In practice, the maximum heap size and heap structure of large applications are influenced as much by garbage collector behavior as by resource availability.

We present an alternate approach to garbage collection wherein the programmer provides untrusted *deallocation hints*. Usage of deallocation hints is similar to trusted manual deallocation, but the consequence of an inaccurate hint is lost performance not correctness. Our hinted collector algorithm uses these hints to identify a subset of unreachable objects with both better parallel asymptotic complexity and practical performance. On some benchmarks, our prototype collector implementation achieves 10-20% pause time reductions. We close with a discussion of the design trade-offs inherent in our approach and lessons to be learned from our collector.

Categories and Subject Descriptors D.3.4 [*Processors*]: Memory management (garbage collection); D.3.3 [*Language Constructs and Features*]: Dynamic storage management

Keywords hinted collection, deallocation hint, memory management, parallel garbage collection, mark and sweep

1. Introduction

According to one popular language survey [1], eight of the top ten languages in use today use some form of automatic memory management. Tracing garbage collection - in the form of sophisticated generational, concurrent, or incremental collectors, but in some cases in that of relatively simple stop-the-world collectors - is the most common mechanism used.

Several languages support a mixed model of memory deallocation - with some objects deallocated via automatic mechanisms and others deallocated manually - which highlights an interesting middle ground that is not well explored in the memory management literature. One language, Objective-C, uses a mixture of compiler-assisted reference counting and trusted manual deallocation. Other languages have well accepted best practices for nearly automatic memory management without language support. For example, C++ has the widely used std::shared_ptr template which provides a reference counting abstraction. Both schemes are unsound due to the trusted nature of manual deallocation, but not all combined schemes have to be.

In this paper, we propose a new variety of garbage collector which relies on *hints* from programmers for performance, but not for correctness. Often, the developer of a program has a mostly accurate mental model of the lifetimes of objects in their program. We use this knowledge to convert the standard reachability problem of a tracing collector into an alternate form where a subset of hinted objects are confirmed as unreachable. We call such a collector a *hinted collector*.

From the user perspective, a hinted collector is a hybrid between a traditional garbage collector and an explicit memory allocator. Unlike a standard garbage collector, program performance can benefit from users' understanding of object lifetimes. The language is extended with a *deallocation hint* construct which - as its name implies - provides an untrusted hint to the runtime that the annotated object will not be reachable during the next collection. An inaccurate deallocation hint is wrong and should be fixed. Unlike in an explicit memory deallocation scheme, the penalty for being wrong is performance, not correctness.

The expectation is that most user-provided deallocation hints are accurate - i.e. the annotated object will be unreachable before the next collection cycle - and that it is feasible for the user to provide hints for most deallocated objects. Given our collective experience with languages like C & C++ with explicit memory allocation, we believe these to be reasonable assumptions. As we have learned the hard way, programmers' mental models of object lifetimes are not *always* correct. The tremendous prevalence of use-after-free, double-free, and uninitialized memory reads are strong evidence of this. However, the fact that we can write large applications in these languages at all is good evidence that developers' mental models are mostly accurate.

These assumptions allows us to restrict the problem we need to solve. Rather than attempting to reclaim *all* unreachable objects, we will only reclaim a subset of unreachable objects. In particular, we will assume that any object not *hinted* with a deallocation hint is live and will not attempt to reclaim it. As in all collectors, any object reachable from an object assumed to be live must also be assumed live. To do otherwise would be unsound.

This formulation gives fundamentally different scalability limitations than a standard tracing collector. The key advantage of a hinted collector is the removal of a constraint on the order in which edges can be visited. Consider the case of a long linked list which

* Research supported by Microsoft (Award #024263) and Intel (Award #024894) funding and by matching funding by U.C. Discovery (Award #DIG07-10227). Additional support comes from Par Lab affiliates National Instruments, Nokia, NVIDIA, Oracle, and Samsung. Also supported by the National Science Foundation (Award #CCF-1017810).

Traversal Collector

Hinted Collector

Figure 1. Minimum number of parallel steps required by a traversal collector and a hinted collector to explore a long linked list.

is live during the collection (Figure 1). A standard traversal mark algorithm must traverse the list in order from head to tail - likely with low locality and many cache misses - whereas a hinted collector can traverse the edges in the list in any desired serial or parallel order. As a result, heap shape - the structure of references connecting objects in the heap - is largely irrelevant to the performance of a hinted collector. Given that long data structures are not uncommon in real world programs, heap shape has been widely identified as a limit to the parallel performance of tracing collectors [4, 5, 25]. Removing this ordering dependency is a potentially profound change.

We present a working prototype of a hinted collector to illustrate its feasibility and to highlight the interesting properties of such a design. We co-opt the existing free calls in C and C++ programs to act as deallocation hints; this allows us to evaluate the feasibility of hinted collection on large programs. Our prototype achieves pause times which are 40-60% faster than a standard tracing collector on some microbenchmarks, and 10-20% faster on some of the SPEC 2006 benchmarks and one case study. We explore the limits of such a design and highlight opportunities for future exploration.

A hinted collector does need to be paired with a backup collector to recover objects which become unreachable without being hinted. As we show, the actual leak rate of such objects is low in C and C++ programs - around 5% in the case study we considered. When paired with either a low frequency stop-the-world tracing collector or a concurrent collector our collector would achieve better average pause times and overall throughput.

Interestingly, such a combined system would provide a clear path - by inserting additional hints or improving the accuracy of those already present - for performance tuning *without having to sacrifice memory safety*. We consider this to be one of the most exciting potential applications of hinted collection.

The key contribution of this work are:

- We introduce the concept of hinted collection, and frame the implicit graph problem - establishing unreachability for a subset of hinted objects - for comparison with the reachability formulation of standard garbage collectors.

- We present an algorithm for this problem which - when given accurate hints - is asymptotically faster in parallel settings. When given inaccurate hints, the algorithm reduces to a standard reachability traversal over the inaccurately hinted objects.

- We present a mostly serial implementation of a hinted collector which outperforms a well tuned mark implementation by between 40-60% on microbenchmarks, and between 10-20% for some of the SPEC benchmarks and one real world case study.

- We highlight lessons learned with the current collector and propose a modified hinted collector design so inspired.

2. Background

At its most fundamental, a garbage collector is an engine for soundly identifying dead objects which can be reclaimed to recycle their allocated memory for future allocation. Tracing garbage collection - as opposed to the more general term automatic memory management - is specifically the use of the reachability abstraction to arrive at such a sound approximation. At their heart, garbage collectors use some traversal algorithm for solving graph reachability.

2.1 Reachability

The graph reachability problem is the following: given a graph consisting of objects (vertices), directed edges connecting objects, and a set of root objects assumed a priori to be live, mark all objects which are transitively reachable along any path from the root set.

In this paper, we compare against the class of traversal based algorithms (such as breadth-first-search, or depth-first-search). In principle, other classes of reachability algorithms could be used for a garbage collector, but we are not aware of a collector that does so. The closest might be the optimistic marking of [5]. Standard traversal algorithms for solving reachability have a serial complexity of $O(|V_{reachable}| + |E_{reachable}|)$ and a parallel complexity of $O(D)$, where D is the depth of the graph.

Throughout this paper we will use $V_{reachable}$ and $V_{unreachable}$ to describe the set of vertices reachable and unreachable by a traversal. These are not known a priori, but are useful for analysis purposes. An edge is reachable if the source vertex is reachable.

2.2 Garbage Collection

In the garbage collection literature, the application - which is ideally ignorant of all memory management details - is known as the mutator. The reachability problem described above is referred to as the *mark phase* of a tracing collector. Much of the work on garbage collection has been focused on improving two metrics: throughput (the number of dead objects collected per unit time), and pause time (the time during which the mutator can not run). Both of these metrics are usually dominated by time spent in the mark phase. A number of options have been explored for accelerating the reachability traversal including:

- Ordering the traversal to improve cache locality is not addressed in the asymptotic results, but is in practice a major concern. The difference between having an item in cache vs not can be roughly two orders of magnitude. As a result, numerous traversal orders have been explored [7, 10, 17].

- Executing the traversal using multiple hardware threads greatly decreases average pause times. As hinted by the asymptotic results, performance does not continue to scale forever. Even ignoring the costs of coordination, program heaps contain a finite degree of parallelism with deep data structures not being uncommon [4, 5, 20].

- Sub-dividing the heap into sections (as in generational and region-based collectors) which can be collected mostly independently greatly reduces the average pause time, at the cost of requiring some edges between regions to be tracked by the mutator. Worst case pause times are still determined by the overall heap structure and may even be worsened by a poor division.

- Splitting the mark phase into a series of smaller steps which are interwoven with the mutator (as in incremental or concurrent collectors) reduces the average pause time, but often reduces throughput. The fundamental issue is that the mutator is essentially racing with the collector; if the mutator ever exhausts the pool of reclaimed memory before the collector can refill it with unreachable objects, the mutator must block on the collector for an amount of time bounded only by that required to perform a full collection cycle.

Despite their limitations, such collectors are very widely used. Production collectors succeed in reducing pauses times to levels that do not impact most programs, and - with the help of some wasted space - achieve "good enough" throughput rates. Current technology breaks down when applications have little tolerance for pauses, extremely high turnover rates, or heaps measured in GB rather than MB [1]. Painfully long pause times have been seen with nearly every production collector of which we are aware.

As we will explore, hinted collection has a parallel asymptotic complexity favorably comparable to reachability based collection - particularly when given accurate deallocation hints.

3. A Hinted Collector

In this section, we present an idealized hinted collector. We focus on the mark phase of the collector, which must establish the invariant that any unmarked object can be safely reclaimed. A standard sweeping phase (either eager or lazy [7]) can follow the mark to actually do the reclamation. Following the discussion of the algorithm, we explore the fundamental scaling limits of such a collector (both in serial and parallel versions) and then close with a discussion of certain key properties of the algorithm.

3.1 The Problem

The graph problem posed to our collector is slightly different from the standard reachability problem solved by standard collectors. We still have a directed graph consisting of a set of objects (vertices), a set of directed edges, and a set of root objects that are assumed live. However, in addition, some of those objects are *hinted* - meaning the user has given a deallocation hint for that object since the last collection, whereas others are *unhinted*. Rather than seeking to identify all unreachable objects, the collector is only asked to identify a *subset of the hinted objects which are in fact disconnected from the roots - i.e. unreachable*. Another way to view the modified problem is to consider the set of hinted objects as an approximate solution to the standard reachability problem. The task at hand is to refine that approximate solution into a subset of objects which are, in fact, unreachable. It is this slightly modified problem statement that allows us to improve parallel scalability over a standard tracing collector. (See Section 3.3)

3.2 The Abstract Algorithm

The hinted collector marking algorithm (given in Figure 2) conceptually has three main phases: marking unhinted objects, marking objects directly reachable from unhinted objects, and a reachability traversal to locate objects which were hinted, but are actually reachable. When all hints are accurate, only the first two execute. We note that the version presented in this section is organized for ease of discourse and clarity, not efficiency of implementation.

The key assumption made by our hinted collector algorithm is that the sets of hinted objects and unhinted objects can be efficiently tracked and objects within those sets can be cheaply iterated. We discuss one means of achieving this in Section 4.2. As with a standard collector, we associate a mark bit with each object that is set if that object is assumed to be live. The collector starts with all objects unmarked. When the algorithm completes, any reachable object will have been marked.

Phase 1 In the first phase, any unhinted objects are marked. Hinted objects in the root set are also marked. A key observation

---

[1] For non-relocating collectors, one must also add long running applications impacted by fragmentation to this list. This is out of the scope of this work.

```
1  phase 1: /* unhinted objects and roots */
2  for o in unhinted objects:
3    mark(o)
4  mark all roots
5
6  phase 2: /* hinted, directly reach. from unhinted */
7  exact = (are all roots unhinted?)
8  for o in unhinted objects:
9    for e in o.outbound_edges:
10     if not e.target.marked:
11       mark e.target
12       exact = false
13
14 if exact:
15   exit with marking done
16
17 phase 3: /* hinted, reachable from hinted only */
18 for o in hinted objects:
19   if o.marked:
20     push(o)
21 while( mark stack not empty ):
22   o = pop
23   for e in o.outbound_edges:
24     if not e.target.marked:
25       mark e.target
26       push e.target
```

Figure 2. Hinted collection algorithm discussed in Section 3.2.

is that there are no restrictions on the iteration order of unhinted objects; iteration can be done in any serial or parallel order.

Phase 2 In the second phase, all outbound references from unhinted objects are traced and their target marked. The net effect of this phase is to mark any hinted object which is directly reachable from an unhinted object. If no new objects are marked during this phase, we have established that no objects were marked inaccurately and do not need to execute phase 3 at all.

As with the first phase, the iteration order is completely arbitrary. Care must be taken to assure that the marking of an object is idempotent, but once this is true, marking can occur in any order.

Phase 3 In the third phase, any objects reachable from the previously marked objects are marked. The purpose is to prevent objects which were inaccurately hinted, but are only reachable from other inaccurately hinted objects, from being incorrectly reclaimed.

As in a standard collector, a stack-based depth-first-search algorithm is used. A mark stack holds references to objects which have been marked, but not yet scanned for outbound references. For now, we will assume an infinite mark stack to avoid overflow issues; we will return to this in Section 4.3. The first step is to scan the set of hinted objects and push any that have been marked onto the stack. A standard traversal is then initiated. When processing an object from the stack, references to objects which have already been marked are ignored since they have either already been traced, or are currently on the mark stack. Once the depth-first-search has terminated, any reachable object must by definition be marked.

3.3 Asymptotic Scalability

We introduce terms V_{hinted}, and $V_{unhinted}$ with the expected meanings. E_{hinted}, and $E_{unhinted}$ are the set of edges leaving each vertex set respectively. We note that these terms are usually incomparable with the terms for reachability. We term an individual hint *accurate* if the object so hinted is unreachable. We describe an unhinted unreachable object as having a *missing* hint.

	Sequential	Parallel
Phase 1	$|V_{unhinted}|$	1
Phase 2	$|E_{unhinted}|$	1
Phase 3 (Exact)	n/a	n/a
Phase 3 (General)	$|V_{hinted}| + (|V_{hinted}| + |E_{hinted}|)$	D_{hinted}
Overall (Exact)	$|V_{reachable}| + |E_{reachable}|$	1
Overall (General)	$|V| + |E| + |V_{hinted}|$	D_{hinted}
Standard Traversal	$|V_{reachable}| + |E_{reachable}|$	D

Table 1. Summary of asymptotic complexity results for hinted collector mark algorithm using an ideal Parallel Random Access Machine (PRAM). The "Exact" results are for the case where all unreachable objects are hinted, and all reachable objects are unhinted. The "General" results allow both inaccurate and missing hints.

Extending this, the set of objects with inaccurate hints is merely $V_{inaccurate} \equiv V_{hinted} \cap V_{reachable}$. In the case where all hints are accurate then $V_{hinted} \subseteq V_{unreachable}$ and $V_{inaccurate} = \emptyset$. We term a set of hints which is fully accurate and with none missing to be *exact*. We say that the set of hints is mostly accurate if $|V_{inaccurate}| << |V_{reachable}|$. We expect that in the common case, hints will be mostly accurate and few hints will be missing. A detailed analysis of each phase of the algorithm is available in Appendix A and a summary of these results in Table 1.

Taking all three phases together, we are left with a sequential complexity of $O(|V| + |E| + |V_{hinted}|)$. When the hints are exact, this reduces to $O(|V_{reachable}| + |E_{reachable}|)$ since phase 3 does not execute and, by assumption, the unhinted and reachable sets are equivalent. Worth noting, this is exactly the complexity of the standard traversal algorithm.

When it comes to the parallel complexity, the hinted collector comes out ahead. In the general form, the asymptotic complexity is $O(D_{hinted})$, where D_{hinted} is the depth of the hinted subgraph. In the case where the hints are exact, this drops to a mere $O(1)$ since traversal of the hinted subgraph is not required. With an infinite number of processors, the running time of a hinted collector is only influenced by the *subset of the graph inaccurately hinted or reachable from objects with missing hints*.

3.4 Key Observations

It is useful to discuss the impact of hint accuracy on the proposed algorithm. On one extreme, a collection for which all objects are hinted reduces to a standard traversal based collector. Phase 1 and 2 become trivial, and only Phase 3 does useful work. The scanning for marked objects at the beginning of Phase 3 is mostly wasted, but since the roots are marked, the traversal will eventually mark all reachable objects. On the other extreme, if no objects are hinted, then the collector reduces to a pair of scans over the set of objects which mark every object and reclaim nothing.

Given a mixture of accurate (unreachable) and inaccurate (reachable) hints, we claim that all reachable nodes will be marked after the traversal. Each object reachable from the roots must be reachable (without passing through a marked object) from at least one object which would be placed on the mark stack as a result of Phase 2 and Phase 3 combined. To summarize this point, it suffices to say that inaccurate hints are safe for correctness, if not necessarily performance.

4. A Practical Serial Collector

Taking the algorithm from the previous section, we implemented a hinted collector for C and C++ programs.[2] By replacing the nor-

mal "free" routine with one which simply records the deallocation hint for later processing, we are able to evaluate the effectiveness of a hinted collector on real programs with large numbers of deallocation hints. Moving from an abstract collector to a concrete one, there are a few questions we need to address:

- How does one efficiently record membership in the sets of hinted and unhinted objects?
- How does one handle overflow during Phase 3 of the algorithm?
- What are the practical bottlenecks and what key optimizations are relevant?

As before, our discussion will focus nearly exclusively on the mark phase of the collector. The implementation uses lazy-sweeping during allocation to reclaim objects unmarked by the collector. This is not a point of difference with a conventional collector.

4.1 Platform

We have modified the Boehm-Demers-Weiser [8] conservative garbage collector for C/C++. The Boehm-Demers-Weiser collector provides a well tuned implementation of a sequential mark-sweep stop-the-world collector. There is also a parallel mark-sweep implementation available; we do not compare against that in this work.

The Boehm-Demers-Weiser collector provides a free-list style malloc/free allocator. When acting as a pure garbage collector, calls to free are ignored by the allocator. There are a number of predefined size classes. Each size class has an associated set of heap blocks (hblks) which store objects of that size, and a free list threaded through the free objects in those pages. Information about the contents of the hblk are stored in a header (hblkhdr) which is allocated in scratch space. Not every hblk has its own header; when larger blocks of memory are needed, multiple hblks are coalesced with only a single header associated with all of them.

4.2 Set Membership Metadata

By default, all objects are assumed to be unhinted. To record deallocation hints, we modified the allocator to store a boolean flag in the hblkhdr to indicate some object in the hblks associated with that header has been hinted. The advantages of the chosen approach are:

- Adding the flag did not require modifying the heap layout. Room was already available in the hblkhdr for additional flags.
- Iterating through objects in a given set can be done cheaply by iterating through a preexisting table of hblkhdrs.
- The many-to-one nature of the flag increases the odds that the flag will be in cache if checked for many objects at once. This will be useful in implementing an edge-filtering optimization.

The downside of the metadata storage scheme is that - since headers are shared by many objects - when one object is hinted by the user, many objects are actually hinted. A likely effect is that

---

[2] The full source code – including all microbenchmarks, test drivers and most data files – is available for download at the following location: `https://github.com/preames/hinted-collection`.

many of those extra objects were inaccurately hinted - resulting in slightly longer pause times. We will investigate the impact of this, and discuss possible alternative implementations in Section 6.3.

4.3 Mark Stack Overflow

Before introducing the concrete implementation, we need to address a slightly more fundamental issue with the algorithm presented previously. In that discussion, we made the assumption that the mark stack - used during Phase 3 depth first traversal of hinted objects - was infinite. In practice, the mark stack is finite and could potentially overflow.

To understand why overflow can occur, picture a heap graph where the entire space is consumed by an inaccurately hinted long linked list. Unless there is room in the mark stack for every object in the program, the mark stack must overflow[3]. We must preserve correctness in this case without reserving an excessively large amount of memory for the mark stack in the normal case.

The Boehm-Demers-Weiser mark implementation includes a mechanism to restart a general heap mark. Every time an object is to be pushed onto the mark stack, it is marked first. If the mark stack overflows, excess items are dropped and the traversal continues. Once the current mark stack empties - to make as much progress as possible - the mark stack is expanded[4], and the heap is scanned for marked objects. Any unmarked objects directly reachable from a marked object is pushed on the mark stack. The mark stack may overflow again, but some forward progress must be made during the emptying of the mark stack. The process will eventually terminate since there are only a finite number of reachable objects. As should be clear, this is a fairly complex process, and in the worst case, could result in the heap being scanned approximately $O(\log(|V|))$ times for a total runtime of $O(|E| * \log(|V|))$.

We must adapt this handling to our own marking algorithm. Neither Phase 1 or 2 use the mark stack in any way. Phase 3, on the other hand, is an adaption of the classic mark algorithm. We extend it with overflow handling in a similar way to the Boehm-Demers-Weiser mark implementation. For the full version of the modified phase 3, see Figure 3.

To avoid needing a mark stack large enough to hold every hinted object, we interrupt the scan occasionally[5] to empty the mark stack. If despite this measure, the mark stack overflows, any objects which would have otherwise been added are simply discarded and an overflow flag is set. The traversal continues - potentially discarding many objects - until it is once again empty. We then increase the size of the mark stack, and repeat the entire process. Since every object is marked before being placed on the mark stack, we are guaranteed to make progress; since there are a finite number of hinted objects, we will eventually terminate.

Since only edges from hinted objects must be considered when repopulating the mark stack, our fully functional algorithm can execute in $O(|E_{hinted}| * \log(|V_{hinted}|))$ - i.e. potentially significantly less than the standard algorithm.

Worth highlighting is that the mark stack can only overflow if a large number of hinted objects are reachable from those unhinted.

---

[3] As described, the mark stack could consume up to 50% of total memory since every object could contain only a single "next" field and be inaccurately hinted. During the depth-first traversal, every object would be on the mark stack at once. This particular case could easily be avoided by optimizing the traversal to remove single reference objects from the mark stack before exploring their children, but similar cases could be easily constructed for unbalanced trees of arbitrary degree.

[4] We note that expanding the mark stack is not required for correctness. In a low memory situation, the mark stack might not be expanded and more iterations would be required.

[5] We currently perform the modified traversal when the mark stack is 50% full. The performance of the collector is largely insensitive to this parameter.

```
1  func modified_dfs:
2    while( mark stack not empty ):
3      o = pop
4      for e in o.outbound_edges:
5        if not e.target.marked:
6          mark e.target
7          if not mark_stack full:
8            push e.target
9          else:
10            mark_stack_too_small = true;
11
12  func mark_hinted_objects:
13    for o in hinted objects:
14      if o.marked:
15        push(o)
16        occasionally modified_dfs();
17    modified_dfs();
18
19  phase 3:
20  mark_stack_too_small = false
21  mark_hinted_objects()
22  while( mark_stack_too_small ):
23    resize_mark_stack( 2 * mark_stack_size )
24    mark_stack_too_small = false
25    mark_hinted_objects()
```

Figure 3. Phase 3 of the hinted collector with mark stack overflow protection added. The algorithm is otherwise unchanged.

By design, this should be a rare case. Long chains occurring solely within the unhinted (i.e. live) section of the heap graph are never traversed and can not trigger overflow. It is possible such a case would be triggered by imprecision in the stored hint metadata. We have not observed this to be a practical concern.

4.4 Practicalities

In the previous subsections, we have addressed the two key differences between the idealized algorithm and the form we can actually implement. Next, we describe the actual implementation - which has some minor differences from the ideal algorithm - and describe key optimizations which reduce the absolute runtime without changing the asymptotic complexity.

Phase 1 Phase one is the simplest to implement. Conceptually, we simply need to walk the tree of hblkhdrs, select those with the deallocation hint flag not set, iterate over each object they contain, and mark all of them. The naive implementation is correct, but the inner-most loop adds about 20% to the overall runtime. Instead, we can take advantage of the layout of mark bits - which are stored in a contiguous bitmask in the hblkhdr - to set all the mark bits for a given hblkhdr at once with a small handful of assignments. Pseudocode for phase 1 is listed in Figure 4.

In the implementation, the marking of root objects is integrated into the modified depth first search of phase 3. The only reason for this is that it allows us to use a manually unrolled and pipelined routine to process items on the mark stack for marking all objects in the root set quickly. There is no intrinsic reason this code could not be duplicated and executed earlier in the process.

Phase 2 Phase two consumes the majority of runtime for the case study and microbenchmarks we have investigated.

The starting point for optimization is a fairly simple loop that iterates over each unhinted object and marks any unmarked object it references. For simplicity, we re-purposed the mark stack and its supporting routines. This was desirable since the task of filtering

```
1  for hdr in hblkhdrs:
2    if not hdr.hinted:
3      set_all_mark_bits(hdr)
```

Figure 4. Phase 1 of the concrete collector.

the word-sized values to identify potential outbound references -
required by the fact we are targeting an type-unsafe language - is
fairly complex and error prone. The unoptimized version of the
code loops through every object in every hinted hblk, pushes all
the objects onto the mark stack (without marking them again),
and then calls a modified stack processing routine which does not
push outbound edges onto the mark stack. This involves a lot of
redundant memory traffic on the mark stack for no good reason,
but has the benefit of being easy to audit for correctness.

While functionally correct, this version is not sufficiently fast to
be competitive with the well tuned tracing collector baseline. We
therefor incorporated the following two key optimizations:

- **Edge-Filtering** – Before checking to see whether an object
  pointed to by a reference is marked, we check to see whether
  the target is an unhinted object. If so, the target must have been
  marked in phase 1 and we avoid dereferencing the pointer. Since
  it is expected that most hinted objects are unreachable, if we
  can filter edges to objects already known to be marked, we
  can ignore most outbound edges. The set membership check
  reduces to a read of a flag in the hblkhdr. The header check
  itself is relatively cheap since, in practice, there are few enough
  header blocks that most of them fit in cache at any one time.
  By performing the additional check, we can shave about 10%
  of runtime from the full hinted collection. In Section 5.3, we
  discuss alternate designs considered.

- **Object Combining** – Instead of processing individual objects,
  we combine all objects in a hblk into a single contiguous range
  and process all potential references together. Since we have
  to be conservative about what might possibly be an outbound
  reference anyway, this combining of objects allows us to completely forgo the outer loop. Depending on the benchmark, we
  see as much as a 30% improvement from this change alone.

  We believe this to be from a mixture of low level code quality
  improvements (i.e. increased instruction level parallelism and
  overlapping memory loads from a hand unrolled and prefetched
  loop) and decreased memory traffic on the mark stack.

The combined algorithm is shown in Figure 5. One point that
is important to mention is that we do not implement the check
for exactly correct hints shown. The key reason for this check is
to avoid executing phase 3 - which affects the theoretical results
slightly, but does not have a significant impact on the running
time of the practical algorithm. This would likely be worthwhile
to implement at some point, it just has not been done yet.

Phase 3 The implementation of Phase 3 of the algorithm is a
mostly direct translation of the version discussed in Section 4.3.
When tuning Phase 3, there are two major goals. First, we want
the case where very few hinted objects are marked - hopefully the
common case - to mostly reduce to a single pass over each hinted
object. Second, we want the graph traversal to be as fast as possible
when it is forced to execute.

For the scan of hinted objects, we take a similar approach to
the unoptimized algorithm described for Phase 2, but with the
difference that marked objects are pushed onto the mark stack
rather than directly scanned. If we find a marked object, then we
must follow any outbound references to ensure that any reachable
hinted objects are marked. Given the algorithm's similarity to a

```
1  func mark_targets(begin, end):
2    while begin < end:
3      if is_reference(begin):
4        if is_hinted(begin):
5          if not begin.marked:
6            mark(begin)
7            exact = false
8      begin += 1 word
9
10 phase 2:
11 exact = true
12 for hdr in hblkhdrs:
13   if combinable(hdr):
14     mark_targets(hdr.hblk_start, hdr.hblk_end)
15   else:
16     for o in hdr.objects:
17       edges = o.outbound_edges
18       mark_targets(edges.start, edges.end)
19
20 if exact:
21   exit with marking done
```

Figure 5. Phase 2 with Edge-Filtering & Object-Coalescing.

standard reachability collector, we were able to reuse many of the
components of the Boehm-Demers-Weiser collector.

In principle, we could use a variant of the object-combining
optimization to reduce traffic on the mark stack and potentially
improve scan performance, but we have not implemented this. We
have implemented a version of the edge-filtering optimization.

Sweep Once Phase 3 has terminated, any reachable object is
known to be marked. This is the same invariant ensured by the mark
phase of a mark-sweep collector. As a result, we are able to reuse
the sweep phase from the baseline collector without modification.
The Boehm-Demers-Weiser collector uses a lazy sweeping strategy. Control immediately returns to the mutator after marking and
memory is incrementally reclaimed on demand during allocation.

5. Evaluation

In Table 2, we present results from a set of microbenchmarks written to highlight the strengths and weaknesses of hinted collection.
As a reminder, the implementation we evaluate in this section is a
serial collector. Preliminary results with a parallel implementation
can be found in the lead author's forthcoming Master's thesis.

5.1 Methodology & Test Platform

All microbenchmarks were written in C++, but use only mal-
loc/free for memory management. Each benchmark was written
in a style to allow manual memory deallocation, but with the free
call redirected to the hinted collector library as a deallocation hint.
When freeing data structures, we chose not to break internal references; this ensures that the hinted collector results pay the full
possible penalty when inaccurate hints are given for the relevant
benchmarks. All benchmarks were compiled with GCC 4.6.3 with
-O3 specified. We also compiled and ran them with Clang 3.1, but
do not report these results since they were essentially identical.[6]

---
[6] To reproduce our results, we strongly suggest starting with our publicly
available source code. The benchmarks exploit undefined behavior in C++,
and compilers are extremely good at breaking such programs. The benchmarks are carefully engineered to get correct results with the versions of the
compilers used. We assume the compiler can not identify dead stores across
procedure boundaries and that no-inlining directives are respected.

benchmark	heap size	gc	hintgc	**speedup**	no-oc	no-ef	range	both	base
Linked List (Dead, Hinted)	31.8 MB	1.45	2.00	**0.72**	0.15	0.30	2.05	0.15	10.10
Linked List (Dead, Unhinted)	31.8 MB	1.40	7.75	**0.18**	10.30	8.35	7.50	7.60	10.55
Linked List (Live, Hinted)	31.8 MB	11.95	12.10	**0.99**	11.70	12.30	12.25	12.30	12.00
Linked List (Live, Unhinted)	31.8 MB	12.10	7.40	**1.64**	10.70	8.85	7.25	7.05	11.10
Fan In (Dead, Hinted)	23.7 MB	0.00	0.00	**n/a**	0.00	0.00	0.00	0.10	0.00
Fan In (Live, Hinted)	23.7 MB	12.85	12.90	**1.00**	12.35	13.30	12.50	12.15	13.25
Fan In (Live, Unhinted)	23.7 MB	12.50	8.25	**1.52**	9.35	11.10	6.00	6.60	14.60
2560 x 1k element LL	88.6 MB	31.70	19.80	**1.60**	27.70	21.75	18.50	18.05	28.60
256 x 10k element LL	88.6 MB	30.95	18.90	**1.64**	27.35	21.65	18.35	18.50	29.00
1/3 Cleanup	184.6 MB	50.10	31.95	**1.57**	44.60	37.15	35.45	32.55	55.80
Deep Turnover	56.6 MB	20.50	12.30	**1.67**	15.70	16.55	10.00	10.80	16.30
Unbalanced (Live)	744.6 MB	252.85	176.50	**1.43**	223.95	192.15	174.85	174.70	240.05
Unbalanced (Partly Dead)	744.6 MB	246.30	175.25	**1.41**	223.40	187.30	175.90	174.90	237.30

Table 2. Average mark times (in ms). "gc" is the baseline tracing collector. "hintgc" is the hinted collector as described in the text with header edge-filtering and object combining. "speedup" shows the improvement of the hinted collector over the tracing collector. "no-oc" is a variant without object combining, but with header edge-filtering. "no-ef", "range", and "both" are variants of the hinted collector with no edge-filtering, range-filtering, and both header and range filtering respectively; all three use object-combining. "base" is a variant with neither edge-filtering or object-combining and illustrates well the importance of the two optimizations.

The times reported in this section are the pause times of individual collections. We do not report overall runtimes or mutator utilization ratios. Each benchmark is run 20 times, and the arithmetic mean value is reported.

Before each benchmark run, we fragment the relevant size classes by allocating a large number of objects with high average turnover, but randomly chosen lifetimes. We disable garbage collection while building the heap structures and hinting any objects necessary. To prevent accumulation of fragmentation, we use a fork/join wrapper around each iteration. As a result, every data point for a particular benchmark shares the same starting heap state.

All results except the scalability experiment were run on a Lenovo Thinkpad with a Intel(R) Core(TM) i7-2620M CPU which has 2 x86_64 cores, each 2-way SMT. The memory hierarchy is organized as a 32 KB L1, 256 KB L2, and 4 MB L3 cache, backed by 8GB of DDR3-1333 memory. There are two memory channels with a maximum bandwidth of 21.3 GB/s.

5.2 Overall Performance

The first two sets of benchmarks illustrate the fundamental performance trade-off of a hinted collector. The hinted collector is able to outperform a tracing collector when the entire heap is live and unhinted (the common case). In these microbenchmarks, the tracing collector wins in all other cases; this is caused by the fact that we truncate the data structures at the root, leaving no tracing work.

- **Linked List** - If the heap contains a long list of objects which is reachable from the root, then any traversal to establish reachability must traverse every object in turn. The hinted collector is able to avoid this long chain of dependent loads.

- **Fan In** - A heap graph with a single root node with edges to P vertices, all of which have a single reference to a final vertex. While this structure may seem contrived, is actually fairly common. It arises frequently from objects which implement copy-on-write semantics; at least one platform we are aware of uses this to optimize the creation of strings.

The remaining benchmarks highlight cases where a hinted collector has a strong advantage. The first two are useful for understanding properties of the two collectors, while the remaining three highlight behavior relevant in real world programs.

- The **2560 x 1k element LL** and **256 x 10k element LL** benchmarks consist of a set of linked lists reachable directly from the root set. We vary the number of linked lists and the number of elements to produce two different heap configurations with different heap structures. The entire heap is live. It is interesting to note that the tracing collector comparatively performs slightly better with shorter but more numerous linked lists. This is exactly what we would expect.

- **1/3 Cleanup** highlights the performance of the collectors when only a portion of the heap becomes unreachable with non-trivial data structures remaining. To illustrate, we allocated six one-million element linked lists and then deallocated two of them. As expected, the hinted collector outperforms the tracing collector by a significant margin.

- In **Deep Turnover** a relatively small portion of the heap is being deallocated. However, that portion is deep inside a long linked list. (We choose to delete 1000 elements off the end of a 1 million element linked list.) This case was chosen to reflect a common pattern in real programs where most of the heap stays around for a long period with small chunks of it being recycled.

- In the two **Unbalanced** results, we see a benchmark with most live space consumed by a collection of 256 depth-6 octtrees. A similar number of linked lists are allocated, but not retained. The first experiment is with all the lists held live, the second is when they are allowed to die. Interestingly, the percentage difference between the two rows is much higher for the standard traversal than the hinted collector. This highlights the stability of our approach with regards to heap shape.

The key reason the hinted collector outperforms a standard collector on these benchmarks is its ability to explore live objects and edges in any order. There are two key benefits that result:

- As previously discussed, not having to follow edges between live nodes in order of discovery prevents the hinted collector from being sensitive to the depth of the live graph. This would mainly benefit a parallel collector, but we see some benefit in our serial collector due to instruction level parallelism and instruction reordering by the hardware.

- By allowing the collector to explore the live edges in any order, the hinted collector converts a series of dependent loads - which is primarily limited by the latency of a memory access - to a set of parallel loads - which is limited by the bandwidth of the

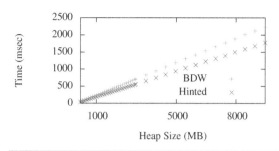

Figure 6. Scalability of hinted and tracing collectors given 10% deallocation rate over range 200 MB to 10GB of allocated data.

memory system. While not reflected in the asymptotic results, this is probably of more practical importance.

We do not directly report the amount of memory reclaimed for each collector on each benchmark. We have manually inspected each benchmark and confirmed that all hinted data is reclaimed for these examples. When unhinted, a small amount of memory (80k) is still reported as being reclaimed, but this is mostly independent of the benchmark. We believe this amount to be from internal approximation in the collector framework; the amount does not vary between collector types.

5.3 Edge-Filtering and Object-Combining

We investigated the impact of the edge-filtering and object-combining optimizations - introduced in Section 4.4 - by running each of the micro benchmarks against versions of the collector with each optimization disabled. We additionally explored an alternate edge-filtering implementation based on tracking a high and low water mark for hinted pointers (henceforth range-based).[7] If during the scan a pointer outside this range was found, it clearly must be un-hinted. Next. we considered the combination of both edge-filtering implementations, with the range check executing first. Finally, we evaluated a version with neither edge-filtering or object-combining.

As can be seen from the results table, edge filtering is clearly advantageous, in some cases contributing a substantial improvement over the base algorithm. When comparing the different implementation options, it is clear the range-based check and the default header flag check both have their own advantages. The combination of the two (in the last column), appears to perform well across the board. Object-combining is clearly also profitable. Note that all the results presented elsewhere in this paper use the header implementation of edge-filtering and object-combining.

5.4 Scalability

We ran an additional experiment with a microbenchmark which allocated reasonably complex heap structures of an arbitrary size and then deallocated a specified amount. In Figure 6, you can see the results of an experiment which varied the heap size from 200 MB to nearly 10 GB while deallocating 10% of the heap at each size. The hinted collector outperforms the standard collector across the entire range. This result is fairly insensitive to the percentage deallocated, but only up to around 90% where the much smaller heap explored by the tracing collector allows it to break even. The exact thresholds are dependent on the structure of the benchmark, but the general pattern was observed across multiple workloads.

---

[7] This implementation was inspired by a similar range base filtering optimization used by the Boehm-Demers-Weiser implementation to quickly discard potential references which could not be actual pointers to objects.

version	min	max	mean	median	95th	99th
Hinted	0.0	490.0	20.42	10.0	70.0	140.0
Tracing	0.0	560.0	24.53	10.0	90.0	170.0

Figure 7. Statistics (across 34861 unique collections) on pause times observed for hinted and tracing collectors for the case study.

5.5 SPEC 2006

Full results from running a subset of the C programs in the SPEC 2006 benchmark suite can be found in Table 3 and 4. Table 3 focuses on the pause times observed, while Table 4 focuses on the amount of memory reclaimed by the hinted collector.

To summarize the results, out of the 10 benchmarks with any deallocation captured by a collection cycle, 9 reclaim 90% or more of the memory hinted as free across the run. The 10th (libquantum) reclaims only 20% of the hinted memory, but the backup collector reclaims only a small amount more. It appears that libquantum is retaining a reference to dead data past the last collection cycle. Across all benchmarks, the largest amount of memory leaked by the hinted collector is 13.15%. Most of the other benchmarks are in the 1-5% range. This leakage is most likely due to hinted objects not actually becoming unreachable until after the next collection.

Pause time results are mixed with several benchmarks taking slightly longer with the hinted collector than the standard collector. A few benchmarks (perlbench, milc, cactusADM) show significant pause time improvement; perlbench improves by nearly 40%.

Methodology Each benchmark was run three times using its reference input set. Statistics were computed across all observed collections for each benchmark. gcc and wrf were excluded since they failed to complete when run with the collector inserted via LD_PRELOAD. gcc is known to use xrealloc which is not currently supported. The cause of failure for wrf has not been investigated.

The tracing collector was run immediately after the hinted collector completed. This was done to remove potential timing differences between runs, but has, in practice, the effect of minorly understating the tracing collector's runtime. There is some noise in the amount of data reclaimed, though we do not believe it to be significant for the overall results. We have seen up to a few hundred KB of space per collection falsely accounted due to marking of collector structures such as free lists. The most likely effect is to overstate the leaked amount slightly.

5.6 Case Study

To highlight the possible impact of hinted collection, we ran a case study with the Clang/LLVM compiler toolchain. We used instrumented versions of Clang 3.1 and the GNU gold linker 1.11 to build Clang itself from source. We instrument the programs to keep track of the amount of data hinted, perform a hinted collection, and then immediately perform a traditional collection.

As can be seen in Table 7, the hinted collector reduced the maximum pause time observed by 12% and 99th percentile pause by 18%. We consider this a strong result. We note that both collectors encountered mark stack overflows during some of the collections; as a result, the reduced overflow cost of the hinted collector was advantageous. Across all the runs, the hinted collector was able to reclaim 95% of all memory hinted, with 5% of memory leaked.

6. Discussion

6.1 Memory Leaks

A hinted collector can leak memory unless paired with a backup collector. Such leaks can come from several sources:

benchmark	Hinted Collector					Tracing Collector				
	count	min	max	average	median	count	min	max	average	median
bzip	36	6.0	118.0	57.03	57.0	36	6.0	116.0	55.58	56.0
cactusADM	33	0.0	183.0	91.52	74.0	33	0.0	194.0	94.76	72.0
calculix	786	0.0	77.0	12.47	0.0	786	0.0	62.0	11.51	0.0
gobmk	156	1.0	21.0	10.46	11.0	156	1.0	20.0	10.88	11.0
gromacs	15	0.0	3.0	0.87	0.0	15	0.0	3.0	1.20	1.0
h264ref	134	0.0	25.0	7.38	5.0	134	0.0	19.0	7.10	5.0
hmmr	1025	0.0	15.0	0.95	0.0	1025	0.0	6.0	0.75	0.0
lbm	3	42.0	42.0	42.00	42.0	3	41.0	41.0	41.00	41.0
libquantum	24	6.0	902.0	121.62	18.0	24	6.0	910.0	123.33	20.0
mcf	3	1.0	1.0	1.00	1.0	3	1.0	1.0	1.00	1.0
milc	181	64.0	562.0	413.34	422.0	181	62.0	607.0	450.71	462.0
perlbench	545	0.0	291.0	101.29	106.0	545	0.0	482.0	122.26	134.0
sjeng	6	12.0	24.0	18.00	18.0	6	12.0	23.0	17.50	17.5
sphinx3	1538	0.0	24.0	11.02	11.0	1538	0.0	16.0	12.47	13.0

Table 3. Statistical summary of pause times observed for each SPEC benchmark. All times are in msec. The first set of columns are from the hinted collector; the second set are a standard collector run immediately after the hinted collector completes. We note that this slightly understates the standard collectors runtime since some garbage has already been reclaimed. Interesting highlights include the sharp drop in maximum pause time for perlbench, and improvement in mean & median pause times for milc.

benchmark	hinted	reclaimed	% rec	leaked	% leaked
bzip	0	0	n/a	0	n/a
cactusADM	7030985408	7000243504	99.56	23867552	0.34
calculix	64077201264	62473916656	97.50	1137503776	1.79
gobmk	2893063104	2892301136	99.97	1761104	0.06
gromacs	14008320	13832240	98.74	621120	4.30
h264ref	3786058800	3411968688	90.12	284106672	7.69
hmmr	8091643648	7898631712	97.61	227583184	2.80
lbm	0	0	n/a	0	n/a
libquantum	2628571280	540985888	20.58	67455024	11.09
mcf	0	0	n/a	0	n/a
milc	260674870560	252234544432	96.76	3103414976	1.22
perlbench	104360698480	100269287632	96.08	15176672352	13.15
sjeng	0	0	n/a	0	n/a
sphinx3	48729799008	48708420560	99.96	101248256	0.21

Table 4. Summary of space reclamation across all collections for each SPEC benchmark. "hinted" is the total number of bytes directly hinted by the application. "reclaimed" is the amount of space reclaimed by the hinted collector. "% rec" is the percentage of hinted data reclaimed; due to collateral hinting, this can be greater than 1.0. "leaked" is the total bytes reclaimed by the tracing collector. "% leaked" is the leaked column divided by the total memory available for collection (leaked + reclaimed).

- Missing hints (direct) - If the user fails to provide a hint for an object, it will not be reclaimed.

- Missing hints (indirect) - If the user provides a hint for a given object, but does not provide a hint for an object which references it, neither object will be reclaimed. The collector can not distinguish between an object being retained due to references from live objects and references from dead objects which are merely unhinted. As one special case of this, any cycle which contains an unhinted object will be retained in its entirety.

- Hint races - If an object is hinted just before a collection, the last reference might survive into the collection where the hint would be cleared without being the object being collected.

- Conservative References - Since our collector is a conservative collector, we may falsely identify a word value as a valid reference. This could cause an object subgraph to be falsely retained.

- Old References - Our collector scans all objects in hblks that contain unhinted objects; it does not distinguish between objects which might be live and those known to be dead - such

as objects on a free list. As a result, references in previously reclaimed objects can force the retention of hinted object.

Out of these sources, only the first two are fundamental to our approach; the latter are artifacts of our particular implementation and could be avoided with an alternate design. As we saw with our case study in Section 5.6, very little memory is leaked in practice. We have not attempted to break down the contributing causes.

During development we did encounter a case where old references triggered retention of large amounts of unreachable objects. In the linked list benchmark, one node from the previous iteration was not reused and by happenstance both lived on an unhinted hblk and pointed into the new list at an early position. We believe this to be a very unusual reuse pattern that is unlikely to arise in real programs. As a safeguard, we plan to introduce a concurrent cleaner to break references in dead objects after they have been reclaimed. This would prevent old references from accumulating over time.

In principle, the hint metadata could be accumulated across multiple collection cycles. This would result in some additional objects being reclaimed over time, but at the cost of inaccurate hints accumulating over time and slowing down the collector. From our experience with patterns of common mistakes in manual deallocation, it is not clear this would be a profitable approach. In practice, we chose to reset the hint metadata on every collection. This is currently a somewhat arbitrary choice.

In a production collector, we would expect to pair a hinted collector with some form of backup collector to ensure that small leaks do not accumulate over time. Conceptually, this is very similar to a manual memory deallocation scheme paired with a background collector to increase the reliability and uptime of a long running process, but without the potential unsoundness of trusted deallocation. Alternatively, one could use a hinted collector as the stop-the-world fallback for a concurrent collector; this would likely reduce stop-the-world pause time when the collector could not keep up. We have not explored the design space of possible pairings, and suggest this would be a profitable area for future work.

6.2 Manual Reasoning

As noted earlier, our entire approach is premised on the assumption that it is reasonable to ask programmers to understand object lifetimes in their programs. We believe the prevalence of programs written in languages with manual deallocation to be conclusive evidence that it is. By that same evidence, we accept the fact that such reasoning is not always simple and that programmers can not in general be *always* correct about object lifetimes. In the context of our current work, we believe that our results clearly demonstrate that real programs provide enough accurate hints to justify the use of a hinted collector.

Taking a step back, we acknowledge that there are times - such as when implementing lock-free data structures - where *not* having to explicitly manage memory greatly simplifies design, reasoning about correctness, and can increase performance. Long term, we would like to explore what programs written from scratch in a language with deallocation hints would look like. We expect that most programmers will rely on common programming idioms or patterns, but not invest in providing deallocation hints in most cases. This is perfectly acceptable; if the concurrent collector can keep up with the application's needs, this is entirely desirable.

In such programs, we foresee deallocation hints coming from two sources. First, library authors are likely to provide hints where possible; widely used libraries already go out of their way to simplify memory management - even in languages with garbage collection. Second, when an application does encounter the limits of the backup collector, we foresee programmers selectively adding deallocation hints to reduce burden on the backup collector. We expect profitable sites would be identified via a profile-guided optimization methodology using some form of an instrumented collector to record reachability. This is similar to how programmers tune the garbage collection performance of Java programs today.

One possibility we would like to explore is how deallocation hints might affect efforts on compile-time object deallocation [11, 12, 18]. If a compiler could predict with high accuracy where an object was likely to become dead, a deallocation hint could be automatically inserted, *even if the compiler could not prove the correctness of deallocation at that point*. We are particular excited by the possibilities of what a just-in-time compiler could do with a combination of runtime profiling and compiler insertion of deallocation hints.

6.3 Metadata Design Alternatives

One of the key design decisions in a hinted collector is how to store the set of hinted objects. As described in Section 4.2, we chose to store a single bit in the hblkhdr - implicitly giving hints for many objects when any one is given. In retrospect, we do not believe this to be the ideal design.

The issue is that phase 3 of the collector algorithm is no longer something which runs only when the user gives inexact hints. While this has not been a problem so far, we are dissatisfied having this case invoked when exact hints have been given. Since its parallel scalability is limited by heap depth, this portion of the algorithm is likely to be a bottleneck in a parallel collector. Another downside, is that the current behavior potentially endangers the tune-ability that is so attractive about a hinted collector.

In many ways, the choice of how to store whether an object has been given a deallocation hint parallels the ways to record mark bits in a standard collector; much of the previous work from that field should carry over. Alternatively, one could take advantage of our tolerance of approximation by using a data structure such as a bloom filter to store an approximate set of deallocation hints.

When we eventually re-implement our collector, we plan to reuse the existing mark bits to store deallocation hints between collections. The basic scheme would be to mark all objects initially on allocation and only unmark an object when a deallocation hint is given. The lack of marking would indicate a deallocation hint had been given for that object and that object only; there would be no collateral damage, as there is now. During collections, the mark state invariant would be restored by marking any hinted objects as in phase 2 & 3 of the current algorithm. Notably, only missing or inaccurate hints would trigger phase 3.

There are two tricks to this representation. First, we would need a way to perform the edge filtering optimization. Assuming that per object mark bits continue to be stored in the page header as a bitmask, this check could be implemented via a series of bit operations. Second, having objects which are live, but unmarked between collections complicates lazy-sweeping to reclaim objects. The easiest solution would be to store a "safe-to-sweep" bit in the hblkhdr that is cleared on the first deallocation hint to a hblk. This same flag could be used for the edge-filtering optimization as well. During hinted collection, this flag could be restored if all objects in the page become marked, potentially improving the efficiency of the edge-filtering optimization within a single collection. The performance of this would need to be explored. An alternate approach would be to use multiple sets of mark bits similar to how one might support concurrent marking and sweeping as in [14].

An additional possibility enabled by this design is the optional integration of a read barrier that could silently fix mistaken deallocation hints if the object is again accessed. This read barrier is not necessary for correctness. It is not clear that it would be a net win, but further investigation is certainly merited.

6.4 Further Discussion

In addition to the serial implementation presented in this paper, we have completed a parallel implementation. Since our parallel implementation is not yet mature, we have chosen not to present those results here. We note that an extended discussion of the implications of hinted collection and full copies of the preliminary performance results for the parallel implementation can be found in the lead author's forthcoming Master's thesis.

7. Related Work

Since we covered much of the related work in garbage collection in Section 2.2, we do not restate it here. Many of the general topics are well covered in Wilson's survey [26].

The only work we know of that directly addresses the fundamental scalability of parallel collection is that of Barabash & Petrank [4, 5]. They propose two techniques. The first is based on inserting shortcut links into the heap dynamically, but does not include any mechanism for keeping links updated between collections. The second uses optimistic marking from randomly chosen heap nodes with spare threads. The issue identified (and not addressed) is a high rate of floating garbage caused by the optimistic marking. Often, a practical responses to heap shape controlled pause times is to simply change the data structure used. We are not aware of research which investigates this approach.

In the realm of systems which combine manual and automatic memory management, probably the best well known is the line of conservative collectors for type-unsafe languages pioneered by Boehm and Weiser [8]. The BDW collector can be used to improve reliability by reclaiming leaks, avoid temporal safety bugs by handling all deallocations, or for reporting leaks during debugging.

In the most recent edition of the C++ standard, support for referencing counting (std::shared_ptr) and unique pointers (std::unique_ptr) has been added to the standard library (but not the language). In recent years, Objective-C has moved from being a language with only manual memory deallocation to a primarily reference counted language (with compiler support) where the use of manual deallocation is strongly discouraged.

There is a wide range of literature on detecting and debugging various classes of deallocation errors (i.e. temporal memory errors) in C and C++ programs [9, 13, 21]. The most relevant for our own work are attempts to create memory allocators which can transparently tolerate deallocation errors in production environments through over-provisioning with randomized object placement [6, 19, 22], type-specific pool allocation [2, 15, 16], checkpointing and environmental perturbation [24], or runtime patching with probability based identification [23]. We do not address spatial memory errors (such as array bounds violations) in this work; our collector would be complemented by approaches such as baggy bounds checking [3] for detecting and tolerating such errors.

8. Conclusion

We have proposed a new approach to the classic problem of automatic memory management. By allowing users to provide hints about object deallocations, we are able to simplify the task that a collector must solve. As we have shown, this leads to better parallel asymptotic bounds and practical performance improvements.

We presented a collector implementation which is both practical and efficient. On a collection of benchmarks and one case study, we are able to show reductions in pause time of up to 10-20%. Remarkably, the current implementation takes advantage of only a small amount of the parallelism enabled by the new algorithm; future collectors could easily outperform this by a large margin.

We used a collection of standard benchmarks and a case study to assess the practical leak rate implied by requiring hints to reclaim an object. As expected, the actual rate of leaked memory was low at less than 5% for most benchmarks. Such a low rate could be easily addressed by pairing a hinted collector with a more standard backup collector. Finally, we closed with a discussion of the lessons learned from the current collector regarding metadata storage and possible directions for followup work.

Acknowledgments

We would like to thank Martin Maas, Joel Galenson, and Krste Asanović for early constructive criticism of the ideas that appeared in this paper. We would also like to thank the anonymous reviewers for their comments.

References

[1] TIOBE Programming Community Index for January 2013. http://www.tiobe.com/content/paperinfo/tpci/. Accessed: 2/1/2013.

[2] P. Akritidis. Cling: A memory allocator to mitigate dangling pointers. In *Proceedings of the 19th USENIX Conference on Security*, USENIX Security'10, 2010.

[3] P. Akritidis, M. Costa, M. Castro, and S. Hand. Baggy bounds checking: an efficient and backwards-compatible defense against out-of-bounds errors. In *Proceedings of the 18th Conference on USENIX Security Symposium*, SSYM'09, 2009.

[4] K. Barabash. Scalable garbage collection on highly parallel platforms. Master's thesis, Technion - Israel Institute of Technology, 2011.

[5] K. Barabash and E. Petrank. Tracing garbage collection on highly parallel platforms. In *Proceedings of the 2010 International Symposium on Memory Management*, ISMM '10, 2010.

[6] E. D. Berger and B. G. Zorn. DieHard: probabilistic memory safety for unsafe languages. In *Proceedings of the 2006 Conference on Programming Language Design and Implementation*, PLDI '06, 2006.

[7] H.-J. Boehm. Reducing garbage collector cache misses. In *Proceedings of the 2nd International Symposium on Memory Management*, ISMM '00, 2000.

[8] H.-J. Boehm and M. Weiser. Garbage collection in an uncooperative environment. *Softw. Pract. Exper.*, Sept. 1988.

[9] J. Caballero, G. Grieco, M. Marron, and A. Nappa. Undangle: early detection of dangling pointers in use-after-free and double-free vulnerabilities. In *Proceedings of the 2012 International Symposium on Software Testing and Analysis*, ISSTA 2012, 2012.

[10] C.-Y. Cher, A. L. Hosking, and T. N. Vijaykumar. Software prefetching for mark-sweep garbage collection: hardware analysis and software redesign. In *Proceedings of the 11th International Conference on Architectural Support for Programming Languages and Operating Systems*, ASPLOS XI, 2004.

[11] S. Cherem and R. Rugina. Compile-time deallocation of individual objects. In *Proceedings of the 5th International Symposium on Memory Management*, ISMM '06, 2006.

[12] S. Cherem and R. Rugina. Uniqueness inference for compile-time object deallocation. In *Proceedings of the 6th International Symposium on Memory Management*, ISMM '07, 2007.

[13] S. Cherem, L. Princehouse, and R. Rugina. Practical memory leak detection using guarded value-flow analysis. In *Proceedings of the 2007 ACM SIGPLAN Conference on Programming Language Design and Implementation*, PLDI '07, 2007.

[14] C. Click, G. Tene, and M. Wolf. The Pauseless GC Algorithm. In *Proceedings of the 1st ACM/USENIX International Conference on Virtual Execution Environments*, VEE '05, 2005.

[15] D. Dhurjati, S. Kowshik, V. Adve, and C. Lattner. Memory safety without runtime checks or garbage collection. In *Proceedings of the 2003 ACM SIGPLAN Conference on Language, Compiler, and Tools for Embedded Systems*, LCTES '03, 2003.

[16] D. Dhurjati, S. Kowshik, and V. Adve. SAFECode: enforcing alias analysis for weakly typed languages. In *Proceedings of the 2006 ACM SIGPLAN Conference on Programming Language Design and Implementation*, PLDI '06, 2006.

[17] R. Garner, S. M. Blackburn, and D. Frampton. A comprehensive evaluation of object scanning techniques. In *Proceedings of the Tenth ACM SIGPLAN International Symposium on Memory Management*, ISMM '11, San Jose, CA, USA, June 4 - 5, jun 2011.

[18] S. Z. Guyer, K. S. McKinley, and D. Frampton. Free-Me: a static analysis for automatic individual object reclamation. In *Proceedings of the 2006 ACM SIGPLAN Conference on Programming Language Design and Implementation*, PLDI '06, 2006.

[19] V. B. Lvin, G. Novark, E. D. Berger, and B. G. Zorn. Archipelago: trading address space for reliability and security. In *Proceedings of the 13th International Conference on Architectural Support for Programming Languages and Operating Systems*, ASPLOS XIII, 2008.

[20] M. Maas, P. Reames, J. Morlan, K. Asanović, A. D. Joseph, and J. Kubiatowicz. GPUs as an opportunity for offloading garbage collection. In *Proceedings of the 2012 International Symposium on Memory Management*, ISMM '12, June 2012.

[21] S. Nagarakatte, J. Zhao, M. M. Martin, and S. Zdancewic. CETS: compiler enforced temporal safety for C. In *Proceedings of the 2010 International Symposium on Memory Management*, ISMM '10, 2010.

[22] G. Novark and E. D. Berger. DieHarder: securing the heap. In *Proceedings of the 17th ACM Conference on Computer and Communications Security*, CCS '10, 2010.

[23] G. Novark, E. D. Berger, and B. G. Zorn. Exterminator: automatically correcting memory errors with high probability. In *Proceedings of the 2007 ACM SIGPLAN Conference on Programming Language Design and Implementation*, PLDI '07, 2007.

[24] F. Qin, J. Tucek, J. Sundaresan, and Y. Zhou. Rx: treating bugs as allergies—a safe method to survive software failures. In *Proceedings of the 12th ACM Symposium on Operating Systems Principles*, SOSP '05, 2005.

[25] F. Siebert. Limits of parallel marking garbage collection. In *Proceedings of the 7th International Symposium on Memory Management*, ISMM '08, 2008.

[26] P. R. Wilson. Uniprocessor garbage collection techniques. In *Proceedings of the International Workshop on Memory Management*, IWMM '92, 1992.

A. Per Phase Asymptotic Analysis

Phase 1 has a serial complexity of $O(|V_{unhinted}|)$ since it must consider every unhinted vertex. Since there is no aliasing of mark bits, the parallel complexity scales inversely with P (the number of processors). As P goes to infinity, the complexity drops to $O(1)$.

Phase 2 has a serial complexity of $O(|E_{unhinted}|)$ since we must explore every outbound edge from every unhinted object exactly once. In the limit, the parallel complexity is again $O(1)$.

Note that unlike Phase 1, there may be aliasing when we add parallel processors. As such, it is likely that the scalability of phase 2 would practically be limited by the contention on updates to mark bits by multiple processors. With a straight-forward implementation, this would be linear in the maximum in-degree ($O(\max_{V \in V} indegree(v))$).

Phase 3 has a sequential complexity of $O(|V_{hinted}| + (|V_{hinted}| + |E_{hinted}|))$. The first term is influenced by the number of hinted objects. The second is driven by the need to perform a graph traversal of the reachable hinted objects. While at first glance it seems like a missing hint could force an exploration of the entire unreachable graph, this is not the case. Any portion of the unreachable graph which was not also hinted has already been marked. The parallel complexity is $O(D_{hinted})$ as P goes to infinity.

As a reminder, if the set of hints is exact phase 3 does not execute. If the given hints were only close to exact, the second term should be small, leaving $O(|V_{hinted}|)$ and $O(1)$ as the dominant terms for the sequential and parallel cases respectively.

Adaptive Scanning Reduces Sweep Time
for the Lisp2 Mark-Compact Garbage Collector

Kazuya Morikawa   Tomoharu Ugawa   Hideya Iwasaki

The University of Electro-Communications

morikawa@ipl.cs.uec.ac.jp   ugawa@cs.uec.ac.jp   iwasaki@cs.uec.ac.jp

Abstract

Mark-compact garbage collection helps long-running programs avoid fragmentation. The Lisp2 mark-compact collector is a classic but still widely-used compaction algorithm. It sequentially scans the entire heap to compact all live objects at one end of the heap while preserving their order of addresses. Since the heap is generally large, this scanning takes a long time. Although some collectors adopt a separate bitmap into which mark bits of objects are stored to reduce the scanning time, we observed that scanning the bitmap can take longer than scanning the heap if objects are densely located. We propose a new scanning method from this observation, which adaptively alternates methods of scanning depending on heap usage; it scans those parts of the heap where live objects are densely located whereas it scans the bitmap for the remaining parts. We implemented this scanning method in the Lisp2 collector of Jikes RVM. The experimental results revealed that the adaptive scanner scanned faster than the method that only scanned the heap and the method that only scanned the bitmap.

Categories and Subject Descriptors D.3.4 [*Programing Languages*]: Processors—Memory management (garbage collection)

General Terms Algorithms, Languages, Performance

Keywords Garbage Collection, Java, Jikes RVM, Lisp2 Algorithm, Compactor

1. Introduction

Automatic heap management, or garbage collection (GC for short), is a fundamental technology adopted in many modern programming languages. Some GC algorithms such as mark-compact GC relocate objects to eliminate fragmentation. Defragmentation is essential for long-running programs that use various sizes of objects to avoid poor use of the heap. Without defragmentation, programs might fail to allocate a large object even if there was enough total amount of free memory. Therefore, real world garbage collectors usually have a compaction mechanism. For example, the HotSpot VM [13] has a mark-compact collector to manage the old generation of its generational heap organization. Mark-compact GC not only eliminates fragmentation but also allows use of bump pointer

allocation. It is known that bump pointer allocation results in good cache behavior [3].

The Lisp2 collector [8] is a widely-used compacting garbage collector. It has to sequentially scan the entire heap to compact all live objects at one end of the heap while preserving their order of addresses. However, since the heap is generally large, this scanning takes a long time. To reduce the scanning time, one might think about using a separate bitmap that holds the mark bits of all objects. In fact, using bitmaps is a well-established idea [1, 5, 10]. Since the bitmap stores the marks at much greater density than if they were stored in the objects, scanning the bitmap is expected to take less time than scanning the entire heap.

We implemented a Lisp2 mark-compact collector in a preliminary experiment using a separate bitmap in the Memory Management Toolkit (MMTk) of Jikes RVM [2] and compared its performance with that of the MMTk's original Lisp2 collector that scanned the entire heap. The results from evaluations indicated that the separate bitmap made GC faster if few objects were live compared to the heap size, i.e., the live objects were less densely located. Otherwise, it was slower than the original Lisp2 collector.

We propose a new scanning method on the basis of these preliminary results, which we call *adaptive scanning*, that combines two scanning methods, i.e., scanning the heap and scanning the bitmap. Adaptive scanning alternates the scanning method depending on the *local* density of live objects; it scans parts of the heap where live objects are densely located while it scans the bitmap for the remaining parts. Adaptive scanning is expected to be effective because objects are likely to survive spatially in clumps based on two well-known hypotheses; (1) many objects live and die in clumps [8][7], and (2) most objects die young [18]. The first hypothesis is reinforced by the second because old objects and new objects are not intermingled due to the main property of the Lisp2 GC in which live objects are compacted toward one end of the heap.

The main contributions of this paper are as follows.

- We found that scanning a bitmap could be slower than scanning the heap if the live objects were densely located. (Section 3). On the basis of this observation, we propose adaptive scanning that can iterate over live objects quickly by switching between bitmap scanning and heap scanning depending on the local density of live objects (Section 4).

- We introduce the *contiguous ratio* that reflects how much the distribution of live objects is skewed. We measured the contiguous ratios of all programs in the DaCapo benchmarks [4] and confirmed that objects live and die in clumps (Section 6.2.1).

- We implemented a Lisp2 collector that employed adaptive scanning in Jikes RVM (Section 5). The experimental results demonstrated that adaptive scanning could scan faster than the method that only scanned the heap and the method that only scanned the bitmap (Section 6).

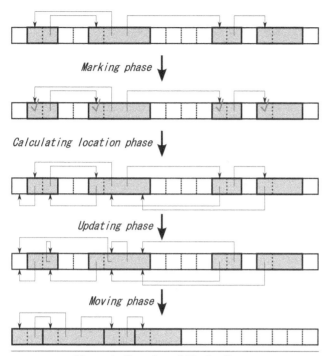

Figure 1. Overview of Lisp2 collector.

2. Lisp2 Mark-Compact Collector

2.1 Overview

Mark-compact collection has a *compaction* phase that relocates live objects at one end of the heap while generally preserving their original order. Compacting live objects creates three main benefits:

(1) fragmentation can be avoided,

(2) good cache behavior can be expected [3], and

(3) allocation is fast.

The Lisp2 collector [8] consists of four phases.

1. *Marking phase* that marks all live objects.

2. *Calculating location phase* that calculates the relocation addresses of live objects.

3. *Updating phase* that updates pointers in the root set and live objects.

4. *Moving phase* that moves every live object to its relocation address.

Every object has an extra word in its header to remember the relocation address calculated in the calculating location phase. This word is called a *forwarding pointer word*.

Figure 1 illustrates the four phases for the Lisp2 collector where live objects are represented in gray and their first word is a forwarding pointer word. Arrows from words other than the first word represent pointers to other objects.

First, starting from the root set, the collector marks the referred objects from already-marked live objects repeatedly in the marking phase until all live objects are marked. Next, the collector searches for live objects in the calculating location phase, computes the address for every live object to which the objects will be moved, and stores it in the forwarding pointer word in the object's header. The collector in this phase has to scan the heap sequentially to keep the original order of objects in the heap. Then, the collector updates every pointer in each live object in the updating phase so

Algorithm 1 Heap scanning.

```
scan() {
  for (obj = Heap.start; obj < Heap.end;
       obj += size(obj))
    if (isLive(obj)) {
      // process the object
    }
}
```

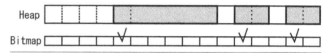

Figure 2. Marking bit in bitmap for each live object.

that it points to the new address that is stored in the forwarding pointer word of the referred object. Finally, the collector moves all live objects to their new addresses in the moving phase. In this last phase, the collector again has to scan the heap sequentially to avoid objects that have not yet been copied to be overwritten by copies of other objects.

The Lisp2 collector generally sequentially scans the entire heap three times, i.e., in the calculating location phase, in the updating phase, and in the moving phase. However, the updating phase does not scan the heap in the implementation of Jikes RVM, but traces live objects, i.e., it follows pointers in a live object recursively. Thus, we will focus on the calculating location and moving phases that scan the heap sequentially in the rest of this paper.

There are many variants of the Lisp2 collector. Some have merged the moving and updating phases [1, 10], others have limited the area of the heap to be compacted [13, 14], and others have coalesced contiguous garbage in the first scanning to skip garbage quickly in the following phases [9]. Because we implemented our Lisp2 collector on Jikes RVM, we used the original Jikes RVM's implementation as a baseline in this paper. We will discuss other variants in Section 7.

2.2 Heap Scanning

The Lisp2 collector scans the entire heap from the start of the heap to search for live objects. Algorithm 1 shows pseudo-code for heap scanning, in which `Heap` represents the heap area, `size` is a function that returns the size of a given object, and `isLive` is a function that checks whether a given object is live or not. For an object that turns out to be live, `scan` calculates its relocation address and stores it in the forwarding pointer word of the object (for the calculating location phase) or it moves the object to its relocation address (for the moving phase).

The collector in this scan algorithm has to check whether each object is live one by one, even if the object is garbage. This is the main reason why heap scanning with the Lisp2 collector is slow [16].

3. Bitmap Scanning

3.1 Overview

It is well-known that the use of a separate bitmap speeds up the scanning process [1, 5, 10]. The collector allocates a bitmap outside the heap. A bit in the bitmap is associated with every *aligned address* at which an object might be allocated. The relationship between the heap and the bitmap is illustrated in Figure 2, where the check marks mean that the bits are set. The bitmap can be regarded as an array of words in which a word is a collection of bits, say 32 bits. ¿From now on, we will assume that a word consists of 32 bits.

Algorithm 2 Bitmap scanning.

```
scan() {
  for (p = Bitmap.start; p < Bitmap.end;
       p += sizeof(word)) {
    w = load(p);
    if (w != 0)
      for (i = 0; w != 0; i++, w >>= 1)
        if (w & 1) {
          obj = getObject(p, i);
          // process the object
        }
  }
}
```

The collector in the marking phase sets the bit for each live object in the bitmap. When scanning, the collector scans the bitmap instead of the heap. If many zero bits appear successively, scanning is expected to proceed rapidly. This is because if a word in the bitmap is zero, the collector can immediately skip 32 aligned addresses in the heap. For instance, if objects are placed at four-byte aligned addresses, the collector can skip 128 bytes in the heap at once. We will call this kind of scanning *bitmap scanning*.

Algorithm 2 is pseudo-code for bitmap scanning to search for live objects, in which `Bitmap` represents the bitmap, `load` is a function that reads a word in the bitmap, and `getObject` is a function that returns an object address that corresponds to its given arguments. If the loaded word is zero, the collector can skip further investigations into the word and proceed to the next word in the bitmap. If the loaded word includes a bit that is set, the collector computes the address of the corresponding object of the bit and processes the object.

3.2 Preliminary Experiments

For the sake of the preliminary experiments, we implemented a Lisp2 mark-compact collector with bitmap scanning (we called it a *bitmap scanning collector*) in the MMTk of Jikes RVM [2]. ¿From the viewpoint of the execution times for DaCapo 2006 benchmarks [4], we compared our implementation with the original Lisp2 mark-compact collector (we called it a *heap scanning collector*) that had already been implemented in Jikes RVM.

The experimental environment involved an Intel Core i7 (4 GHz) and 8 GB of main memory with the Ubuntu 12.04 operating system (kernel version 3.2.0-34-generic-pae). We used four processors[1] with a runtime option of Jikes RVM. The version of Jikes RVM we used was 3.1.2. The word length in this environment was 32 bits.

We executed each benchmark program and measured its GC times during a single iteration after four warm-up iterations. We repeated this five times and averaged all measured GC times. The smallest heap size we used was the minimum size that could execute the benchmark program repeatedly ten times. We have presented the results with their breakdowns for the pmd benchmark in Figure 3 as typical experimental results.

The allocation time for the bitmap was very short and negligible in the bitmap scanning collector. When the heap size was large in pmd, the GC time for the bitmap scanning collector became shorter than that for the heap scanning collector due to the reduced scanning time in the calculating location and moving phases. This demonstrates the effectiveness of bitmap scanning. In contrast, when the heap size was small and, as a result, the live objects in the heap were denser after GC, heap scanning was faster than bitmap scanning but not by much.

---
[1] We also experimented with a single processor, but the results had almost the same tendency as those presented in this paper.

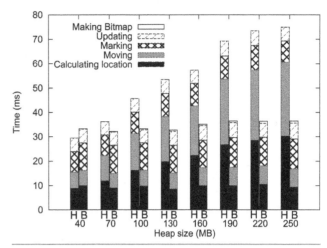

Figure 3. Elapsed time spent in single GC cycle on average for pmd. H and B correspond to heap and bitmap scanning.

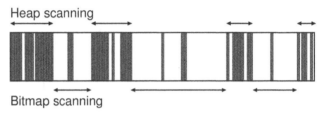

Figure 4. Choosing scanning method depending on local density of live objects in heap.

4. Adaptive Scanning

4.1 Key Underlying Idea

Through the experiments discussed in Section 3.2, we found that bitmap scanning could be faster if the live objects were less dense, and heap scanning could be faster if the live objects were denser. This observation led us to combine both scanning methods and to dynamically alternate the two scanning methods according to how dense live objects in the heap were.

It is well-known that many objects tend to live and die in clumps [8][7]. Thus, how dense the live objects are is considered to vary from place to place within the heap. It is also well-known that many objects soon become garbage, and old objects live for a long time [18]. Older objects in the mark-compact collector are compacted toward one end of the heap after GC. Thus, around this end of the heap, the live objects are expected to be denser because live objects successively exist there. In contrast, the live objects in the rest of the heap are expected to be less dense because new objects, most of which will soon die, are allocated in this area.

On the basis of these observations, adaptive scanning uses heap scanning for places in the heap where live objects are densely located and uses bitmap scanning for other places, as is illustrated in Figure 4.

During scanning, adaptive scanning measures the density of live objects and switches the scanning method at each point where this density changes from low to high or high to low. There may be several strategies for determining changes in density.

4.2 Strategies

We adopted the following simple strategy.

17

Algorithm 3 Adaptive scanning.

```
scanHeap(obj) {
  while (obj < Heap.end)
    if (isLive(obj)) {
      // process the object
      obj += size(obj);
    } else
      return obj + size(obj);
  return NULL;
}

scanBitmap(p, j) {
  for (; p < Bitmap.end; p += sizeof(word)) {
    w = load(p) >> j;
    if (w != 0) {
      for (i = j; (w & 1) == 0; i++, w >>= 1)
        ;
      return getObject(p, i);
    }
    j = 0;
  }
  return NULL;
}

scan() {
  obj = Heap.start;
  while (true) {
    obj = scanHeap(obj);
    if (obj == NULL) return;
    (p, j) = toBitmap(obj);
    obj = scanBitmap(p, j);
    if (obj == NULL) return;
  }
}
```

- We switched the scanning method from heap to bitmap scanning when we encountered a garbage object and continued to use bitmap scanning as long as garbage objects followed.

- We switched from bitmap to heap scanning when we encountered a live object and continued to use heap scanning as long as live objects followed.

There could be various alternatives. For example, the collector might switch the scanning method based on the *n*-grams of object states (live or garbage), i.e., states of *n* consecutive objects. In the case of using trigrams, the collector switches from bitmap to heap scanning after it found three consecutive objects of states "live → garbage → live" but does not switch even if it found "live → garbage → garbage". Our simple strategy switches as soon as it finds a garbage object or a live object. It might switch too soon because the object is an isolated island in the sea of garbage objects. If the collector uses *n*-grams, the above problem can be avoided.

Another alternative is to take register width and cache behavior into account. Once the collector loads a word from the bitmap when scanning the bitmap, it is quite cheap to examine all the bits in the word as it requires no more loads from memory. Similarly, it is cheap to examine all the bits in the cache line that have already been loaded.

We only adopted the above simple strategy in this research. Implementations and evaluations of more sophisticated strategies have been left for future work.

4.3 Algorithm

Algorithm 3 has pseudo-code for adaptive scanning. The collector starts with heap scanning. If it finds a garbage object, it switches to bitmap scanning. It continues to use bitmap scanning while garbage objects successively exist, but switches to heap scanning if it encounters a live object.

In Algorithm 3, scan calls scanHeap and scanBitmap alternately. Given the address of the first object, scanHeap processes live objects as long as they successively exist in the heap. If it encounters garbage, it returns the address of the next object. If it gets to the end of the heap, it returns NULL. After returning from scanHeap, scan calculates using toBitmap the position of the bit in the bitmap for the next object to be investigated. toBitmap returns a pair (p, j) for a given object, where the object corresponds to the j-th bit of the word pointed at by p. The calculated position is passed to scanBitmap, which scans the words in the bitmap as long as they are zero, i.e., garbage objects successively exist. It returns the address of the next live object, or NULL if it gets to the end of the bitmap.

5. Implementation

5.1 MMTk

We implemented the adaptive scanning collector on MMTk, which is the memory management toolkit used by Jikes RVM [2]. MMTk has a variety of garbage collectors including the Lisp2 collector with heap scanning (we called it the *heap scanning collector* in Section 3.2). We replaced its method of scanning in the calculating location and moving phases with the adaptive scanning. This section provides details of the heap scanning collector.

5.1.1 Space

MMTk uses a contiguous memory area for storing everything, i.e., Java objects, VM internal objects, loaded classes, compiled code fragments, and metadata for memory management. The size of this area is bounded by maxHeapSize, which can be set by using the -Xmx command line parameter.

MMTk partitions the contiguous memory area into several *spaces*, each of which stores objects with the same properties and is managed by its own GC algorithm. Each space is not necessarily contiguous but may consist of a number of contiguous memory chunks.

The *small object space* is the one for small Java objects that can be relocated. Most objects are generally stored in this space, and thus the GC time for this space is dominant. We implemented the Lisp2 collector for this space. We will use the term *heap* for this space in the rest of this paper.

5.1.2 Region

MMTk's collector manages the heap as a set of 32 KB memory blocks, called *regions*. When a new object is required, the collector tries to allocate it in the same region as the one where the last object was allocated. If this attempt fails, the collector acquires a new region for the underlying memory manager, or it performs a GC if it is not available.

Regions are connected to one another to form a linked list. The collector compacts objects toward the head of the list, possibly moving objects across regions. After that, all regions in which no objects remain are returned to the underlying memory manager.

5.1.3 Updating Pointers

It is straightforward to implement compaction except for the updating phase.

As we described in Section 2.1, MMTk does not scan the heap in the updating phase but traces pointers so that it can also update pointers in spaces other than the small object space. The collector uses mark bits in the objects' headers with opposite meanings, i.e., it clears the marks of visited objects.

5.1.4 Parallel Collection

The heap scanning collector carries out GC using multiple collector threads in parallel. The set of regions is divided into n subsets, where n is the number of collector threads. Each thread is assigned a subset and compacts only this subset. Thus, strictly speaking, the order of addresses for live objects may not be preserved. Nevertheless, the order is nearly preserved and the property of the skewed distribution of live objects is still expected to be satisfied.

5.2 Adaptive Scanning Collector

The implementation of the adaptive scanning collector consists of two parts: bitmap scanning and a dynamically alternating mechanism. This section only gives details on the former because the implementation of the latter is straightforward. Note that all the implementation details are common to the bitmap scanning collector that we used for the preliminary experiment discussed in Section 3.2.

5.2.1 Allocation of Bitmap

The adaptive scanning collector uses a contiguous bitmap covering the entire small object space. The bitmap is allocated in the space for metadata. This design may waste memory since the space consists of several discontiguous chunks of regions. However, this is not a serious problem because the distribution of the regions is bounded by the parameter, -Xmx.

Another option is to allocate a distinct bitmap in the header area of each region. However, according to the literature [8], placing the bitmap at a fixed position in each region poses the risk of degrading performance due to contention by the same set in a set-associative cache. This is because a set-associative cache maps many memory addresses of the same lower bits to a limited number of cache lines.

5.2.2 Marking the Bitmap

The adaptive scanning collector marks a bit in the bitmap for the first address of each live object in the marking phase. It also marks a mark bit in the object's header. This does not cause any extra overhead compared to the heap scanning collector. This is because the heap scanning collector employs tracing rather than scanning in the updating phase, and this tracing assumes that the mark bit in every live object's header is set at the beginning as we described in Section 5.1.3. If multiple collector threads are running, marking the bitmap needs synchronizations, e.g. atomic test-and-set instructions, to avoid the race. Synchronizations are not needed to mark an object's header. We will demonstrate that synchronizations are the main overhead with our implementation in Section 6.2.4.

5.2.3 Scanning

To quickly scan the bitmap, the adaptive scanning collector uses a pre-calculated table that provides the position of the least significant bit set to one in a given byte as an index of the table. Once the collector finds the bitmap word to be examined is not zero, the collector examines it byte by byte from the least significant byte to the most significant using the table. We also tried the bitwise algorithm that counted the number of 0-bits in parallel. However, we found that looking up a pre-calculated table was faster.

We could use hardware dependent instructions such as BSF (Bit Scan Forward), which searches its source operand for the least significant set bit (1 bit), in the Intel processors. However, we did not use such instructions for the sake of portability.

6. Experiments

We evaluated the adaptive scanning collector in the same environment as that for the preliminary experiment presented in Sec-

tion 3.2. We used a small program as a micro-benchmark and the DaCapo benchmark suite [4] as macro-benchmark programs. We compared the adaptive scanning collector with the heap scanning and bitmap scanning collectors. Although we could introduce techniques listed in Section 7 to polish the baseline collectors, we did not because we wanted our evaluation to be faithful to the original Jikes RVM, which did not adopt these techniques. We will use HS for heap scanning, BS for bitmap scanning, and AS for adaptive scanning in this section.

6.1 Micro-benchmark

We made a small micro-benchmark program in order to compare the elapsed times spent for the heap scan (*not* for the entire GC) of AS with those of HS and BS in various situations including the worst case for AS.

The micro-benchmark program allocates lots of small objects in the heap. The size of each object is four words (16 bytes). First, the program allocates m objects and threads them to form a live linked list, then allocates additional n objects but does not link them to the list so that they can become garbage. The program repeats the above allocations until the heap consists of m contiguous live objects, n contiguous garbage objects, m contiguous live objects, n contiguous garbage objects, and so forth. We call a heap in this state an "m-live-n-dead heap".

After the program allocates N objects,[2] it explicitly calls System.gc() to compact live objects, and removes some of these compacted objects from the live linked list to form an m-live-n-dead heap. Then, the program again repeats allocations of m contiguous live objects and n contiguous garbage objects until the heap is occupied by N objects, and it calls System.gc() again. The program repeats the above procedure ten times.

For various combinations of m and n, we measured elapsed times spent in simply scanning the heap (without any processing on each live/garbage object) by using the three scanning methods. Figure 5 (a) presents the results where m (the number of contiguous live objects) was one and n (the number of contiguous garbage objects) was varied from one to 32. The case of $m = n = 1$ can be regarded as the worst case for AS because it has to switch its scanning method whenever it identifies an object. The greater n becomes, the more advantageous for both AS and BS because they can skip garbage chunks. As expected, we can see the tendencies described above from the results. In the worst case for AS, large overhead, viz., $AS/HS = 2.12$ was observed. However, as n increased, this overhead drastically decreased; when $n = 3 - 4$, the scanning times for HS and AS were comparable, and when $n \geq 9$, AS/HS was less than 0.50.

Figure 5 (b) has the results where n was fixed to one and m was varied from one to 32. The greater m becomes, the more advantageous this is for HS. In fact, HS exhibited the shortest scanning time for the three methods. BS slowed as m increased because many bits were set in the bitmap table. In contrast, AS approached HS as m increased whereas it was a great deal slower than HS when m was small. This is because AS could adaptively switch its scanning method to heap scanning.

Figure 5 (c) gives the results for various combinations of m and n where the level area with the dotted line indicates the elapsed time for HS where $m = n = 1$. We can see that AS became faster as n increased regardless of m due to the effect of bitmap scanning. We can also see that AS approached HS; AS became faster as m increased when AS was slower than HS (n was small), and AS became slower as m increased when AS was faster than HS (n was large).

---

[2] In this experiment, we allocated 2,540,000 objects ($N = 2,540,000$) so that we did not cause GC to run due to lack of free memory.

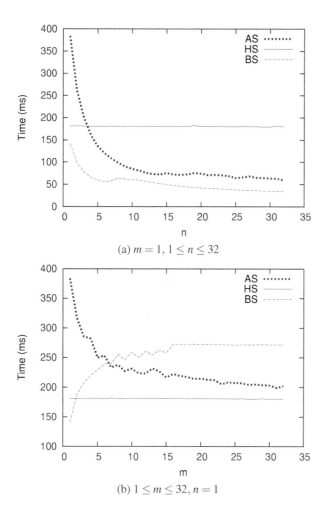

(a) $m = 1, 1 \le n \le 32$

(b) $1 \le m \le 32, n = 1$

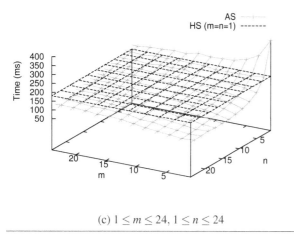

(c) $1 \le m \le 24, 1 \le n \le 24$

Figure 5. Results for Micro-benchmark (*m*-live-*n*-dead heap).

6.2 Macro-benchmarks

We used the DaCapo 2006 benchmark suite [4], which consisted of the eleven benchmark programs antlr, bloat, chart, eclipse, fop, hsqldb, jython, luindex, lusearch, pmd, and xalan. Please go to DaCapo benchmarks home page for the details on these programs.

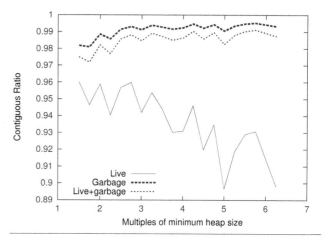

Figure 6. Contiguous ratios for pmd.

6.2.1 Object Distribution

We decided to use a simple strategy in AS on the basis of the assumption that live objects would likely appear in succession and so would garbage. To ensure this assumption would be the case, we measured the ratio of objects whose successors were in the same category with respect to their liveness. We have called this ratio the *contiguous ratio* throughout the rest of this paper. For example, the contiguous ratio of live objects is defined as the ratio of the number of live objects that follow another live object to the number of all live objects. To calculate contiguous ratios, we executed all benchmarks at a variety of heap sizes with HS.

Figure 6 plots the contiguous ratios for pmd with respect to live objects, garbage objects, and all (live + garbage) objects, which are typical results. We can see that the contiguous ratio for all objects was more than 97%. Even though this ratio for live objects decreases as the heap size increases, this is not a problem because the amount of garbage becomes much larger than the number of live objects.

We also measured contiguous ratios for the other benchmarks with two heap sizes, i.e., twice and five times the minimum heap size. The ratios were more than 93.9%.

6.2.2 Overall Performance

We measured the total execution times and total GC times for all benchmarks for seven sizes of available memory area: from twice to five times, with 0.5 intervals, the minimum heap size.[3] The memory area included not only the small object space (heap) but also the other spaces such as metadata space for the bitmap (see Section 5.1.1). Nevertheless, most of the areas were used for the heap. Figures 7 to 8 show the medians with the first and third quartiles.

Among these benchmarks, hsqldb showed clearly different behavior from the others. This may be because it explicitly invoked GC by calling System.gc() independent of the heap size, and its alloc/live ratio was very small (i.e., 2.0) [4].

All the other benchmarks except antlr, fop, and xalan showed a similar tendency. When the heap was large for these benchmarks, AS and BS were much faster than HS, and AS was a little faster than BS. This is because the live objects were less dense, and AS behaved like BS. In contrast, when the heap size was small, HS

---

[3] Since the mark-compact collector of Jikes RVM 3.1.2 could not run properly with a 500 MB heap in our environment, we modified Jikes RVM so that it could run with this heap size and used it for the measurement of eclipse and hsqldb with a 500 MB heap.

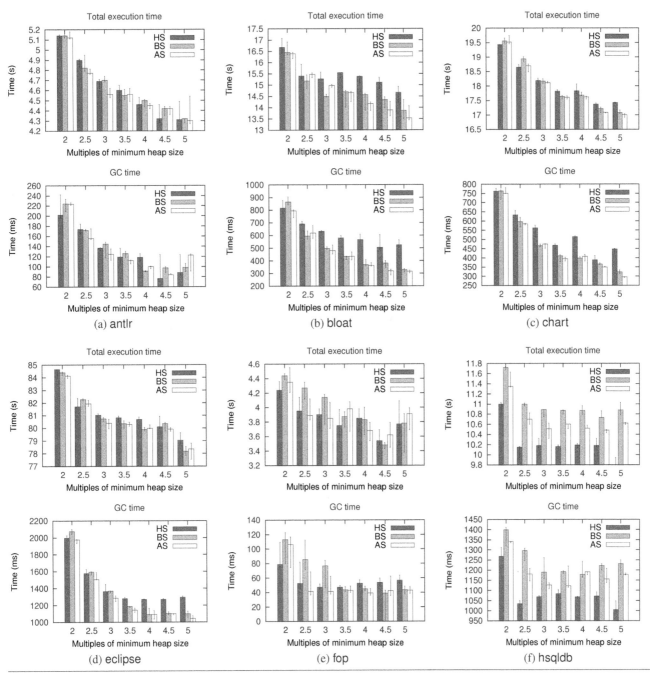

Figure 7. Total Execution Time and Total GC Time for DaCapo benchmarks (1).

demonstrated superior performance because the live objects were denser. Nevertheless, AS behaved like HS and outperformed BS.[4]

For xalan, although AS did not outperform HS even when the heap was large, AS approached HS as the heap size became larger. Antlr with large heap sizes and fop with all heap sizes showed different behavior from the others. This was because only a small number of GCs are invoked. For instance, the average number of GCs per benchmark was 3.2 for antlr (heap size = minimum heap size × 5) and 2.7 for fop (heap size = minimum heap size × 2).

6.2.3 Breakdown of GC Time

Figure 9 shows the average elapsed time for pmd that was spent performing one GC cycle for each size of the available memory area. Each bar is broken down into the elapsed times for individual phases. We arranged the elapsed times for phases that scanned the heap, i.e., for the calculating location and moving phases at the bottom of each bar to clarify the tendency of scanning time.

AS performed consistently and distinctly better than HS and BS for phases that scanned the heap. This meant that AS successfully overcame the degradation in performance of HS for large heaps and BS for small heaps. The reason for AS's superiority over BS is as

---

[4] luindex was an exception.

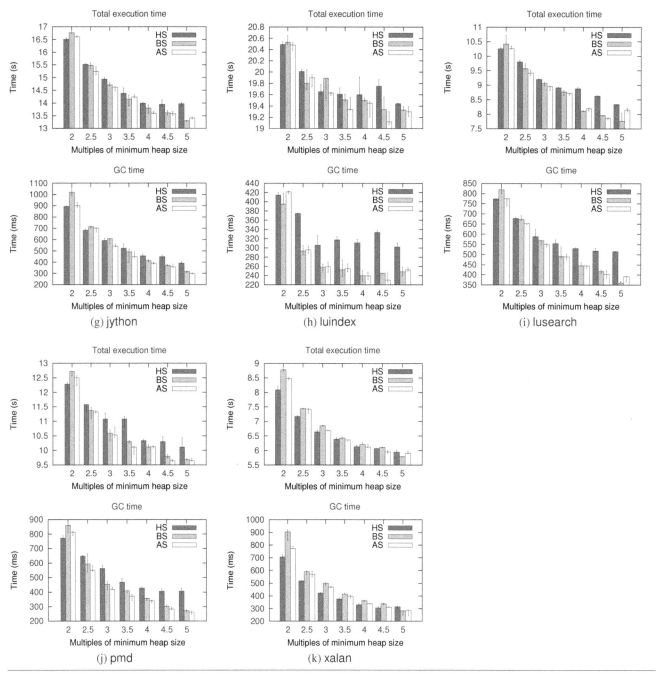

Figure 8. Total Execution Time and Total GC Time for DaCapo benchmarks (2).

follows. A certain fraction of a tight heap is occupied by clumps of live objects, which can be scanned more quickly by HS than BS. AS successfully used heap scanning for the clumps. This suggests the effectiveness of dynamically alternating between the two scanning methods during a single scan.

The overall elapsed time for GC with AS was, however, not always outstanding; HS was as fast as AS with a 40-MB heap. Figure 9 shows that the marking phases of collectors that use bitmaps, i.e., AS and BS, are longer than those of HS.

There are two reasons for that. The first is the double marking that we described in Section 5.1.3. The second is synchronization on the bitmap.

Since our collector has multiple collector threads, markings on the bitmap need synchronization, or a bit set by one thread might be overwritten with zero by another thread that attempted to set another bit in the same word. We used an atomic test-and-set instruction to avoid a race. However, this instruction sacrificed the advantage of the cache. We will show in the next subsection that synchronization was a significant overhead of the marking phase of AS and BS. In fact, our further measurements showed that almost all slowdowns for pmd and about three-quarters of the slowdowns for hsqldb were caused by synchronization.

Synchronization is needed not only for our adaptive scanning but for any GC where two or more collector threads may change

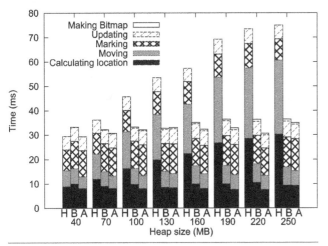

Figure 9. Elapsed time spent in single GC cycle in average for pmd. H, B, and A correspond to heap, bitmap, and adaptive scanning.

different bits of a word concurrently. To the best of our knowledge, the only alternative would be to replace a bit vector with a larger structure such as a byte-vector [15].

6.2.4 Performance of Single-threaded Collector

In order to factor out the costs of synchronization, we modified the implementations of AS and BS by replacing test-and-set instructions in the bitmap operations with write instructions. We measured the total execution times and total GC times for DaCapo benchmarks using a single collector thread with the same heap sizes as those we used in Section 6.2.2. Figures 10 and 11 show the results. We can see the performance superiority of AS more clearly than Figures 7 and 8. These results indicate that synchronization overhead was high.

It is worth noting that, in hsqldb, AS was faster than HS while BS was not. This is a clear evidence of the effectiveness of alternating two scanning methods dynamically during a single scanning. This is because objects tend to locate densely in hsqldb since its alloc/live ratio was very small as we mentioned in Section 6.2.2. Thus, AS behaved like HS more often than other benchmark programs.

7. Related Work

Much work has been done in the area of mark-compact GC. The Compressor [10] is a state of the art concurrent compaction algorithm. In addition to concurrent behavior, the Compressor achieves one-heap-pass compaction, i.e., the Compressor combines the updating and moving phases into a single phase. Objects do not have forwarding pointers so that the Compressor can move objects while updating pointers. Instead, the Compressor has a small vector called the *offset vector* [1] from which the Compressor can compute the new address of each object. Though the offset vector has to be built prior to the actual compaction, the Compressor can build it efficiently because the Compressor does not touch the actual objects but only scans the bitmap. Nevertheless, according to our experimental results, we can expect that the Compressor can build the offset vector faster by using adaptive scanning if the live objects are dense. We can also expect that adaptive scanning may reduce scanning time of the actual compaction phase. Evaluation of a combination of the Compressor and adaptive scanning is one of our plans for future work.

It is a well-known technique to coalesce contiguous garbage objects in the first scanning phase so that they can be skipped quickly in the following phases [9]. Even though this technique can reduce the total scanning cost, it cannot remove the cost of scanning over uncoalesced garbage objects in the first scanning phase. Adaptive scanning can reduce the cost of the first scanning.

Ripley et al. [14] mentioned the same observation as the one we described in Section 4.1, i.e., live objects are expected to be denser around one end of the heap. They proposed a collector that compacts the entire heap other than the area occupied by objects that have survived the last GC. Based on the same observation, the HotSpot VM [13] avoids compacting a prefix of the heap (from its beginning to some point) whose density of live objects is higher than a user-defined threshold. This technique can be incorporated with the adaptive scanning so that it can avoid compacting the prefix and scan the rest of the heap by using adaptive scanning. It is expected that this combination improves performance because there may be clumps of live objects in the scanning area.

Some state of the art collectors employ bitmaps of mark bits [10, 13]. No extra costs are incurred for such collectors in preparing properly marked bitmaps to introduce adaptive scanning. Li et al. [11] presented a fully parallel Lisp2 collector with a non-bitmap approach, i.e., it places a mark bit in the header of each object to avoid atomic operations on a bitmap. However, we demonstrated that adaptive scanning could be faster than heap scanning even though it needs atomic operations for preparing the bitmap.

Chung et al. [6] presented a technique that quickly scans a nearly empty heap for the sweep phase of the mark-sweep collector. This technique stores the addresses of live objects into a table in the mark phase and sorts the addresses. It scans the sorted table instead of the heap in the sweep phase. They also proposed a method that can select whether to use this technique or to use ordinary mark sweep collection depending on heap usage. In contrast to adaptive scanning, their method applied a single strategy to the entire heap. The index-compact collector [16] is a Lisp2 mark-compact collector that uses the same table as Chung et al. for scanning.

Bitmaps are widely-used in mark-sweep collectors. Many mark-sweep collectors that used a bitmap were introduced in Section 2.4 of Jones and Lins [8]. SML# [17] has a mark-sweep collector that uses bitmaps for allocation, i.e., it searches the bitmaps for an unset bit. Bitmaps are organized on multiple levels. A bit in a higher level bitmap is unset if and only if there is at least one unset bit in the area of the lower level bitmap corresponding to the higher's bit. This enables the allocator to quickly skip an area filled with live objects.

Mark-compact collectors are often used for major collection in generational collectors as well as used as stand-alone collectors. The Java HotSpot VM adopts the Lisp2 mark-compact collector for its major collection. Mark-compact collectors are also used for minor collections to more efficiently use space in some situations [12].

8. Conclusion

We proposed an adaptive scanning method that combines scanning the heap and scanning a bitmap. It alternates the scanning method depending on the local density of live objects. We also implemented the Lisp2 compactor that uses adaptive scanning for the calculating location and moving phases in Jikes RVM. The results of our experiments with a hand-made micro benchmark program revealed that adaptive scanning scanned fast when live and/or garbage objects are located contiguously. The results also revealed that adaptive scanning was slow in the worst case where all live objects were adjacent to garbage objects and vice versa, which is an unusual case, The results of our experiments with the DaCapo benchmarks showed the

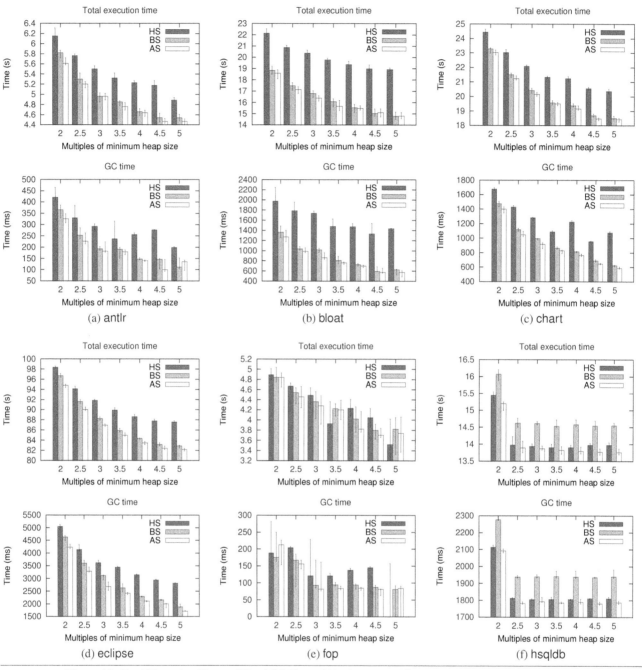

Figure 10. Total Execution Time and Total GC Time of Single-threaded Collector for DaCapo benchmarks (1).

tendency that adaptive scanning scanned faster than heap scanning and as fast as bitmap scanning when the heap was large. When the heap was small, adaptive scanning scanned faster than bitmap scanning. Therefore, we conclude the adaptive scanning is an efficient scanning method if the well-known hypothesis that objects live and die in clumps holds.

We found that the main reason why the Lisp2 compactor with adaptive scanning was slower than that with heap scanning when the heap was small was the cost of synchronization needed for parallel bitmap operations. To reduce this overhead is a topic of future work. We also surveyed some variants of mark-compact collectors. Implementation and evaluation of combinations of our Lisp2 compactor and those variants are also left for future work.

Acknowledgments

We would like to thank Richard Jones and anonymous reviewers for their valuable comments and feedback on this paper. This research was partly supported by JSPS KAKENHI Grant Numbers 22700026 and 23500038.

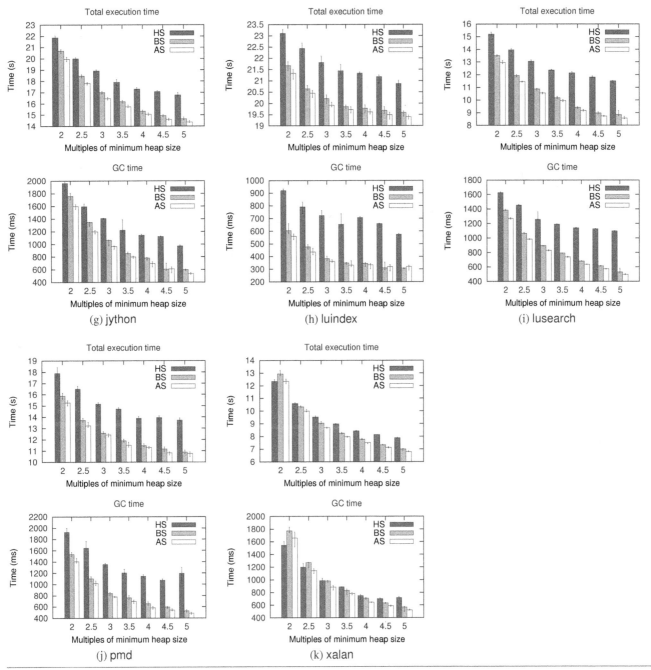

Figure 11. Total Execution Time and Total GC Time of Single-threaded Collector for DaCapo benchmarks (2).

References

[1] D. Abuaiadh, Y. Ossia, E. Petrank, and U. Silbershtein. An efficient parallel heap compaction algorithm. *Proceedings of the 19th Annual ACM SIGPLAN Conference on Object-Oriented Programming Systems, Languages, and Applications Languages, and Applications (OOPSLA 2004)*, 224–236, 2004.

[2] B. Alpern et al. The Jikes research virtual machine project: building an open source research community. *IBM Systems Journal*, 44(2):399–417, 2005.

[3] S. M. Blackburn, P. Cheng, and K. S. McKinley. Myths and realities: The performance impact of garbage collection. *Proceedings of the ACM International Conference on Measurements and Modeling Computer Systems (SIGMETRICS 2004)*, 25–36, 2004.

[4] S. M. Blackburn et al. The DaCapo benchmarks: Java benchmarking development and analysis. *Proceedings of the 21st Annual ACM SIGPLAN Conference on Object-Oriented Programming Systems, Languages, and Applications (OOPSLA 2006)*, 169–190, 2006.

[5] H. J. Boehm and M. Weiser. Garbage collection in an uncooperative environment. *Software: Practice and Experience*, 18(9):807–820, 1988.

[6] Y. C. Chung, S.-M. Moon, K. Ebcioğlu, and D. Sahlin. Reducing sweep time for a nearly empty heap. *Proceedings of the 27th ACM*

SIGPLAN-SIGACT Symposium on Principles of Programming Languages (POPL 2000), 378–389, 2000.

[7] B. Hayes. Using key object opportunism to collect old objects. *Proceedings of the 6th Annual ACM SIGPLAN Conference on Object-Oriented Programming Systems, Languages, and Applications (OOP-SLA 1991)*, 33–46, 1991.

[8] R. Jones, A. Hosking, and E. Moss. *The Garbage Collection Handbook.* Chapman and Hall/CRC Press, 2012.

[9] R. Jones and R. Lins. *Garbage Collection Algorithms for Automatic Dynamic Memory Management.* John Wiley and Sons, New York, 1996.

[10] H. Kermany and E. Petrank. The Compressor: concurrent, incremental, and parallel compaction. *Proceedings of the ACM SIGPLAN 2006 Conference on Programming Language Design and Implementation (PLDI 2006)*, 354–363, 2006.

[11] X.-F. Li, L. Wang, and C. Yang. A fully parallel LISP2 compactor with preservation of the sliding properties. *Proceedings of Languages and Compilers for Parallel Computing (LCPC 2008)*, LNCS 5335, 264–278, 2008.

[12] P. McGachey and A. L. Hosking. Reducing generational copy reserve overhead with fallback compaction. *Proceedings of the 5th Inter-*

national Symposium on Memory Management (ISMM 2006), 17–28, 2006.

[13] Sun Microsystems. Memory management in the Java HotSpot(TM) virtual machine. http://www.oracle.com/technetwork/java/javase/memorymanagement-whitepaper-150215.pdf, 2006.

[14] G. D. Ripley, R. E. Griswold, and D. R. Hanson. Performance of storage management in an implementation of SNOBOL4. *IEEE Transactions on Software Engineering*, 4(2):130–137, 1978.

[15] P. G. Sobalvarro. A lifetime-based garbage collector for lisp systems on general-purpose computers. Technical report, MIT, 1988.

[16] L. Tong and F. C. M. Lau. Index-compact garbage collection. *Proceedings of the 8th Asian conference on Programming Languages and Systems (APLAS 2010)*, LNCS 6461, 271–286, 2010.

[17] K. Ueno, A. Ohori, and T. Otomo. An efficient non-moving garbage collector for functional languages. *Proceedings of the ACM SIGPLAN Conference on Functional programming (ICFP 2011)*, 196–208, 2011.

[18] D. Ungar. Generation scavenging: A non-disruptive high performance storage reclamation algorithm. *Proceedings of the first ACM SIG-SOFT/SIGPLAN Software Engineering Symposium on Practical Software Development Environments (SDE 1984)*, 157–167, 1984.

Control Theory for Principled Heap Sizing

David R. White   Jeremy Singer

School of Computing Science
University of Glasgow
{david.r.white,jeremy.singer}@glasgow.ac.uk

Jonathan M. Aitken

Department of Computer Science
University of York
jonathan.aitken@york.ac.uk

Richard E. Jones

School of Computing
University of Kent
r.e.jones@kent.ac.uk

Abstract

We propose a new, principled approach to adaptive heap sizing based on control theory. We review current state-of-the-art heap sizing mechanisms, as deployed in Jikes RVM and HotSpot. We then formulate heap sizing as a control problem, apply and tune a standard controller algorithm, and evaluate its performance on a set of well-known benchmarks. We find our controller adapts the heap size more responsively than existing mechanisms. This responsiveness allows tighter virtual machine memory footprints while preserving target application throughput, which is ideal for both embedded and utility computing domains. In short, we argue that formal, systematic approaches to memory management should be replacing ad-hoc heuristics as the discipline matures. Control-theoretic heap sizing is one such systematic approach.

Categories and Subject Descriptors   D.3.4 [*Programming Languages*]: Processors—Memory management (garbage collection); D.4.2 [*Operating Systems*]: Storage Management—Allocation / deallocation strategies

Keywords   Heap Size; Control Theory; Virtual Machines; Jikes RVM; HotSpot; Ergonomics

1. Introduction

The dynamic heap size of a garbage-collected program can have a significant impact on its execution time. We believe that optimization of per-program heap size will become more important with the increasing use of garbage collection (GC) on embedded systems, as well as the growth of utility computing via the cloud. The dominant customer billing model for the latter is likely to be based on CPU cycles and memory space rental [2, 6, 13, 16].

Unfortunately there is no general technique to determine, ahead-of-time, the expected impact of a particular heap size on the execution time of a given program. Factors such as the dynamic allocation behavior of the software, the GC policy of the managed runtime, and the underlying memory manager in the host OS complicate the relationship between heap size and execution time. Many programs proceed through distinct phases of dynamic allocation behavior [15, 26, 28], thus it is important that the heap size *adapts* to accommodate shifts in application allocation characteristics.

A good heap sizing mechanism should minimize the overhead of GC, make efficient use of memory and avoid problems such as

paging [36]. Setting a large static heap size is an inefficient use of memory; this should be avoided.

This paper proposes the use of *control theory* [24] to adjust heap sizes dynamically. In contrast to existing, heuristic-based techniques for heap sizing, control theory provides a principled mathematical approach. As virtual machines (VMs) become more sophisticated and widespread, a progression from expert-designed, hand-tuned heuristics to rigorous autonomic mechanisms is increasingly appealing.

We implement a particular controller that monitors short-term GC overhead, and seeks to maintain this at a pre-defined level by adjusting the heap size accordingly. Using this controller, we are able to maintain target levels of application throughput. This is ideal for a high-level quality-of-service agreement, such as might be required in a utility computing context [25].

With the exception of HotSpot's *ergonomics* functionality [30] most VMs do not provide users with the facility to specify where an application's execution should lie on the time-space tradeoff curve. Alonso and Appel [3] describe the concept of flexible working sets when employing garbage collection. There is a minimum heap size below which an application cannot execute, and increasing the heap size above this value reduces GC overhead, hence reducing overall application time. Generally the garbage collector is tuned by an expert, to give some average, acceptable level of performance. Unless a fixed heap size is set, the user has no fine grained control over tradeoff between memory and execution time. Whilst HotSpot does provide this functionality, its implementation shares some of the weaknesses of other heap sizing mechanisms, as we discuss later.

This paper makes two main contributions:

1. It motivates and describes the use of a proportional-integral-derivative (PID) controller for runtime heap sizing, including high-level theory and low-level implementation details in Jikes RVM.

2. It provides an empirical characterization of PID controller heap sizing on a selection of DaCapo benchmark workloads, and compares full-heap GC behavior with Jikes RVM and HotSpot ergonomics heap sizing mechanisms.

2. Heap Size Sweet-Spots

If we consider the large-scale behavior of software, then we may assess the impact of a (fixed) heap size on execution time. Figure 1 illustrates this relationship on a Linux system limited to 300MB RAM by a kernel boot parameter, running Jikes RVM with the antlr and lusearch benchmarks from the DaCapo suite (v2006-10-MR2 [9]) using a full-heap mark/sweep collector, default inputs and 30 repetitions. There is a balance to be struck between a small heap, where GC overhead is high, and a large heap, where paging may occur if limited memory is available. Each graph shows a

ISMM'13,   June 20–21, 2013, Seattle, Washington, USA.
Copyright © 2013 ACM 978-1-4503-2100-6/13/06... $15.00

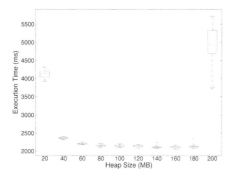

(a) DaCapo 2006 antlr

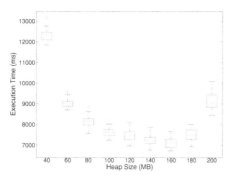

(b) DaCapo 2006 lusearch

Figure 1: Heap size vs execution time for two benchmarks

		Heap Occupancy					
		0.00	**0.10**	**0.30**	**0.60**	**0.80**	**1.00**
GC Overhead	**0.00**	0.90	0.90	0.95	1.00	1.00	1.00
	0.01	0.90	0.90	0.95	1.00	1.00	1.00
	0.02	0.95	0.95	1.00	1.00	1.00	1.00
	0.07	1.00	1.00	1.10	1.15	1.20	1.20
	0.15	1.00	1.00	1.20	1.25	1.35	1.30
	0.40	1.00	1.00	1.25	1.30	1.50	1.50
	1.00	1.00	1.00	1.25	1.30	1.50	1.50

Table 1: Jikes RVM heap sizing look-up table

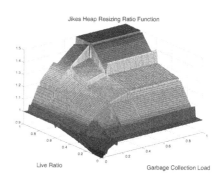

Figure 2: Visualizing the Jikes RVM heap resizing function

'sweet-spot' at a specific heap size, where overall execution time is minimized. This behavior is also reflected in realistically sized, production configurations [10].

This curve will be affected by the VM's environment, particularly the amount of available memory. Issues with paging frequently occur when many applications are executing concurrently on a machine, e.g. a compute node in a cloud data center, or where memory is limited in embedded systems, e.g. an Android device.

While these graphs give us an idea of 'optimal' heap size if we were forced to select a constant value ahead-of-time, in practice the problem is dynamic and this optimum changes at different points during execution. Therefore it is essential that any heap sizing mechanism is *adaptive* and able to respond efficiently to changes in application behavior.

3. Heap Sizing in Deployed VMs

In this section, we survey how two popular production VMs adapt their heap sizes. This is generally a combination of both user-specified thresholds (such as the `-Xmx` maximum heap size parameter to the Java VM) and hand-crafted heuristics encoded within the memory manager.

As a rule, such systems tend to be *improvized*, in that they are not based on any underlying theory. Further, they are usually *conservative* in that they prefer to increase heap size rather than decrease it, and often at a slower rate than may be desired.

3.1 Jikes RVM

Throughout this paper, we use Jikes Research Virtual Machine (RVM) [4, 5], in combination with the Memory Management Toolkit (MMTk) [8] as our experimentation platform. First, we consider how it currently implements heap resizing. After each GC, the `HeapGrowthManager` class is queried to determine a suitable

resize ratio for the heap based on two variables: these are 'short-term GC overhead', g, and 'current live ratio', l. The resize ratio $r(g, l)$ is a function of these two variables. The function inputs are calculated immediately after each GC has completed, as follows:

$$g = \frac{\text{Time taken for the most recent GC}}{\text{Time since the last GC}} \quad (1)$$

$$l = \frac{\text{Amount of live data on the heap}}{\text{Current heap size}} \quad (2)$$

The resize ratio r is calculated by using these two values as indices into a look-up table. One version of the RVM look-up table is illustrated in Table 1. The two variables are matched to the values in bold, which represent interval boundaries, and the resize ratio is generated based on this look-up table with some interpolation. By calling the RVM source from Matlab, we can visualize this function, as shown in Figure 2. The visualization shows that this function is essentially a discrete valued function using linear interpolation between values. We can also see the discontinuities in the function, due to a small interpolation bug in the source code.

The values in the look-up table are hardcoded in the VM and, according to a private communication [18], were the result of trial-and-error experimentation several years ago. We observe that:

- The system is not goal-oriented; there is no target state that it aims to achieve, for example a particular heap size or value of g.

- The mechanism is *stateless*: i.e. it does not take past behavior into account.

- Trial and error is not an objective approach to determining good coefficients.

- Hand-crafted heuristics are susceptible to programming errors, unanticipated situations and pathological cases (for example, the programming error above is only exposed when the input variables are specific values).

- There is no evidence to believe that the heuristic is still valid. The GC implementation has changed considerably since the table was established. Why should we believe it still works?

Perhaps in view of these limitations, the resize function is clearly conservative. When profiling the behavior of DaCapo benchmarks, we have found this that the heap is rarely shrunk significantly, and heap size growth lags behind application behavior.

3.2 HotSpot

Since version 1.5, the Sun (Oracle) HotSpot JVM features an adaptive heap sizing policy known as *GC ergonomics* [30]. The user can specify ahead-of-time values for three targets: (1) maximum GC pause time goal, (2) application throughput goal (i.e. proportion of overall execution time spent in application code), and (3) minimum heap size. According to Sun's published documentation [30], the ergonomics system applies the following heuristics (in this order). (a) If the GC pause time is greater than the pause time goal then *decrease heap size* to attain the goal. (b) If the pause time goal is being met, then consider the application's throughput goal. If the application's throughput goal is not being met, then *increase heap size* to attain the goal. (c) If both the pause time goal and the throughput goal are being met, then *decrease heap size* to reduce memory footprint.

The heap sizing policy is implemented in the `AdaptiveSize-Policy` class and its subclasses. We have examined code from the OpenJDK v6 open-source release: it consists precisely of the above series of hard-coded, case-based rules. The heap resize ratios are less flexible than for Jikes RVM. In steady state, the heap growth ratio is fixed at 1.2 for increases and at 0.95 for decreases. In the early stages of execution, there is a supplementary value added to the growth ratio for increases, so the first time the heap grows the ratio will be 2.0. However this supplementary value decays towards 0 as further GCs occur. In summary, HotSpot heap sizing is more goal-oriented than Jikes RVM, but still lacks a rigorous mathematical model. Vengerov [33] notes that the ergonomics policy is based on 'some heuristic rules that do not guarantee that the GC throughput [or pause time] will actually be maximized [or minimized] as a result.'

4. Heap Sizing as a Control Problem

We propose that heap sizing should be treated as a *control problem*. Control theory is a well-established branch of engineering that can be used to vary an input control signal to a system in order to obtain a desired output signal. Commonly, feedback is employed in what is known as a *closed-loop* controller. Figure 3 illustrates an abstract control system. The deviation from the desired behavior (the error of the output when compared to a reference signal) is used as a feedback signal to adjust the input control signal. We rely on existing work in control theory to produce a simple, elegant, efficient and well-founded solution to the problem of adaptive heap sizing.

A change in the system, such as a software phase change or increased demand from other applications, can be considered as a change in the optimal heap size. In this sense, we are attempting to control a dynamic system such as those that may be encountered in the field of control theory. The controller must respond effectively to changes while ignoring spurious noise. Figure 4 illustrates this situation.

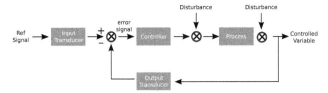

Figure 3: A closed-loop control system

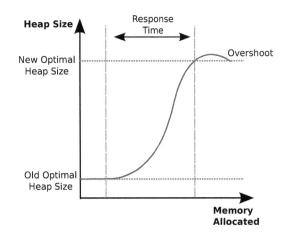

Figure 4: Heap sizing as a control problem

Traditional control theory is concerned with designing effective controllers with regard to the following characteristics:

- Steady-state error: a system is said to have zero steady state error if it eventually settles to the target value. In the case of a mechanical lift system we would wish to have it stop exactly at each floor. In the case of our system, we may expect to settle at the desired value of g (for instance).

- Transient response characteristics: i.e. how quickly a system responds to an input. In the case of a lift, if the response time is slow the passengers may grow bored waiting to reach their destination. However, they will feel uncomfortable acceleration if the response time is too fast. In this terminology, current heap sizing methods can be considered conservative, in that they have a long response time.

4.1 Formulating the Problem

To consider heap sizing as a control problem, we must decide upon the input control variable we will use to manipulate the system, and the output measurement variable we will use as feedback to modify the control variable. Our chosen control variable is the heap resize ratio and in this work we will focus on g, the short-term GC overhead as our measurement variable (alternatives might include mark/cons ratio). This decision is partly based on the use of g in the existing Jikes RVM heap sizing function and in the ergonomics system provided by HotSpot. Any deployed controller is likely to consider at least one other measured variable, but for the moment we focus on g only. Note that we intend to demonstrate the effectiveness of control theory in regulating the system, rather than recommending one variable over another.

We make one modification to the GC overhead variable, i.e. we calculate a *median* average over a sliding window of size five. The sliding window is initialized with the GC overhead target value in all five slots, and then updated with the most recent GC overhead measurement in a FIFO style after each GC. This filtered average was implemented after an empirical evaluation found excessive noise in the GC overhead signal for controller tuning (see later, Section 5.3). The sliding window average dampens this signal somewhat. We denote this average as $\hat{g}$. HotSpot employs a similar smoothing mechanism via its `AdaptiveWeightedAverage` class. It computes average GC overhead x in terms of most recently measured GC overhead g via the recurrence relation $x_{n+1} = \alpha g + (1 - \alpha)x_n$. The default α value is 0.5. Such exponentially decaying sample calculations are common for lightweight overhead management in software systems, e.g. QVM [7].

Controller design usually considers the evolution of the controlled system in the time domain (before moving to the Laplace domain). However, we adopt *memory allocated* as a proxy for time, due to the variable nature of execution time across different processors. This is common practice in GC analysis literature ([22] p145).

5. Designing a Heap Size Controller

There is limited existing work on the mathematical characterization of heap sizes for Java applications [32], and it is not clear whether such formulations are generally applicable. It appears that the equations describing heap size are tied to a particular system configuration, for a fixed benchmark/input combination, with no external dynamic variation. Instead we chose to treat the system as a *black box*, and apply a popular and robust controller known as a PID (proportional-integral-derivative) controller [14, 24].

We attempt to achieve and maintain a *target* GC overhead g^* as set by the user. Thus we do not model the system using differential equations (for example), but rather we rely on empirical work to tune the controller to the system. Similarly, we do not consider the application of more sophisticated control methods such as a state-space controller or the formulation of the problem as one of optimal control. These may prove useful avenues for further research.

In our implementation, a decision about resizing the heap only occurs immediately after a GC. This is consistent with the standard Jikes RVM behavior. This ensures that we isolate the effect of the controller as the single change to the system.

5.1 PID Controller

5.1.1 Why a PID Controller is Appropriate

The PID controller is an ideal selection for this problem; it offers a three-term controller with zero-steady state error provided by extra integral action and is proportionate to the time history and predicted progression of the system response. Additionally it requires no model of the system, in effect performing black-box control, albeit one that is tuned rather than designed for the system.

5.1.2 PID Controller Theory

PID controllers implement a control technique that builds upon compensator design. It used both proportional plus integral and proportional plus derivative control to achieve improvements in steady-state error and transient response time. A PID controller uses the following time-domain equation:

$$u(t) = K_c \left(\epsilon(t) + \frac{1}{T_i} \int_0^t \epsilon(t) \, dt + T_d \frac{d\epsilon(t)}{dt} \right) + b \quad (3)$$

The PID controller operates on an error signal $\epsilon(t)$, developed from the difference in the system input and output. This error value is minimized by the three terms in the PID equation, which adjust how quickly the controller reacts to a change in input, and therefore a change in the error signal. The proportional term K_c provides a term which is a linear multiplier of the error value at the current time-step. This is a simple traditional gain control block. The value of this gain adjusts the responsiveness of the controller and there is a distinct trade-off that must be made: too small a value and the system will respond slowly to an input, but too large a value and the system will become unstable due to a phase inversion producing positive rather than the desired negative feedback and thus signal amplification rather than reduction.

The integral component, T_i, controls responsiveness to the time history of the error signal. If the error signal is growing, it provides an extra gain relative to the summation of the duration and magnitude of this error. This helps provide an extra boost in reducing the error to zero. As the integrative term only uses time history, a high value may well produce overshoot in the desired value resulting in the system hunting for and oscillating towards a zero error. Due to the introduction of an integral term this reduces any steady-state error to zero. Any controller lacking an extra integral will contain a steady-state error, a constant difference between desired and achieved value when the system is allowed to settle.

The differential component, T_d, controls responsiveness to a predication made about the error signal. This helps add stability and make the system more responsive to changes that diverge from a zero steady state error. The derivative within the calculation makes it very susceptible to measurement noise on the output. The differential could produce a much larger signal that the actual system response.

Our control signal, $u(t)$, is the heap resize ratio at time t, i.e.

$$\text{new heap size} = u(t) \times \text{old heap size} \quad (4)$$

The control signal $u(t)$ is given relative to a setpoint of b, which in our case is a unitary resize ratio. The error measure $\epsilon(t) = g^* - \hat{g}(t)$ is the deviation at time t from the desired garbage collection overhead g^*. This error is calculated at the end of each garbage collection, since g and hence $\hat{g}$ only change after a garbage collection event.

The constants K_c, T_i and T_d control a proportional, integral and derivative response to the error signal. The balancing of these constants defines the controller behavior. K_c is referred to as the overall 'gain' of the controller.

5.2 Controller Implementation

We instrumented the `MemoryManager` and `HeapGrowthManager` classes from Jikes RVM and MMTk respectively to analyze the behavior of the existing system and to allow us to perform the design and tuning of our controller. In terms of the PID itself, we made the following changes:

1. The `MemoryManager` class was modified to keep a running count of total bytes allocated, to serve as a proxy for time.

2. The `HeapGrowthManager` class was modified to measure, record and transmit values for the short-term GC load to the PID controller, along with the count from `MemoryManager`. This class also maintains a sliding window to calculate average value $\hat{g}$.

3. The `HeapGrowthManager` class was also modified to use the PID controller when considering a heap resize. Any resizing respects the maximum and minimum heap sizes as specified in the boot image and commandline parameters of the VM. When heap size hits the lower or upper value, the PID controller integral term is reset to zero to prevent `integral windup`, which causes errors when signals are clipped at boundary values.

4. A `PID` class was created to maintain the controller operation.

A patch adding this controller to Jikes RVM is available online [1] along with our source code, experimental scripts, analysis scripts and output data.

5.3 Controller Tuning

The tuning process aims to tailor the controller to the characteristics of the underlying system. We use the empirical tuning method by Ziegler and Nichols [38] to determine the constants used in the PID controller. This involves controlling the system with no integral or derivative component. The gain K_c is adjusted until it reaches the ultimate gain K_u, when the output signal begins to oscillate with period T_u. The parameters for the PID controller in Equation 3 can then be calculated as shown below:

$$
\begin{aligned}
K_c &= 0.6K_u \\
T_i &= 0.5T_u \\
T_d &= 0.125T_u
\end{aligned}
\qquad (5)
$$

This method is not favored for mechanical systems where there is a risk of damaging the system by applying excess strain in reaching the point of oscillation. This is especially true of high frequency oscillations, which could damage mechanical components. Also, the onset of the oscillations may prove difficult to identify if they have a long time period. Additionally sharp-fronted input signals may cause excessive strain by exceeding rates of demands on the system, e.g. consider the situation when turning a car into a corner, mechanical limitations will mean that too high a rate of turning force from the driver will result in loss of control.

However this is an ideal approach for a software system, where there is less concern about mechanical strain. Though this method provides no guarantees about whether control of the system will be optimal, rather it provides a good rule of thumb tuning process for a system to be controllable without knowledge of the underlying system model. The trade-off with developing the control this way means that there is no guaranteed response, as we have not developed the controller with any particular desired dynamics in mind. Additionally the non-linearities in the underlying system will change the dynamics of the controller response across the operational range meaning the controller will behave with different responses in different regions of operation.

6. Evaluation

6.1 Setup

In all these experiments, we execute the `FastAdaptiveMarkSweep` configuration of Jikes RVM hg tip of 25th March 2013 with the GNU Classpath library. We used the simple mark-sweep GC in order to best expose the behavior of the PID controller (and other) heap expansion managers. In particular, at this stage we wanted to avoid any complexities of separately controlling the size of more than one space (as would be necessary for a generational GC). As above, the test machine is lightly loaded (although the load should not affect our results provided that paging of the heap does not occur), Mac OS X 10.8.2, 2GHz quad-core Intel Core i7, 4GB 1333MHz DDR3. In the interest of repeatability, we provide all our code, scripts and data online [1].

We first run experiments using individual benchmarks from the DaCapo suites with `large` inputs, and then create a 'phased' benchmark for further evaluation in Section 6.5. We use 3 benchmarks from the DaCapo 9.12 suite and 8 benchmarks from the DaCapo 2006-10-MR2 suite; thus we used 11 benchmarks from the 25 in the suites. Of the 14 excluded, 10 were not used because the Jikes RVM or the supporting Classpath library were incapable of executing the benchmarks. A further 3 were not memory intensive enough to provide sufficient data, and one was too slow and memory intensive to use efficiently. Full details are available online [1].

DaCapo v.	Benchmark	Target g	K_c	K_c/T_i	K_cT_d
2009	pmd	0.09	6.6	0.01	1300
	sunflow	0.03	9.0	0.03	750
	xalan	0.04	8.4	0.02	1100
2006-10-MR2	bloat	0.11	6.0	0.02	620
	eclipse	0.14	5.4	0.01	810
	fop	0.06	7.8	0.01	1300
	jython	0.21	4.8	0.00	1200
	luindex	0.09	7.2	0.06	230
	lusearch	0.05	5.4	0.01	980
	pmd	0.15	5.4	0.01	950
	xalan	0.04	8.4	0.01	1820

Table 2: Target GC Overhead Values and Tuned PID Parameters for each Benchmark

6.2 Experiment A: Establishing Realistic Overhead Targets

We ran each benchmark on the standard RVM for an unlimited number of iterations, until 100 garbage collections had been completed, with the heap size limited to the range [50, 250MB]. The average GC load in these runs was calculated, and subsequently used to provide a realistic target value for the PID in controller in Experiment C. Table 2 shows the resulting target values. Each value is the median of our 'sliding window' GC overhead $\hat{g}$, hence each value in the table is actually a median of medians.

6.3 Experiment B: Tuning the PID Controller

Next, we enabled the PID controller and ran the same benchmarks in order to follow the Ziegler-Nichols method of PID tuning as described in Section 5.3. The heap size was limited to [50, 500MB], and we increased the gain K_c until the system began oscillating around the goal values derived in Experiment A. Figure 5 gives an example of an oscillating system; the quality of the oscillations achieved varied between benchmarks, and the noise in the signal made tuning a subjective and imperfect process.

We took three measurements of the period for each benchmark (example shown in Figure 5) and took the median period as our final measurement. This allowed us to calculate coefficients for the PID equation on a per-benchmark basis. Note that if we were to deploy the PID controller generally, we would choose an average or other summary statistic of these values, but here we were interested in (i) a limit study of the optimal application of the technique, and (ii) whether tuning varies with the application.

6.4 Experiment C: Evaluation

We then enabled the PID controller with the coefficients derived from Experiment B; we set the goal value g^* of the controller to be the target values from Experiment A. The results for the eleven benchmarks are given in Figure 6.

There is a pair of graphs for each benchmark: the top graph of a pair shows how the garbage collection overhead varies with time, as the PID controller attempts to achieve the designated target. The bottom graph of a pair shows how the heap size is changed to achieve this goal. Each point represents a single garbage collection. Note that the graphs have different scales.

The PID controller adjusts the size of the heap in response to any deviations from the target GC overhead. Over time, we would expect adjustments to decrease provided that the software does not exhibit large variations in memory consumption. Thus, a smoother graph on the left should be reflected in a converging heap size on the right; this is what we see.

For the 2009 and 2006 xalan benchmarks the PID controller rapidly reduces the error and converges the heap size to a reason-

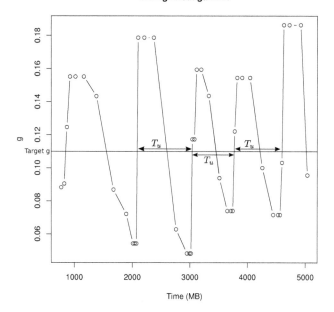

Tuning: bloat gain=10

Figure 5: Experiment B: Example of an Oscillating System During Controller Tuning

able value. Note the decreasing amplitude as time progresses for both xalan graphs. There is an initial start-up period, which varies in length between the two. Similarly, the 2009 pmd and 2006 fop benchmarks, for example, settle well and the PID maintains a low error.

In contrast, the 2006 bloat and 2006 jython benchmarks are less stable and result in dramatic changes in heap size; the PID controller struggles to reduce the error that results from large temporal variations in GC overhead. The PID has a natural responsiveness defined by its parameters; in this case the PID provides very light damping which results in the poor, oscillating, response.

In these experiments, we allowed the PID to resize the heap almost without restraint, and we apply the calculated resize at every possible opportunity (i.e. immediately after every GC event). However, the main purpose of the PID is to provide a better calculation of what the heap size should be, rather than determining how frequently we resize the heap. Hence, it is possible to imagine subsampling the PID output, i.e. only executing a subset of the resizes indicated by the lower graphs. This would lead to a more stable heap size, at a potential cost of reducing the responsiveness of the PID and increasing deviation from the target g^* value. Another way to reduce the variation in heap size would be to further smooth the measurement of GC overhead, by further filtering of g.

To summarize, the PID works well at controlling the median GC overhead, but when g is subject to a large amount of variation, heap size will also vary greatly. This is likely due to high frequency content in the input signal causing some instability in the controller, which could be rectified by using a slightly smaller gain at the potential expense of some responsiveness. Alternatively it may be necessary to incorporate further control logic surrounding the PID or more intensive filtering, to find a balance the stability of heap size versus the efficiency gains of using a more responsive controller.

6.5 Experiment D: Comparative Evaluation on Phased Benchmark

In this study, we compose two DaCapo 2009 benchmarks to induce phased behavior. The artificial workload is two iterations of xalan followed by two iterations of sunflow, both with large inputs, The sequence is repeated many times, within the same VM instance. This behavioral profile may be similar to a Java application server which runs diverse jobs. Our objective is to provide an empirical comparison of different heap sizing mechanisms: default RVM/MMTk, Ergonomics, and PID controller.

We run all the phased benchmark experiments with the modified Jikes RVM build outlined above, using a full-heap mark/sweep GC. We set the initial and minimum heap size to 50MB, and the maximum heap size to 500 MB. We run each phased benchmark test for 500 full-heap GCs, which is always enough to change phase from xalan to sunflow several times.

For the RVM/MMTk default heap sizing policy (as outlined in Section 3.1) there are no parameters to set apart from the minimum and maximum heap size.

For the Ergonomics policy, we implement a simple case-based ergonomics scheme (as outlined in Section 3.2) in Jikes RVM. We use the same hard-wired parameters as in HotSpot, The full source code for this cut-down ergonomics reimplementation is available in our online repository [1]. Our ergonomics system does not support a GC pause time goal since we have no nursery generation to resize, but specifies an application throughput goal (from which we derive a GC overhead target) and a minimum and maximum heap size.

For the PID controller, we initially used the mean value of the corresponding PID parameter settings for xalan and sunflow as reported in Table 2. However we have reduced the proportional controller gain K_c to prevent the system clipping; this aids stability. We have reduced K_c to 0.75 times the mean value of xalan and sunflow gains from Ziegler-Nichols tuning, to iterate towards more desirable behavior. This is a common process in controller design, especially for non-linear systems where some manual tuning is often necessary to produce improved responses.

We set the GC overhead target g^* to 0.05, which is a representative value. We use this g^* value for both the PID controller and the ergonomics mechanism.

Figure 7 shows how the heap size changes over time with each policy. Workload phases are clearly marked on the graph. From the graph, we see that Ergonomics and PID heap sizing are more responsive than Jikes RVM. This is particularly noticeable at the beginning of a phase. Further, we see that Ergonomics is more conservative than PID in its heap size decrease actions (PID generally decreases earlier and further). Finally, there is a memory leak in this phased benchmark since the overall trend for all policies is to converge on the maximum heap size. This is caused by repeated classloader and recompilation activity bloating the immortal data region.

6.6 Discussion

One might ask why we did not use a *replay compilation* methodology when generating these heap sizing graphs. Our answer is that we want to demonstrate that our PID controller can be deployed in realistic (i.e. adaptive compilation) scenarios, rather than constrained experimental environments. Rather than steady state behavior, we are interested in the dynamic unstable behavior of initialization and phase change. In real use, the adaptive compiler operates and affects heap expansion. We did not want to ignore this.

Similarly, one might ask why the results for each heap sizing policy are not drawn from multiple runs, and displayed with *confidence intervals*. The difficulty is that, in Jikes RVM, GC does not occur deterministically in relation to memory allocation (even when replay compilation is enabled). So each run of a benchmark

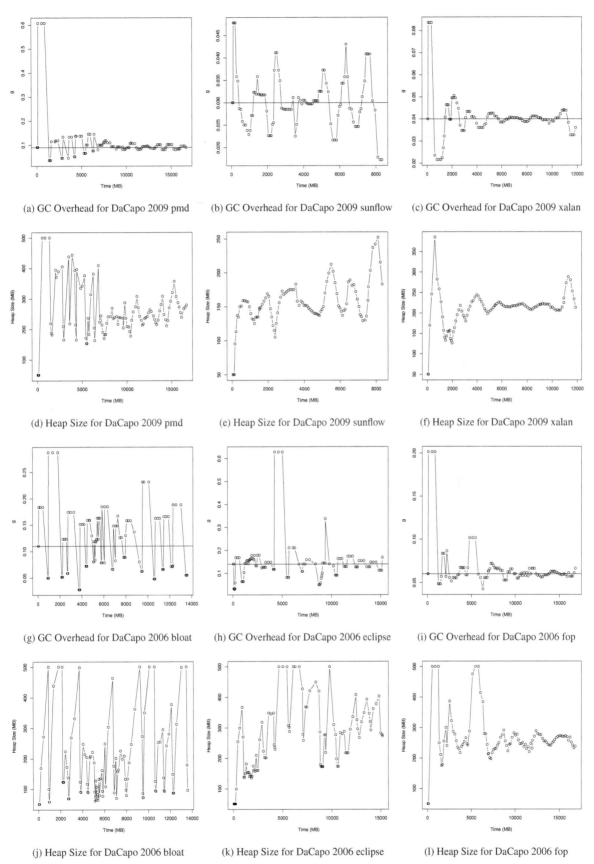

(a) GC Overhead for DaCapo 2009 pmd   (b) GC Overhead for DaCapo 2009 sunflow   (c) GC Overhead for DaCapo 2009 xalan

(d) Heap Size for DaCapo 2009 pmd   (e) Heap Size for DaCapo 2009 sunflow   (f) Heap Size for DaCapo 2009 xalan

(g) GC Overhead for DaCapo 2006 bloat   (h) GC Overhead for DaCapo 2006 eclipse   (i) GC Overhead for DaCapo 2006 fop

(j) Heap Size for DaCapo 2006 bloat   (k) Heap Size for DaCapo 2006 eclipse   (l) Heap Size for DaCapo 2006 fop

Figure 6: Evaluating the PID Controller on the DaCapo Benchmarks

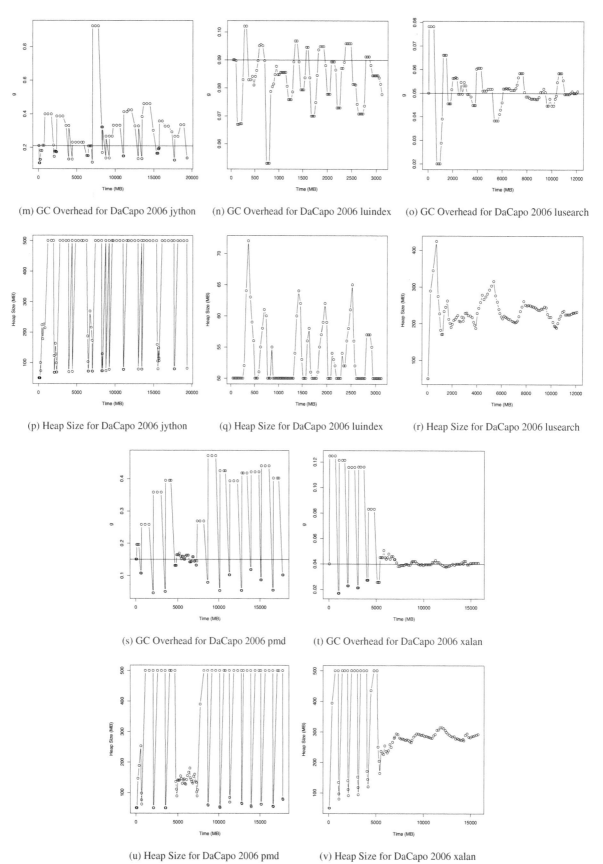

(m) GC Overhead for DaCapo 2006 jython   (n) GC Overhead for DaCapo 2006 luindex   (o) GC Overhead for DaCapo 2006 lusearch

(p) Heap Size for DaCapo 2006 jython   (q) Heap Size for DaCapo 2006 luindex   (r) Heap Size for DaCapo 2006 lusearch

(s) GC Overhead for DaCapo 2006 pmd   (t) GC Overhead for DaCapo 2006 xalan

(u) Heap Size for DaCapo 2006 pmd   (v) Heap Size for DaCapo 2006 xalan

Figure 6: Evaluating the PID Controller on the DaCapo Benchmarks (continued)

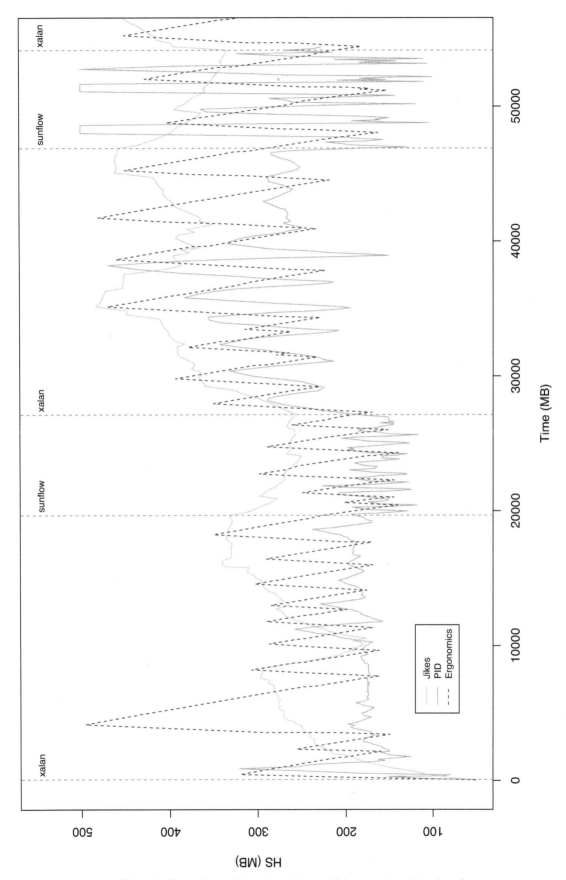

Figure 7: Comparison of three heap sizing policies on a phased benchmark

with a particular heap growth policy will give a different curve, with points at different x values.

We have deliberately omitted any evaluation of benchmark execution times with the three heap sizing policies. In truth, they are all largely similar. The key point is that, to reduce execution time, the goal-oriented policies (PID, Ergonomics) enable the user to specify a lower GC overhead target which will result in a correspondingly larger heap size. Jikes RVM on the other hand has no such facility, apart from the coarse-grained initial and maximum heap size parameters.

We measured the overhead of the heap resizing calculation and found it to be negligible. In a micro-benchmarking test, we ran 10 million iterations of each heap resizing method, supplying randomized input. The Ergonomics and PID resizing methods each took around 1 second to complete 10 million iterations. The default Jikes RVM resizing method took around 2 seconds to complete 10 million iterations. Jikes RVM takes longer because it does multiple array lookups for bounding, followed by multiple floating-point operations for interpolation. However the overhead of a single resize calculation (which happens once per GC) is minimal in comparison to the total cost of a GC.

7. Related Work

Heap sizing is a well-studied problem, and many researchers have attempted to provide better mechanisms. Most of these techniques have not been adopted by commercial VMs to our knowledge. (Note that we have already reviewed existing VM techniques in Section 3.)

7.1 Heuristic Approaches to Heap Management

Brecht et al. [12] discuss the concept of a 'sweet-spot' in heap size, similar to our own discussion in Section 2. They introduce a novel, heuristic-based, heap sizing mechanism for the Boehm GC. The heap grows by different amounts, depending on its current size in relation to a set of threshold values. The threshold values are hand-tuned for each system configuration, with the aim of reducing GC overhead while avoiding paging. Note that the heap size is never reduced; this is a restriction of the Boehm GC [11].

Most recent work on dynamic heap sizing has the explicit goal of avoiding paging (e.g. [19, 21, 34, 35]). Yang et al. [34, 35] employ reuse distance histograms and a simple linear model of the heap required; their approach requires modifications to the underlying OS. The Page-level Adaptive Memory Manager (PAMM) attempts to discover the optimal heap size for a number of applications running on a machine, taking advantage of software phase behavior [36]. The Isla Vista system uses allocation stalls as a warning of impending GC-induced paging [19] and resizes the heap accordingly. Isla Vista uses an additive increase / multiplicative decrease heap sizing policy, based on TCP congestion control. The heap grows linearly when there are no allocation stalls, and shrinks aggressively as soon as allocation stall activity is detected. Hertz et al. [21] use a region of shared scratchpad memory to allow concurrently executing VMs to exchange page fault and resident set size information in order to coordinate collections and heap sizes. The cooperative aspects of the memory manager are encoded using a fixed set of rules, known as Poor Richard's memory manager.

Alonso and Appel [3] describe a user-level advice service, that concurrent garbage-collected ML applications can query to determine whether to grow or shrink their runtime heaps. When an application requests advice, it passes the parameters describing its current state with respect to GC (e.g. current GC overhead and the proportion of live data on its heap). The advisor returns a ΔS value that specifies a heap size change for the application. The advisor uses a hard-coded, hand-tuned equation to determine values for ΔS

based on this application's CPU time and memory size, in relation to the other concurrent applications.

7.2 Mathematical Models for Heap Management

Although it may seem like a somewhat subjective distinction, the following papers deal with heap resizing using principled mathematical models, rather than arbitrary heuristics.

Sun et al. [31] consider the problem of a single Java application server that has isolated, per-application heaplets within a single JVM. Each heaplet's size can be set independently. They introduce a simple analytical model, which adapts the size of all heaplets in order to equalize the GC frequency over all applications.

Tay and Zong [32] demonstrate how to derive a page fault equation that relates the number of page faults to actual heap size and resident heap size. Such an equation characterizes the behavior of a single program run with a specific input, given fixed GC and OS policies. Tay and Zong introduce a heap sizing rule (an equation that uses the same parameters as the page fault equation) and provide a coherent interpretation for its formulation. When the heap sizing rule is applied, the number of page faults during execution is minimized. The weakness in this approach is that the equations are not readily transferable to another situation, i.e. a change in application input, or transient system load would necessitate retuning to generate new parameter values for the page fault equation and heap sizing rule.

Vengerov [33] derives a mathematical equation to characterize the throughput (proportion of time spent in application execution rather than GC, i.e. $1 - g$ in our notation) of the generational collector in HotSpot. Based on this model, Vengerov then develops a mechanism for tuning the GC parameters so as to optimize the throughput. The major difficulty in estimating and optimizing throughput in HotSpot arises from its multiple generation spaces and decoupled GC policies in each space. Vengerov's work is relevant to ours, in that it controls heap size parameters and seeks to minimize GC time. However he tackles the problem in an entirely different way, using a *white-box* approach. As an expert GC analyst, he constructs a mathematical model of the whole system, then designs a custom tuning algorithm. We feel that our *black-box* approach is simpler. However we have only demonstrated it on a full-heap collector (i.e. no young generational spaces) where all throughput measurements are precise.

Singer et al. [27] use microeconomic supply and demand theory to characterize GC behavior. They apply the concept of elasticity to heap size, and devise a new elasticity-based approach to heap expansion. In the reported experiments, heap growth is rapid and difficult to control. Damping is required: this is not envisaged in their crude microeconomic framework, but would be implicitly provided in a PID controller. Another shortcoming of their heap sizing approach is that a target elasticity value is not an intuitive parameter for a user or system administrator to set. On the other hand, a controller target GC overhead is much easier to understand.

7.3 Control Theory for Heap Management

As far as we are aware, there are only two other instances of control-theoretic approaches to memory resource allocation [17, 29]. These are application-specific optimizations, rather than general VM mechanisms.

Storm et al. [29] deal with *autonomic database* configuration. They use control theory to implement a self-tuning memory manager that handles adaptive heap sizing for databases. A typical enterprise database has distinct heaps for various memory-intensive features. e.g. compiled SQL cache, buffer pool, sort memory. The solution proposed by Storm et al. uses a cost/benefit estimation model for resizing individual heaps, with an overall tuning objective of equalizing the cost/benefit metrics for all heaps. The tuning is accomplished using a multi-input multi-output (MIMO) controller with an integral control law (cf. the I component of a PID controller). They enumerate the advantages of a controller-based tuning approach as (i) fast convergence, (ii) rapid adaption, and (iii) stable response to noise.

Gandhi et al. [17] use control theory to improve performance of the *Apache web server*. The two high-level system outputs that their controller attempts to optimize are CPU and memory utilization metrics. The system administrator must set desired values for CPU and memory utilization. The two controller inputs are Apache tuning parameters for (i) the maximum number of simultaneous clients, and (ii) the pause time on an http client connection before it is closed. The web server is modeled as a black box, and characterized using experimental data. The controller is a simple MIMO proportional integral controller (cf. the P and I components in a PID controller). Controller parameter values are tuned using pole placement and linear quadratic regulator techniques. There is limited system performance evaluation in the paper.

We note that the application of control theory to computer systems, and particularly cloud-based resource sharing virtualized systems, is a growing area of research activity [20, 23, 25, 37].

8. Conclusion

8.1 Summary

In this paper, we have proposed the use of control theory for dynamic heap sizing of garbage-collected applications. We have described the deployment of a PID controller in the Jikes RVM memory management system. We have characterized the behavior of this heap size controller on a set of standard Java benchmarks, and compared it with two existing, heuristic-based heap sizing mechanisms.

Our goal in employing control theory is as much to *provide a rigorous approach* as it is to provide a near-optimal solution. So long as our controller is robust and competitive with hand-crafted alternatives, then we propose that its solid foundation should prove a compelling argument for its adoption.

8.2 Discussion of Limitations

In one sense, it is difficult to make a fair comparison between our PID controller and the existing heap sizing mechanism in Jikes RVM, since it is not clear what the current system is trying to optimize, whereas the PID controller has an explicit goal. We hope eventually to design a controller that frees the user of the need to specify a target GC overhead, which will enable a more straightforward comparison. This may require the application of *optimal control theory*.

An obvious limitation is the need to *tune* a PID controller for a specific scenario. As we discuss in Section 6.3, the parameter values are fairly similar across the range of DaCapo benchmark workloads. For clearly distinct workloads, one can use *gain scheduling* to swap in a new set of parameters. In general, most heuristic-based approaches require some amount of tuning effort, so this is a common weakness. All tuning was performed manually in our experiments, however automated PID tuning packages are widely used in industrial settings.

All the experiments reported in this paper use a full-heap, mark/sweep GC. This seems to be a useful base case to demonstrate our new control-theoretic technique. We have not examined generational copying collection at all. We expect that the same techniques should be applicable to generational GC, but that the process of interacting with the controller will be more complex. We note that both Jikes RVM and HotSpot use their heuristic heap sizing mechanism for both generational and non-generational GC, possibly with different growth ratio parameters. We also note that

Vengerov's work [33] on computing overall GC overhead from nursery GC overhead may be applicable.

Another potential concern is the possibility of address space fragmentation caused by excessively frequent heap size changes, particularly with non-moving collectors. In defense of our scheme, we observe that all production VMs support adaptive heap sizing, and there is a general complaint from users that VMs are 'not ramping up the heap size quickly enough.' Further, modern memory managers like MMTk support the mapping of logical heap spaces onto discontiguous region in virtual address space.

So far, our controller does not support paging avoidance, i.e. it does not account for the right-hand half of the sweet-spot curves in Section 2. The currently deployed Jikes RVM heap resizing mechanism is also oblivious to paging. For future work, we hope to incorporate a second controller (using a subsumption model) that will reduce the heap size if it detects paging activity. Such a compound controller would drive an application's heap size towards the sweet-spot region of execution automatically and adaptively.

8.3 Future Work

In addition to extending our control-theoretic system to handle generational collectors and paging avoidance, we have a more ambitious objective.

We envisage a set of VM instances, executing concurrently on a manycore server. Each VM has its own low-level heap resizing mechanism, similar to the PID controller described in this paper. However a higher-level meta-controller is needed at the system level, to ensure that all the VMs co-operate fairly, or in a manner that satisfies (possibly diverse) client policies. We imagine this meta-controller will drive the target variables of the underlying controllers, using some kind of statistical, economic or game theory model.

Acknowledgments

We are grateful to Tony Printezis and Mario Wolczko for confirming our understanding of the HotSpot heap resizing mechanism. We thank David Matthews and Sophia Drossopoulou for commenting on an early draft of this paper. We also acknowledge the help of the anonymous referees.

This research was partly supported by the London Mathematical Society and the Scottish Funding Council through the SICSA project.

References

[1] Experimental resources. `http://sf.net/p/jikesrvm/research-archive/40`.

[2] O. Agmon Ben-Yehuda, M. Ben-Yehuda, A. Schuster, and D. Tsafrir. The resource-as-a-service (RaaS) cloud. In *USENIX Conference on Hot Topics in Cloud Computing*, 2012.

[3] R. Alonso and A. W. Appel. An advisor for flexible working sets. In *Proceedings of the 1990 ACM SIGMETRICS Conference on Measurement and Modeling of Computer Systems*, 1990.

[4] B. Alpern, C. R. Attanasio, J. J. Barton, M. G. Burke, P. Cheng, J.-D. Choi, A. Cocchi, S. J. Fink, D. Grove, M. Hind, S. F. Hummel, D. Lieber, V. Litvinov, M. F. Mergen, T. Ngo, J. R. Russell, V. Sarkar, M. J. Serrano, J. C. Shepherd, S. E. Smith, V. C. Sreedhar, H. Srinivasan, and J. Whaley. The Jalapeño virtual machine. *IBM Systems Journal*, 39(1), 2000.

[5] B. Alpern, S. Augart, S. M. Blackburn, M. Butrico, A. Cocchi, P. Cheng, J. Dolby, S. Fink, D. Grove, M. Hind, K. S. McKinley, M. Mergen, J. E. B. Moss, T. Ngo, V. Sarkar, and M. Trapp. The Jikes research virtual machine project: Building an open source research community. *IBM Systems Journal*, 44(2):1–19, 2005.

[6] M. Armbrust, A. Fox, R. Griffith, A. D. Joseph, R. Katz, A. Konwinski, G. Lee, D. Patterson, A. Rabkin, I. Stoica, and M. Zaharia. A view of cloud computing. *Communications of the ACM*, 53:50–58, 2010.

[7] M. Arnold, M. Vechev, and E. Yahav. QVM: an efficient runtime for detecting defects in deployed systems. In *Proceedings of the 23rd ACM SIGPLAN Symposium on Object-Oriented Programming Systems, Languages, and Applications (OOPSLA)*, pages 143–162. ACM, 2008.

[8] S. M. Blackburn, Perry Cheng, and K. S. McKinley. Oil and water? high performance garbage collection in Java with MMTk. In *Proceedings of the 26th International Conference on Software Engineering*, pages 137–146. ACM, 2004.

[9] S. M. Blackburn, R. Garner, C. Hoffman, A. M. Khan, K. S. McKinley, R. Bentzur, A. Diwan, D. Feinberg, D. Frampton, S. Z. Guyer, M. Hirzel, A. Hosking, M. Jump, H. Lee, J. E. B. Moss, A. Phansalkar, D. Stefanović, T. VanDrunen, D. von Dincklage, and B. Wiedermann. The DaCapo benchmarks: Java benchmarking development and analysis. In *Proceedings of the ACM SIGPLAN Symposium on Object-Oriented Programming Systems, Languages, and Applications (OOPSLA)*. ACM, 2006.

[10] S. M. Blackburn, R. E. Jones, K. S. McKinley, and J. E. B. Moss. Beltway: Getting around garbage collection gridlock. In *ACM SIGPLAN Conference on Programming Language Design and Implementation (PLDI)*, pages 153–164. ACM, 2002.

[11] H.J. Boehm and M. Weiser. Garbage collection in an uncooperative environment. *Software: Practice and Experience*, 18(9):807–820, 1988.

[12] T. Brecht, E. Arjomandi, C. Li, and H. Pham. Controlling garbage collection and heap growth to reduce the execution time of Java applications. *ACM Transactions on Programming Languages and Systems*, 28:908–941, 2006.

[13] R. Buyya, S. Y. Chee, and S. Venugopal. Market-oriented cloud computing: Vision, hype, and reality for delivering IT services as computing utilities. In *Proceedings of High Performance Computing and Communications*, pages 5–13, 2008.

[14] A. Datta, M.T. Ho, and S.P. Bhattacharyya. *Structure and synthesis of PID controllers*. Springer, 2000.

[15] E. Duesterwald, C. Cascaval, and Sandhya Dwarkadas. Characterizing and predicting program behavior and its variability. In *Proceedings of Parallel Architectures and Compilation Techniques*, 2003.

[16] D. Durkee. Why cloud computing will never be free. *Queue*, 8:20:20–20:29.

[17] N. Gandhi, D.M. Tilbury, Y. Diao, J. Hellerstein, and S. Parekh. MIMO control of an Apache web server: modeling and controller design. In *Proceedings of the American Control Conference*, 2002.

[18] David Grove. Private Communication, 2011.

[19] C. Grzegorczyk, S. Soman, C. Krintz, and R. Wolski. Isla vista heap sizing: Using feedback to avoid paging. In *Proceedings of the International Symposium on Code Generation and Optimization*, 2007.

[20] J. Hellerstein, S. Singhal, and Qian Wang. Research challenges in control engineering of computing systems. *IEEE Transactions on Network and Service Management*, 6(4):206–211, 2009.

[21] M. Hertz, S. Kane, E. Keudel, T. Bai, C. Ding, X. Gu, and J. E. Bard. Waste not, want not: resource-based garbage collection in a shared environment. In *Proceedings of the 11th ACM SIGPLAN International Symposium on Memory Management (ISMM)*.

[22] R. Jones, A. Hosking, and E. Moss. *The Garbage Collection Handbook: The Art of Automatic Memory Management*. Chapman & Hall, 2012.

[23] C. Karamanolis, M. Karlsson, and X. Zhu. Designing controllable computer systems. In *Proceedings of the 10th conference on Hot Topics in Operating Systems*, 2005.

[24] N. S. Nise. *Control Systems Engineering*. John Wiley & Sons, Inc., 3rd edition, 2000.

[25] P. Padala, K. G. Shin, X. Zhu, M. Uysal, Z. Wang, S. Singhal, A. Merchant, and K. Salem. Adaptive control of virtualized resources in utility computing environments. In *Proceedings of the 2nd ACM SIGOPS/EuroSys European Conference on Computer Systems*. ACM, 2007.

[26] S. P. Reiss. Dynamic detection and visualization of software phases. In *Proceedings of the 3rd International Workshop on Dynamic Analysis*. ACM, 2005.

[27] J. Singer, R. E. Jones, G. Brown, and M. Luján. The economics of garbage collection. In *Proceedings of the 10th ACM SIGPLAN International Symposium on Memory Management (ISMM)*. ACM, 2010.

[28] S. Soman, C. Krintz, and D. F. Bacon. Dynamic selection of application-specific garbage collectors. In *Proceedings of the 4th ACM SIGPLAN International Symposium on Memory Management (ISMM)*. ACM, 2004.

[29] A. J. Storm, C. Garcia-Arellano, S. S. Lightstone, Y. Diao, and M. Surendra. Adaptive self-tuning memory in DB2. In *Proceedings of the 32nd International Conference on Very Large Data Bases*, 2006.

[30] Sun. Garbage collector ergonomics. `http://docs.oracle.com/javase/1.5.0/docs/guide/vm/gc-ergonomics.html`.

[31] K. Sun, Y. Li, M. Hogstrom, and Y. Chen. Sizing multi-space in heap for application isolation. In *Companion to the 21st ACM SIGPLAN Symposium on Object-Oriented Programming Systems, Languages, and Applications (OOPSLA)*. ACM, 2006.

[32] Y.C. Tay and X.R. Zong. A page fault equation for dynamic heap sizing. In *Proceedings of the first joint WOSP/SIPEW International Conference on Performance Engineering*, 2010.

[33] D. Vengerov. Modeling, analysis and throughput optimization of a generational garbage collector. In *Proceedings of the 9th ACM SIGPLAN International Symposium on Memory Management (ISMM)*. ACM, 2009.

[34] T. Yang, E. D. Berger, S. F. Kaplan, and J. E. B. Moss. Cramm: virtual memory support for garbage-collected applications. In *Proceedings of the 7th Symposium on Operating Systems Design and Implementation*. ACM, 2006.

[35] T. Yang, E.D. Berger, M. Hertz, S.F. Kaplan, and J.E.B. Moss. Automatic heap sizing: Taking real memory into account. In *Proceedings of the 4th ACM SIGPLAN International Symposium on Memory Management (ISMM)*. ACM, 2004.

[36] C. Zhang, K. Kelsey, X. Shen, C. Ding, M. Hertz, and M. Ogihara. Program-level adaptive memory management. In *Proceedings of the 5th ACM SIGPLAN International Symposium on Memory Management (ISMM)*. ACM, 2006.

[37] X. Zhu, M. Uysal, Z. Wang, S. Singhal, A. Merchant, P. Padala, and K. Shin. What does control theory bring to systems research? *SIGOPS Operating Systems Review*, 43:62–69, 2009.

[38] J. G. Ziegler and N. B. Nichols. Optimum settings for automatic controllers. *Transactions of the American Society of Mechanical Engineers*, 64:759–768, 1942.

Pacman: Program-Assisted Cache Management *

Jacob Brock

Department of Computer Science
University of Rochester
Rochester, NY, USA
jbrock@cs.rochester.edu

Xiaoming Gu [†]

Azul Systems, Inc.
Sunnyvale, CA, USA
xiaoming@azulsystems.com

Bin Bao [†]

Adobe Systems Incorporated
bbao@adobe.com

Chen Ding

Department of Computer Science
University of Rochester
Rochester, NY, USA
cding@cs.rochester.edu

Abstract

As caches become larger and shared by an increasing number of cores, cache management is becoming more important. This paper explores collaborative caching, which uses software hints to influence hardware caching. Recent studies have shown that such collaboration between software and hardware can theoretically achieve optimal cache replacement on LRU-like cache.

This paper presents Pacman, a practical solution for collaborative caching in loop-based code. Pacman uses profiling to analyze patterns in an optimal caching policy in order to determine which data to cache and at what time. It then splits each loop into different parts at compile time. At run time, the loop boundary is adjusted to selectively store data that would be stored in an optimal policy. In this way, Pacman emulates the optimal policy wherever it can. Pacman requires a single bit at the load and store instructions. Some of the current hardware has partial support. This paper presents results using both simulated and real systems, and compares simulated results to related caching policies.

Categories and Subject Descriptors B.3.2 [*MEMORY STRUCTURES*]: Design Styles - Cache memories; D.3.4 [*PROGRAMMING LANGUAGES*]: Processors - Compilers, Optimization

General Terms Algorithms, Performance, Theory

Keywords cache replacement policy, collaborative caching, optimal caching, priority cache hint

---

* The research is supported in part by the National Science Foundation (Contract No. CCF-1116104, CCF-0963759, CNS-0834566), IBM CAS Faculty Fellowship and a grant from Huawei.

[†] The work was done when Xiaoming Gu and Bin Bao were graduate students at the University of Rochester.

1. Introduction

There are two basic strategies to reduce the number of cache misses: locality optimization and cache management. In cases where locality optimization falls short (e.g. when loop tiling and loop fusion cannot reduce the working set size to fit in the cache), improved cache management can pick up the slack by storing as much of the active data as possible.

In this paper, we present program-assisted cache management (Pacman), a practical solution to approximate optimal cache management. It solves mainly two problems: at compile time, deciding how to best cache data, and at run time, communicating the decision to hardware.

To decide whether or not to cache data, we employ a comparison with OPT, the optimal caching policy. Under this policy, the stack distance of a block at any access (which we will call the OPT distance) represents the smallest cache size for which the access will be a cache hit [19].

We present profiling techniques that collect and identify patterns in the OPT distance for individual references over the program. Two training runs with different program inputs show linear patterns for some references that allow the inference of patterns for future runs with any input. The decision of whether to cache the data is then simple: If the OPT distance is less than the cache size, the data is cached. Otherwise, it is not.

In order to communicate this decision to the hardware, Pacman divides each loop into two parts at compile time: a high-locality part with short OPT distances, and a low-locality part with long OPT distances. At run time, the loop boundaries are adjusted based on the input and cache size, and high-locality accesses are cached, while low-locality accesses are not.

Pacman requires hardware support, in particular, a single bit at each instruction to control whether cache should store the accessed data. A limited form of such an interface is the non-temporal stores on Intel machines, which have recently been used to reduce string processing and memory zeroing time [21, 30]. A number of other systems have been built or proposed for software hints to influence hardware caching. Earlier examples include the placement hints on Intel Itanium [7], bypassing access on IBM Power series [23], the evict-me bit of [26]. Wang et al. called a combined software-hardware solution *collaborative caching* [26].

Past collaborative caching solutions have used the dependence distance [4] and the reuse distance [7, 26] to distinguish between high and low-locality data and to cache the former more securely over the latter. However, in an optimal cache policy, low-locality data is not always thrown out (consider a program, e.g. streaming, that has *only* low locality data). A reuse distance based hint would mark all data as low locality and does not exploit the fact that a portion of it can fit in cache and benefit from cache reuse. Pacman conducts partial data caching by mimicking OPT management (as illustrated in Figure 4). In addition, unlike the previous solutions, the Pacman hints change with the cache and the input size (which are the two parameters to loop splitting).

Pacman optimizes loop code by performing different types of cache accesses based on the loop index. In this paper, we analyze and evaluate scientific loop kernels and benchmark programs. For loops in other types of programs, the Pacman framework can be applied without change, but the effect depends on whether Pacman can identify exploitable patterns for cache management. Another possible use of Pacman is to augment the implementation of the array abstraction in higher level languages (Section 4.5).

The rest of the paper first characterizes OPT caching and then describes the Pacman system that allocates cache among data within an array and across multiple arrays.

2.   Pacman System Overview

Cache management is traditionally done online in hardware. Unfortunately, the optimal caching solution is impossible to compute online, because it requires knowledge of future memory accesses. Pacman circumvents this problem by computing the optimal solution at profiling time and then applying the solution at run time. Figure 1 shows an overview of the system, and the three phases are outlined as follows:

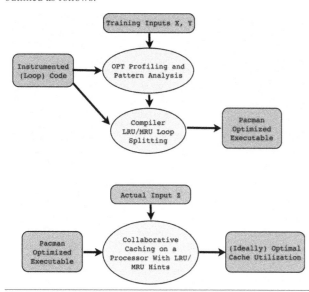

Figure 1. Overview of the Pacman system with OPT pattern profiling, LRU/MRU loop splitting, and collaborative caching

1. **Profiling Time** At a training run, the memory access trace is profiled to determine the OPT distance at each access. Patterns are then identified in these OPT distances. With multiple training runs using different input array sizes, patterns for other inputs can be extrapolated.

2. **Compile Time** Based on the patterns, a compiler performs loop splitting so that at run time, the loop iterations can be divided into groups where each static memory reference in the loop is tagged with a hint (for either LRU or MRU eviction).

3. **Run Time** At run time, based on the cache size and the input, a Pacman-optimized loop determines the actual division of loop splitting to guide the cache with the hints to approach optimal cache management.

3.   Optimal Caching and the OPT Distance

The optimal (OPT) algorithm replaces the block that is accessed furthest in the future whenever a replacement was necessary. Another way to put it is that OPT evicts the *least imminently used* block, instead of the least recently used one that the *least recently used* (LRU) policy would. This is the basis of the optimal caching algorithm of [5].

The idea was expanded by [19] with the concept of the OPT stack, a priority list for what blocks should be the cache at any given time; A cache of size (1, 2, 3, ...) will contain the first (1, 2, 3, ...) blocks in the stack, thus an access to a data block is a miss when its stack position (OPT distance, or OPTD) is greater than the size of the cache. Figure 2 shows a memory access trace for a simple streaming program and demonstrates the application of three rules for managing the OPT cache stack:

- **Upward Movement:** *A block can only move up when accessed, and then it moves to the top.* Moving upward implies entering a cache (of size less than its current stack position), and this can only happen if the block is accessed. The block goes to the top of the OPT stack because it needs to be accessible by a cache of size 1.

- **Downward Movement:** *Vacancies are filled by whichever block above it will not be used for the longest time in the future.* A new block is treated as having vacated a new spot at the bottom (in order to usurp the top position). Moving a block downward to fill a vacancy represents its eviction from all caches smaller than the position of the vacancy (and the block with the most remote future use is evicted).

- **Tiebreaking:** *When there is a tie due to two infinite forward distances, it may be broken arbitrarily.*

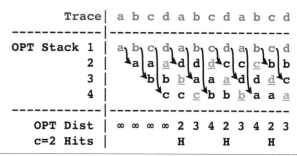

Figure 2. An example memory access trace for a simple streaming application. Because a block must always be loaded into the cache for the processor to use it, the top stack position is always given to the current memory block. When they are necessary, demotions are given to the block in the stack which will not be needed for the longest time in the future. For a cache size of 2, this program would cause cache thrashing under an LRU policy, but under the OPT policy, every third access is a hit once the cache is warm. This is a result of the $(2, 3, 4)$ pattern in the OPT distances which arises for streaming accesses, as explained the appendix. Demotions are shown with arrows, and the next access is shown in red with underline.

To demonstrate the practical difference between the optimal policy and the LRU policy, consider a simple streaming application which repeatedly traverses a 5MB array. Figure 3 compares

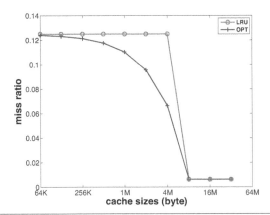

Figure 3. LRU & OPT miss ratios of a streaming application on power of 2 cache sizes from 64KB to 32MB (64-byte blocks, 16-way set associative). LRU does not benefit from a larger cache unless/until the working set fits in completely. OPT fully utilizes the available space to cache the working set as much as possible.

the cache performance of LRU and OPT for 16-way set associative cache with 64-byte cache blocks (8 data elements per block). The figure shows the miss ratio for all power-of-two cache sizes between 64KB and 32MB. When the cache size is less than 5MB, the LRU cache has a constant miss ratio of $\frac{1}{8} = 12.5\%$, but there is a sharp drop in the miss ratio at 5MB because the whole array then fits in the cache.

The OPT distances in this example vary from 2 cache blocks to roughly the data size. To show why this is the case, we demonstrate in Figure 2 how the OPT distances vary from 2 to roughly the data size in a smaller access trace. As the OPT distance varies between 128 bytes and 5MB in the streaming application, those accesses whose OPT distance is below the cache size will be cache hits. As the cache size grows, more accesses will be hits, so there is a more gradual reduction in the miss ratio.

Another way to view the performance discrepancy is that at the end of the array, LRU is acting on the assumption that the array will now be traversed backwards, while OPT knows that it will be traversed forwards again from the beginning.

4. OPT-based Hint Insertion

This section describes the theory, analysis, transformation, and two extensions of Pacman.

4.1 Optimal Collaborative Caching

Collaborative caching may obtain the performance of OPT on LRU like caches, as proved for several papers including the bypass and trespass LRU caches [10] and the LRU/MRU cache [11]. Instead of clairvoyance and complex cache replacement as required by OPT (described in Section 3), the collaborative cache uses two alternatives more amenable to hardware implementation:

- *1-bit hint.* A memory access is marked by a single bit to be either a normal (LRU) access or a special (MRU, e.g.) access.

- *LRU-like hardware.* The deviation from LRU involves only actions affecting the boundary positions of the stack (while OPT requires reordering in the middle of the stack) [11]. In fact, limited implementations are already available on existing hardware (see Section 5.6).

Pacman uses the LRU/MRU cache and the OPT distance for hint insertion. As an example, consider Pacman being given the

data access trace in Figure 4. To make it interesting, the trace has mixed locality: 2 blocks xy are reused frequently, having high locality; while the other 7 blocks abcdefg (highlighted in red) have a streaming pattern and low locality. Pacman first computes the forward OPT distances, which are shown below the trace.

trace	xyaxybxycxydxyexyfxygxyaxybxycxydxye ...
fwd. optd	2342352362372382392342352362372382 39 ...
hint (c=5)	LLLLLLLMLLMLLMLLMLLLLLLLLLMLLMLLMLLM ...

Figure 4. Since the non-xy accesses (highlighted in red) all have reuse distances greater than the cache size, a reuse distance based hint would cache none of them. A better solution is to cache some, but not all of them.

Suppose that the cache size is 5. For each access, Pacman inserts either an LRU or an MRU hint, shown in the table below the distances, by checking whether the distance is over 5. Being so hinted, the cache keeps xy and 2 of the streaming data in cache while leaving the others out, despite the fact that each of the streaming data have reuse distances larger than the cache size. In this way, the cache stores as much data in the cache as can benefit from it.

To quantify cache performance, the following table gives the stack distances for LRU (i.e. the reuse distance), MRU, OPT [19], and Pacman (i.e. the LRU/MRU distance) [11]. Capacity misses happen on accesses whose distance exceeds the cache size (miss iff $dis > c = 5$). The miss counts are 5 and 10 for LRU and MRU but just 3 for OPT and Pacman. Where Pacman accurately predicts the OPT distance, it gives the optimal cache hint. [1] OPT and Pacman distances differ, because the Pacman cache has LRU-like logic, while OPT does not.

trace	xyaxybxycxydxyexyfxygxyaxybxycxydxye	miss (c=5)
lru	---33-33-33-33-33-33-119119119119119	5
mru	---23-34-45-56-67-78-892924345456567	10
opt	---23-23-23-23-23-23-234235236237238	3
pac.	---33-33-32-32-32-32-325334336327328	3

Figure 5. Comparison of caching policies, demonstrating that, with correct OPTD predictions, Pacman can match the optimal policy.

The distances explain the inner workings of the cache management. The high distances in LRU show its inability to cache any low-locality data. The high distances in MRU show its problem with caching high-locality data. Both OPT and Pacman treat the two working sets separately and always have low distances for high-locality data and linearly increasing distances for low-locality data. The varying distances are effectively priorities through which these policies select program data to cache.

4.2 OPT Pattern Recognition

In an execution, a reference in a loop may make many accesses, each with a forward OPT distance. Pattern analysis uses training runs to find the correlation between the loop index and the OPT distance so the OPT distance can be predicted when the program is run for real.

OPT Forward Distance Profiling The profiling step records the forward OPT distance and the iteration count at all enclosing loops. Each reference-loop pair provides one sequence of <index, distance> pairs for the next step of pattern analysis. The profiling mechanism and cost are described in Section 4.4.

---

[1] In fact, it can be proved that the LRU/MRU cache will miss if and only if the OPT cache does (for the chosen cache size, 5 in this case). [11]

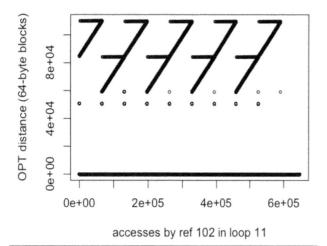

y-axis label: OPT distance (64-byte blocks)
x-axis label: accesses by ref 102 in loop 11

Figure 6. The OPT distances exhibited by a reference in *Swim*. The bounded pattern is between 5 and 10. The linear pattern has a slope of 38 cache blocks for every 100 iterations.

Linear and Bounded Patterns The OPT distances of a reference have mainly two types of patterns. The first is bounded length. For example, as a loop traverses a (8-byte) double precision array, it moves to a different (64-byte) cache block at every eighth access. The seven preceding accesses are spatial reuses. The length of these OPT distances are bounded. The eighth access, however, has an OPT distance that varies and can be as large as the size of the array. The first case is a *bounded pattern*, and the latter a *linear pattern*. We define the bounded pattern by the upper bound of the distances and the linear pattern by an intercept α and a slope β. An <index, distance> pair $< i, d >$ belongs to a linear pattern $< \alpha, \beta >$ if $d \approx \alpha + \beta i$.

As an example, Figure 6 plots the OPT distances for 647 thousand accesses by one of the 197 references in the SPEC 2000 benchmark program *Swim*. The 647 thousand distances are drawn as circles on a 2D plot, with the distance on the y-axis and the iteration count on the x-axis.

The bounded pattern is visible as the line at the bottom of the figure. The distances are between 5 and 10. The pattern contains about 7/8 (88%) of all points. The 5 diagonal lines (from lower left to upper right) show five linear patterns. The common slope (0.38) shows that the distance increases by 38 cache blocks for every 100 iterations. Although it is not visually apparent, the two patterns include most of the points on the plot. The points outside these two patterns account for less than 0.001% of the total (262 out of 646,944).

Grid Regression Most OPT distances are part of some linear pattern: Either they stay within a constant range, as in the case of spatial reuse, or they grow at a constant rate, as in the case of an array traversal. However, in real data the intermingling of multiple patterns (as in Figure 6) makes linear regression difficult. The problem can be solved by separating the data points into their pattern groups and then applying linear regression within each group. Based on this observation, we developed a technique we call *grid regression*.

```
algorithm grid_regression(set)

  tile_partition(set) #3 rows x 40 cols

  for each tile
    slope = regression(tile).slope
    intercept = regression(tile).intercept
```

```
    y_pred(x) = slope*x + intercept
    for each point
      if abs(y - y_pred) < 100
        add point to pattern

  combine_tile_patterns

end algorithm
```

Given a set of (x,y) coordinates for iteration index and OPT distance of the reference at that access, the data set is divided into 40 rows and 3 columns. Each tile is assigned a slope and intercept based on standard linear regression. Each point in each tile is then accepted as "in the pattern" if the OPT distance is within 100 of the regression line. If more than 90% of the points in a region are in the pattern, the tile is considered to have a pattern. Next, each pattern merges with each neighbor if the neighbor's smallest and largest points are within 100 of the first pattern's regression line. After as many patterns have merged as possible, each pattern's *accuracy* is defined as the percentage of points in the set that lie in the pattern.

An Example in Swim *Swim* is a SPEC 2000 benchmark, adapted from vectorized code for shallow water simulation. It has 197 references to 14 arrays in 22 loops. As an example profiling analysis, we run the program on the input 256 by 256. Each array is 524KB in size. The following table shows OPT distance patterns for a 2-level nested loop, with 18 references at the inner loop (Loop 3) and 6 more at the outer loop (Loop 4).

```
Loop 4: r257 to r262
  Loop 3: r251 to r256
```

ref	loop	alloc	intercept	accuracy/size
251	4	48.6%	534kb	96.2%
252	4	24.4%	1620kb	99.6%
253	4	48.6%	534kb	97.0%
254	4	24.4%	1613kb	99.2%
255	4	77.3%	186kb	22.2%
256	4	24.4%	1620kb	99.2%
257	4	48.9%	545kb	100.0%
258	4	32.3%	3789kb	100.0%
259	4	48.9%	540kb	100.0%
260	4	24.5%	1620kb	100.0%
261	4	48.8%	540kb	100.0%
262	4	24.5%	1628kb	100.0%

The multi-level grid regression found patterns (third to fifth columns) for these references (first column). The patterns show an elaborate size-dependent cache allocation. If the cache size is smaller than 186KB, all these references are MRU. Between 186KB and 540KB, *r255* in the inner loop is allocated in cache. From 540KB to 1.6MB, *r251* and *r253* in the inner loop and *r257, r259* and *r261* in the outer loop all take an equal share, 49%. These six references access only two arrays, with the inner-loop ones accessing the body and outer-loop ones the boundary of the arrays. As the cache size increases beyond 1.6MB, more referenced data is allocated into cache. Using *Swim* as a non-trivial example, we next discuss the issues in analyzing programs with more complex loop structures.

Nested Loops For each reference, all enclosing loops are analyzed for patterns. The loop whose pattern has the highest accuracy is considered *pattern carrying*. Its loop index and those of the inner loops are used for the OPT distance prediction. As an example, Figure 7 shows a reference in a two-level i, j loop that traverses a matrix. In the inner j loop, the iteration count ranges from 0 to n_j,

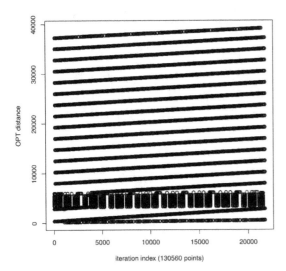

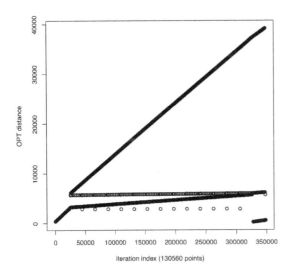

Figure 7. The OPT distance patterns of a reference in a nested loop. The x-axis shows the inner-loop iteration count in the upper graph and the cumulative iteration count in the lower graph. The outer loop (cumulative iteration count) is selected for Pacman to predict the OPT distance.

the number of j iterations. In the outer i loop, the iteration count is cumulative and ranges from 0 to $n_j n_i$. Grid regression identifies many linear patterns at the inner loop, one for each loop instance, but no majority pattern. At the j loop, it finds a single (linear) pattern. The patterns in *Swim* are all carried by the outer loop as in this example, as stated by the second column in the previous table.

Non-contiguous access, Non-perfect Nesting, Branches, and Indirection Linear patterns are fairly robust against code complexity. The previous *Swim* loop nest processes the boundary elements differently than the body elements outside the inner loop (r257–r262). These accesses form a regular linear pattern since their processing recurs at regular intervals. Similarly, if there is conditional processing, an array is accessed by multiple references in branches or switch cases. If some of those references access each

element, then they will all have the same linear pattern. Still, the linear pattern may fail in two cases. The first is when an array is accessed only partially *and* at irregular intervals, e.g. through indirection. Linear regression would show an accuracy proportional to the degree of regularity. The second is when the same reference, through indirection, accesses two different arrays at different regular intervals. The analysis can detect multiple linear patterns, but each pattern is small in size and unsuitable for prediction.

Conservative Pattern Selection Pacman uses a pattern only if the accuracy is above a threshold, e.g. 90%. When the pattern accuracy is low, we may not know which access should be labeled MRU. To be conservative, we make them LRU, so at least not to perform worse than the original program. A compiler solution may remedy this. Beyls and D'Hollander developed conditional hints for loop references that have mixed reuse-distance patterns [7]. To use it here, we need compiler analysis of the OPT distance, which we leave as future work.

Whole-array and Priority-array Patterns Two characteristics in the *Swim* example are common in programs we have tested. First, the linear patterns occur at the whole-array level, e.g. the outer loop in *Swim*. The OPT distance grows with the array *size*, independent of the array *shape*. We call it the *whole-array pattern*. Second, the intercept represents a kind of stratification — lower priority arrays (because of the greater intercepts) are cached only after all higher priority arrays have been. We call it the *priority-array* pattern. These two properties are important in cross-input pattern analysis.

Cross-Input Pattern Prediction When the input changes, a reference may access the same array but with a different shape and size. The shape does not affect whole-array patterns. The size affects the intercept of priority-array patterns. The intercept changes proportionally to the size of the high priority arrays.

To predict the change in the intercept, Pacman uses multiple training runs. Each provides an <intercept, input size> pair. Then the pattern is established by standard linear regression. The minimum number of tests needed is two. Our test programs in Section 5 are mostly scientific simulations on some dense physical grid. We use the total grid size as the input size in the experiment. It can be automated by examining the loop bounds in training and using them to calculate the input size before executing the loop.

The predictability of loop bounds has been carefully studied by Mao and Shen. They gave a three-step solution — feature extraction, incremental modeling and discriminative prediction — and showed accurate prediction of the loop bounds in a set of Java program from just a few extracted parameters [17].

4.3 Loop Splitting and Hint Insertion

After Pacman finds a linear pattern for a reference, it uses a compiler to split the pattern-carrying loop. The following function finds the break point before which a reference should make LRU accesses and after which it should make MRU accesses. In the formula, p is a pattern with *intercept* and *slope*. The two splitting parameters are the cache size c and the input size n.

```
function lru-mru-split( p, c, n )
    return (c - p.intercept * n) / p.slope
end
```

A loop may have k references that require loop splitting. Pacman produces at most k different breakpoints. The reference is LRU in the loops before its breakpoint and MRU in the loops after its breakpoint. Of the $k + 1$ loops, the first will have all LRU accesses, and the last will have MRU accesses.

```
for i in 1, n  // loop x
  body
end
```

is transformed to

```
b1,..,bk = lru-mru-split( p1,...,pk, n, c )
sort(b1,...,bk)
for i in 1, b1
    body-1
end
...
for i in bk-1, bk
  body-k
end
for i in bk, n
  body-k+1
end
```

Loop splitting increases the code size as the loop body is duplicated for every breakpoint. However, the degree of splitting is limited. First, not all references require splitting. It is required only for references that have a linear OPT distance pattern. Second, references with similar patterns can use the same breakpoint. For the example shown in Section 4.2, the loop nest from *Swim* has 18 references in the inner loop. Twelve have linear patterns and require loop splitting. Five of them have a similar pattern, so they can use the same split. The other 7 have 2 additional patterns, so this example would take 4 replicated loops. Third, loop code is compact and has good spatial locality. As the execution moves from one to the next, the active code size does not change. Forth, some of the loops may not be executed. In the *Swim* example, the largest pattern (of the 3) has an intercept of 3.8MB. At a smaller input size or a larger data size, the last replicated loop would have zero iteration. Finally, if a loop has a large body and requires a large number of splits, we may choose a subset of splits by weighing on the relative importance of the references. In evaluation, we will show that loop code tends not to incur misses because the instruction cache on modern machines is large.

4.4 OPT Forward Distance Profiling

OPT profiling (i.e. stack simulation [19]) takes a data access trace as the input and computes the OPT distance for each access. The distance is *backward* because it is computed at the end of each data reuse pair. Pacman converts it to a forward distance by recording it at the start of the data reuse pair. Since a program trace is too large to fit in main memory, Pacman dumps the access time and OPT distance pairs to a file. While the backward distance is ordered, the forward distance is not. Pacman uses the Unix sort command in a second pass to order the pairs by the access time in preparation for pattern analysis.

We can reduce the cost of storing the OPT distance traces by ignoring short distances if needed but by far the greatest cost in Pacman is the OPT simulation. For fastest OPT profiling, we use the tool by Sugumar and Abraham [25]. It implements the OPT stack using a splay tree for cache efficiency and a novel technique to update stack layout quickly. Profiling times for each workload are shown in Table 1.

Accompanying the OPT distance, Pacman records three types of program information: memory reference, loop, and function call. For memory profiling, we instrument every load and store. For function profiling, we insert profiling calls before and after every call site. Loop profiling captures 3 events: loop entry, loop exit, and a loop tick for every iteration.

The purpose of function profiling is to detect context-sensitive patterns in loops. In the following we discuss only loop pattern

analysis, which is the same once the context is fixed. A function may be called inside a loop. There are two effects. First, the same function may be called by multiple loops. Pacman treats it in each loop context as a different function so not to mix their patterns. Second, a function may be executed multiple times in the same loop iteration. Pacman records these OPT distances as happening at the same time (measured by the iteration count).

4.5 Non-loop Pacman

We discuss an extension that takes advantage of the flexibility of program control: the support of non-loop code. In modern languages, most array operations are implemented in libraries such as the Vector class in Java and Array class in Ruby. Some of the functions traverse the entire array. These functions can take the LRU/MRU breakpoint as an optional parameter. The implementation would access the array using LRU access up to the breakpoint and MRU afterwards. A recent paper discusses the modern implementation of dynamically sized array [22]. Pacman may be added as another optimization technique to enable programmer control over the cache allocation for the array.

5. Evaluation

5.1 Experimental Setup

Workloads To evaluate Pacman, we simulate its use with 8 workloads. As the commonly used benchmark to measure memory bandwidth, *stream* repeatedly traverses a set of large arrays. Our version uses just one array. *SOR* implements Jacobi Successive Over-relaxation modified from SciMark 2.0 [1]. *Swim, mgrid,* and *applu* are from SPEC CPU 2000 [2] and *bwaves, leslie3d* and *zeusmp* from SPEC CPU 2006 [3]. For each workload, we have 3 different input sizes: small, medium, and large. Table 1 shows the number of references and loops and the size of their executions.

We chose these programs because their data size and running length can be adjusted by changing the input parameters. The training uses OPT, so Pacman cannot profile programs on overly large inputs. The testing of Pacman can be done on any size input. In order to compare with OPT, however, we choose small enough inputs in testing as well.

Pacman Implementation We implemented the profiling support a version of the LLVM compiler [15]. We did not implement loop splitting. Instead, all loop accesses are processed during simulation, and the splitting is done by the simulator. The simulated cache has 64-byte blocks, 16- way set associativity for cache sizes between 2MB and 16MB. The block size and associativity are based on the x86 machine we use for the simulation. Since we simulate only (data) cache, not the CPU, we cannot evaluate the looping overhead. We do not expect a significant overhead for the list of reasons given in Section 4.3. In Section 5.6, we will use a simple test to measure the complete effect of Pacman on a real system.

The OPT profiling times shown in Table 1 were measured on a 3 GHz AMD Opteron Processor 4284 with a 2 MB L3 cache.

Dynamic Insertion Policy (DIP) We compare Pacman with a hardware solution called Dynamic Insertion Policy (DIP) by Qureshi et al. [20]. DIP divides the cache into three sets: (1) a small set of cache blocks dedicated to the LRU policy, (2) another small set of cache blocks dedicated to a mostly-MRU policy called Bimodal Insertion Policy (BIP), and (3) the majority of cache blocks which will follow whichever of the first two policies is performing best at any point in time.

For workloads that are LRU-averse during any phase in their execution, DIP can outperform LRU by adaptively choosing BIP. For workloads that are LRU-friendly throughout, DIP consistently allocates the majority of cache blocks to LRU, but can in rare

Workload	Mem. Ref's (Num.)	Loops (Num.)	Input Size	Trace Length (M)	Data Set Size (MB)	OPT Profile Time (s)
streaming	1	2	small	5.2	2.1	11.7
			med.	10.5	4.2	18.1
(C)			large	21.0	8.4	35.0
SOR	7	5	small	10.7	2.1	10.8
			med.	42.8	8.4	35.3
(C)			large	171.7	33.6	149.7
swim	341	33	small	42.5	7.6	50.8
			med.	95.5	16.9	151.7
(F77)			large	169.6	29.9	306.6
mgrid	418	46	small	5.1	0.2	5.7
			med.	39.5	1.1	37.9
(F77)			large	312.2	7.6	323.5
applu	1858	125	small	42.2	2.8	50.9
			med.	62.9	4.1	74.9
(F77)			large	163.1	10.3	213.2
bwaves	630	96	small	25.6	1.1	33.4
			med.	52.9	2.2	69.0
(F77)			large	389.6	16.6	631.4
leslie3d	3718	295	small	31.1	1.9	32.7
			med.	64.9	3.7	72.9
(F90)			large	147.6	6.9	171.4
zeusmp	10428	446	small	13.9	2.1	19.4
			med.	39.5	2.9	53.8
(F77)			large	85.5	4.2	117.6

Table 1. The statistics of the 8 workloads

instances even be outperformed by LRU because of misses incurred by BIP dedicated blocks.

For our comparisons, we used a DIP implementation of Xiang et al. [28], which follows the description in the original paper and selects the parameters the paper mentioned: a policy selection threshold of 1024 (so that the LRU set must have 1024 more misses than the BIP set in any time window to trigger a policy switch to BIP), and "bimodal throttle parameters" of 1/16, 1/32, and 1/64 (so that each BIP block randomly uses LRU instead of MRU with this probability). The lowest miss rate between these three options is always reported, although there is only small variation.

Estimated Reuse Distance Hint Policy (RDE-Hint) We compare Pacman with a software solution by Beyls and D'Hollander [7]. They proposed a reuse distance based hint. If over 90% of memory accesses generated by an instruction have reuse distances greater than the cache size, the instruction is given a cache hint of "MRU". Pacman works similarly, but using the OPT distance metric described in Section 3 instead of reuse distance.

The estimated reuse distance hint (*RDE-Hint*) policy is a modification of Pacman and an approximation of the Beyls and D'Hollander method. Figure 4 shows an example where the reuse distance for certain accesses (`abcdefg`) remains constant (and large), but the OPT distance forms a linear pattern peaking above the reuse distance. When an OPTD pattern is identified in the Pacman policy, these references will likely have large reuse distances, as demonstrated above, so they are tagged by the RDE-Hint policy for MRU eviction.

5.2 Pacman for Swim

Figure 8 shows the percent reduction of misses for four cache sizes. When training and testing on the same input, Pacman reduces the number of misses by 3%, 6%, 22% and 39%. When training on two small inputs and testing on a large input, the reduction becomes 3%, 5%, 41% and 58%. The larger reduction has to do with the relation between the data size and cache size and does not mean the predicted OPT distance is more accurate for the larger input.

We use the total grid size as the data size for *swim*. Two grids may have different shapes but the same size. We have tested two

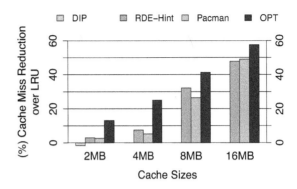

(a) Swim, training on input 256 by 256 and 384 by 384 and testing on 512 by 512

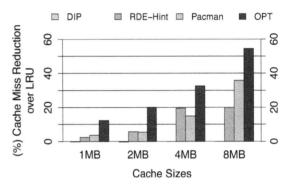

(b) Swim, training on input 384 by 384 and testing on 200 by 737

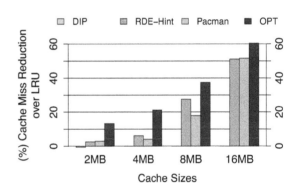

(c) Swim, training on input 256 by 256 and 384 by 384 and testing on 300 by 873

Figure 8. DIP, RDE-Hint, Pacman and OPT tested on *swim* when the input size (a), array shape (b) and both (c) change from training to testing.

other inputs. The first is 200 by 737, which we choose to have the same total size as 384 by 384. Pacman predicts the same linear patterns for the two executions. Similarly, we choose 300 by 837 to have the same size of 512 by 512. We test Pacman by changing just the grid shape, just the input size, and both. The reduction numbers are shown in Figure 8. There is no significant loss of Pacman benefits as a result of these changes. It demonstrates the robustness of the Pacman pattern analysis and the cross-input prediction for this program.

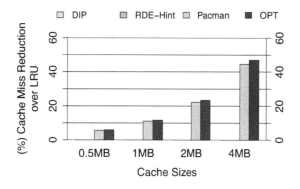

(a) Streaming, training on *SIZE*=256 and *SIZE*=512 and testing on *SIZE*=1024

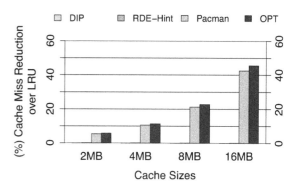

(b) SOR, training on *SIZE*=512 and 1024 and testing on *SIZE*=2048

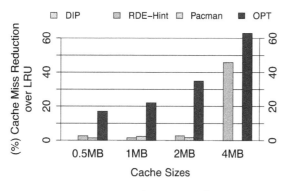

(c) Mgrid, training on $SIZE=2^4$ and $SIZE=2^5$ and testing on $SIZE=2^6$

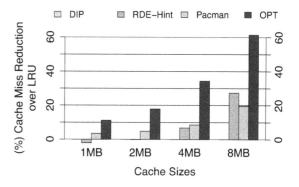

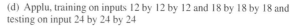

(d) Applu, training on inputs 12 by 12 by 12 and 18 by 18 by 18 and testing on input 24 by 24 by 24

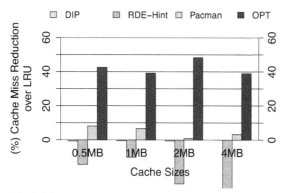

(e) Leslie3d, training on inputs 21 by 21 by 2 and 31 by 31 by 2 and testing on 41 by 41 by 3

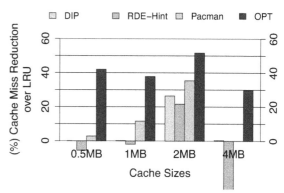

(f) Zeusmp, training on inputs 8 by 8 by 8 and 12 by 12 by 12 and testing on 16 by 16 by 16

Figure 10. The improvements by DIP, RDE-Hint, Pacman and OPT over LRU. The input size is given by grid dimensions. The total size is used by the run-time predictor.

5.3 Other Programs

We show the results for 6 programs in Figure 10. Stream has the simplest pattern. Pacman obtains a performance close to optimal. In *SOR*, most computation happens in a 3-nested loop in Figure 11.

In the j loop, all 6 array references have group spatial reuse. Pacman profiling shows that the LLVM compiler generates 3 references for the loop. Two of the references have only short OPT distances. Only the third reference shows a linear pattern. Pacman

recognizes it and reduces the miss ratios by 5%, 11%, 21% and 43% for the four cache sizes from 2MB to 16MB.

A more powerful compiler can apply loop tiling and reduce the size of the working set to fit entirely in cache. Pacman would find no linear pattern. On the other hand, there are iterative computations not amenable to tiling (e.g. k-means) and programs not amenable to compiler analysis. For those, Pacman provides the benefit of better cache management as in this example.

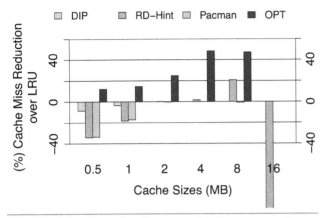

Figure 9. DIP, RDE-Hint, Pacman and OPT tested on *bwaves* (training on input 9 by 9 by 4 and 9 by 9 by 8 and testing on 17 by 17 by 16).

```
for (p=0; p<TIME; p++) {
  for (i=1; i<SIZE-1; i++) {
    for (j=1; j<SIZE-1; j++)
      G[i][j] = omega_over_four * (G[i-1][j] +
                G[i+1][j] + G[i][j-1] +
                G[i][j+1]) + one_minus_omega
                * G[i][j];
  }
}
```

Figure 11. The main loop in SOR, where Pacman inserts MRU hints for 3 of the references

The other four programs are physical simulations. *Mgrid* is a multi-grid solver that computes a three dimensional scalar potential field. *Applu, bwaves, zeusmp,* and *leslie3d* are all fluid dynamical simulations. *Applu* solves five coupled nonlinear PDEs on a three dimensional grid, *bwaves* and *zeusmp* both simulate blast waves (*zeusmp* does so specifically for astrophysical scenarios), and *leslie3d* simulates eddy flows in a temporal mixing layer.

There are 418 references in 46 loops in *mgrid* and 1858 references in 125 loops in *applu*. The types of patterns are more complex than those of *SOR*. Many references in *applu* have a similar look as shown by an example one in Figure 7. *Mgrid* does not have as many strong linear patterns, partly because of its divide-and-conquer type computation. As a result, the reduction by Pacman is higher in *applu*, from 2% to 34%, than in *mgraid*, from -6% to 10%.

There are a few cases of negative impacts on cache whose size is small. The reason is an error in cross-input analysis which predicts MRU for LRU access. For large set-associative cache, an over-use of MRU is not immediately harmful. The chance is that the following accesses would visit somewhere else in cache. For small cache, however, the incorrect MRU accesses may cause the eviction of high locality data and hence increase the miss rate.

Pacman obtains significant miss-ratio reductions over LRU, 11% to 24% for *leslie3d* and 0% to 26% for *zeusmp*. As members of SPEC2006, their code is larger. *Zeusmp* has as many as 10 thousand (static) references in nearly 500 loops.

Pacman does not improve the last program, *bwaves*, as shown in Figure 9. *Bwaves* has 260 references in 68 loops; most of the loops are nested 4 to 6 levels deep, and the input grid has just 3 dimensions. Although the performance is worse than LRU for caches of 0.5 MB and 1 MB, for larger caches, Pacman does no worse than LRU. Figure 12 shows the OPT distances for one of the

14 references in a 5-nested loop indexed by the combined iteration count from the outermost loop. In this and most other references, Pacman could not find a usable pattern because of the low accuracy (as low as 20% in the largest pattern).

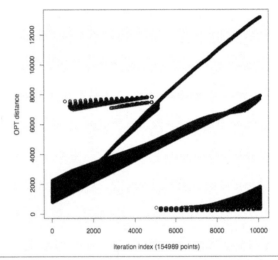

Figure 12. The OPT distances of a reference-loop pair in *bwaves*. Pacman finds multiple linear patterns but none is usable because of low accuracy.

5.4 Comparison to Dynamic Insertion Policy

In the SOR workload outlined above, DIP gives nearly the same miss rate as LRU because during the traversal of G, there are a significant number of immediate reuses (causing misses in the BIP blocks). While there are also low locality accesses, BIP never outperforms LRU strongly enough to trigger a policy switch to BIP. DIP does not reduce the number of misses in our test suite, with the exception of *zeusmp*, for which it makes a significant reduction for two of the cache sizes shown in Figure 10. The changes in all other programs are less than 1%. While DIP does not improve the performance, it does not degrade it, which makes it a safe policy.

Pacman outperforms DIP in most of our trials. It has the advantage of gathering program information through profiling (where DIP uses on-line execution history). On the other hand, the mechanism differs. DIP applies a single policy across the board at any one point in program execution. The goal is to find the better solution of two policies. Pacman assigns an eviction policy to each access. The goal is the best solution of all policies.

To be fair, we limited our tuning of DIP to the parameters specified in that paper. DIP was not developed with our tests, with the exception of *swim*. *Swim* was deemed "inherently LRU" as DIP was not able to improve its performance [20]. Nonetheless, this does demonstrate that, due to its fine-grained policy selection (as shown for the specific *Swim* loop in Section 4.2), Pacman has the edge for "inherently LRU" programs.

5.5 Comparison to Estimated Reuse Distance Hint Policy

RDE-Hint performed at or above the level of Pacman for some trials. There is only one trial (Mgrid, 4MB) where Beyls significantly outperforms Pacman.

The difference between RDE-Hint and Pacman is that whenever Pacman *might* provide an MRU hint (when there is a linear OPTD pattern), RDE-Hint *does*. In the example in Figure 4, RDE-Hint will provide MRU hints to the high reuse distance data `abcdefg`, just like the LRU policy. This similarity is shown in the results for the Streaming and SOR benchmarks, where RDE-Hint performs on par with LRU. Like the OPT policy of Mattson [19], Pacman places a portion of the high reuse distance data in the cache. While RDE-Hint beats Pacman in some tests, the possibility of throwing out too much data makes it more volatile, as seen in the results for Leslie3d and Zeusmp

RDE-Hint can do worse than LRU because LRU evicts unused data, whereas RDE-Hint does not cache data in the first place if it is predicted to be unused. Overclassification of data as low locality then results in throwing out data that could have been used. For example, when there is both low and high-locality data as in Figure 5, LRU eviction is better than MRU eviction, but RDE-Hint will flag the low-locality data for MRU eviction. In contrast, Pacman will almost never do worse than LRU; since only a portion of the low-locality data is flagged for MRU, it is unlikely that too many accesses will be uncached.

5.6 Performance on Real Hardware

The x86 ISA provides non-temporal store instructions which can bypass cache. They write to memory without loading the corresponding cache line first. SSE4.1 adds a non-temporal read instruction which is limited to write-combining memory area. For regular data that resides in main memory, the non-temporal read does not bypass the cache hierarchy [13]. There are also non-temporal prefetch instructions on x86, but they do not provide the full functionality of a non-temporal read. Still, we can evaluate the effect of Pacman using just the non-temporal store.

We run our tests on a machine with an Intel Xeon E5520 processor. The processor contains 4 symmetric 2.27GHz cores which share an 8MB L3 cache. With Hyper-Threading enabled, the processor can support up to 8 hardware threads.

Figure 13 shows the kernel of our test program. The outer loop advances in time step. In each time step, the inner loop updates each element of array A based on its old value. The inner loop is parallelized with OpenMP. The size of array A is set to 12MB, which is too large for cache reuse under LRU.

$$for(t = 0; t < MAXITER; t++)$$
$$\#pragma\ omp\ parallel\ for$$
$$for(i = 0; i < N; i++)$$
$$A[i] = foo(A[i]);$$

Figure 13. An OpenMP loop nest: the inner loop updates the array element by element; the outer loop repeats each the inner loop at each time step.

To enable the outer loop reuse, Pacman splits the inner loop into two, each of which is still an OpenMP parallel loop. The first loop writes to the first 8MB of array A using the normal (LRU) access, and the second loop the last 4MB of A using the non-temporal access. In the second loop, the non-temporal store is via the GCC intrinsic _mm_stream_pd. We unroll the inner loop 8 times, and the non-temporal stores happen once for each cache block rather than each element. To exclude the unrolling effect from the performance comparison, we perform the same loop unrolling on the original program. After loop splitting, Pacman keeps the first 8MB of A in the last level cache for reuse throughout the time steps.

Figure 14 gives the performance comparison between the original program and the optimized version. Another version, which only naively replaces the regular stores with non-temporal ones without splitting the inner loop, is also included in Figure 14 for comparison.

Figure 14(a) depicts the performance data with hardware prefetching on and in Figure 14(b) without prefetching. In the second case, we turn off all four kinds of hardware prefetchers by setting the corresponding Model-Specific Register (MSR) on all cores, similar to the approach in [27]. We test our programs for up to 8 threads,

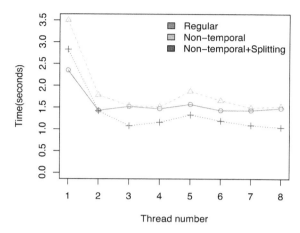

(a) Performance with hardware prefetching

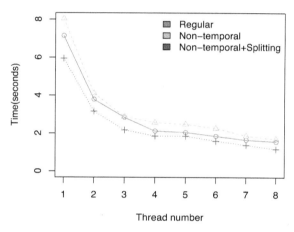

(b) Performance without hardware prefetching

Figure 14. The performance comparison on Intel Xeon E5520.

threads 1-4 are assigned to four physical cores, and threads 5-8 are bound to four hyper-threads.

First let's consider single-thread performance. For the experiment, we turn on and off prefetching to measure its effect. With prefetching, the Pacman code is 19% slower than the original program when using 1 thread. Without prefetching, Pacman is 17% faster. The difference shows that for single-thread execution, prefetching is more effective than Pacman despite the fact that it improves the locality. The 19% slowdown suggests that non-temporal accesses either have a higher overhead or interfere with prefetching (which must be designed to maximize performance for sequential streaming access).

Prefetching requires sufficient memory bandwidth to be effective. In the single-thread test, one CPU core has the memory bandwidth of the entire system. Once the memory bandwidth is shared by more cores, cache management becomes important because better caching reduces the bandwidth demand and hence the contention on memory bandwidth. At more than 2 threads, Pacman is clearly better, as shown in Figure 14(a). At 3 and 8 threads, Pacman reduces the parallel execution time by over 30%. The results show the relation between cache management and prefetching. When there is enough bandwidth, prefetching is sufficient, at least for contiguous memory traversals; when the bandwidth is under contention, caching is effective in further improving performance (by over 30% in this test).

Loop splitting by Pacman is also important. Without it, the performance is as much as 47% lower than the original program. If we turn off prefetching, the better cache management by Pacman is uniformly beneficial, from 17% improvement in one thread to 25% improvement at 8 threads, as shown in Figure 14(b).

We have tested the overhead of loop splitting by running the sequential version with one loop doing all the work and with eight replica loops each doing one eighth of the work. In addition, each loop is unrolled 8 times, so each loop body has 8 statements. The binary size is 7583 bytes before loop splitting and 8159 bytes after splitting. The running time is completely identical between the two versions. There is no visible run-time overhead from loop splitting. We also tested on an AMD Opteron machine and found no overhead by loop splitting. The reason is that the total code size, despite unrolling and splitting, is still small compared to the size of L1 instruction cache (32KB on Intel Xeon and 64KB on AMD Opteron). Furthermore, loop code has good instruction locality. As long as the size of a single loop does not exceed 32KB or 64KB, we do not expect repeated misses in the instruction cache.

On multicore machines, the memory bandwidth is shared among all co-run programs. By reducing the memory bandwidth demand of one program, Pacman improves not only the cache performance for the program but possibly its co-run peers because they can now use a greater share of the available memory bandwidth.

6. Related Work

Several previous solutions used reuse distance analysis, either by a compiler [7, 26] or by profiling [6, 7, 16], to distinguish between high locality and low locality accesses. The different caching mechanisms include Itanium placement hints [6, 7], evict-me tags [26] and cache partitioning through page coloring [16].

The reuse distance shows the program locality independent of cache management and size. When data larger than cache size have the same locality (reuse distance), it is unclear how to select a subset for caching. If we choose one group of accesses for LRU and the others for MRU, the cache locality changes for affected data but also for other data. This common problem when optimizing a tightly coupled system is described in a Chinese adage: "pulling one hair moves the whole body".

Reuse distance has been used to predict cross-input locality from the whole program to individual references (e.g. [8, 18]. Pacman uses the same training strategy but predicts the change in a linear pattern rather than in a histogram.

Optimal collaborative caching has been studied as a theoretical possibility [10–12]. Gu et al. proved the theoretical optimality in bypass and trespass LRU cache [10], the LRU-MRU cache [11], which we use in Pacman, and the priority LRU cache [12]. They designated each reference as LRU or MRU based on whether the majority of its OPT distances is greater than a threshold [11], following the technique of Beyls and D'Hollander [7]. A reference is always MRU or always LRU. The drawback is the same with the reuse distance: there is no partial caching of a working set. The optimality requires re-inserting hints for each different input and cache size. A recent solution allowed the same hints to optimize for caches of an arbitrary size but required passing integer-size priority hints rather than a single bit [12]. Pacman uses linear-pattern analysis and loop splitting to adapt cache hints across input and cache sizes. It addresses practical problems such as non-unit size cache blocks, nested loops, and cross-array and cross-program cache allocation.

Cache can implement adaptive solutions entirely in hardware with no visible overhead and with transparency to the user program. Indeed, perhaps no modern cache is implemented strictly as LRU.

Techniques such as DIP [20] (compared in Section 5.4), recently reuse-time predictor [9] and many previous techniques improve over LRU by revising the LRU strategy or switching among multiple strategies. For memory management, elaborate strategies have been developed for paging, including EELRU [24], MRC [31], LIRS [14], and CRAMM [29]. While these previous policies are based on heuristics, Pacman is based on the optimal strategy, which it computes at the profiling time (to obtain program information and tolerate the OPT overhead). It inserts program hints so the hardware can obtain optimal management without needing program analysis or computing the optimal strategy. The empirical comparison shows the need for program-level control to allocate cache among differently for different groups of arrays and use different LRU/MRU policies within the same array. Finally, collaborative caching permits direct software control.

7. Summary

In this paper, we have presented the Pacman system for program-assisted cache management. It uses profiling to obtain the forward OPT distances, grid regression and cross-input analysis to identify linear patterns, and loop splitting to enable the dynamic designation of LRU/MRU accesses for each original data reference. Pacman needs the hardware to support LRU/MRU access interface. The interface requires at most one bit for each memory access. Most of the analysis and all program transformation are done off-line before a program executes.

By evaluating the system using simple and complex benchmark programs, we found that most programs exhibit strong linear patterns that can be captured by profiling. The reduction over LRU is significant and becomes as much as 40% to 60% when managing a large cache. Real-machine experiments suggest that MRU access incurs an overhead. Still, the improved cache reuse can improve performance when prefetching is difficult or when the contention on memory bandwidth is high. While Pacman is not the first caching policy to make use of program profiling, its unique contribution is in its use of the OPT distance for providing cache hints.

From these results, we believe that computer architects should consider supporting LRU/MRU hints to enable collaborative caching. The interface enables new types of cache memory management by a program or a compiler.

Acknowledgments

The authors would like to thank Yaoqing Gao, Xipeng Shen the anonymous ISMM reviewers, and our colleagues and visitors at the University of Rochester: Lingxiang Xiang, Xiaoya Xiang, Sandhya Dwarkadas, Engin Ipek, Jorge Albericio, and Li Shen for their insightful ideas, questions, and comments, and the use of code.

References

[1] SciMark2.0. http://math.nist.gov/scimark2/.

[2] SPEC CPU2000. http://www.spec.org/cpu2000.

[3] SPEC CPU2006. http://www.spec.org/cpu2006.

[4] R. Allen and K. Kennedy. *Optimizing Compilers for Modern Architectures: A Dependence-based Approach.* Morgan Kaufmann Publishers, Oct. 2001.

[5] L. A. Belady. A study of replacement algorithms for a virtual-storage computer. *IBM Systems Journal,* 5(2):78–101, 1966.

[6] K. Beyls and E. D'Hollander. Reuse distance-based cache hint selection. In *Proceedings of the 8th International Euro-Par Conference,* Paderborn, Germany, Aug. 2002.

[7] K. Beyls and E. D'Hollander. Generating cache hints for improved program efficiency. *Journal of Systems Architecture,* 51(4):223–250, 2005.

[8] C. Fang, S. Carr, S. Önder, and Z. Wang. Instruction based memory distance analysis and its application. In *Proceedings of PACT*, pages 27–37, 2005.

[9] M. Feng, C. Tian, C. Lin, and R. Gupta. Dynamic access distance driven cache replacement. *ACM Trans. on Arch. and Code Opt.*, 8(3):14, 2011.

[10] X. Gu, T. Bai, Y. Gao, C. Zhang, R. Archambault, and C. Ding. P-OPT: Program-directed optimal cache management. In *Proceedings of the LCPC Workshop*, pages 217–231, 2008.

[11] X. Gu and C. Ding. On the theory and potential of LRU-MRU collaborative cache management. In *Proceedings of ISMM*, pages 43–54, 2011.

[12] X. Gu and C. Ding. A generalized theory of collaborative caching. In *Proceedings of ISMM*, pages 109–120, 2012.

[13] A. Jha and D. Yee. Increasing memory throughput with intel streaming simd extensions 4 (intel sse4) streaming load, 2007. Intel Developer Zone.

[14] S. Jiang and X. Zhang. Making lru friendly to weak locality workloads: A novel replacement algorithm to improve buffer cache performance. *IEEE Trans. Computers*, 54(8):939–952, 2005.

[15] C. Lattner and V. S. Adve. Automatic pool allocation: improving performance by controlling data structure layout in the heap. In *Proceedings of PLDI*, pages 129–142, 2005.

[16] Q. Lu, J. Lin, X. Ding, Z. Zhang, X. Zhang, and P. Sadayappan. Soft-OLP: Improving hardware cache performance through software-controlled object-level partitioning. In *Proceedings of PACT*, pages 246–257, 2009.

[17] F. Mao and X. Shen. Cross-input learning and discriminative prediction in evolvable virtual machines. In *Proceedings of CGO*, pages 92–101, 2009.

[18] G. Marin and J. Mellor-Crummey. Cross architecture performance predictions for scientific applications using parameterized models. In *Proceedings of SIGMETRICS*, pages 2–13, 2004.

[19] R. L. Mattson, J. Gecsei, D. Slutz, and I. L. Traiger. Evaluation techniques for storage hierarchies. *IBM System Journal*, 9(2):78–117, 1970.

[20] M. K. Qureshi, A. Jaleel, Y. N. Patt, S. C. S. Jr., and J. S. Emer. Adaptive insertion policies for high performance caching. In *Proceedings of ISCA*, pages 381–391, 2007.

[21] S. Rus, R. Ashok, and D. X. Li. Automated locality optimization based on the reuse distance of string operations. In *Proceedings of CGO*, pages 181–190, 2011.

[22] J. B. Sartor, S. M. Blackburn, D. Frampton, M. Hirzel, and K. S. McKinley. Z-rays: divide arrays and conquer speed and flexibility. In *Proceedings of PLDI*, pages 471–482, 2010.

[23] B. Sinharoy, R. N. Kalla, J. M. Tendler, R. J. Eickemeyer, and J. B. Joyner. Power5 system microarchitecture. *IBM J. Res. Dev.*, 49:505–521, July 2005.

[24] Y. Smaragdakis, S. Kaplan, and P. Wilson. The EELRU adaptive replacement algorithm. *Perform. Eval.*, 53(2):93–123, 2003.

[25] R. A. Sugumar and S. G. Abraham. Efficient simulation of caches under optimal replacement with applications to miss characterization. In *Proceedings of SIGMETRICS*, Santa Clara, CA, May 1993.

[26] Z. Wang, K. S. McKinley, A. L.Rosenberg, and C. C. Weems. Using the compiler to improve cache replacement decisions. In *Proceedings of PACT*, Charlottesville, Virginia, 2002.

[27] C.-J. Wu and M. Martonosi. Characterization and dynamic mitigation of intra-application cache interference. In *Proceedings of ISPASS*, pages 2–11, 2011.

[28] L. Xiang, T. Chen, Q. Shi, and W. Hu. Less reused filter: improving L2 cache performance via filtering less reused lines. In *Proceedings of ICS*, pages 68–79, New York, NY, USA, 2009. ACM.

[29] T. Yang, E. D. Berger, S. F. Kaplan, and J. E. B. Moss. CRAMM: Virtual memory support for garbage-collected applications. In *Proceedings of OSDI*, pages 103–116, 2006.

[30] X. Yang, S. M. Blackburn, D. Frampton, J. B. Sartor, and K. S. McKinley. Why nothing matters: the impact of zeroing. In *OOPSLA*, pages 307–324, 2011.

[31] P. Zhou, V. Pandey, J. Sundaresan, A. Raghuraman, Y. Zhou, and S. Kumar. Dynamic tracking of page miss ratio curve for memory management. In *Proceedings of ASPLOS*, pages 177–188, 2004.

A. Two Properties of OPT Distance

OPT distance is a foundational concept in the paper. We present two of its theoretical properties to aid its understanding. First, we show a general relation with the reuse distance.

PROPOSITION 1. *At each access, the OPT distance is no more than the reuse distance.*

Proof Without loss of generality, consider an access of the data element x and the reuse window from the last access to the current access of x. At the start of the window, x is just accessed, so it is at the top position in both the LRU and the OPT stacks. Next we compare the movement of x in these two stacks.

The movement is based on priority. LRU ranks data by the last access time. OPT ranks by the next access time. As the other data are accessed, they come to the top of the stack. In LRU, they always gain a higher priority than x, so they stay over x in the LRU stack. In OPT, depending on the next access time, they may rank lower than x and drop below x. As a result, x always stays at the same or a higher stack position in OPT than in LRU until the end of the reuse window. At the end, the OPT distance is smaller than or equal to the reuse distance.

The next proposition states the exact OPT distance formula for repeated streaming accesses. We have seen this pattern in a specific example in Section 3. Here we prove a general result.

PROPOSITION 2. *When repeatedly traversing n data $a_1 \ldots a_n$, the OPT distance is ∞ for the first n accesses and then repeats from $2 \ldots n$ until the end of the trace.*

Proof It is trivial to show the pattern if $n = 2$. Next we assume $n > 2$. At the nth position, a_n is accessed. All n blocks are in cache. The OPT stack, from top to bottom, is $a_n, a_1 \ldots a_{n-1}$. Except for a_n, the elements are ordered by the next access time. Now we examine the OPT distance and the stack layout in the following $n - 1$ accesses: $a_1, \ldots, a_{n-1}$. At a_1, the OPT distance is 2, and the top two stack entries are changed to a_1, a_n. At a_2, the OPT distance is 3, and the top 3 spots are changed to a_2, a_n, a_1. The pattern continues. At a_{n-1}, the OPT distance is n, and the stack is $a_{n-1}, a_n, a_1, \ldots, a_{n-2}$. Now, the next $n - 1$ accesses in the trace are $a_n, a_1, \ldots, a_{n-2}$. Comparing to the last $n - 1$ accesses, we see the identical configuration of the stack and the upcoming $n - 1$ accesses, if we re-number data blocks from $a_n, a_1, \ldots, a_{n-1}$ to $a_1, \ldots, a_n$. The same reasoning applies, and hence the pattern of OPT distances repeats.

We note that the periodicity of the OPT distances is $n - 1$. As a result, the same datum does not have the same OPT distance over time. Its OPT distance increases by 1 each time the datum is reused in cache. For any cache size, every datum will alternate to stay in and out of the OPT cache. The optimal caching is not by a preference of a data subset but a rotation of all data over time. In fact, it can be shown that choosing a preferred subset is an inferior solution. If we phrase this theoretical result in political terms, we have a proof that democracy outperforms aristocracy in data caching.

Generating Sound and Effective Memory Debuggers

Yan Wang   Iulian Neamtiu   Rajiv Gupta

Department of Computer Science and Engineering
University of California, Riverside, CA, USA
{wangy,neamtiu,gupta}@cs.ucr.edu

Abstract

We present a new approach for constructing debuggers based on declarative specification of bug conditions and root causes, and automatic generation of debugger code. We illustrate our approach on several classes of bugs, memory or otherwise. For each bug class, bug conditions and their root cause are specified declaratively, in First-order logic, using 1 to 4 predicates. We employ a low-level operational semantics and abstract traces to permit concise bug specification and prove soundness. To facilitate locating bugs, we introduce a new concept of value propagation chains that reduce programmer burden by narrowing the fault to a handful of executed instructions (1 to 16 in our experiments). We employ automatic translation to generate the debugger implementation, which runs on top of the Pin infrastructure. Experiments with using our system on 7 versions of 4 real-world programs show that our approach is expressive, effective at finding bugs and their causes, and efficient. We believe that, using our approach, other kinds of declaratively-specified, provably-correct, auto-generated debuggers can be constructed with little effort.

Categories and Subject Descriptors   D.2.5 [*Testing and Debugging*]: Debugging aids, Monitors;   D.3.1 [*Formal Definitions and Theory*]: Semantics

General Terms   Languages, Reliability, Theory, Verification

Keywords   Debugging; Fault Localization; Logic Specification; Operational Semantics; Runtime Monitoring

1. Introduction

Debugging is a tedious and time-consuming process for software developers. Debugging-related tasks (i.e., understanding and locating bugs, and correcting programs) can take up to 70% of the total time of software development and maintenance [18]. Therefore, providing effective debugging tools is essential for improving productivity. To assist in the debugging task, both general-purpose debuggers [10, 15, 18, 37], and specialized tools targeting memory bugs (e.g., buffer overflows [6, 25], dangling pointer dereferences [5], and memory leaks [29, 36]) have been developed.

These current debugging approaches have several shortcomings which are more pronounced in the context of memory-related bugs. First, detection of memory-related bugs is tedious using general-

ISMM'13,   June 20–21, 2013, Seattle, Washington, USA.
Copyright © 2013 ACM 978-1-4503-2100-6/13/06... $10.00

purpose debuggers, so programmers have to use tools tailored to specific kinds of bugs; however, to use the appropriate tool the programmer needs to first know what kind of bug is present in the program. Second, when faulty code is encountered during execution, its impact on program execution might be observed much later (e.g., due to a program crash or incorrect output), making it hard to locate the faulty code. Third, debuggers are also written by humans, which has two main disadvantages: (a) adding support for new kinds of bugs entails a significant development effort, and (b) lack of formal verification in debugger construction makes debuggers themselves prone to bugs, which limits their effectiveness.

We propose a novel approach to constructing debuggers that addresses the above challenges, and provide an illustration and evaluation on memory-related bugs. We allow bugs[1] and their root causes to be specified declaratively, using just 1 to 4 predicates, and then use automated translation to generate an actual debugger that works for arbitrary C programs running on the x86 platform. We have proved that bug detection is sound with respect to a low-level operational semantics, i.e., bug detectors fire prior to the machine entering an error state. Our work introduces several novel concepts and techniques, described next.

Declarative debugger specification. In our approach, bugs are specified via *detection rules*, i.e., error conditions that indicate the presence of a fault, defined as First-order logic predicates on abstract states. In Section 2 we show how bug specifications can be easily written. Using detection rules as input, we employ automated translation to generate the debugger implementation; thanks to this translation process, explained in Section 4.1, from 8 lines of specification about 3,300 lines of C code are generated automatically.

Debugger soundness. We use a core imperative calculus that models the C language with just a few syntactic forms (Section 3.1) to help with specification and establishing correctness. We define an operational semantics (Section 3.2) which models program execution as transitions between abstract states Σ; abstract states form the basis for specifying debuggers in a very concise yet effective way. Next, we define error states for several memory bugs, and use the operational semantics (which contains transitions to legal or error states) to prove that the detectors are sound (Section 3.3).

Value propagation chains. In addition to bug detection rules, our specifications also contain *locator rules*, which define value propagation chains pointing to the root cause of the bug. These chains drastically simplify the process of detecting and locating the root cause of memory bugs: for the real-world programs we have applied our approach to, users have to examine just *1 to 16* instructions (Section 5.2).

Section 4 describes our implementation and online debugger usage. After a debugging session starts, a monitoring component maps the actual execution to the abstract machine state. The detec-

---

[1] We define a *bug* to be a class of faults, for example, a double-free bug refers to all double-free faults present in the program.

tors generated from the bug specification perform online bug detection, i.e., while the program is running. Note that we detect bugs *before* they actually manifest, when the abstract machine is about to enter an error state—this prevents faults from silently propagating and accumulating. Moreover, when a fault is detected, we suspend the execution using a breakpoint, so that developers can examine the state and, with help from bug locators, get to the bug's root cause. Our approach works for arbitrary C programs. The task of monitoring is carried out by an automatically-generated Pin tool.

Experiments with using our system to detect actual bugs in real-world programs show that it is expressive, effective at finding bugs, and has acceptable performance overhead (Section 5).

Prior efforts in this area include memory bug detectors, algorithmic debugging, and monitoring-oriented programming; we provide a comparison with related work in Section 6. However, to the best of our knowledge, our work is the first to combine a concise, declarative debugger specification style with automatic generation of bug detectors and locators, while providing a correctness proof.

Our approach has the following advantages:

1. *Generality.* As we show in Section 2, bug specifications consist of 1 to 4 predicates per bug. Thus, specifications are easy to understand, scrutinize, and extend. Formal definitions of program semantics and error states show that bug detection based on these bug specifications is correct.

2. *Flexibility.* Instead of using specialized tools for different kinds of bugs, the user generates a single debugger that still distinguishes among many different kinds of bugs. Moreover, bug detectors can be switched on and off as the program runs.

3. *Effectiveness.* Bug detectors continuously evaluate error conditions and the user is informed of the error condition (type of bug) encountered before it manifests, e.g., via program crash. Bug locators then spring into action, to indicate the value chains in the execution history that are the root causes of the bug, which allow bugs to be found by examining just a handful of instructions (1 to 16), a small fraction of the instructions that would have to be examined when using dynamic slicing.

2. Bug Specification

Figure 1 provides an overview of our approach. As the program executes, its execution is continuously monitored and x86 instructions are mapped to low-level operational semantics states Σ (described in Section 3.2). For most memory bugs, programmers use an abstraction of the semantics (execution trace σ and redex e), to write bug specifications; the full semantics is available to specify more complicated bugs. Bug detectors and bug locators are generated automatically from specifications. During debugging, detectors examine the current state to determine when an error condition is about to become true, i.e., the abstract machine is about to enter an error state. When that is the case, locators associated with that error condition report the error and its root cause (location) to the programmer. Our debugger is able to simultaneously detect multiple kinds of bugs, as illustrated by the stacked detectors and locators in the figure.

We now present the user's perspective to our approach. Specification is the only stage where the user needs to be creatively involved, as the rest of the process is automatic, thanks to code generation. We first describe the specification process (Section 2.1). Next, we illustrate how our approach is used in practice for memory bugs (Section 2.2) and other kinds of bugs (Section 2.3). Later on (Section 5.2), we demonstrate the effectiveness of our approach by comparing it with traditional debugging and slicing techniques.

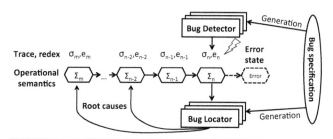

Figure 1. Overview of bug specification, detection and location.

2.1 Specifying Debuggers via Rules

Traces and redexes. To simplify specification, for most memory bugs, the programmers can describe bugs by just referring to traces σ and redexes e. The trace σ records the execution of relevant memory operation events—write for memory writes, malloc for allocation, free for deallocation—which are germane to memory bugs. Redexes e indicate the expression to be reduced next, such as function entry/exit, allocation/deallocation, memory reads and writes; when e is a memory operation, it contains a location r signifying the pointer to be operated on, e.g., freed, read from, or written to. The scarcity of syntactic forms for redexes and execution trace events provide a simple yet powerful framework for specifying C memory bugs.

Rules. To specify a bug kind, the user writes a rule (triple): *<detection point, bug condition, value propagation>*. The first two components, *detection point* and *bug condition*, specify a bug detector, while the third component, *value propagation*, specifies a bug locator. Figure 2 shows how detection points, bug conditions and bug locators are put together to form rules and specify six actual classes of memory bugs. We now proceed to defining each component of a rule.

Detection points specify the reductions where bug detection should be performed, as shown below.

Detection point	Next reduction e	Semantics
$deref\_r\ r$	$*r$	memory read
$deref\_w\ r$	$r := v$	memory write
$deref\ r$	$*r / r := v$	memory access
$free\ r$	free r	deallocation
$call\ z\ v$	$z\ v$	function call
$ret\ z\ v$	ret $z\ e$	function return

The programmer only needs to specify the detection point (left column). Our debugger will then evaluate the bug condition when the operational semantics's next reduction is e (middle column). For example, if the programmer wants to write a detector that fires whenever memory is read, she can use $deref\_r\ r$ as a detection point. Detection points which can match multiple reduction rules, coupled with the simple syntax of our calculus, make for brief yet effective specification; for example, using a single detection point, $deref\ r$, the user will at once capture the myriad ways pointers can be dereferenced in C.

Bug conditions are First-order logic predicates which allow memory bugs to be specified in a concise, declarative manner, by referring to the detection point and the trace σ. First, in Figure 2 (bottom) we define some auxiliary predicates that allow more concise definitions for bug detectors. $Allocated(r)$ checks whether pointer r has been allocated. The low-level semantics contains mappings of the form $r \mapsto (bid, i)$, i.e., from pointer r to the block bid and index i it points to; $Bid(r)$ returns r's block in this mapping. Therefore, $Allocated(r)$ is true if the block r is currently pointing into a block bid that according to the trace σ has previ-

Rules	Detection point	Bug condition	Value propagation
[UNMATCHED-FREE]	$detect\langle\sigma; free\ r\rangle:$	$\neg Allocated(r) \vee r \neq Begin(r)$	$VPC(r)$
[DOUBLE-FREE]	$detect\langle\sigma; free\ r\rangle:$	$Allocated(r) \wedge Freed(r, r_1)$	$VPC(r), VPC(r_1)$
[DANGLING-POINTER-DEREF]	$detect\langle\sigma; deref\ r\rangle:$	$Allocated(r) \wedge Freed(r, r_1)$	$VPC(r), VPC(r_1)$
[NULL-POINTER-DEREF]	$detect\langle\sigma; deref\ r\rangle:$	$r = NULL$	$VPC(r)$
[HEAP-BUFFER-OVERFLOW]	$detect\langle\sigma; deref\ r\rangle:$	$Allocated(r) \wedge \neg Freed(r, \_) \wedge (r < Begin(r) \vee r \geq End(r))$	$VPC(r)$
[UNINITIALIZED-READ]	$detect\langle\sigma; deref\_r\ r\rangle:$	$\neg FindLast(\_, \mathsf{write}, r, \_,)$	

$$\underline{\text{Auxiliary predicates}} \qquad \begin{aligned} Allocated(r) &\doteq \exists\,(\_, \mathsf{malloc}, \_, bid) \in \sigma : bid = Bid(r) \\ Freed(r, r_1) &\doteq \exists\,(\_, \mathsf{free}, r_1, bid) \in \sigma : bid = Bid(r) \end{aligned}$$

Figure 2. Bug detection rules and auxiliary predicates.

ously been allocated, i.e., it contains a malloc event for this bid; '$\_$' is the standard wildcard pattern. $Freed(r, r_1)$ is true if the block bid that r is currently pointing into has been freed, i.e., the trace σ contains a free event for this bid. Note that free's argument r_1, the pointer used to free the memory block, is not necessarily equal to r, as r could be pointing in the middle of the block while r_1 is the base of the block (cf. Section 3.2).

With the auxiliary predicates at hand, we define First-order logic conditions on the abstract domain, as illustrated in the bug condition part of Figure 2. Note that $FindLast(ts, event)$ is a built-in function that traverses the trace backwards and finds the last matching event according to given signature. For example, a dangling pointer dereference bug occurs when we attempt to dereference r whose block has been freed before; this specification appears formally in rule [DANGLING-POINTER-DEREF], i.e., the bug is detected when the redex is $*r$ or $r := v$ and the predicate $Allocated(r) \wedge Freed(r, r_1)$ is true. Note that r_1 is a free variable here and its value is bound to the pointer which is used to free this block for the first time.

Bug locators. The last component of each rule specifies *value propagation chains* (VPC) which help construct bug locators. The VPC of variable v in a program state Σ is the transitive closure of value propagation edges ending at Σ for variable v. The VPC is computed by backward traversal of value propagation edges ending at Σ for variable v. Note that dynamic slicing does not distinguish data dependences introduced by computing values from dependences introduced by propagating existing values. Value propagation edges capture the latter—a small subset of dynamic slices.

For each bug kind, the VPC specifies how the value involved in the bug manifestation relates to the bug's root cause. For example, in [DOUBLE-FREE], the root cause of the bug can be found by tracing the propagation of r (the pointer we are trying to free) and r_1 (the pointer that performed the first free). In [NULL-POINTER-DEREF], it suffices to follow the propagation of the current pointer r which at some point became $NULL$.

2.2 Memory Debuggers in Practice

We now provide a comprehensive account of how our approach helps specify, detect and locate the root causes of memory bugs using three examples of actual bugs in real-world programs.

Double-free. Attempting to free an already-freed pointer is a very common bug. In Figure 2, the rule [DOUBLE-FREE] contains the specification for the bug: when the redex is free r and the predicates $Allocated(r)$ and $Freed(r, r_1)$ are both true, we conclude that r has already been freed.

The real-world program *Tidy-34132* contains a double-free memory bug which manifests itself when the input HTML file contains a malformed *font* element, e.g., $< font\ color = "green" <$ $? font >$. The relevant source code for this bug is presented in the left column of Figure 3. The program constructs a *node* structure

for each element (e.g., *font*) in the HTML file. An element may contain multiple attributes corresponding to the *attributes* field of the *node* structure, which is a pointer to the *attribute* structure. The program pushes a deep copy of the *node* structure onto the stack when encountering an inline element (i.e., *font* in our test case) by calling *PushInline* (line 057). The deep copy is created by duplicating the dynamically allocated structure pointed to by each field in the *node* structure as well as fields of fields recursively. For example, the program duplicates the *node*'s *attributes* fields and fields of the *attributes* structures, as shown in line 092. However, the programmer makes a shallow copy of the *php* field in the *attribute* structure by mistake in line 033 because of a missing statement, as shown in line 039. All the copies of *node* structure pushed onto the stack by *PushInline* will be subsequently popped out in function *PopInline* (line 097), where all the allocated regions will be freed recursively. In some situations, due to the shallow copy, the *php* field of some *node* structures will contain dangling pointers. If some element in the HTML file is empty and can be pruned out, the program removes the node from the markup tree and discards it by calling *TrimEmptyElement* (line 309), which eventually calls *DiscardElement* at line 316. Node deletion is just a reverse process of node deep copy—it will free all the dynamically-allocated memory regions in the *node* structure in a recursive fashion, including the structures pointed to by the *php* fields. When providing certain HTML files as input, the program crashes when it tries to trim the empty *font* element because the *php* field of the *attributes* field of the *font* element has been freed in *PopInline*.

The second column of Figure 3 shows the events added to our trace σ during execution (irrelevant events are omitted). As we can see, the bug condition specified in rule [DOUBLE-FREE] is satisfied because σ contains events malloc, n, 1_H, and free, ptr, 1_H (1_H is the heap block id), indicating that block 1_H has been allocated and then freed, which makes $Allocated(r) \wedge Freed(r, r_1)$ true.

The root cause of the double-free bug is the shallow copy in line 033, and the fix (line 039 in istack.c) calls for far more program comprehension (why, when and how the two different pointers wrongly point to the same heap block) than just the positions of the two *free* calls (line 136 in parser.c), which is the best bug report that current automatic debugging tools (e.g., Valgrind) can achieve. With the help of our bug locators, programmers need to examine just 16 instructions to figure out how and when the two pointers used in *free* point to the same memory region by following the value propagation chains for the two pointers (the two pointers can be the same in some situations, in which case the two value propagation chains are exactly the same). We show the value propagation chains for this execution in the third column of Figure 3; in our actual implementation, this value chain is presented to the user. Note that the value of the pointer *ptr* used in the *free* function is first generated in function *malloc* and propagates to pointer p in function *MemAlloc*, and so on. The right child of node $\boxed{attrs \rightarrow php}$ is exactly the place where the shallow copy comes from (shallow copy

C code	Relevant events added to the trace σ

savedir.c:
76: char * savedir (const char *dir){
         DIR *dirp;
85:      dirp = opendir (dir);
86:      if (dirp == NULL)
87:         return NULL;
129: ...}
increment.c:
173: get_directory_contents (char *path){ ...
180:     char *dir = savedir (path);   ...
205:     for (entry = dirp; entrylen =
206:        strlen (entry))!= 0; //**crash**
207:        entry +=entrylen +1)
	write, $dirp$, _, savedir $retval$
	write, $entry$, _, $dirp$
	write, str, _, $entry$
	
	bug detected at strlen(str)

Value Propagation Chain

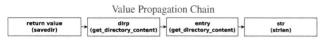

Figure 4. Detecting, and locating the root cause of, a NULL pointer dereference bug in *Tar-1.13.25*.

from $attrs \rightarrow php$ to $newattrs \rightarrow php$). Hence, with the help of our bug locators, programmers can quickly understand the root cause and fix the bug.

NULL pointer dereference. In Figure 2, the rule [NULL-POINTER-DEREF] is used to express and check for NULL pointer dereference bugs. The real-world program *Tar-1.13.25* contains a NULL pointer dereference bug which causes a crash when the user tries to do an incremental backup of a directory without having read access permissions to it. A source code excerpt containing the bug is shown in the first column of Figure 4. If the user does not have read access to the specified directories, the function *opendir* will return a NULL pointer. This causes the program to crash at line 206 when passing this pointer to function *strlen*.

With the help of our debugger, programmers can figure out the bug type, and get significant insight about the failure via bug locators. The trace of an execution which triggers this bug is shown on the right side of Figure 4. The NULL pointer bug detector will detect this bug when the NULL pointer is dereferenced in *strlen*. The value propagation chain of the NULL pointer, shown on the bottom of Figure 4, indicates where the NULL pointer originates (*line 87 in savedir.c*) and how it propagates to the crash point.

Unmatched free. Attempting to free an illegal pointer is a very common bug. In Figure 2, the rule [UNMATCHED-FREE] contains the declarative specification for the bug: whenever the evaluation reaches a point where the next expression is free r, if at least one of two conditions is met, the rule fires. If $Allocated(r)$ is false, the program tries to free something that has not been allocated in the first place. If $r \neq Begin(r)$, the program attempts to free a pointer that has been allocated, but instead of pointing to the malloc'd block (i.e., the base), r points somewhere in the middle of the block.

The real-world Python interpreter *Cpython-870c0ef7e8a2*, contains an unmatched free bug (freeing something that has not been allocated) that leads to a crash. The bug manifests when the *type.__getattribute__* function is misused (e.g., *type.__getattribute__(str, int)*) in the input Python program. The *type.__getattribute__(typeName, attrName)* function finds the attribute associated with *attrName* in *typeName*'s attribute list. However, passing a type name, e.g., *int*, as attribute name crashes the program.

A source code excerpt containing the bug is shown in the first column of Figure 5. Encountering a *type.__getattribute__(typeName, attrName)* statement, the Python interpreter invokes the *type_getattro* function at line 2483 to find the attribute associated with *name* in *type*'s attribute list at line 2517. When no attribute is found, an er-

C code	Relevant events added to trace σ
unicodeobject.c: 1353: PyUnicode_Ready(PyObject *unicode){... 1389: _PyUnicode_CONVERT_BYTES(...) 1405: free((PyASCIIObject*)unicode→wstr); 1479: ...} typeobject.c: 2483: type_getattro(type, PyObject* name){ /***the following statements are missing in buggy code**/ 2488: **if (!PyUnicode_Check(name)) {** ... 2492: **return NULL;}** 2517: attribute = _PyType_Lookup(type, name); 2551: PyErr_Format(PyExc_AttributeError, 2552: "type object '%.50s' has no attribute '%U'", 2553: type→tp_name, name);	write, ptr, _, $unicode \rightarrow wstr$ **bug detected at** free(ptr)

Value Propagation Chain

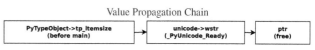

Figure 5. Detecting, and locating the root cause of, an unmatched free bug in *Cpython-870c0ef7e8a2*.

ror message will be printed at line 2551 by calling *PyErr_Format*; *PyErr_Format* will eventually call *_PyUnicode_Ready* to prepare an Unicode string and print it. *_PyUnicode_Ready* converts the Unicode string stored in *unicode→wstr buffer*, and then finally frees the buffer. However, the programmer has wrongly assumed that the *name* object at line 2483 must be an object of type *PyUnicodeObject* or subclass of it (e.g., *PyASCIIObject*), and has forgotten to add a type check at line 2488. When a type name is passed as the attribute name, the *unicode* at line 1405 is an object of type *PyTypeObject*, rather than *PyASCIIObject*. Thus, the programmer thinks *free* is invoked on *PyASCIIObject*'s *wstr* field when in fact it is invoked on *PyTypeObject*'s *tp_itemsize* field.

The second column shows the relevant events added to σ. As we can see, there is no event malloc, n, _ to make $Allocated(r)$ true. The value propagation chain of ptr (bottom of figure), shows how the wrong value of ptr is propagated from $unicode \rightarrow wstr$, which is a global variable and initialized before the execution of main (by the program loader), rather than dynamically allocated.

2.3 Other Classes of Bugs

While the core of our work is centered around the six classes of memory bugs we have just presented, programmers can use our approach to easily specify debuggers for other classes of bugs. We now proceed to briefly discuss examples of such classes; the bug specifications are presented in Figure 6.

Memory leaks. The rule [POSSIBLE-LEAK] specifies possible leaks as follows: if main is about to exit while the heap H contains one or more blocks that have not been freed, i.e., the heap domain is not empty, the rule fires.

With rule [DEFINITE-LEAK], we report leakages if, at the end of program execution, the heap H contains some blocks that no pointer in P points to. In other words, if there is no live pointer pointing to a block, we report the block as a definite leak.

The rule [LEAK-IN-TS] can be used to detect leaks in transactions. For simplicity, we assume that the scope of a transaction spans the entire body of a function denoted by metavariable ts. The programmer can easily specify that all the blocks allocated inside the transaction (body of ts) should be freed at the end of the transaction. We report leaks if, when function ts returns, the heap H contains some blocks which are allocated inside this function and have not been freed yet. Note that $FindLast(k, \text{call}, ts, \_)$ matches the latest event which calls function ts, and the free variable k is bound

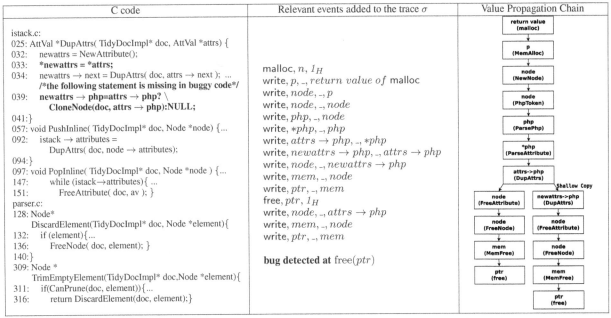

Figure 3. Detecting, and locating the root cause of, a double-free bug in *Tidy-34132*.

to the timestamp for this event. $Time(bid) > k$ checks whether this block is allocated inside this function (or transaction).

Garbage collector bugs. [GC-BUG] illustrates how to specify one of the basic correctness properties for garbage collector implementations, that the alive bits are set correctly. Consider, for example, a mark-and-sweep garbage collector that uses the least significant bit of each allocated block to mark the block as alive/reachable (bit = 1) or not-alive (bit = 0). We can check whether the alive bits are set correctly at the end of a GC cycle before resetting them (bit = 0), as shown in rule [GC-BUG]: all blocks in H are marked as alive and all blocks in F are marked as freed.

3. Formalism

We now present our formalism: a core imperative calculus that models the execution and memory operations of C programs. We introduce this calculus for two reasons: (1) it drastically simplifies programmer's task of expressing bugs in C programs, by reducing the language to a few syntactic constructs and the dynamic semantics to a handful of abstract state transitions, and (2) it helps prove soundness.[2]

3.1 Syntax

We adopt a syntax that is minimalist, yet expressive enough to capture a wide variety of bugs, and powerful enough to model the actual execution. The syntax is shown in Figure 7. A program consists of a list of top-level definitions d. Definitions can be main, whose body is e, global variables g initialized with value v, and functions f with argument x (which is a tuple in the case of multiple-argument functions) and body e.

Expressions e can take several syntactic forms: values v, explained shortly; variable names x (which represent local variables or function arguments, but not global variables); let bindings; stack

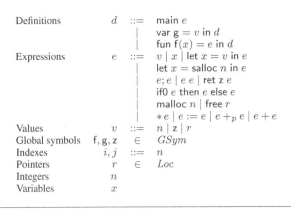

Figure 7. Syntax.

allocations let $x = $ salloc n in e, where variable x is either a local variable or a function argument, n is its size (derived from the x's storage size), and e is an optional initializer; sequencing $e; e$ and function application e e; function return ret z e; conditionals if0 e then e else e; malloc n, allocating n bytes in the heap; free r, deallocating a heap block; pointer dereference $*e$; assignment $e := e$; pointer arithmetic $e +_p e$, and integer arithmetic $e + e$. Values v can be integers n, global symbols z, or pointers r. Indexes, e.g., i, j, are integers and are used to specify the offset of a pointer in a memory block. Pointers r range over locations Loc, and are used as keys in a pointer map, as described next; note that we do not assume a specific type (e.g., integer, long) for pointers, as it is not relevant for defining the abstract machine.

3.2 Operational Semantics

The operational semantics consists of state and reduction rules. The semantics is small-step, and evaluation rules have the form:

$$\langle H; F; \overline{S}; P; k; \sigma; f; e \rangle \longrightarrow \langle H'; F'; \overline{S}'; P'; k'; \sigma'; f'; e' \rangle$$

which means expression e reduces in one step to expression e', and in the process of reduction, the heap H changes to H', the freed

---

[2] Soundness refers to detectors being correct with respect to the operational semantics to help catch specification errors; it does not imply that we certify the correctness of auto-generated and manually-written code for the Pin-based implementation, which operates on the entire x86 instruction set.

Rules	Detection point	Bug condition
[POSSIBLE-LEAK]	$detect\langle H; \sigma; \mathsf{ret}\ main\ v\rangle$:	$dom(H) \neq \emptyset$
[DEFINITE-LEAK]	$detect\langle H; P; \sigma; \mathsf{ret}\ main\ v\rangle$:	$\exists\ bid\ \in\ H : \neg(\exists\ r \mapsto (bid, \_)\ \in\ P)$
[LEAK-IN-TS]	$detect\langle H; \sigma; \mathsf{ret}\ ts\ v\rangle$:	$\exists\ bid\ \in\ H : FindLast(k, \mathsf{call}, ts, \_) \wedge Time(bid) > k$
[GC-BUG]	$detect\langle H; F; \sigma; \mathsf{ret}\ gc\ v\rangle$:	$\neg((\forall\ bid\ \in\ H : IsAlive(bid) \wedge (\forall\ bid\ \in\ F : \neg IsAlive(bid)))$
	Auxiliary predicates	$IsAlive(bid)\ \doteq\ bid\ \&\ 0x1 = 1$

Figure 6. Bug detection rules and auxiliary predicates for other classes of bugs.

blocks set F changes to F', the stack $\overline{S}$ changes to $\overline{S}'$, the pointer map P changes to P', the timestamp changes from k to k', the trace changes from σ to σ' and the value origin f changes to f'. We now provide definitions for state elements and then present the reduction rules.

Definitions. In Figure 8 we present the semantics and some auxiliary definitions. In our memory model, memory blocks b of size n are allocated in the heap via malloc n or on the stack via salloc n. Block id's bid are keys in the domain of the heap or the stack; we denote their domain Bid, and represent elements in Bid as $1_H, 2_H, 3_H, \ldots$ (which indicates heap-allocated blocks) and $1_S, 2_S, 3_S, \ldots$ (which indicates stack-allocated blocks). Memory blocks are manually deallocated from the heap via free r and automatically from the stack when a function returns (the redex is ret $z\ v$). All the deallocated heap and stack blocks are stored in F—the "freed" set—as (bid, h) and (bid, s) respectively. Block contents b are represented at byte granularity, i.e., $\boxed{v_0, \ldots, v_{n-1}}$; a freshly-allocated block is not initialized, and is marked as $\boxed{\text{junk}}$. The heap H contains mappings from block id's bid to tuples (b, n, k); tuples represent the block contents b, the block size n and the timestamp k when the block was created. A stack frame S consists of mappings $bid \mapsto (b, n, k)$, just like the heap. The stack $\overline{S}$ is a sequence of stack frames.

We keep a pointer map P with entries $r \mapsto (bid, n)$, that is, a map from references to block id bid and offset n. Timestamps k are integers, incremented after each step. The trace σ records timed events ν, i.e., (timestamp, event) pairs. Events ν can be memory writes write, r, v, f which indicate that value v, whose origin was f, was written to location r; if-conditions $n == n'$ which indicate that the value of the if guard n was n', allocations malloc, n, bid, deallocations free, r, bid, function calls call, z, v and function return ret, z, v. At each step we keep a value origin f that tracks where the last value v comes from: a constant, a global variable, or the prior step(s), as explained shortly. Runtime expressions e are the expressions defined in Figure 7.

We use several notational shorthands to simplify the definition of the rules; they are shown in the top-middle part of Figure 8. Given a pointer r, we can look it up in the heap H or stack $\overline{S}$, extract its bid and index i, and contents $\boxed{v_0, \ldots, v_{n-1}}$. We now explain the shorthands: $Bid(r)$ is the block id; $Idx(r)$ is the pointer's offset; $Begin(r)$ is the beginning address of a block r refers to; $End(r)$ is the end address of a block; $Size(r)$ is the size of the block; $Time(bid)$ is the timestamp at which the block was allocated; $Block(r)$ is the whole block contents; $Value(r)$ is the value stored in the memory unit pointed to by r.

Several other shorthands are defined in the top-right part of Figure 8 as follows: "bid fresh" means the bid is not in the domain of H, F, and $\overline{S}$, and bid has never been used before; $popStack(S, F)$ is used to deallocate all the blocks in the stack S, i.e., for all $bid \in dom(S)$, add (bid, s) to F.

We define a notion of the origin of a value v, denoted $orig(v, f)$, as follows: given a prior origin f, if v is a constant n, then the ori-

gin of value v is *gen* (value v is newly *generated* here); if v is a variable z, then the origin of value v is z (value v is propagated from variable z); otherwise, the origin of value v is f, i.e., the prior origin, indicating it is the result of a prior computation. This origin information is instrumental for constructing bug locators, as it helps track value propagation and hence bug root causes.

We use evaluation contexts $\mathbb{E}$ to indicate where evaluation is to take place next; they are modeled after expressions, and allow us to keep reduction rule definitions simple.

Evaluation rules. Further down in Figure 8 we show the reduction rules. The rule [LET] is standard: when reducing let $x = v$ in e, we perform the substitution $e[x/v]$. The rule [LET-SALLOC] is used to model the introduction of local variables and function arguments; it is a bit more complicated, as it does several things: first it allocates a new block bid of size n on the stack, initialized to junk, then it picks a fresh r and makes it point to the newly allocated block bid and index 0, and finally substitutes all occurrences of x with r. The allocation rule, [MALLOC], is similar: we model allocating n bytes by picking a fresh bid, adding the mapping $[bid \mapsto (\boxed{\text{junk}}, n, k)$ to the heap, creating a fresh pointer r that points to the newly-allocated block at offset 0, recording the event $(k, \mathsf{malloc}, n, bid)$ in the trace σ, and updating the f to *gen*, meaning r is newly generated at this step. The deallocation rule, [FREE], works as follows: we first identify the bid that r points to, and then remove the $bid \mapsto (b, n, k_1)$ mapping from the heap, and add the (bid, h) tuple to F; we record the event by adding $(k, \mathsf{free}, r, bid)$ to the trace.

The function call rule, [CALL], works as follows: create an empty stack frame S and push it onto the stack, then rewrite z v to be let $x = \mathsf{salloc}\ n$ in $(x := v; e)$, which means we allocate a new block for the function argument x on the stack, and set up the next reductions to assign (propagate) the value v to x, and then evaluate the function body e; we record the call by adding (k, call, z, v) to the trace, and propagate v's origin; we assume each function body e contains a return expression ret z e'. The converse rule, [RETURN], applies when the next expression is a return marker; it pops the current frame S off the stack, deallocates all the blocks allocated in S before, record the return by adding (k, ret, z, v) to the trace, and updates the f to $orig(v, f)$.

Dereferencing, modeled by the rule [READ], entails returning the value pointed to by r, and updating the f to be r, denoting that the origin of value v comes from r. When assigning value v to the location pointed to by r (which resides at block id bid and index i), modeled by the rule [ASSIGN], we change the mapping in the heap or stack (whichever r points to) to b', that is the block contents value at index i is replaced by v; we also record the write by adding $(k, \mathsf{write}, r, v, orig(v, f))$ to the trace, and record the assignment-induced value propagation by setting f to $orig(v, f)$.

Integer arithmetic ([INT-OP]) does the calculation, and updates the f to *gen* to mark the fact that n_3 is newly generated here; actually this rule is only necessary for purposes of value propagation, as most components of Σ remain unchanged. Pointer arithmetic ([PTR-ARITH]) is a bit more convoluted: we first find out bid and i—the block id and index associated with r, create a fresh r_2 that

Definitions

Block id	bid	$\in$	Bid
Block contents	b	::=	$\boxed{v_0, \ldots, v_{n-1}}$
Heap	H	::=	$\emptyset$
			$\mid bid \mapsto (b, n, k), H$
Freed blocks	F	::=	$\emptyset \mid (bid, h), F$
			$\mid (bid, s), F$
Stack frame	S	::=	$\emptyset$
			$\mid bid \mapsto (b, n, k), S$
Stack	$\overline{S}$	::=	$\emptyset \mid \overline{S}, S$
Pointers	P	::=	$\emptyset \mid r \mapsto (bid, i), P$
Timestamp	k	::=	n
Events	ev	::=	write, r, v, f
			$\mid n == n'$
			$\mid$ malloc, n, bid
			$\mid$ free, r, bid
			$\mid$ call, z, v
			$\mid$ ret, z, v
Timed events	ν	::=	(k, ev)
Traces	σ	::=	$\emptyset \mid \nu \cup \sigma$
Value origin	f	::=	$gen \mid z \mid r$
Expressions	e	::=	...

Shorthands

Given $P[r \mapsto (bid, i)]$

$Bid(r) \doteq bid$

$Idx(r) \doteq i$

Given $H[bid \mapsto (b, n, k)] \vee \overline{S}[bid \mapsto (b, n, k)]$
and $P[r \mapsto (bid, i)], b = \boxed{v_0, \ldots, v_{n-1}}$

$Begin(r) \doteq bid$

$End(r) \doteq bid + n$

$Size(r) \doteq n$

$Time(bid) \doteq k$

$Block(r) \doteq b$

Given $H[bid \mapsto (b, n, k)] \vee \overline{S}[bid \mapsto (b, n, k)]$
and $P[r \mapsto (bid, i)], b = \boxed{v_0, \ldots, v_{n-1}}$
and $Begin(r) \leq r < End(r)$

$Value(r) \doteq v_i$

Shorthands (contd.)

bid fresh $\doteq$ $bid \notin Dom(H) \wedge$
$\qquad bid \notin Dom(F) \wedge$
$\qquad bid \notin Dom(\overline{S})$

$popStack(S, F) \doteq F \cup \left(\bigcup_{bid \in dom(S)} (bid, s) \right)$

$orig(v, f) \doteq \begin{cases} gen, & \text{if } v \text{ is a const. } n \\ z, & \text{if, } v \text{ is a gvar. } z \\ f, & \text{otherwise} \end{cases}$

Evaluation contexts

$\mathbb{E}$ ::= $[] \mid$ let $x = \mathbb{E}$ in e
$\mid \mathbb{E} \ e \mid v \ \mathbb{E} \mid$ ret $z \ \mathbb{E}$
$\mid \mathbb{E}; e \mid v; \mathbb{E}$
$\mid$ malloc $\mathbb{E} \mid$ salloc $n \ \mathbb{E}$
$\mid$ free $\mathbb{E}$
$\mid \mathbb{E} := e \mid r := \mathbb{E} \mid *\mathbb{E}$
$\mid \mathbb{E} +_p e \mid r +_p \mathbb{E}$
$\mid \mathbb{E} + e \mid n + \mathbb{E}$
$\mid$ if0 $\mathbb{E}$ then e else e

Evaluation

[LET]	$\langle H; F; \overline{S}; P; k; \sigma; f; \text{let } x = v \text{ in } e \rangle \longrightarrow \langle H; F; \overline{S}; P; k+1; \sigma; f; e[x/v] \rangle$	
[LET-SALLOC]	$\langle H; F; \overline{S}, S; P; k; \sigma; f; \text{let } x = \text{salloc } n \text{ in } e \rangle \longrightarrow$ $\langle H; F; \overline{S}, S[bid \mapsto (\boxed{junk}, n, k)]; P[r \mapsto (bid, 0)]; k+1; \sigma; f; e[x/r] \rangle$	$r \notin Dom(P)$ $\wedge \ bid$ fresh
[MALLOC]	$\langle H; F; \overline{S}; P; k; \sigma; f; \text{malloc } n \rangle \longrightarrow$ $\langle H[bid \mapsto (\boxed{junk}, n, k)]; F; \overline{S}; P[r \mapsto (bid, 0)]; k+1; \sigma, (k, \text{malloc}, n, bid); gen; r \rangle$	$r \notin Dom(P)$ $\wedge \ bid$ fresh
[FREE]	$\langle H \uplus bid \mapsto (b, n, k_1); F; \overline{S}; P[r \mapsto (bid, 0)]; k; \sigma; f; \text{free } r \rangle \longrightarrow$ $\langle H; F \cup (bid, h); \overline{S}; P; k+1; \sigma, (k, \text{free}, r, bid); f; 0 \rangle$	
[CALL]	$\langle H; F; \overline{S}; P; k; \sigma; f; z \ v \rangle \longrightarrow$ $\langle H; F; \overline{S}, S; P; k+1; \sigma, (k, \text{call}, z, v); orig(v, f); \text{let } x = \text{salloc } n \text{ in } (x := v; e) \rangle$	$z = \lambda x.e, S = \emptyset$
[RETURN]	$\langle H; F; \overline{S}, S; P; k; \sigma; f; \text{ret } z \ e \rangle \longrightarrow$ $\langle H; F'; \overline{S}; P; k+1; \sigma, (k, \text{ret}, z, v); orig(v, f); v \rangle$	$F' = popStack(S, F)$
[READ]	$\langle H; F; \overline{S}; P; k; \sigma; f; *r \rangle \longrightarrow \langle H; F; \overline{S}; P; k+1; \sigma; r; v \rangle$	$Value(r) = v \wedge v \neq junk$
[ASSIGN]	$\langle H[bid \mapsto (b, n, k_1)]; F; \overline{S}[bid \mapsto (b, n, k_1)]; P[r \mapsto (bid, i)]; k; \sigma; f; r := v \rangle \longrightarrow$ $\langle H[bid \mapsto (b', n, k_1)]; F; \overline{S}[bid \mapsto (b', n, k_1)]; P; k+1;$ $\sigma, (k, \text{write}, r, v, orig(v, f)); orig(v, f); v \rangle$	$b' = b[i \mapsto v]$ $\wedge v \neq junk$
[INT-OP]	$\langle H; F; \overline{S}; P; k; \sigma; f; n_1 + n_2 \rangle \longrightarrow \langle H; F; \overline{S}; P; k+1; \sigma; gen; n_3 \rangle$	$n_3 = n_1 + n_2$
[PTR-ARITH]	$\langle H; F; \overline{S}; P; k; \sigma; f; r +_p n \rangle \longrightarrow$ $\langle H; F; \overline{S}; P[r_2 \mapsto (bid, i+n)]; k+1; \sigma; gen; r_2 \rangle$	$Bid(r) = bid,$ $Idx(r) = i, r_2 \notin Dom(P)$
[IF-T]	$\langle H; F; \overline{S}; P; k; \sigma; f; \text{if0 } n \text{ then } e_1 \text{ else } e_2 \rangle \longrightarrow$ $\langle H; F; \overline{S}; P; k+1; \sigma, (k, n == 0); f; e_1 \rangle$	$n = 0$
[IF-F]	$\langle H; F; \overline{S}; P; k; \sigma; f; \text{if0 } n' \text{ then } e_1 \text{ else } e_2 \rangle \longrightarrow$ $\langle H; F; \overline{S}; P; k+1; \sigma, (k, n == n'); f; e_2 \rangle$	$n' \neq 0$
[CONG]	$\langle H; F; \overline{S}; P; k; \sigma; f; \mathbb{E}[e] \rangle \longrightarrow \langle H'; F'; \overline{S}'; P'; k'; \sigma'; f'; \mathbb{E}[e'] \rangle$	$\langle H; F; \overline{S}; P; k; \sigma; f; e \rangle \longrightarrow$ $\langle H'; F'; \overline{S}'; P'; k'; \sigma'; f'; e' \rangle$

Error rules

[BUG-UNMATCHED-FREE]	$\langle H; F; \overline{S}; P[r \mapsto (bid, j)]; k; \sigma; f; \text{free } r \rangle \longrightarrow Error$	$(bid \notin Dom(H)$ $\wedge (bid, h) \notin Dom(F))$ $\vee r \neq Begin(r)$
[BUG-DOUBLE-FREE]	$\langle H; F; \overline{S}; P[r \mapsto (bid, 0)]; k; \sigma; f; \text{free } r \rangle \longrightarrow Error$	$(bid, h) \in Dom(F)$
[BUG-DANG-PTR-DEREF]	$\langle H; F; \overline{S}; P[r \mapsto (bid, j)]; k; \sigma; f; *r \rangle \longrightarrow Error$	$(bid, h) \in Dom(F)$
[BUG-DANG-PTR-DEREF2]	$\langle H; F; \overline{S}; P[r \mapsto (bid, j)]; k; \sigma; f; r := v \rangle \longrightarrow Error$	$(bid, h) \in Dom(F)$
[BUG-NULL-PTR-DEREF]	$\langle H; F; \overline{S}; P; k; \sigma; f; *r \rangle \longrightarrow Error$	$r = NULL$
[BUG-NULL-PTR-DEREF2]	$\langle H; F; \overline{S}; P; k; \sigma; f; r := v \rangle \longrightarrow Error$	$r = NULL$
[BUG-OVERFLOW]	$\langle H; F; \overline{S}; P[r \mapsto (bid, j)]; k; \sigma; f; *r \rangle \longrightarrow Error$	$bid \in Dom(H) \wedge$ $(r < Begin(r) \vee r \geq End(r))$
[BUG-OVERFLOW2]	$\langle H; F; \overline{S}; P[r \mapsto (bid, j)]; k; \sigma; f; r := v \rangle \longrightarrow Error$	$bid \in Dom(H) \wedge$ $(r < Begin(r) \vee r \geq End(r))$
[BUG-UNINITIALIZED]	$\langle H; F; \overline{S}; P; k; \sigma; f; *r \rangle \longrightarrow Error$	$Value(r) = junk$

Figure 8. Operational semantics (abstract machine states and reductions).

now points to block *bid* and index $i + n$ and add it to P and finally update the f to *gen*, to record that r_2 is newly generated here.

The conditional rules [IF-T] and [IF-F] are standard, though we record the predicate value and timestamp, i.e., $(k, n == 0)$ and $(k, n! = n')$, respectively, into the trace; predicate values serve as a further programmer aid. The congruence rule, [CONG], chooses where computation is to be applied next, based on the shape of $\mathbb{E}$.

Error rules. The bottom of Figure 8 shows the error state reduction rules. When one of these rules applies, the abstract machine is about to enter an error state—in our implementation, the debugger pauses the execution (breakpoint) just before entering an error state. These rules are instrumental for proving soundness (Section 3.3) as they indicate when bug detectors should fire. For brevity, we only define error rules and prove soundness for the bugs in Figure 2. We now proceed to describing the error rules. [BUG-UNMATCHED-FREE] indicates an illegal free r is attempted, i.e., r does not point to the begin of a legally allocated heap block. [BUG-DOUBLE-FREE] indicates an attempt to call free r a second time, i.e., the block pointed to by r has already been freed. [BUG-DANG-PTR-DEREF] and [BUG-DANG-PTR-DEREF2] indicate attempts to dereference a pointer (for reading and writing, respectively) in an already-freed block. Similarly, [BUG-NULL-PTR-DEREF] and [BUG-NULL-PTR-DEREF2] indicate attempts to dereference (read from/write to) a null pointer. Rules [BUG-OVERFLOW] and [BUG-OVERFLOW2] indicate attempts to access values outside of a block. Rule [BUG-UNINITIALIZED] applies when attempting to read values inside an uninitialized block (allocated, but not yet written to).

3.3 Soundness

We use Σ as a shorthand for a legal state $\langle H; F; \overline{S}; P; k; \sigma; f; e \rangle$, and *Error* as a shorthand for an error state. Hence, the condensed form of the reduction relation for legal transitions is $\Sigma \longrightarrow \Sigma'$, while transitions $\Sigma \longrightarrow Error$ represent bugs. At a high level, our notion of soundness can be expressed as follows: if the abstract machine, in state Σ, would enter an error state next, which is the "ground truth" for a bug, then the user-defined bug detectors, defined in terms of just e and σ, must fire.

The proof of soundness relies on several key definitions and lemmas. We define a notion of a well-formed state, then we prove that reductions to non-error states preserve well-formedness, and finally the soundness theorem captures the fact that the premises of error transition rules in fact satisfy the user-defined bug specification, hence bugs will be detected.

We begin with the definition of well-formed states:

Definition 3.1 (Well-formed states). *A state* $\Sigma = \langle H; F; \overline{S}; P; k; \sigma; f; e \rangle$ *is well-formed if:*

1. $H \cap F = \emptyset$
2. $(H \cup F) \cap (\bigcup_{S \in \overline{S}} S) = \emptyset$

Intuitively, the first part says that block id's cannot simultaneously be in the heap H and in the freed set F, while the second part ensures that the set of heap pointers (allocated or freed) does not overlap with the set of stack pointers.

Next, we introduce a lemma to prove that non-error transitions keep the state well-formed.

Lemma 3.2 (Preservation of well-formedness). *If* Σ *is well-formed and* $\Sigma \longrightarrow \Sigma'$, *and* Σ' *is not an error state, then* Σ' *is well-formed.*

The proof is by induction on the reduction $\Sigma \longrightarrow \Sigma'$. Intuitively, this lemma states that, since the state always stays well-formed during non-error reductions, memory bugs cannot "creep in" and manifest later, which would hinder the debugging process. We now proceed to stating the main result, the soundness theorem.

Theorem 3.3 (Soundness). *Let the current state be* Σ, *where* $\Sigma \neq Error$, *the current trace be* σ *and the redex be* e. *Suppose* **p** *is a bug detector, i.e., a predicate on* σ *and* **e**, *and* [BUG-P] *is an error rule associated with the detector. If the machine's next state is an* Error *state* $(\Sigma \longrightarrow Error)$ *then the detector fires, i.e., predicate* **p** *is true.*

Put otherwise, the soundness theorem states that an error in the concrete domain of the operational semantics is detected in the abstract domain of the bug detector. Some auxiliary lemmas and the complete proof can be found in the companion technical report [35]. In a nutshell, in the proof we proceed by case analysis on the given error state transition, then appeal to various lemmas to show how the trace σ correctly captures the events that, when examined together with the redex e, will lead to the bug detector's predicate **p** becoming true and hence ensure the correctness of bug detection.

4. Implementation

We now describe our implementation; it consists of an offline translation part that generates the detectors and locators from a bug specification, and an online debugger that runs the program and performs detection/location.

4.1 Debugger Code Generation

From bug specification rules, described in Section 2.1, automated translation via Flex[13] and Bison[14] is used to generate a **detector** and **locator** pair. We illustrate this process using Figure 9 which contains the full bug specification text for double-free bugs as written by the developer.

The translator first generates two helper functions for the *Allocated* and *Freed* predicates, respectively. The *Allocated* helper function parses the tracked event trace (realized by the *state monitoring* runtime library, explained shortly) to find out whether the block associated with r is allocated in the heap. The generated detector checks whether the block pointed to by pointer r is allocated in the heap and freed later whenever the program's execution reaches the start of the *free* function.

Each generated locator computes several value propagation chains based on the bug specification. For example, as shown in Figure 9, two value propagation chains are computed for the two pointers (r and $r1$) which are used to deallocate the same memory block. Each write event write, r, _, z in the captured trace represents a value propagation edge from z to r. Value propagation chains are computed by traversing the value propagation edges back starting from the error detection point, until *gen* is encountered.

4.2 Online Debugging

Figure 10 shows an overview of the online debugger. The implementation runs as two separate processes (GDB and Pin) and consists of several parts: a GDB [15] component, that provides a command-line user interface and is responsible for interpreting the target program's debugging information; a *state monitoring* component, that tracks program execution and translates it into the abstract machine state of our calculus; and a *detector control* component that helps programmers turn detectors on and off on-the-fly. The generated bug detectors, together with the state monitoring and detector control component are linked and compiled to a pintool (a shared library) which is dynamically loaded by the Pin [20] dynamic binary instrumentation tool. Both our state monitoring component and automatically-generated bug detectors are realized by instrumenting the appropriate x86 instructions in Pin. The GDB component communicates with the Pin-based component via GDB's remote debugging protocol.

define	Allocated(r)	=	**exists** event(_ , malloc, _ , bid) in Trace **suchthat** (bid == Bid(r))
define	Freed(r, r1)	=	**exists** event(_ , free , r1, bid) in Trace **suchthat** (bid == Bid(r))
[double_free] **detect** <Trace; free r>:			Allocated(r) && Freed(r, r1) :VPC(r), VPC(r1)

Figure 9. Actual bug specification input for double-free bugs.

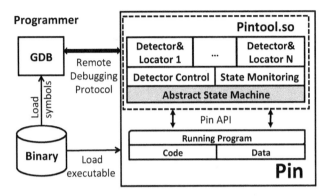

Figure 10. Online debugging process.

The *detector control* module allows programmers to turn detectors on and off at runtime. When the program's execution reaches a detection point, all the detectors associated with that detection point are evaluated in the specified order. Whenever any specified bug condition is satisfied, i.e., a bug is detected, our implementation first calls `PIN_ApplicationBreakpoint` to generate a breakpoint at the specified statement, and then generates a bug report which consists of all the concerned events in the bug specification, as a well as the source file name and line number.

The *state monitoring* component, a runtime library, observes the program execution at assembly code level and maps it back to transitions and state changes in the abstract machine state (e.g., H, P, σ) described in Section 3.2. Figure 11 shows a null pointer dereference bug to illustrate how the native x86 execution is mapped to the abstract state transitions in our calculus, as well as the detection points in the detection rules. The first three columns show the code in C, in our calculus, and assembly. Because C implicitly uses dereferenced pointers for stack variables (e.g., *p=1* in C is really **(&p)=1*), and our calculus make the implicit dereference explicit, code in our calculus needs one more dereference than code in C (e.g., *w:=***p* in our calculus corresponds to *w=**p* in C). In the second column of Figure 11 we append the *_addr* suffix to variables from the first column (e.g., *p* becomes *p_addr*) to avoid confusion.

As we can see, the x86 execution has a straightforward mapping to the state transition in our calculus. For example, the execution of the first *mov (%eax),%eax* instruction is mapped back to the [READ] evaluation rule with *r* being *p_addr* (where *r* is stored in register *eax* here), while the second *mov (%eax),%eax* is mapped back to the same rule with *r* being **p_addr* in our calculus. Meanwhile, each binary instruction has a natural mapping to the detection points (shown in the fourth column). For example, the first *mov (%eax),%eax* instruction corresponds to both *deref_r p_addr* and *deref p_addr* detection points. That is, all the bug detectors associated with *deref_r r* or *deref r* detection points are evaluated when the program is about to execute this instruction.

We generate the recording infrastructure after parsing the specifications, and only activate the required event trackers (e.g., we only activate *malloc* and *free* event trackers for double-free bugs).

Next we describe maintaining state transitions for the pointer mapping P. A block id is assigned to each allocated block, and the block id is increased after each allocation. Unique block ids ensure the detection of dangling pointer dereference bugs even

when a memory block is reused. Each pointer is bound with the block id and index of the block pointed to by shadow memory. We implement the pointer mapping transition by propagating the shadow value of each pointer along with the pointer arithmetic operation. Although we only need the mapping for pointers, we temporarily maintain mapping information for registers. The fifth column in Figure 11 shows an example of how the pointer mapping is changed by propagating the shadow value for the execution of assembly code given in the third column. For example, the *malloc* function returns the address of the allocated block (e.g., the block id is 1_H) in the register *%eax*, we shadow *%eax* to (1_H, 0), denoted by $P[\%eax \mapsto (1_H, 0)]$ in Figure 11. The mapping info is propagated from register *%eax* into *p* after the execution of *mov %eax, -0x10(%ebp)*, denoted by $P[-0x10(\%ebp) \mapsto (1_H, 0)]$ in Figure 11, which means that pointer *p* points to the first element inside block 1_H. Suppose two bug detectors are generated based on the buffer overflow and null pointer dereference specifications in Figure 2. Then when the program's execution reaches the first *mov (%eax),%eax* instruction, we are at a `deref` r detection point (*r* is stored inside register *%eax*), and pointer mapping information for register *%eax* contains the pointer mapping information for *r* here($P[\%eax \mapsto (1_H, 0)]$). By evaluating the two detectors, none of the bug conditions are satisfied. The pointer mapping for register *%eax* is set to invalid (denoted by (x,x) in Figure 11) due to the assignment. The execution continues to the second *mov (%eax),%eax* instruction, and the null pointer dereference bug is reported because *r == 0* is satisfied here (*r* is stored in register *%eax* and its value equals zero).

Value origin tracking is implemented similarly to pointer mapping. Each variable and register is tagged with a shadow origin of its value, and whenever the next expression to reduce is *r := v*, we update the origin (shadow value) of *r* to be the origin of *v*, and we record *r* and its new origin in the trace.

Storing all the tracked events and value propagations in memory may cause the debugger to run out of memory for long-running programs. Older events, which are unlikely to be accessed, can be dumped to disk and reloaded into memory if needed. However, we did not encounter this problem for our examined programs.

5. Experimental Evaluation

We evaluate our approach on several dimensions: *efficiency*, i.e., the manual coding effort saved by automated generation; *effectiveness/coverage*, i.e., can we (re)discover actual bugs in real-world programs; and *performance* overhead incurred by running programs using our approach.

5.1 Efficiency

We measure the efficiency of our debugger code generation by comparing the lines of code of the bug specification and the generated C implementation. For each kind of bug, we specify the bug detector and bug locator as shown in Figure 2. Table 1 shows the comparison of lines of codes for bug specification and generated debugger for each kind of bug and all bugs combined.

Since detectors use the same model (detection point and predicates on the abstract machine state), and share the code for the state monitoring library, the generated code for all detectors combined is 3.3 KLOC, while for a single detector, the code size ranges from 2.2 to 2.4 KLOC. Note that the generated implementations are orders of magnitude larger than the bug specifications.

C	Our calculus	Assembly code	Detection points	Tracked pointer mapping	Additions to σ

int w;
int **p;
p=(int**)
malloc(4);
*p=0;
 	
w=**p;
	let w_addr=salloc 4 in
	let p_addr=salloc 4 in
	p_addr:=malloc 8;
	
	*p_addr:=0;
	
	w_addr:=***p_addr;
		call malloc
		mov %eax, −0x10(%ebp)
		mov − 0x10(%ebp), %eax
		movl $0x0, (%eax)
		mov − 0x10(%ebp), %eax
		mov (%eax), %eax
		mov (%eax), %eax
		mov %eax, −0xc(%ebp)
			deref_w / deref p_addr
			deref_r / deref p_addr
			deref_w / deref *p_addr
			deref_r / deref p_addr
			deref_r / deref *p_addr
				$P[\%eax \mapsto (1_H, 0)]$
				$P[−0x10(\%ebp) \mapsto (1_H, 0)]$
				$P[\%eax \mapsto (1_H, 0)]$
				$P[(\%eax) \mapsto (x, x)]$
				$P[\%eax \mapsto (1_H, 0)]$
				$P[\%eax \mapsto (x, x)]$
					(malloc, n, 1_H)
					(write, p_addr, _,
					malloc *retval*)
					(write, *p_addr, _,
					gen)
					bug detected at
					deref * p_addr

Figure 11. State transition for a null pointer dereference bug.

Lines of code	Unmatched Free	Double Free	Dangling Ptr. Deref.	Null Ptr. Deref.	Heap Buffer Overflow	Uninitialized Read	Total
Specification	2	3	3	1	3	1	8
Generated debugger	2.3K	2.4K	2.4K	2.2K	2.3K	2.2K	3.3K

Table 1. Debugger code generation efficiency: comparison of lines of specification and generated debuggers for different bugs.

Program Name	LOC	Bug type	Bug location	Bug source	Program description
Tidy-34132	35.9K	Double Free	istack.c:031	BugNet [27]	Html checking & cleanup
Tidy-34132	35.9K	Null Pointer Dereference	parser.c:161	BugNet [27]	Html checking & cleanup
Bc-1.06	17.0K	Heap Buffer Overflow	storage.c:176	BugNet [27]	Arbitrary-precision Calculator
Tar-1.13.25	27.1K	Null Pointer Dereference	incremen.c:180	gnu.org/software/tar/	Archive creator
Cpython-870c0ef7e8a2	336.0K	Unmatched Free	typeobject.c:2490	http://bugs.python.org	Python interpreter
Cpython-2.6.8	336.0K	Double Free	import.c:2843	http://bugs.python.org	Python interpreter
Cpython-08135a1f3f5d	387.6K	Heap Buffer Overflow	imageop.c:593	http://bugs.python.org	Python interpreter
Cpython-83d0945eea42	271.1K	Null Pointer Dereference	_pickle.c:442	http://bugs.python.org	Python interpreter

Table 2. Overview of benchmark programs.

Program name	Traditional debugging	Dynamic slicing	VPC
Tidy-34132-double-free	28,487	4,687	16
Tidy-34132-null-deref	55,777	13,050	4
Bc-1.06	42,903	19,988	1
Tar-1.13.25	74	7	4
Cpython-870c0ef7e8a2	20,719	13,136	2
Cpython-2.6.8	1,083	444	10
Cpython-08135a1f3f5d	270,544	135,366	1
Cpython-83d0945eea42	11,916	7,285	2

Table 3. Debugging effort: instructions examined.

5.2 Debugger Effectiveness

A summary of benchmarks used in our evaluation is shown in Table 2; each benchmark contains a real reported bug, with the details in columns 3–6. We now provide brief descriptions of the experience with using our approach to find and fix these bugs. Note that three of the bugs were presented in detail in Section 2.2, hence we focus on the remaining five bugs.

In addition to the double-free bug, *Tidy-34132* also contains a NULL pointer dereference which manifests when the input HTML file contains a nested *frameset*, and the *noframe* tag is unexpectedly included in the inner *frameset* rather than the outer one, which causes function *FindBody* to wrongly return a null pointer.

Bc-1.06 fails with a memory corruption error due to heap buffer overflow (variable *v_count* is misused due to a copy-paste error).

Cpython-2.6.8 has a double-free memory bug when there is a folder in the current directory whose name is exactly the same as a module name, and this opened file is wrongly closed twice, resulting in double-freeing a *FILE* structure. *Cpython-08135a1f3f5d* crashes due to a heap buffer overflow which manifests when the *imageop* module tries to convert a very large RGB image to an 8-bit RGB. *Cpython-83d0945eea42* fails due to a null pointer derefer-

ence when the *_pickle* module tries to serialize a wrongly-initialized object whose *write_buf* field is null.

It can be easily seen that the benchmark suite includes bugs from our detector list and that all the bugs come from widely-used applications. Thus, this benchmark suite is representative with respect to debugging effectiveness evaluation.

All the bugs were successfully detected using the debuggers generated from the specifications in Figure 2. However, we did find several cases of false positives. Because our approach is based on Pin, which cannot track code execution into the kernel for system calls, our generated debuggers detected some false positives (uninitialized reads). This limitation can be overcome by capturing system call effects [26], a task we leave to future work.

We now quantify the effectiveness of our approach by showing how locators dramatically simplify the process of finding bug root causes. We have conducted the following experiment: we compute the number of instructions that would need to be examined to find the root cause of the bug in three scenarios: *traditional debugging*, *dynamic slicing*[38], and *our approach*. We present the results in Table 3. Traditional debugging refers to using a standard debugger, e.g., GDB, where the programmer must trace back the execution starting from the crash point to the point that represents the root cause. For the bugs considered, this would require tracing back through the execution of 74 to 270,544 instructions, depending on the program. When dynamic slicing is employed, the programmer traces back the execution along dynamic dependence edges, i.e., only a relevant subset of instructions need to be examined. Breadth-first traversal of dependence chains until the root cause is located leads to tracing back through the execution of 7 to 135,366 instructions, depending on the program. In contrast, in our approach, the programmer will trace back through the execution along value propagation chains which amounts to the examination of just 1 to 16 instructions. Hence, our approach reduces the debugging effort significantly, compared to traditional debugging and dynamic slicing.

Program name	Null Pin seconds	Bug detect seconds (factor)	Bug detect&VP seconds (factor)
Tidy-34132-double-free	0.77	6.05 (7.9x)	7.62 (9.9x)
Tidy-34132-null-deref	0.62	4.52 (7.3x)	5.58 (9.0x)
Bc-1.06	0.62	4.61 (7.4x)	5.70 (9.2x)
Tar-1.13.25	1.08	5.89 (5.5x)	7.43 (6.9x)
Cpython-870c0ef7e8a2	3.95	59.21 (15.0x)	80.84 (20.5x)
Cpython-2.6.8	3.31	33.16 (10.0x)	41.35 (12.5x)
Cpython-08135a1f3f5d	2.95	32.03 (10.9x)	40.13 (13.6x)
Cpython-83d0945eea42	3.17	54.21 (17.1x)	63.83 (20.1x)

Table 4. Program execution times (from start to bug-detect), when running inside our debugger.

5.3 Performance

The focus of our work was efficiency and effectiveness, so we have not optimized our implementation for performance. Nevertheless, we have found that the time overheads for generated monitors and locators are acceptable for interactive debugging. When measuring overhead, we used the same failing input we had used for the effectiveness evaluation. We report the results in Table 4. We use the "Null Pin" (the program running under Pin without our debugger) time overhead as the baseline, which is shown in the first column, and the time overhead with all detectors on is in the second column. The third column shows the time overhead with all detectors on and value propagation on. All experiments were conducted on a DELL PowerEdge 1900 with 3.0GHz Intel Xeon processor and 3GB RAM, running Linux, kernel version 2.6.18.

From Table 4, we can see that the time overhead incurred by all bug detectors ranges from 5.5x to 17.1x compared to the baseline, while the time overhead incurred by all bug detectors and value propagation ranges from 6.9x to 20.5x. We believe this overhead is acceptable and a worthy tradeoff for the benefits of our approach.

When running the programs inside our debugger we have found that (1) running time increases linearly with the number of bug detectors enabled, and (2) even with the overhead imposed by our dynamic approach with all detectors and value propagation on, real-world programs took less than 81 seconds to crash on inputs that lead to bug manifestation. These results demonstrate that the overhead is acceptable and our approach appears promising for debugging tasks on realistic programs.

6. Related Work

Memory debuggers. A number of works aim to handle multiple kinds of memory bugs [2, 11, 28]. DieHard [2] is a unified algorithm for memory management for avoiding memory errors. Purify [11] and Valgrind Memcheck [28] detect memory bugs using dynamic binary instrumentation. Bond et al.'s approach [3] tracks the origins of unusable values; however, it can only track the origin of Null and undefined values while our VPCs capture not only origin, but propagation for any specified variable. VPCs are therefore much more useful. E.g., for a double-free bug, the origin of pointer *r* used in the second free is always the return value of *malloc* (which is not very informative). These approaches are specialized to find a reduced class of memory bugs, and the bug detection is "hardcoded". Our approach permits very easy extensibility to new kinds of bugs via specification and code generation; we also present a soundness proof to show that the debuggers specification are correct.

Advanced debugging and bug finding. MemTracker [34] provides a unified architectural support for low-overhead programmable tracking to meet the needs for different kinds of bugs. Find-Bugs [12] leverages bug patterns to locate bugs and Algorithmic (or declarative) debugging [32] is an interactive technique where the user is asked at each step whether the prior computation step was correct [33]. Program synthesis has been used in prior work to automatically generate programs from specifications at various levels: types [21], predicates or assertions/goals [22]; however no prior work on synthesis has investigated specification at the operational semantics level in the context of debugging.

Runtime verification and dynamic analysis. Monitor-oriented programming (MOP) [24] and Time Rover [16] allow correctness properties to be specified formally (e.g., in LTL, MTL, FSM, or CFG); code generation is then used to yield runtime monitors from the specification. Monitor-oriented programming (MOP) [4, 24] combines formal specification with runtime monitoring. In MOP, correctness properties can be specified in LTL, or as FSM, or as a CFG. Then, from a specification, a low-overhead runtime monitor is synthesized to run in AspectJ (i.e., use aspect-oriented programming [17] in JavaMOP [4]) or on the PCI bus (in BusMOP [30]) to monitor the program execution and detect violations of the specification. Time Rover [7, 16] combines LTL, MTL and UML specification with code generation to yield runtime monitors for formal specifications.

PQL [23] and PTQL [9] allow programmers to query the program execution history, while tracematches [1] allows free variables in trace matching on top of AspectJ. GC assertions [31] allow programmers to query the garbage collector about the heap structure. Jinn [19] synthesizes bug detectors from state machine for detect foreign function interface.

Ellison and Roşu [8] define a general-purpose semantics for C with applications including debugging and runtime verification; in our semantics we only expose those reduction rules that help specify memory debuggers, but our approach works for the entire x86 instruction set and sizable real-world programs including library code.

Compared to all these approaches, our work differs in several ways: the prior approaches are adept at specifying properties and generating runtime checkers (which detect what property has been violated), whereas ours points out *where*,*why*, and *how* a property is violated; also, we introduce value propagation chains to significantly reduce the effort associated with bug finding and fixing.

7. Conclusions

We have presented a novel approach to constructing memory debuggers from declarative bug specifications. We demonstrate that many categories of memory bugs can be specified in an elegant and concise manner using First-order logic; we then prove that bug specifications are sound, i.e., they do not miss bugs that manifest during execution. We show that from the concise bug specifications, debuggers that catch and locate these bugs can be generated automatically, hence programmers can easily specify new kinds of bugs. We illustrate our approach by generating debuggers for six kinds of memory bugs. Experiments with using our approach on real-world programs indicate that it is both efficient and effective.

Acknowledgments

This research is supported by the National Science Foundation grants CCF-0963996 and CCF-1149632 to the University of California, Riverside.

References

[1] C. Allan, P. Avgustinov, A. S. Christensen, L. Hendren, S. Kuzins, O. Lhoták, O. de Moor, D. Sereni, G. Sittampalam, and J. Tibble. Adding trace matching with free variables to aspectj. OOPSLA '05, pages 345–364.

[2] E. D. Berger and B. G. Zorn. DieHard: Probabilistic memory safety for unsafe languages. *PLDI'06*, pages 158–168.

[3] M. D. Bond, N. Nethercote, S. W. Kent, S. Z. Guyer, and K. S. McKinley. Tracking bad apples: reporting the origin of null and undefined value errors. OOPSLA '07, pages 405–422.

[4] F. Chen and G. Roşu. MOP: An Efficient and Generic Runtime Verification Framework. In *OOPSLA'07*, pages 569–588.

[5] D. Dhurjati and V. Adve. Efficiently detecting all dangling pointer uses in production servers. In *DSN '06*, pages 269–280.

[6] D. Dhurjati and V. Adve. Backwards-compatible array bounds checking for c with very low overhead. In *ICSE '06*, pages 162–171, 2006.

[7] D. Drusinsky. The temporal rover and the atg rover. In *SPIN 2000*.

[8] C. Ellison and G. Roşu. An executable formal semantics of C with applications. In *POPL '12*, pages 533–544.

[9] S. F. Goldsmith, R. O'Callahan, and A. Aiken. Relational queries over program traces. OOPSLA '05, pages 385–402.

[10] R. Hähnle, M. Baum, R. Bubel, and M. Rothe. A visual interactive debugger based on symbolic execution. In *ASE '10*, pages 143–146.

[11] R. Hastings and B. Joyce. Purify: Fast detection of memory leaks and access errors. *USENIX Winter Tech. Conf.*, pages 125–136, 1992.

[12] D. Hovemeyer and W. Pugh. Finding bugs is easy. *OOSPLA'04*, pages 92–106.

[13] http://flex.sourceforge.net/. Flex homepage.

[14] http://www.gnu.org/software/bison/. Bison homepage.

[15] http://www.gnu.org/software/gdb/. Gdb homepage.

[16] http://www.time-rover.com. Time Rover homepage.

[17] G. Kiczales, J. Lamping, A. Mendhekar, C. Maeda, C. V. Lopes, J.-M. Loingtier, and J. Irwin. Aspect-oriented programming. In *ECOOP'97*, pages 220–242.

[18] A. Ko and B. Myers. Debugging reinvented: Asking and answering why and why not questions about program behavior. *ICSE'08*, pages 301–310.

[19] B. Lee, B. Wiedermann, M. Hirzel, R. Grimm, and K. S. McKinley. Jinn: synthesizing dynamic bug detectors for foreign language interfaces. PLDI '10, pages 36–49.

[20] C.-K. Luk, R. Cohn, R. Muth, H. Patil, A. Klauser, G. Lowney, S. Wallace, V. J. Reddi, and K. Hazelwood. Pin: building customized program analysis tools with dynamic instrumentation. In *PLDI '05*, pages 190–200.

[21] D. Mandelin, L. Xu, R. Bodík, and D. Kimelman. Jungloid mining: helping to navigate the api jungle. In *PLDI '05*, pages 48–61.

[22] Z. Manna and R. Waldinger. A deductive approach to program synthesis. *ACM Trans. Program. Lang. Syst.*, pages 90–121, 1980.

[23] M. Martin, B. Livshits, and M. S. Lam. Finding application errors and security flaws using pql: a program query language. OOPSLA '05, pages 365–383.

[24] P. O. Meredith, D. Jin, D. Griffith, F. Chen, and G. Roşu. An overview of the MOP runtime verification framework. *International Journal on Software Techniques for Technology Transfer*, pages 249–289, 2011.

[25] S. Nagarakatte, J. Zhao, M. M. Martin, and S. Zdancewic. Softbound: highly compatible and complete spatial memory safety for c. *PLDI'09*, pages 245–258.

[26] S. Narayanasamy, C. Pereira, H. Patil, R. Cohn, and B. Calder. Automatic logging of operating system effects to guide application-level architecture simulation. In *SIGMETRICS'06*, pages 216–227.

[27] S. Narayanasamy, G. Pokam, and B. Calder. BugNet: Continuously recording program execution for deterministic replay debugging. *ISCA'05*, pages 284–295, 2005.

[28] N. Nethercote and J. Seward. Valgrind: A framework for heavyweight dynamic binary instrumentation. *PLDI'07*, pages 89–100.

[29] G. Novark, E. D. Berger, and B. G. Zorn. Efficiently and precisely locating memory leaks and bloat. In *PLDI '09*, pages 397–407.

[30] R. Pellizzoni, P. Meredith, M. Caccamo, and G. Rosu. Hardware runtime monitoring for dependable cots-based real-time embedded systems. In *RTSS'08*, pages 481–491.

[31] C. Reichenbach, N. Immerman, Y. Smaragdakis, E. E. Aftandilian, and S. Z. Guyer. What can the gc compute efficiently?: a language for heap assertions at gc time. OOPSLA '10, pages 256–269.

[32] E. Y. Shapiro. *Algorithmic Program DeBugging*. MIT Press, 1983.

[33] J. Silva. A survey on algorithmic debugging strategies. *Adv. Eng. Softw.*, pages 976–991, 2011.

[34] G. Venkataramani, I. Doudalis, Y. Solihin, and M. Prvulovic. Memtracker: An accelerator for memory debugging and monitoring. *ACM Trans. Archit. Code Optim.*, pages 5:1–5:33, 2009.

[35] Y. Wang, I. Neamtiu, and R. Gupta. Generating sound and effective memory debuggers. Technical report, University of California, Riverside, Department of Computer Science and Engineering, http://www.cs.ucr.edu/~neamtiu/pubs/memdebug-tr.pdf, 2013.

[36] G. Xu, M. D. Bond, F. Qin, and A. Rountev. Leakchaser: helping programmers narrow down causes of memory leaks. In *PLDI '11*, pages 270–282.

[37] C. Zhang, D. Yan, J. Zhao, Y. Chen, and S. Yang. Bpgen: an automated breakpoint generator for debugging. In *ICSE '10*, pages 271–274.

[38] X. Zhang, R. Gupta, and Y. Zhang. Precise dynamic slicing algorithms. *ICSE '03*, pages 319–329, May 2003.

Rigorous Benchmarking in Reasonable Time

Tomas Kalibera

University of Kent, Canterbury

t.kalibera@kent.ac.uk

Richard Jones

University of Kent, Canterbury

r.e.jones@kent.ac.uk

Abstract

Experimental evaluation is key to systems research. Because modern systems are complex and non-deterministic, good experimental methodology demands that researchers account for uncertainty. To obtain valid results, they are expected to run many iterations of benchmarks, invoke virtual machines (VMs) several times, or even rebuild VM or benchmark binaries more than once. All this repetition costs time to complete experiments. Currently, many evaluations give up on sufficient repetition or rigorous statistical methods, or even run benchmarks only in training sizes. The results reported often lack proper variation estimates and, when a small difference between two systems is reported, some are simply unreliable.

In contrast, we provide a statistically rigorous methodology for repetition and summarising results that makes efficient use of experimentation time. Time efficiency comes from two key observations. First, a given benchmark on a given platform is typically prone to much less non-determinism than the common worst-case of published corner-case studies. Second, repetition is most needed where most uncertainty arises (whether between builds, between executions or between iterations). We capture experimentation cost with a novel mathematical model, which we use to identify the number of repetitions at each level of an experiment necessary and sufficient to obtain a given level of precision.

We present our methodology as a cookbook that guides researchers on the number of repetitions they should run to obtain reliable results. We also show how to present results with an effect size confidence interval. As an example, we show how to use our methodology to conduct throughput experiments with the DaCapo and SPEC CPU benchmarks on three recent platforms.

Categories and Subject Descriptors C.4 [*Performance of Systems*]: Measurement Techniques.

Keywords Benchmarking methodology; statistical methods; DaCapo; SPEC CPU.

1. Introduction

Experimental evaluation is key to programming language and systems research. It has proved hard to do well. Programs are (possibly surprisingly) non-deterministic, and their execution times can vary significantly from run to run, or with different builds. Such variation makes it uncertain what the effect of, say, a particular optimisation might be. The challenge to experimental computer scientists

is to deal with this uncertainty, and to provide reliable estimates of program speedup. The difficulty is to know how many experiments to run, and to minimise the cost in experiment time without compromising the validity of the results. We show that, in most cases, good experimental methodology is feasible without excessive cost.

We focus on execution time, the key measurement in, for example, 90 out of 122 papers presented in 2011 at PLDI, ASPLOS and ISMM, or published in TOPLAS (nos. 1–4) and TACO (nos. 1–2). Unfortunately, the overwhelming majority of these papers reported results in ways that seem to make their work impossible to repeat, or did not convincingly demonstrate their claims for performance improvement: 71 failed to provide any measure of variation (such as variance or a confidence interval) for their results. This is unparalleled in most other scientific and social scientific fields. It risks reporting misleading results.

These risks are real. Advances in performance in our field are often small (Mytkowicz et al [20] report a median of 10%) and so can fall within the bounds of measurement error. In a case study of Java VM/DaCapo benchmarking, Georges et al [9] show how poor methods of repeating and summarising experiments led to misleading results. Ignoring systematic bias in code layout in experiments with SPEC CPU benchmarks can also deliver misleading results [20]. Even if reported speedups are relatively large, a rigorous study should estimate the measurement error.

While it is disappointing that all this evidence seems to have had little impact on practice in our field, maybe it is understandable. Researchers find themselves faced with the task of running ever more experiments in order to deal with these problems. Thus they run multiple iterations of a benchmark for each VM execution and run each VM execution multiple times. Variations in Unix environment size and in link order, and randomised algorithms in compilers (producing different binaries for the same code) all seem to impose further requirements for repetition [1, 9, 15, 20]. For example, running the SPEC INT benchmarks to measure speedup of a compiler optimisation against a base, using 30 different linking orders, takes 3 days on a recent platform. Running the DaCapo 2006 and 2009 benchmarks [3] to compare two systems, using 20 executions and 10 iterations, also takes almost 3 days.

We renounce any catalogue of despair. We show that good experimental methodology is feasible: we can cater for variation in performance without excessive repetition in most cases. Our approach is to adapt experiment design to the problems that a particular platform and benchmark present. In our experience, research groups run the same benchmarks on the same systems for years. This is done for a good reason, as otherwise the performance changes due to, say, improvements of a garbage collector under study could be confused with performance changes due to operating system upgrades. In this setting, an initial investment into dimensioning benchmark experiments will pay off. As common in most statistical analyses of data, this does involve some manual steps. In most projects this is a one-off investment but, of course, any major change to the system would necessitate re-dimensioning.

Note that repetition is most needed where most non-determinism occurs in the experiment. We show how to establish the repetition counts necessary for any evaluation to be valid, and sufficient to provide the most precise result for a given experimentation budget. We show how to estimate the error bounds both to evaluate the performance of a single system and to compare execution times of a baseline and a new version of a system: such ratios are commonly used but hardly ever qualified with error bounds. As an example, we apply our methodology to a case study of the performance of DaCapo and SPEC CPU benchmarks. Our contributions are:

- We explain the shortcomings of statistical methods commonly used in our field. Instead, we offer a sound method based on effect sizes and confidence intervals.
- We provide an observational study of non-determinism in the DaCapo and SPEC CPU benchmarks.
- We offer a sound experimental methodology that makes best use of experiment time. We establish, both formally and in practice, the optimum number of repetitions of experiments to achieve the most precise results for a given experiment time.
- We compare our methodology with heuristics-based practice, and show that the latter often leads to either too few or too many experiments.
- We revisit the question of the effect of code layout on the performance of DaCapo and SPEC CPU and show that it is less important than prior work had shown.

2. Related Work

When running SPEC CPU benchmarks, Mytkowicz et al [20] found a number of sources of significant *measurement bias*, i.e. a systematic error in the measurement of systems that might favour one system over another. These included the Unix environment size and the link order (the order in which .o files are given to the linker), which affect the memory layout of data and code, and hence memory hierarchy (cache, virtual memory) performance. Mytkowicz et al suggest eliminating this bias by randomising the experimental set-up. Because of the expense of running benchmarks with many different link orders, they used only the 'training' sizes for the benchmarks. We repeated their experiments and confirmed the impact of link order for training sizes. However, our experimental methodology made it feasible to consider SPEC's full 'reference' sizes, where we found that, although there was variation, it was very small (Section 7.2).

Getting the experimental methodology right is crucial because, as Georges et al [9] demonstrate, different methodologies can lead to different conclusions. They advocate running multiple iterations of each Java benchmark within a single VM execution, and multiple VM executions. In each execution, a number of initial iterations is dropped to *warm up* the benchmark before it is deemed to have converged to steady state. They establish the warm-up number on the fly by finding the first window of N (say, 10) iterations that seems stable (the relative width of 95% confidence interval for the mean is less than 5%). The sample mean of such a window is used to summarise this execution of the VM.

The DaCapo'09 benchmark harness also tries to detect steady state automatically, but reports one iteration per VM execution. It keeps calculating relative variation (the ratio of standard deviation and mean) over windows of three iterations until it drops below 3%, at which point the benchmark is deemed to have converged: the time of one iteration is used as the summary. We observe that these two automated methods do not perform well, as they often lead to either too few experiments, hence failing to get to a steady state, or far too many (Section 6.3).

The compilation strategy of Java VMs is non-deterministic. Which methods are JIT-compiled and when is determined by sampling method execution. One way to reduce variation between VM executions is always to compile to the same plan. Ogata et al [22] use a sampling compiler to capture a compilation plan and then, for measurements, a replay compiler which compiles methods according to this plan. Georges et al [10] advocate compiler replay with multiple plans to avoid any bias introduced by a fixed compilation plan. They summarise with fixed-effects analysis of variance. However, this technique can be used only for very similar systems, where forcing the same compilation plan could still give results representative of real executions.

Stabiliser [7] is an LLVM-based compiler and runtime environment for code, stack and heap layout randomisation. It changes the layout randomly at regular intervals during one execution of a benchmark, in order to reduce the need for repeated execution. One benefit is that the sources of layout bias (such as the environment size [20] or link order) need not be identified by the experimenter. On the other hand, the results may include far more variation than in real systems, and hence can mislead. Our approach is less intrusive, but expects the experimenter to find potential sources of bias. If layout is the cause of bias, our methodology could be combined with Stabiliser. Our approach also applies to systems where online re-randomisation is not yet available, such as JVMs.

3. The Challenge of Reasonable Repetition

We have seen how variation can be introduced at several stages of a benchmark experiment (iteration, execution, compilation and so on). Three kinds of variables influence the outcomes of experiments. Values of *controlled variables* (such as the platform we choose, the heap size or compiler options) and how they impact the results are of interest for the evaluation. *Random variables* (such as the time between hardware interrupts or scheduling order on a multi-processor) change frequently in a random or non-deterministic manner. We are interested in the statistical properties of our results in face of random variables, but not in the individual values of these variables. *Uncontrolled variables* happen to be fixed for most or all of an experiment, but are beyond our control. If these impact the results, they cause bias and mislead. Hence, the experimenter's first task is to identify uncontrolled variables that impact results and modify the experimental system so that these become either controlled or random. For example, randomising link order turns an uncontrolled variable into a random one.

Experiment design is a statistical discipline which deals with how to run experiments efficiently given a set of controlled and random variables (see e.g. Maxwell & Delaney [18] for more details and references to the literature). The goal of benchmarking experiments is typically to estimate (a confidence interval for) the mean execution time of a given benchmark on one or more platforms, that is for a relatively small set of combinations of values of controlled variables. Note that the mean is a property of the underlying probability distribution of the population of random execution times. In practice we can never know this mean or the distribution, but a confidence interval can tell us something about what that mean might be. If we use sound experimental methodologies in our studies, each time constructing a 95% confidence interval for the mean, we can expect that overall in 95% of cases our intervals will have covered the true means. Often the goal is also to estimate speedup (65 of the 90 papers in our survey): such an estimate should also be qualified by a confidence interval.

The challenge we address here, and also the next step of the experimenter, is to design efficient experiments (repetitions and repetition counts) given the random variables present. A further challenge is to identify and get rid of the uncontrolled variables.

Think of a benchmarking experiment as a sequence of actions, starting with building the benchmark and system under test (e.g. a virtual machine or a compiler — we call this *compilation*) and ending with providing a single execution time measurement. If this sequence included neither random nor uncontrolled variables turned to random, the design would be trivial — just run once and take the result. But in reality a number of random variables in the sequence will influence the measurement. Some take effect before the measured operation starts and influence it indirectly, others act during it.

This necessitates repeating the sequence a number of times, at least from the point where the first random variable takes effect. Suppose compilation was not random (it was deterministic and performance did not depend on code layout): in this case we would not have to repeat it. In contrast if, say, the start-up of a VM execution includes some random variation, then we must repeat VM *executions* but can do this with the same binary. We refer to points of potential repetition as *levels* of the experiment (not to be confused with a 'factor level' in ANOVA). The *highest* level is the first source of variation in the experiment sequence, e.g. compilation. The *lowest* level is the operation measured (e.g. an *iteration* of a benchmark).

Through repetition we get a number of measurements and typically we calculate a confidence interval. The more repetitions made, the narrower ('more precise') is the interval. At the very least, repetition must be done at the highest level that has random variation to avoid bias, but sometimes repeating at lower levels can reduce experimentation time without sacrificing precision.

In the rest of this paper, we consider how to design experiments that will deliver reliable results at the least cost in experimentation time. We explore how many repetitions are needed, at which levels, and for what price in terms of experimentation time. Although our approach is general, as an example we consider benchmarking with two suites, DaCapo and SPEC CPU, and three levels (repeating iteration, execution and compilation).

4. The Challenge of Summarising Results

As we observed above, it is still uncommon in our discipline to report results with any degree of statistical rigour despite the efforts of Georges, Mytkowicz and others [9, 10, 20]. Often the plausible argument is made that, if performance improvements are large (e.g. $2\times$ or more), there is no need for statistical machinery to prove that they are real. However, improvements reported in the programming languages field are often small enough (e.g. about 10% [20]) to necessitate some statistical demonstration that they do not come about by chance. Moreover, even a large speedup should come with error bounds estimate to allow rigorous quantification and comparison of different studies. Where researchers have used statistical techniques, these have often been significance tests.

Significance testing. Quantification of performance change with statistical significance [13, 16] tests whether it is likely that two systems have different performance. The decision is based on the probability that the observed difference (or a larger one) in the (sample) means of the two systems would occur if the (true) means were the same. This probability, the p-value, is compared against a pre-defined threshold, the significance level (i.e. 5%). If the p-value is smaller then the null hypothesis, that the two systems have the same performance, is rejected.

Problems with statistical significance testing have long been known. The method is deprecated in other disciplines [5, 6, 21, 25], and some journals explicitly require alternative methods [12]. First, significance testing does not provide the metric we are ultimately interested in, a reliable estimate of e.g. the ratio of the execution times of two systems. The test is also vulnerable to the number of measurements used. The larger the sample size is (the more measurements we have), the more unlikely even a very small difference becomes. In practice this means that a large sample size (and in our field it is easy to generate very large samples) will nearly always

lead to the decision that there is a 'statistically significant' difference in performance, even if the true difference is so small that it is of little interest; statistical significance methods confuse sample size and practical relevance [6]. Statistical significance tests are also notoriously hard to interpret. This may be because they do not give us the answer to what we want to know but instead offer temptations, such as the belief that the p-value is actually the probability that the systems have the same performance. The interpretation of the results of statistical tests is sufficiently tricky that even some statistics textbooks have got it wrong (examples are given by Cohen [6]).

Visual tests. An alternative is to construct confidence intervals for the two systems under test and to examine whether they overlap. If they do not, then one can conclude that it is likely that the systems differ in performance [9, 16]. Jain [13] adds another step, falling back to a statistical test if the intervals overlap only slightly, i.e. if the centre of neither interval lies within the other. An advantage of the visual test is that it gives a clear measure of the size of the difference in mean performance, while the intervals also show the uncertainty of the systems in isolation. However, although this is a useful aid for an analyst, a visual test still does not tell us what we want to know (an estimate for the ratio of the performances of the two systems and its error bound) and, in contrast to a statistical test, lacks any rigorous semantics as its error is not known. It is actually rather conservative. For example, with 95% confidence intervals, the probability of error is not 5%, but less than 1% under the normality assumption [23].

Normality. Researchers in our field commonly assume that the Central Limit Theorem justifies their use of parametric methods such as a t-test or analysis of variance on data that is not normally distributed. Informally, the theorem states that the average of a sufficiently large number of independent and identically distributed (i.i.d.) random variables tends to follow a Normal distribution. Although the theorem does not fully justify this assumption, parametric methods have been found to be robust under various sets of conditions [2, 24]. Our summarising method is based on analysis of variance, and we provide a full derivation and discuss its assumptions in our technical report [14]; we also demonstrate an alternative non-parametric method.

Effect size. Better methods are available. In section 9.3, we show how to construct an *effect size* confidence interval. Summaries can be as simple as "we are 95% confident that system A is faster than system B by 5.5% $\pm$ 2.5%". Such a statement is more natural than those derived from significance testing and less open to misinterpretation: it quantifies the size of the change, gives its error bound and indicates how certain this result is.

> RECOMMENDATION: Analysis of results should be statistically rigorous and in particular should quantify any variation. Report performance changes with effect size confidence intervals.

In summary, sound experimental methodology is an increasing concern for the computer science research community. On one hand, it is clear that our field lags behind the standards expected by other sciences for reporting experimental evaluations. This has led to the foundation of *Evaluate Collaboratory* (http://evaluate.inf.usi.ch/) to promote better experimental practice. On the other hand, researchers are unclear as to how to make best use of their time to run and report experiments without sacrificing rigour. This paper is a contribution towards resolving that dilemma.

5. Benchmarks and Platforms

Benchmarks For JVM experiments we use DaCapo 2006 and 2009 benchmarks (2006-10-MR2 and 9.12-bach) running on Open-JDK 7 (version 7u2, build 13, November 17, 2011) compiled with

Table 1. Platforms Used in the Case Study.

	Linux		CPU	GHz	LLC	Mem.
P1	3.0.0	64bit	4x16(x1) AMD Opteron	2.1	12M L3	64G
P2	2.6.38	64bit	2x4(x2) Intel Xeon	2.27	8M L3	12G
P3	3.0.0	64bit	1x4(x2) Intel Core i7	3.4	8M L3	16G
P4	2.6.35	64bit	1x2(x1) Intel Core 2	2.4	4M L2	4G
P5	2.6.35	32bit	1x1(x2) Intel Pentium 4	3.2	1M L2	4G

gcc version 4.7. These benchmarks are widely used in garbage collection and VM research. We report only those benchmarks that run without crashing on the VM. We run the 'large' and 'small' sizes of each workload, using the default production settings of the VM and letting the benchmark harness scale the workloads to all available processors.

For gcc experiments we use CINT (integer benchmarks) from the SPEC CPU2006 benchmark suite, version 1.2. SPEC CPU benchmarks are widely used for C/Fortran compiler and CPU performance measurements. We build the benchmarks with gcc 4.7 using the O3 optimisations, and run the 'train' (smallest) and the 'reference' (standard) sizes.

Platforms We use 5 different platforms, each running a version of Ubuntu Linux. In Table 1, '2x4(x2)' denotes a system with 2 physical processors, each with 4 cores and 2-way hyper-threading. Platforms P1 and P2 have non-uniform memory access. We disable all system services that might interfere with measurements.

6. Repeating Iterations

Researchers are typically interested in steady state performance, so we restrict our study to this case. Performance in the steady state should be 'somewhat' stable, without clear trends, and particularly without any obvious overhead of VM or application initialisation. We cannot take *live* measurements before this state is reached.

We identify an initialised state and an independent state of benchmark execution. We call a state *independent* if the execution times of the benchmark iterations are (statistically) independent and identically distributed. A state is *initialised* — the lower bar — when iterations are no longer subject to obvious and significant initialisation overhead. Such overhead may be due to dynamic linking, filling I/O buffers for data/code, or just-in-time compilation. Independence means that the duration of an iteration is not affected by earlier iterations in the same execution. By definition, 'independent' implies 'initialised'. We believe that most researchers would regard an independent state as 'steady', and so i.i.d. is a well-defined sufficient condition for the steady state. We also believe that 'initialised' would be widely accepted as a necessary condition for a steady state.

Random factors, such as context switches, scheduling order or Java heap layout, can affect performance, so repetition at the iteration level or higher is needed. Repeating iterations is experimentally cheaper since there is no need to wait for a new execution (or higher level operation) to reach a steady state.

Note that it does not makes sense to repeat measurements unless the system has reached an independent state. If measurements are not i.i.d., the variance and confidence interval estimates will be biased. The first question to ask is, therefore, *does a benchmark reach an independent state and, if so, after how many iterations?*

Aside: some researchers might repeat statistically dependent iterations and then include, say, their average in further summary [9]. This approach is not incorrect if the results are correctly interpreted, but the risk of misinterpretation is high. It redefines what is measured. For example, rather than asking "how long does it take to run 1 iteration", it asks "how long does it take to run 10 iterations" (divided by 10). Any variance then relates to the '10 iterations' rather than the 'one iteration'. This approach always requires repetition at

a higher level to avoid bias and to form the confidence interval. We would not encourage this practice.

6.1 Independent State

Our first study is to investigate whether DaCapo benchmarks reach independent state. We run three executions of each benchmark with 300 iterations per execution (note that we do not expect researchers to run this many iterations). DaCapo and other Java benchmark suites (such as the SPEC JVM ones) allow iterations to be repeated within a single VM execution. On the other hand, SPEC CPU benchmarks provide only one measurement per execution of a benchmark binary: we address this later.

In the first step, we inspect run-sequence plots (of iteration duration against iteration number), looking for an iteration after which the data seem stable, that is with no regularities or patterns. We always take the maximum of the three executions, but in most benchmarks the executions agree very closely. We discard the unstable prefix. In the second step we check whether the remaining data are statistically independent. If they are, we have found the point at which the benchmark iterations become independent. Otherwise, we conclude that the benchmark does not reach an independent state in reasonable time (running 300 iterations of many of the large-size DaCapo benchmarks takes far more time than is feasible for a particular experiment).

To reduce time, we support this manual process with an interactive R script. In the first step, the user clicks on a run-sequence plot to indicate the point at which the data seem stable (this takes a few seconds per benchmark execution). In the second step, the script displays three plots for each benchmark execution: an autocorrelation function (ACF) plot, a lag plot, and a run-sequence plot with the consecutive measurements connected (details below). Each of these plots can reveal dependencies, and each is offered in two versions — one for the measured data and one for that data randomly reordered. The two versions make the interpretation easier: the experimenter simply looks for a systematic, significant difference between the real and the randomised plots. With some practice this takes less than a minute per benchmark (for all 3 executions).

Lag plots and ACF plots (also called correlograms) are commonly used to detect whether a time-series data set is random or not. Given a series Y, a *lag plot* for a given lag h plots the points (Y_t, Y_{t-h}). Interpretation is easy: any pattern detected in a lag plot indicates some dependency. We check lag plots for lags 1–4, using both iteration order and randomly reordered data (all plotted on one screen by our script). For example, the lag plots in Figure 1(a) show strong auto-dependency in iterations of lusearch9.[1]

An *auto-correlation plot* shows, for each lag h, the correlation of the series Y_t with its lagged version Y_{t-h}: $cor(Y_t, Y_{t-h}) = E[(Y_t - \mu_Y)(Y_{t-h} - \mu_Y)]/\sigma_Y^2$, where μ and σ^2 are the mean and variance of Y. By definition, the value is always between -1 and 1. It is 1 for lag $h = 0$, but for larger values of h, independent data should have correlations mostly small in absolute value and in the range shown between the horizontal dotted lines (which bound the values expected from random noise) in Figure 1(b). Any systematic structure in the correlations, even if small, is an additional indication of a dependency. Figure 1(b) shows the ACF for the same lusearch9 data as the lag plot.

We applied this method to 'small' and 'large' DaCapo benchmarks on platforms P1 and P2. Table 2 shows which combinations reached an independent state. We found that the (in)dependence patterns agreed in most cases for different benchmark executions. However, results for 'small' sizes disagreed significantly with those for 'large' sizes: clearly one cannot use the 'small' sizes as a shortcut to identify the number of iterations required by 'large' bench-

---

[1] Lusearch9 stands for lusearch from DaCapo 2009.

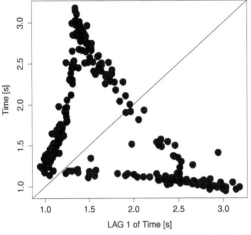 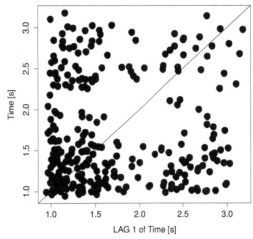

(a) Lag plots show how one measurement (x-coordinate) depends on its preceding measurement (y-coordinate). Any pattern in the plot suggests a strong dependency (left figure); a more random scatter indicates no dependency (right figure).

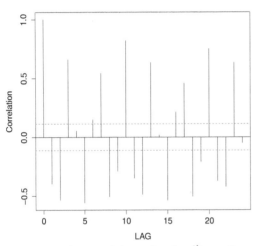 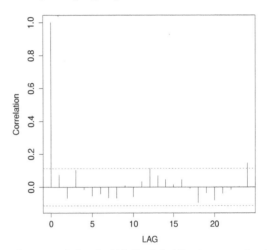

(b) ACF plots show correlation against the xth preceding measurements. Large correlations (outside the dashed lines) or any pattern in the correlations marks a dependency (left figure). In contrast, the right-hand figure shows no dependency.

Figure 1. Iteration durations for lusearch9 (left) and randomly re-ordered (right), large size, Jikes RVM running on P2.

marks to achieve independence. The patterns also disagree between platforms.

Over half the DaCapo/OpenJDK benchmarks reach an independent state. Column 2 of Table 3 shows the number of iterations required for this *independent warmup*. These figures are JVM dependent: Jikes RVM gave different results.

> **RECOMMENDATION: Use this manual procedure just once to find how many iterations each benchmark, VM and platform combination requires to reach an independent state.**

In our previous research, manual inspection of detailed performance data also helped to reveal bugs that did not lead to crashes, thus saving not only experimentation but also debugging time.

6.2 Initialised State

Many benchmarks do not reach an independent state in reasonable time (Table 2). So how should we run these benchmarks? Most have strong auto-dependencies: a gradual drift in times, trends (gradual increase and decrease), state changes (abrupt change in results after some number of iterations), systematic transitions between

durations (e.g. odd-numbered iterations show one time and even-numbered ones another), and so on. By choosing which iterations to take, we influence the result significantly (by *tens* of percent). This is problematic for on-line algorithms that often choose different iterations in different runs, platforms or VMs — they use an expensive methodology to distinguish performance differences of only a few percent, but the algorithm incorporates noise many times larger.

> **RECOMMENDATION: If a benchmark does not reach an independent state in a reasonable time, take the same iteration from each run.**

The trends tend to be consistent across runs, and so we would take the first iteration for which each benchmark is initialised, i.e. the largest initialised warmup over all VMs and platforms in our experimental setting. Column 1 of Table 3 shows the initialised warmups of all the 'large' benchmarks on our platforms, established manually through inspection of the first 50 iterations of each execution (from their run-sequence plots). This took only a few seconds per benchmark execution.

Table 2. Independent State in DaCapo/OpenJDK.

	Small		Large	
	P2	P1	P2	P1
avrora9	x	x	x	x
bloat6	-	-	x	x
chart6	-	-	-	x
eclipse6	x	x	x	x
eclipse9	x	x	x	x
fop6	x	-	x	-
fop9	-	-	-	-
h29	x	x	x	x
hsqldb6	-	-	x	-
jython6	x	x	-	-
jython9	-	x	-	-
luindex6	x	x	-	-
luindex9	-	x	x	x
lusearch6				
lusearch9	x	x	x	x
pmd6	-	-	-	x
pmd9	-	-	-	x
sunflow9	-	x	x	-
tomcat9	x	-	-	x
tradebeans9	x	x	-	x
tradesoap9	x	x	-	x
xalan6	-	-	x	x
xalan9	-	-	x	x

x reached independent state
- did not reach independent state

Table 3. Number of Iterations to Warmup DaCapo/OpenJDK.

	Platform P1				Platform P2			
	Initial.	Indep.	Harness	Georges	Initial.	Indep.	Harness	Georges
avrora9	2	128	4	1	3	8	3	6
bloat6	2	3	9	∞	2	4	8	∞
chart6	10	88	10	7	3		4	1
eclipse6	3	14	5	11	5	7	7	4
eclipse9	3	9	4	1	2	14	4	1
fop6	6		6	4	10	180	7	8
fop9	6		10	20	6		9	16
h29	0	19	3	0	3	0	4	0
hsqldb6	3		4	1	6	6	8	15
jython6	3		5	2	3		5	2
jython9	3		4	1	3		4	1
luindex6	6		4	48	13		4	8
luindex9	11	19	7	8	10	85	7	8
lusearch9	3	5	5	247	2	37	5	33
pmd6	3	134	4	1	7		4	1
pmd9	3	48	5	2	5		5	3
sunflow9	3		10	∞	0	0	20	∞
tomcat9	5	39	8	8	9		6	8
tradebeans9	2	5	4	5	2		4	1
tradesoap9	3	5	5	1	2		4	1
xalan6	2	2	29	∞	6	13	15	139
xalan9	3	9	8	42	3	31	5	2

6.3 Experimentation Time Savings

Table 3 shows number of iterations for warmup determined by the DaCapo'09 harness and by Georges' method [9]. We show maximums over three runs. We observe that the heuristics do not do very well. There are cases when they give a warmup longer than the independent warmup (e.g. lusearch9 on P1), which would waste experimentation time. In other cases they give a warmup shorter than the initialised warmup (e.g. luindex6 on P2), making any results prone to initialisation noise and hence unusable. This is not to pick particularly on these two heuristics. Automated on-line heuristics attempt to take a decision after a few iterations, as they are designed for real runs. This renders them less reliable than our once per benchmark/JVM/platform manual method where we look at 300 iterations. The heuristics sometimes detect independence too late, but will always waste time on benchmarks that never reach independence.

The second question to ask is, therefore, *how many iterations should be run with benchmarks that do reach an independent state?* We can run a benchmark to independence and then collect a number of iterations, or we can repeatedly run it only to its initialised state and collect one iteration. The former method can save experimentation time if there is higher variation between iterations rather than between executions, the initialised warmup plus the VM initialisation before the first iteration is large, and the independent warmup is small. We examine the tradeoffs between the levels to repeat below.

7. Repeating Executions

The lowest level at which we can repeat a SPEC CPU benchmark is executing a binary; thus the issues are similar to those faced when repeating DaCapo iterations. For DaCapo, the interest is whether there are any random factors that impact results at the execution level. Hence, we discuss repeating executions for these two suites separately.

7.1 Variation in Execution (DaCapo)

We focus on DaCapo benchmarks that reach an independent state by their 11th iteration or sooner. If a benchmark does not reach independence by this time, we simply run it to its initialised state, and take only one live iteration. Our approach is however independent of such a threshold.

To find out if there is random variation exclusively at the execution level, we ran 30 executions of each benchmark, each with 40 iterations, on OpenJDK/P1. We compare the execution variation with the iteration variation (Table 4). By *iteration variation* we mean the variation of iterations within a single execution. By *execution variation* we mean the variation between means of executions. A non-trivial execution variation that is much larger than the iteration variation shows that there are random factors that impact results at the execution level that we need to handle. The variations in Table 4 are normalised by the mean. We define these measures mathematically in Section 9.4 and give more sophisticated estimates in Section 9.2.

Table 4 shows that lusearch9 has very high execution variation (30%) and much higher than the iteration variation (3%). Xalan6 and bloat6 also have high variation at execution level, as does xalan9 to some extent. The execution variations of the remaining three benchmarks are below 0.5%, so we conclude that they do not have significant random variation at the execution level.

7.2 Initialisation, Independence (SPEC CPU)

SPEC CPU benchmarks can run only one iteration per execution. Under SPEC rules each binary should be executed 3 times (5 executions were used in [20]). The benchmarks are quite long

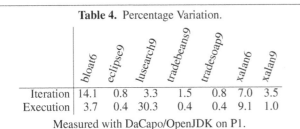

Table 4. Percentage Variation.

	bloat6	eclipse9	lusearch9	tradebeans9	tradesoap9	xalan6	xalan9
Iteration	14.1	0.8	3.3	1.5	0.8	7.0	3.5
Execution	3.7	0.4	30.3	0.4	0.4	9.1	1.0

Measured with DaCapo/OpenJDK on P1.

running, so we first check if repetition is really needed, i.e. if there is any initialisation noise (necessitating warmup) and if the measurements are i.i.d.. For this we ran 30 executions of each 'large' CINT benchmark binary on platforms P3 and P4. On P3, all the measurements from each benchmark were i.i.d. so warmup was unnecessary, allowing us to execute each binary only once. On P4, 10 out of 12 CINT benchmarks had the same nice property.

The exceptions were mcf and gobmk, both of which still can be immediately considered in an initialised state, but then are auto-dependent through at least the first 20 executions (mcf increasing, gobmk decreasing execution times). It would be infeasible with these two benchmarks to reach an independent state as the 20 iterations already take nearly 4 hours (even if they became independent later, which we did not check). As in the case of the DaCapo benchmarks that do not reach independent state in reasonable time, we would just take the first execution in the initialised state, that is the first execution.

Thus, in summary, on our two platforms, it is reasonable to use only one execution of each benchmark binary rather than the default of 3 (2 as warmup), thereby saving about 7 hours of experiment time.

It may be regarded as questionable whether reaching a steady state is even desirable with the SPEC benchmarks. Although the SPEC rules require repetition, the start-up performance of these benchmarks may be closer to their real usage. Our numbers suggest that this discussion is a distraction: based on results on our platforms, only one execution is necessary.

8. Repeating Compilation

If any random variation is due to compilation of our VM, compiler or benchmark, we must repeat the compilation and evaluate multiple binaries. The same applies if performance depends on code layout, in which case we should randomise the layout to avoid bias.

To investigate the performance implications of code layout we patched the `gcc` compiler to randomise the order of functions within each module (source file) compiled, the order of modules compiled/linked and the order of functions globally during link-time optimisations (LTO), a recent feature of `gcc`. We use LTO with the SPEC CPU benchmarks thus randomising their layout fully. OpenJDK does not yet build with LTO, but its modules are linked in large batches, so the layout is substantially randomised by our patch as well. This randomises the VM itself but not the application code's layout, and thus there is no direct runtime overhead.

8.1 DaCapo

To check whether DaCapo/OpenJDK benchmarks are sensitive to code layout, we compared relative variation in 30 executions, each with a different binary, against variation in 30 executions of the same binary on platform P1. We always took the 10th iteration from each execution. Of 24 DaCapo benchmarks, 8 had a variation over binaries larger than that over executions, but the difference was never more than a single percentage point, except for antlr6 where the variation was 9% over binaries and 3% over executions. We also

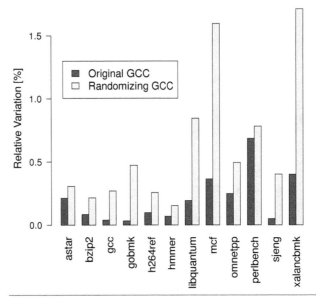

Figure 2. Relative variation with randomising and original `gcc` (reference size).

carried out a similar experiment with Jikes RVM, randomising the layout of the VM classes, but the variation over binaries was only up to one percentage point larger than that over executions.

In summary, while code layout performance impact has been reported for other systems [11, 15, 20], we found little evidence of this problem with DaCapo on our platforms despite looking hard.

8.2 SPEC CPU

We repeated Mytkowicz et al's experiment with link order [20] on platforms P3, P4 and P5 to see if our systems' performances are sensitive to link order. We ran all the 'training' CINT benchmarks, with 30 binaries differing in link order, each binary 5 times, and taking the 5th execution from each. We calculated the relative variation for each benchmark. As a baseline, we repeated exactly the same experiment without link order randomisation. We confirmed the earlier result that nearly all the benchmarks had a higher variation with the link order randomisation than without, and some by a large margin (e.g. xalancbmk 4% vs. 1% and libquantum 1.9% vs. 0.3% on P3). Furthermore, we found that some benchmarks had statistically significantly worse performance with randomised link order (xalancbmk by 4% and libquantum by 2.6%). An experimenter would clearly have to decide if the goal of their study is performance, independent of code layout (as we believe is commonly the case), or the performance of a given layout. Note that the `gcc` compiler would not normally change the code layout (these experiments were performed without LTO).

However, real benchmarking must use reference size benchmarks. Does code layout impact them in the same way? The experiments above cannot be run with reference sizes, because the benchmarks run for too long. However, we showed in Section 7.2 that it suffices to run each binary just once with the reference size. So we ran every benchmark 30 times on platform P3, each time for a different binary. We repeated this once for randomised builds and once for non-randomised (the default) in order to compare the variations again. As we used LTO for our randomised binaries, we also used it with the baseline binary. With each benchmark the variation was higher with the randomised layout (Figure 2), although the variation was quite small overall (1.7% with xalancbmk, 1.6% with mcf and below 1% with all the other benchmarks). Only with xalancbmk and mcf was the performance with randomisation consistently worse – by 3.3% with xalancbmk and by 6.8% with mcf (both statistically significant).

Nevertheless, repeating with different code layouts is still useful to avoid bias if the goal is to evaluate layout-independent performance. It can be done quite cheaply as there is no need for per-execution warmup. The only added cost is re-compiling a benchmark before execution, which is comparably cheap as these benchmarks are long running. However, the experimenter needs to be aware that layout randomisation can impact performance *consistently*, and not just introduce noise. To find out the case on a given platform, one would have to run initial experiments.

9. Multi-level Repetition

With many experiments (such as those DaCapo benchmarks that reach an independent state), we want to repeat executions and take multiple measurements from each. Adding repetition at the highest level will always increase the precision of the result (narrow the confidence interval). But, in some cases, increasing repetition at a lower level may do so more cheaply. The trade-off is between the degree of variation caused at each level and the cost of repetition. Repetition at the iteration level is cheap (once a benchmark has reached independence, the added cost is just the measured time of that new iteration). Repetition at the execution level is more expensive because, as we add a new execution, we have to wait for it to reach independence — the cost depends on the length of the independent warmup and also on application initialisation before the first iteration (non-trivial in e.g. tradebeans9 and tradesoap9). The cost of repetition at the compilation level is the time to compile, which again can be non-trivial (e.g. OpenJDK takes about 20 minutes to compile on our platforms).

These trade-offs can be formulated mathematically in order to determine the optimum number of repetitions that should be performed at each level to get the most precise result for a given experimentation time. The inputs for this optimisation are the costs (independent warmup, time to compile, etc.) and measurements from an *initial experiment*. From these measurements, one can estimate the variances at the different levels. The outputs are the optimum repetition counts (at all but the highest level) to use for *real experiments* later. As long as the variances in the real experiments are similar to those in the initial experiments, the repetition counts remain optimal. The interval estimation, however, uses only estimates/data from the real experiments, so that the results are sound even if the variances change.

Such a method has been derived for three-level experiments [15]. Here we generalise that method to an arbitrary number of levels and make a technical improvement to the variance estimators. Kalibera and Tuma [15] used statistically biased variance estimators when calculating the repetition counts, and hence the counts established were not optimal (the expected value of a biased estimator of the sample variance is not equal to the true variance of the underlying distribution). Their variance estimator of the sample mean was also biased, making the confidence interval too wide. Too wide an interval would lead to wasting experimental time and increase the chance of failing to detect a true difference in systems. Full proofs and derivations are available in our technical report [14] and more background can be found in McCulloch et al [19] or Searle et al [26]. In Section 9.4 we show how to apply our general method to find optimum repetition counts for DaCapo.

9.1 Initial experiment

Let us consider repetition at levels 1 (the lowest) to n (the highest). First, run an initial experiment. We denote parameters of the initial experiment in sans serif font (e.g. 'r_1') and those for the real experiment in serif font (e.g. 'r_1'). Choose the repetition counts (exclusive of any warm-up iterations needed), $r_1, \ldots, r_n$, at each of these levels to be some arbitrary yet sufficient value; 20 may be a good choice but use 30 if possible. If there are many levels for the initial experiment, reduce experimental time by using fewer repetitions (say, 10) at lower levels if you must. It makes sense only to include a level at the top of the hierarchy (n) where you know some repetition is needed. For example, we ruled out the impact of VM code layout on DaCapo benchmarks earlier (on our platform), so we would not include compilation.

Including other levels ($n - 1$ and below) is purely for optimisation of the experimental time, as repetition there is never needed for correctness. If including all levels where repetition is possible would be infeasible, design several initial experiments with different inner levels omitted (though always including the highest level), e.g. just compilation and iterations, but not executions. If the optimal repetition count at any level in these partial experiments ends up being 1, it is best not to repeat at that level in the real experiment.

In the initial experiment, gather the costs of repetition at each level, $c_1, \ldots, c_{n-1}$, i.e. the time added exclusively by that level. The dimensioning process assumes that these costs do not change much between experiments, which follows our experience. With a 3-level experiment (iterations, executions and compilations), we have:

c_1 time to get an iteration (iteration duration)
c_2 time to get an execution (time to independent state)
c_3 time to get a binary (build time)

In this initial experiment, also take the measurement times, which we denote $Y_{j_n \ldots j_1}$, where $j_1 = 1 \ldots r_1$ to $j_n = 1 \ldots r_n$. These are indexed by the experiment levels (highest to lowest), e.g. $Y_{2,1,3}$ would be the third non-warmup iteration time from the first execution of the second binary in that 3-level experiment.

Calculate arithmetic means of these measurements for different levels. For instance, the mean across experiments at all but the highest level (for which the j_n^{th} repetition is used) is denoted $\overline{Y}_{j_n \underbrace{\bullet \cdots \bullet}_{n-1}}$, i.e. indexes that vary are denoted by bullets.

9.2 Variance Estimators

After running the initial experiments, we calculate n unbiased variance estimators, $T_1^2, \ldots, T_n^2$ from the costs c_i and the measurements $Y_{j_n \ldots j_1}$. These estimators describe how much each level contributes independently to variability in the result. First, calculate S_i^2, the *biased* estimator of the variance at each level i, $1 \leq i \leq n$:

$$S_i^2 = \frac{1}{\prod_{k=i+1}^{n} r_k} \frac{1}{r_i - 1} \qquad (1)$$

$$\sum_{j_n=1}^{r_n} \cdots \sum_{j_i=1}^{r_i} \left(\overline{Y}_{j_n \ldots j_i \underbrace{\bullet \cdots \bullet}_{i-1}} - \overline{Y}_{j_n \ldots j_{i+1} \underbrace{\bullet \cdots \bullet}_{i}} \right)^2$$

Then obtain each T_i^2 through an iterative process:

$$T_1^2 = S_1^2,$$
$$\forall i \, . \, 1 < i \leq n, T_i^2 = S_i^2 - \frac{T_{i-1}^2}{r_{i-1}}. \qquad (2)$$

If $T_i^2 \leq 0$ (or at least very small — note T_i^2 denotes an estimator, *not* some value squared), then this level of the experiment induces little variation so repetitions at this level can be removed from the real experiment. This is semantically equivalent to running the initial experiment again with fewer levels.

9.3 Real Experiment: Confidence Interval

Once we have these variance estimators and costs, the optimum numbers of repetitions at levels 1 to $n-1$ for the *real* benchmarking experiments on the same platform are $r_1, \ldots, r_{n-1}$:

$$\forall i . 1 \le i < n, \; r_i = \left\lceil \sqrt{\frac{\mathsf{c}_{i+1}}{\mathsf{c}_i} \frac{\mathsf{T}_i^2}{\mathsf{T}_{i+1}^2}} \right\rceil. \qquad (3)$$

In the real experiment, we use these optimal repetition counts, $r_i, \ldots, r_n$. Note that this formula does not give the optimum repetition count for the highest level. This is because the optima found $(r_1, \ldots, r_{n-1})$ are independent of the number of repetitions chosen at that level. More repetitions can always be added at that level during the real experiment to improve the results' precision and the counts already found will remain optimal.

Recalculate the variance estimator S_n^2 in the same way as before but using the optimal repetition counts and the measurements from the real experiment. Note that although S_n^2 is a biased estimator of the variance at the highest level, it is the right estimator to use in the confidence interval formula (4): technical details can be found in our technical report [14]. Then calculate as before the arithmetic means, $\overline{Y}_{j_n \underbrace{\bullet \cdots \bullet}_{n-1}}$ and $\overline{Y}_{\underbrace{\bullet \cdots \bullet}_{n}}$ (denoted $\overline{Y}$ hereafter).

The asymptotic confidence interval with confidence $(1 - \alpha)$ is:

$$\overline{Y} \;\pm\; t_{1-\frac{\alpha}{2},\nu} \sqrt{\frac{S_n^2}{r_n}} = \qquad (4)$$

$$\overline{Y} \;\pm\; t_{1-\frac{\alpha}{2},\nu} \sqrt{\frac{1}{r_n(r_n-1)} \sum_{j_n=1}^{r_n} \left(\overline{Y}_{j_n \underbrace{\bullet \cdots \bullet}_{n-1}} - \overline{Y} \right)^2}$$

where $t_{1-\frac{\alpha}{2},\nu}$ is the $(1 - \frac{\alpha}{2})$-quantile of the t-distribution with $\nu = r_n - 1$ degrees of freedom.

Observe that, for a single-level experiment, the interval is the standard asymptotic interval based on Student's t distribution (used in most statistical literature and elsewhere [9, 13, 16]). Note also that the multi-level interval is the same as if we had used a single-level interval for the means of all data from all but the highest level (e.g. binary means).

> **RECOMMENDATION: For each benchmark/VM/platform, conduct a dimensioning experiment to establish the optimal repetition counts (equation 3) for each but the top level of the real experiment. Re-dimension only if the benchmark/VM/platform changes.**

9.4 DaCapo Executions vs. Iterations

We applied our optimisation method to suitable DaCapo benchmarks, i.e. those with random variation at the execution level and which reach independence in a reasonable time. In Section 7.1 we identified these as bloat6, lusearch9, xalan6 and xalan9 (on P1). In Section 8.1 we found no random variation at the compilation level with these benchmarks, so we are optimising a 2-level experiment, looking for the optimum number of iterations per execution.

Cost c_1 is the iteration duration: we use the average of all live measurements. Cost c_2 is the time to the first live measurement, which includes VM startup, application startup, and iterations for independent warmup. We take the average from all executions (we instrumented DaCapo to print the current time when an iteration starts, relative to VM start). We show the results in Table 5. We normalise the variance estimates T_1^2 and T_2^2 by the mean iteration duration giving variations $\mathsf{t}_i = \sqrt{\mathsf{T}_i^2}/\overline{\mathsf{Y}}$. They are very similar to the biased estimators $\sqrt{S_i^2}/\overline{\mathsf{Y}}$ in Table 4, so the less sophisticated method we used for that table worked quite well. Count r_1 is the optimum number of live iteration measurements to take from

Table 5. Optimum Iteration Count with DaCapo.

	$\mathsf{c}_1[s]$	$\mathsf{c}_2[s]$	$\mathsf{t}_1[\%]$	$\mathsf{t}_2[\%]$	r_1
bloat6	35.5	110.0	14.0	2.7	**10**
lusearch9	1.7	12.3	3.4	30.3	**1**
xalan6	10.8	24.6	7.2	8.9	**2**
xalan9	6.7	71.8	3.5	0.8	**15**

each of the benchmarks. Note that lusearch9 has an optimum of only 1 measurement: it has a very high execution variation so experimenter time is much better spent repeating whole executions rather than iterations.

10. Measuring Speedup

Typically, we want to compare two systems, e.g. one with a new optimisation against a base system without, and usually in terms of the ratio of their execution times. Of the 90 papers from our survey that evaluated execution time, 65 reported execution time ratios. Unfortunately, confidence intervals for the execution time ratio are rarely shown in our field (only 3 papers from our survey attempted that). Here we show one way to calculate such intervals and derive how to choose repetition counts.

The interval we show is by Fieller [8] and has been known since the 1950s, though it has not to our knowledge been used before for computer performance evaluation. The calculation of another confidence interval for the ratio has been proposed for computer simulations [17]. That interval is based on the delta method, but their case was sampling from a finite population rather than infinite which we need here. Also, their interval depends on the normal distribution of the ratios (more details in Cochran [4]). The Fieller interval which we show here does not make this assumption. Our technical report [14] includes more details.

10.1 Confidence Interval

A confidence interval for the ratio can be constructed as follows. Let $\overline{Y}$ be the average of all live measurements from the old system and $\overline{Y'}$ that from the new system. We estimate the ratio as $\overline{Y'}/\overline{Y}$. We can calculate an asymptotic $(1 - \alpha)$ confidence interval as:

$$\frac{\overline{Y} \cdot \overline{Y'} \mp \sqrt{\left(\overline{Y} \cdot \overline{Y'} \right)^2 - \left(\overline{Y}^2 - h^2 \right)\left(\overline{Y'}^2 - h'^2 \right)}}{\overline{Y}^2 - h^2} \qquad (5)$$

where

$$h = t_{\frac{\alpha}{2},\nu} \sqrt{\frac{S_n^2}{r_n}} \qquad\qquad h' = t_{\frac{\alpha}{2},\nu} \sqrt{\frac{S_n'^2}{r_n}}$$

The variance estimators for the old and new system, S_n^2 and $S_n'^2$ are derived as in Sections 9.2 and 9.3. h and h' are the half-widths of the confidence intervals for the single systems (Section 9.3).

10.2 Repetition Counts

We have shown how to establish repetition counts for single systems in isolation. With a little algebra, it can be shown how the relative half-widths of the single-system intervals relate to the half-width of the interval for the ratio. Let e, e' be the relative half-widths of the systems in isolation:

$$e = h/\overline{Y} \qquad e' = h'/\overline{Y'}$$

The half-width of the interval for the ratio, $\mathbf{e}$, is

$$\mathbf{e} = \frac{\overline{Y'}}{\overline{Y}} \cdot \frac{1}{1 - e^2} \cdot \sqrt{e^2 + e'^2 - e^2 e'^2}$$

We are normally interested only in narrow intervals for the single systems, say with a half-width below 10%. Hence, we can approx-

Table 6. Suggested Repetitions with DaCapo.

	Warmup	Iterations	Executions for precision			
			1%	1.5%	2.5%	5%
avrora9	2	1	14	18	5	
bloat6	3	10	99	46	18	7
chart6	10	1	8	5		
eclipse6	3	1	33	16	8	
eclipse9	3	1	6			
fop6	6	1	10	6		
fop9	6	1	12	7		
h29	0	1	13	7	5	
hsqldb6	3	1	12	7		
jython6	3	1	15	8	5	
jython9	3	1	10	6		
luindex6	6	1	8	5		
luindex9	11	1	9	6		
lusearch9	3	1	∞	∞	548	139
pmd6	3	1	52	25	11	5
pmd9	3	1	5			
sunflow9	3	1	70	33	14	6
tomcat9	5	1	14	8	5	
tradebeans9	2	1	24	12	6	
tradesoap9	3	1	5			
xalan6	2	2	311	140	52	15
xalan9	9	15	10	6		

Table 7. Suggested Repetitions SPEC CPU.

	Executions = Builds for precision			
	0.5%	1%	1.5%	2%
astar	4 (5)			
bzip2	4 (5)			
gcc	4 (5)			
gobmk	6			
h264ref	4 (5)			
hmmer	3 (5)			
libquantum	14	6		
mcf	42	13	7	5
omnetpp	7			
perlbench	12	5		
sjeng	6			
xalancbmk	48	14	8	6

imate the second term: $(1 - e^2) \approx 1$. Similarly, $e^2 e'^2 \approx 0$. Hence,

$$\mathbf{e} \approx \frac{\overline{Y'}}{\overline{Y}} \sqrt{e^2 + e'^2} \qquad (6)$$

Note that, if we were comparing one system with itself, the relative width of the ratio interval would be $\sqrt{2}$ times wider than the interval for the system itself. If two systems have similar performance and their intervals are no wider than ϵ relative to the mean, then the ratio interval would be no wider than $\epsilon\sqrt{2}$. The better (faster) the new system is, the narrower will be the confidence interval for the ratio.

Finally, and fortunately, this result says that optimising the number of repetitions for a single system, as described in previous sections, also optimises for the ratio of execution times in two systems.

RECOMMENDATION: Always provide effect size confidence intervals for results (equation 4 for single systems or 5 for speedups).

11. Good Repetition Counts

As we have shown, the required and optimum numbers of repetitions depend on the platform, VM, and benchmark.

Table 6 summarises the repetition counts we established for the DaCapo benchmarks on platform OpenJDK/P1. The highest experimental level here is execution — the more executions we take, the narrower confidence interval we get. The table shows approximately how many repetitions would be needed to get a confidence interval with a half-width that is within 1%, 1.5%, 2.5% or 5% of the mean. We do not show counts of fewer than 5 executions as they could hardly be used to get the variance estimate right (the confidence interval uses only the variance estimate at the highest level, so it is fine to have smaller repetition counts at the other levels). If 1000 iterations are not enough for a given precision, the table shows the ∞ symbol. The number of executions (highest-

level repetitions) can be established on-line, by adding repetitions until the confidence interval is sufficiently narrow.

Table 7 summarises the repetition counts for SPEC CPU benchmarks on platform P3, compiling with a layout randomising gcc. The counts are those required to provide 95% confidence intervals with half-widths of 0.5%, 1%, 1.5% and 2% of the mean; each binary is executed exactly once. Five of the benchmarks are so stable that fewer than 5 executions already give a half-width of 0.5%. We would still run 5 executions of these, though, to get the confidence interval estimate. For half-widths of 1% and higher, we again do not show repetition counts below 5. The benchmarks are much more stable than DaCapo. Xalancbmk and mcf have consistently worse performance with randomisation — if benchmarking of a fixed layout is sought, the variance would be smaller and it would suffice to run 5 executions of both for a 0.5% interval half-width.

12. Summary

Rigorous performance evaluation requires benchmarks to be built, executed and measured multiple times in order to deal with random variation in execution times. Researchers should provide measures of variation when reporting results.

Benchmarks such as DaCapo or SPEC CPU require very different repetition counts on different platforms before they reach an initialised or independent state. Iteration execution times are often strongly auto-dependent: i.e. the benchmark does not reach a steady state, and hence automatic detection of steady state, such as that used in the DaCapo harness or the method recommended by Georges [9], is not applicable. By choosing different iterations in different runs, these heuristics can create an error of tens of percent. We believe that currently proposed or implemented heuristics have proved insufficient to detect independence accurately. We show that manual identification of independence is both necessary and provides a feasible technique, when applied as a one-off analysis for each system. Accurate and robust automation of this inspection is an open problem.

One benefit of our technique is that it made it feasible to repeat earlier experiments on the effect of code layout [20], but using the reference size of SPEC CPU benchmarks. In contrast to the earlier experiments that could use only training sizes, we find the effect of code layout to be small for reference sizes. Similarly, we found no significant impact on the performance of DaCapo benchmarks when we used the gcc compiler to randomise the code layout of the HotSpot JVM.

To capture variation, experiments need to be repeated. Experimentation time can be reduced by repetition at multiple levels (e.g.

compilation, execution, iteration) rather than always repeating at the highest level (e.g. compilation). However, there is no need to repeat at a level if the variation introduced by that level is small (e.g. at the compilation level when the effect of code layout is small). We provide a statistically rigorous method that identifies the optimal number of repetitions to perform at each level for a given experimentation budget. Our method saves experimenter time. Although this dimensioning experiment is expensive, it does not need to be repeated unless the system (e.g. benchmark/VM/platform) changes. For most research groups, this investment will be amortised over a few years. We have applied our method to the DaCapo and SPEC CPU benchmarks on several platforms. However, it is essential that experimenters do not use our dimensioning results at face value but apply our method to their systems, where their results are likely to differ.

RECOMMENDATION: Benchmark developers should include our dimensioning methodology as a one-off per-system configuration requirement.

We exhort researchers to report confidence intervals for their results and show how to derive these for experiments repeated at multiple levels, both for single systems and for reporting speedups between systems. Our methods reported here correct, generalise and extend earlier work [15]; a full description and proofs are available in our technical report [14].

Acknowledgements We thank the anonymous reviewers for their thoughtful comments and suggestions which have improved the presentation of this work. We are also grateful to Howard Bowman and to members of the Evaluate Collaboratory for many useful discussions. Finally, we are grateful for the support of the EPSRC through grant EP/H026975/1.

References

[1] M. Arnold, M. Hind, and B. G. Ryder. Online feedback-directed optimization of Java. In *Proceedings of the 17th annual ACM SIGPLAN conference on Object-Oriented Programming Systems, Languages and Applications (OOPSLA)*. ACM, 2002.

[2] S. Basu and A. DasGupta. Robustness of standard confidence intervals for location parameters under departure from normality. *Annals of Statistics*, 23(4):1433–1442, 1995.

[3] S. M. Blackburn, R. Garner, C. Hoffman, A. M. Khan, K. S. McKinley, R. Bentzur, A. Diwan, D. Feinberg, D. Frampton, S. Z. Guyer, M. Hirzel, A. Hosking, M. Jump, H. Lee, J. E. B. Moss, A. Phansalkar, D. Stefanović, T. VanDrunen, D. von Dincklage, and B. Wiedermann. The DaCapo benchmarks: Java benchmarking development and analysis. In *Proceedings of the 21nd annual ACM SIGPLAN conference on Object-Oriented Programming Systems, Languages and Applications (OOPSLA)*, pages 169–190. ACM, 2006.

[4] W. G. Cochran. *Sampling Techniques: Third Edition*. Wiley, 1977.

[5] R. Coe. It's the effect size, stupid: What effect size is and why it is important. In *Annual Conference of the British Educational Research Association (BERA)*, 2002.

[6] J. Cohen. The Earth is round (p < .05). *American Psychologist*, 49(12):997–1003, 1994.

[7] C. Curtsinger and E. D. Berger. Stabilizer: Statistically sound performance evaluation. In *Proceedings of the eighteenth international conference on Architectural support for programming languages and operating systems (ASPLOS)*. ACM, 2013.

[8] E. C. Fieller. Some problems in interval estimation. *Journal of the Royal Statistical Society*, 16(2):175–185, 1954.

[9] A. Georges, D. Buytaert, and L. Eeckhout. Statistically rigorous Java performance evaluation. In *Proceedings of the 22nd annual ACM SIGPLAN conference on Object-Oriented Programming Systems, Languages and Applications (OOPSLA)*. ACM, 2007.

[10] A. Georges, L. Eeckhout, and D. Buytaert. Java performance evaluation through rigorous replay compilation. In *Proceedings of the 23rd ACM SIGPLAN conference on Object-Oriented Programming Systems, Languages and Applications (OOPSLA)*. ACM, 2008.

[11] D. Gu, C. Verbrugge, and E. Gagnon. Code layout as a source of noise in JVM performance. In *Component And Middleware Performance Workshop, OOPSLA*, 2004.

[12] C. Hill and B. Thompson. Computing and interpreting effect sizes. In *Higher Education: Handbook of Theory and Research*, volume 19, pages 175–196. Springer, 2005.

[13] R. Jain. *The Art of Computer Systems Performance Analysis*. Wiley, 1991.

[14] T. Kalibera and R. E. Jones. Quantifying performance changes with effect size confidence intervals. Technical Report 4–12, University of Kent, 2012.

[15] T. Kalibera and P. Tuma. Precise regression benchmarking with random effects: Improving Mono benchmark results. In *Proceedings of Third European Performance Engineering Workshop (EPEW)*, volume 4054 of *LNCS*. Springer, 2006.

[16] D. J. Lilja. *Measuring Computer Performance: A Practitioner's Guide*. Cambridge University Press, 2000.

[17] Y. Luo and L. K. John. Efficiently evaluating speedup using sampled processor simulation. *IEEE Computer Architecture Letters*, 3(1):6–6, 2004.

[18] S. E. Maxwell and H. D. Delaney. *Designing Experiments and Analyzing Data: a Model Comparison Perspective*. Routledge, 2004.

[19] C. E. McCulloch, S. R. Searle, and J. M. Neuhaus. *Generalized, Linear, and Mixed Models*. Wiley, 2008.

[20] T. Mytkowicz, A. Diwan, M. Hauswirth, and P. F. Sweeney. Producing wrong data without doing anything obviously wrong! In *Proceeding of the 14th international conference on Architectural Support for Programming Languages and Operating Systems (ASPLOS)*. ACM, 2009.

[21] S. Nakagawa and I. C. Cuthill. Effect size, confidence interval and statistical significance: a practical guide for biologists. *Biological Reviews*, 82(4):591–605, 2007.

[22] K. Ogata, T. Onodera, K. Kawachiya, H. Komatsu, and T. Nakatani. Replay compilation: Improving debuggability of a just-in-time compiler. In *Proceedings of the 21st annual ACM SIGPLAN conference on Object-Oriented Programming Systems, Languages and Applications (OOPSLA)*. ACM, 2006.

[23] M. E. Payton, M. H. Greenstone, and N. Schenker. Overlapping confidence intervals or standard error intervals: What do they mean in terms of statistical significance? *Journal of Insect Science*, 3(1996), 2003.

[24] D. Rasch and V. Guiard. The robustness of parametric statistical methods. *Psychology Science*, 46(2):175–208, 2004.

[25] R. M. Royall. The effect of sample size on the meaning of significance tests. *American Statistician*, 40(4):313–315, 1986.

[26] S. R. Searle, G. Casella, and C. E. McCulloch. *Variance Components*. Wiley, 1992.

ACDC: Towards a Universal Mutator for Benchmarking Heap Management Systems

Martin Aigner   Christoph M. Kirsch

University of Salzburg

firstname.lastname@cs.uni-salzburg.at

Abstract

We present ACDC, an open-source benchmark that may be configured to emulate explicit single- and multi-threaded memory allocation, sharing, access, and deallocation behavior to expose virtually any relevant allocator performance differences. ACDC mimics periodic memory allocation and deallocation (AC) as well as persistent memory (DC). Memory may be allocated thread-locally and shared among multiple threads to study multicore scalability and even false sharing. Memory may be deallocated by threads other than the allocating threads to study blowup memory fragmentation. Memory may be accessed and deallocated sequentially in allocation order or in tree-like traversals to expose allocator deficiencies in exploiting spatial locality. We demonstrate ACDC's capabilities with seven state-of-the-art allocators for C/C++ in an empirical study which also reveals interesting performance differences between the allocators.

Categories and Subject Descriptors   D.3.4 [*Programming Languages*]: Memory management

General Terms   Performance, Measurement

Keywords   benchmark; explicit heap management; multicore

1. Introduction

ACDC is an open-source benchmark that may be configured to emulate virtually any single- and multi-threaded mutator behavior for measuring allocation, deallocation, and memory access throughput as well as memory consumption and multicore scalability of an allocator. ACDC itself is designed and implemented to introduce negligible temporal and bounded spatial overhead and to scale to large numbers of threads on multicore hardware. In particular, ACDC implements all per-object operations in constant time, pre-allocates all memory for bookkeeping during initialization, and minimizes contention on shared memory for bookkeeping by bulk processing shared objects.

ACDC emulates the lifecycle of dynamically allocated objects which, as shown in Figure 1, begins with the allocation of memory for storing an object on the heap, followed by read and write

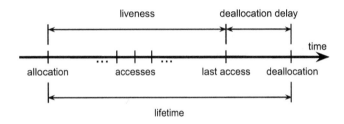

Figure 1: The lifecycle of an object

accesses to the allocated memory, and ends with the deallocation of the allocated memory. The time from allocation to deallocation is called the lifetime of an object. The time from allocation to last access is called the liveness of an object which ACDC, unlike other benchmarking tools, also emulates explicitly by controlling object access. The difference between lifetime and liveness of an object, here called deallocation delay, emulates mutator inefficiencies in identifying dead objects for deallocation which may in turn expose allocator inefficiencies in handling dead memory.

ACDC allocates objects of different size and may do so periodically at different configurable frequencies for temporary use with finite lifetime (AC) as well as for permanent use with infinite lifetime (DC), hence the name. Size, lifetime, and number of objects are determined according to configurable random distributions that mimic typical behavior observed with allocation-intensive C programs where smaller and short-living objects are more likely to occur than larger and long-living objects [3, 21].

Time in ACDC is logical. Time advances when a configurable amount of memory, called the ACDC time quantum, has been allocated [11]. The allocation and deallocation frequencies are derived from the time quantum. Objects are allocated at the rate of the time quantum and deallocated at the rate of their lifetimes which are multiples of the time quantum.

We present experimental evidence that ACDC is able to reveal the relevant performance characteristics of seven state-of-the-art allocators for C/C++. Our experiments are thus firstly about the capabilities of ACDC and only secondly about the allocators although seeing their relative performance turns out to be interesting and valuable, in particular the time-space trade-offs of scalability versus memory consumption as well as spatial locality versus false sharing. The few unexplained anomalies are to the best of our knowledge artifacts caused by the allocators, not ACDC.

The structure of the paper is as follows. ACDC is described in detail in Section 2. Related work is discussed in Section 3. The allocators and experiments are described in Section 4. Conclusions are in Section 5.

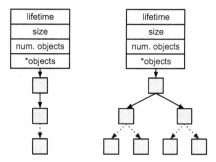

Figure 2: A lifetime-size-class is implemented by either a linked list or a binary tree

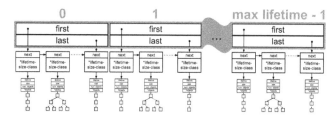

Figure 4: A heap-class is an array of lifetime-classes where the index represents a lifetime

2. ACDC

ACDC allocates sets of objects with the same size and lifetime and gathers the objects in so-called lifetime-size-classes. In particular, each ACDC thread first determines the number of objects that are to be allocated next based on size and lifetime values obtained by configurable random distributions and then allocates the objects one by one and stores them in a lifetime-size-class. In order to implement the logical time in ACDC each thread maintains a thread-local clock. After a thread allocated the objects for a lifetime-size-class the thread checks if it has allocated the amount of memory given by the ACDC time quantum since the last time advance, independently of the memory other threads have allocated. If yes, the thread advances the clock and proceeds to share, access, and deallocate objects. If not, the thread allocates objects for another lifetime-size-class until time is advanced. The logical time in ACDC is thus thread-local and approximative since clocks may be late up to the amount of memory allocated for the objects of the largest lifetime-size-class. The drift between clocks is bounded by a configurable amount through a barrier. The lifetime of a shared object ends when it has ended for all threads sharing the object.

As shown in Figure 2, a lifetime-size-class may be configured to be implemented by either a linked list or a binary tree of objects to facilitate subsequent memory access and eventual deallocation either in the exact (list) or mirrored, depth-first (tree) order of allocation. In particular, the tree is constructed in pre-order, left-to-right and subsequently traversed in pre-order, right-to-left. Other choices are possible but remain for future work. Multiple lifetime-size-classes containing objects of different size but all with the same lifetime are gathered in so-called lifetime-classes which are linked lists of such lifetime-size-classes, as shown in Figure 3. Lifetime-classes facilitate constant-time insertion of lifetime-size-classes and deallocation of all objects in a given lifetime-class in time linear in the number of objects. The objects in a lifetime-class

are deallocated when their lifetime ends in which case the lifetime-class is said to have expired.

ACDC distinguishes a configurable amount of lifetime-classes of which one is dedicated to permanent objects. Each ACDC thread maintains its own lifetime-classes stored in an array, called heap-class, which is indexed by lifetime for constant-time access, as shown in Figure 4.

For benchmarking single-threaded allocation and deallocation throughput and memory consumption ACDC may be configured to emulate a single-threaded mutator that allocates and deallocates objects but never actually accesses the allocated memory, as shown in Figure 5a. For benchmarking memory access throughput to expose differences in memory layout quality ACDC may also be configured to read and write allocated memory between allocation and deallocation. In configurations with a single ACDC thread, as shown in Figure 5b, ACDC may thus expose allocator inefficiencies in accommodating spatial locality.

In multi-threaded configurations, for benchmarking multi-threaded allocation and deallocation throughput as well as memory consumption and multicore scalability, as shown in Figure 5c, ACDC may expose allocator inefficiencies in avoiding contention on allocator data structures (through concurrent allocation and deallocation), blowup memory fragmentation [5] (through deallocation of objects allocated by other threads), and false sharing of allocated objects (through thread-local access of unshared objects). All three types of inefficiencies may prevent multicore scalability.

Sharing objects in multi-threaded ACDC works by having each ACDC thread allocate a configurable number of objects for shared rather than thread-local use. In addition to the thread-local heap-classes each thread also maintains a second, lock-protected heap-class. The lock-protected heap-classes of all threads together serve as distribution pool for shared objects, as shown in Figure 6. Each thread (producer) inserts lifetime-size-classes of objects that are

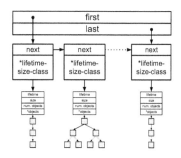

Figure 3: A lifetime-class is a linked list of lifetime-size-classes with the same lifetime

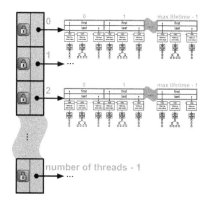

Figure 6: The distribution pool is an array of lock-protected heap-classes, one per thread.

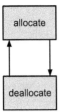

(a) Control-flow view of a single ACDC thread allocating and deallocating objects

(b) A single ACDC thread allocating, accessing, and deallocating objects

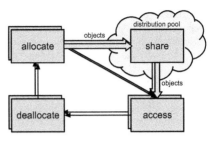

(c) Multiple ACDC threads allocating, sharing, accessing, and deallocating objects

Figure 5: ACDC in a nutshell

Parameter	Range	Default
mode	ACDC or false-sharing	ACDC
number of threads	1 to 64	1
number of objects	0 to int-max	0
min. size	8 to int-max	16 B
max. size	min. size to int-max	256 B
min. liveness	1 to benchmark duration	1
max. liveness	min. liveness to int-max	10
deallocation delay	0 to benchmark duration	0
time quantum	1 to int-max	256 KB
benchmark duration	1 to int-max	50
max. time drift	1 to benchmark duration	10
list-based ratio	100% - tree-based ratio	100%
access live objects	TRUE or FALSE	TRUE
write access ratio	0% to 100%	10%
shared objects	TRUE or FALSE	FALSE
shared objects ratio	0% to 100%	100%
retrieving threads ratio	0% to 100%	100%

Table 1: ACDC runtime options and default settings

meant to be shared into the lock-protected heap-classes of (a subset of) all threads and retrieves (consumer) possibly many lifetime-size-classes inserted by others packaged as lifetime-classes from its own lock-protected heap-class. Insertion is linear in the number of threads and retrieval is linear in the number of lifetime-classes. The retrieved lifetime-classes are then inserted into the thread-local heap-class in constant time for further thread-local processing.

2.1 Configuration

ACDC offers extensive configuration of its allocation, sharing, access, and deallocation behavior. Table 1 shows the relevant options along with their default values. We briefly describe each parameter.

The mode parameter switches between ACDC's default mode in which object sizes and lifetimes are determined by random distributions and a mode for exposing allocator inefficiencies due to false sharing. In this mode ACDC only allocates small objects with the same, fixed lifetime.

The number of threads defines how many concurrent threads ACDC creates and runs. The upper bound of 64 threads is explained in Section 2.3. The number of objects defines how many objects ACDC allocates in a lifetime-size-class. With the default of zero ACDC determines the number dynamically based on object size and lifetime. The minimum and maximum size and liveness define the range of the random distributions that determine the size and liveness, respectively, of the objects ACDC allocates. The deallocation delay extends the lifetime of all objects such that ACDC

stops accessing the objects when their liveness ended but deallocates them only after their lifetime ended.

The time quantum defines the amount of memory that each thread needs to allocate to advance its thread-local clock by one unit of time. The benchmark duration defines the time to terminate the benchmark by how often each thread needs to advance its clock before termination. The maximum difference between the clock value of a given thread and the value of any other thread's clock is bounded by the maximum time drift.

ACDC gathers allocated objects with the same size and lifetime in lifetime-size-classes that may be implemented by a linked list or a binary tree. The data structure is chosen randomly according to the configured list-based and tree-based ratio.

By default ACDC accesses live objects in between allocation and deallocation as shown in Figure 5b. A behavior where objects are not accessed at all, as shown in Figure 5a, may also be configured by setting access live objects to FALSE. In this case the write access ratio, which controls the fraction of the live heap that will be modified upon access, is ignored. Otherwise, 10% of the live memory are by default written during access.

The behavior illustrated in Figure 5c can be configured by setting shared objects to TRUE. In this case the shared objects ratio defines the number of allocated lifetime-size-classes that will be shared with other threads. The receiving threads ratio controls the number of threads that will receive references to the shared objects through the distribution pool.

2.2 Metrics and Probes

ACDC explores the basic performance dimensions time and space. Time is reported in normalized total allocation time, normalized total deallocation time, and normalized total access time in milliseconds (also consistently in all experiments). Note that unlike the logical time of ACDC, temporal performance is reported in real time. By allocation time we mean the time an allocator spends in allocating objects. Total allocation time is the sum of the allocation time the allocator benchmarked by ACDC spends in all threads. The normalized total allocation time is the total allocation time divided by the number of threads. Total allocation time is thus equal to normalized total allocation time in single-threaded configurations. Allocation time is measured in CPU cycles by reading the CPU time stamp counter before and after allocating a lifetime-size-class of objects. The CPU cycles are scaled to milliseconds during normalization. Normalized total deallocation time and normalized total access time are defined similarly. Here the time stamp counter is read before and after deallocating expired lifetime-classes and accessing objects, respectively. The time spent in sharing lifetime-size-classes, controlling the time drift, and other bookkeeping is thus not considered.

Space is reported in normalized average memory consumption in megabytes (again also consistently in all experiments). By memory consumption we mean the memory consumption of ACDC without the overhead of the bookkeeping data structures. For measuring memory consumption we have implemented an interface to the Linux proc filesystem that provides the resident set size, i.e., the number of virtual memory pages ACDC maintains in real memory. ACDC samples memory consumption at each time advance starting after a warm-up phase of twice the maximum liveness. The average memory consumption is the arithmetic mean of the samples without the bookkeeping overhead. The normalized average memory consumption is the average memory consumption again divided by the number of threads.

For simplicity, we do not allocate permanent objects in our experiments so that the arithmetic mean is a useful metric and the memory required for bookkeeping overhead is bounded in ACDC's configuration parameters and can thus be pre-allocated. Although the required amount may be estimated for each configuration we determined an amount that works for all experiments (500 MB) and then only used that amount. We employ the brk system call for pre-allocating the memory for bookkeeping to avoid performance impacts on the allocators under test. All bookkeeping objects are allocated by ACDC's own memory management in the pre-allocated space and aligned and padded to cache lines to avoid false sharing.

2.3 Implementation details

ACDC constructs lifetime-size-classes by approximating empirical findings that suggest objects allocated by real applications are more likely to be small and short-living than large and long-living [3, 21]. ACDC determines size, lifetime, and number of objects of a lifetime-size-class in constant time in three steps. First, ACDC selects the size from a uniformly distributed, discrete interval $[2^r, 2^{r+1}]$ where r is selected from a uniformly distributed, discrete interval $[log_2(\text{min. size}), log_2(\text{max. size}))$. Next, ACDC randomly selects the liveness from a uniformly distributed, discrete interval [min. liveness, max. liveness] and adds the deallocation delay to obtain the lifetime. In the last step, ACDC calculates the number of objects based on the selected size and liveness with the following formula:

$$\text{number of objects} = (log_2(\text{max. size}) - log_2(\text{selected size}) + 1)^2 *$$
$$(\text{max. liveness} - \text{selected liveness} + 1)^2$$

The formula yields a large number of objects if the distance of the selected size to the maximum size is large (the objects are small) or if the distance of the selected liveness to the maximum liveness is large (the objects are short-living).

ACDC may run up to 64 threads. The upper bound enables lock-free deallocation of shared objects through atomic operations on 64-bit words storing 64-bit bitmaps with one bit for each thread. Each lifetime-size-class maintains such a bitmap where the thread that allocates the lifetime-size-class sets the bits that are assigned to the threads that are selected to share the lifetime-size-class. Each sharing thread resets its assigned bit when the lifetime-class that contains the shared lifetime-size-class expires without deallocating the objects unless the thread determines the word storing the bitmap to be zero. On platforms that support atomic operations on 128-bit words ACDC may run up to 128 concurrent threads.

3. Related Work

3.1 Empirical studies

Empirical studies on memory allocators are typically performed as part of the literature on new allocators. To the best of our knowledge there is no recent academic study of the relative performance of explicit memory allocators. The Oracle Technology Network contains a recent article on the performance impact of memory allocation in multi-threaded applications [20]. However, it only compares three allocators namely Hoard [5], libumem [6] (based on the SunOS slab allocator), and mtmalloc (part of Oracle Solaris 10). The study concludes that in terms of latency and scalability mtmalloc outperforms the other two allocators and in terms of memory efficiency libumen does best. A different benchmark performed by Berger [4] on the same allocators showed speedups of 2.74 and 3.13 comparing Hoard to libumem and mtmalloc, respectively.

3.2 Benchmarks

The literature on memory management systems contains a large and diverse set of benchmarking programs for evaluating the performance of allocators. We focus our discussion on synthetic programs that appeared in well-known allocator papers, e.g. Hoard [5], LKmalloc [13], Streamflow [18], and the allocator by Michael [17].

The Larson benchmark [13] aims at simulating the behavior of a server responding to a client request. A worker thread in the Larson benchmark receives a set of objects from another thread, performs random deallocations and allocations on this set and writes two words in each newly allocated object. Then it passes the set of objects to a new thread performing the same routine and terminates. The benchmark may run multiple workers in parallel. The threads allocate objects of different size which are uniformly distributed in a configured range. This may be an unrealistic assumption according to previous results on object lifetime characteristics [3, 21]. Also, this benchmark does not allow to control the lifetime of the allocated objects and does not implement heap access.

Sh8bench is the latest version of a synthetic benchmark by MicroQuill [2]. It computes a simple object size distribution based on a statically predefined enumeration of only 12 different sizes ranging from 8 to 168524 bytes. In each round, the mutator deallocates a portion of the objects allocated in the previous round and also allocates new objects. The mutator does not involve access to the requested dynamic memory. Like the Larson benchmark, sh8bench offers no control over object lifetimes.

Lever and Boreham presented a performance study of ptmalloc [15] using three benchmarking programs as part of the Linux scalability project. The first program, called malloc-test, runs multiple threads that all allocate a fixed number of objects of fixed size and deallocate each object right after allocation. The goal is to examine malloc and free latency for an increasing number of threads. The second program is a simplified version of the Larson benchmark using only a fixed object size. The goal of this benchmark is to expose blowup memory fragmentation [5], i.e., increasing memory consumption when deallocating threads are different from allocating threads. Finally, the third program tests for false sharing effects where a set of objects is allocated and each object is accessed by a different thread. However, only malloc-test is available for download on the Linux scalability project webpage [1].

These commonly used benchmarking programs achieve similar goals in different ways but, unlike ACDC, do not allow to evaluate all relevant allocator performance criteria in isolation. The Larson benchmark only provides a throughput metric counting the number of allocations and deallocations. The malloc-test and Sh8bench benchmarks accumulate all performance information in total execution time. Effects related to spatial locality cannot be explicitly studied with any of these tools. Moreover, the liveness of objects is not modeled explicitly. In contrast, ACDC is an attempt to enable emulation of mutator behavior that reveals all relevant allocator performance characteristics.

For garbage-collected programming languages like Java there exist standardized evaluation suites like SPECjvm2008 [19]. However, ACDC currently does not support benchmarking implicit memory management systems.

4. Experiments

All experiments ran on a server machine with four 6-core 2.1 GHz AMD Opteron 8425 processors, 64 KB L1 and 512 KB L2 data cache per core, 6 MB shared cache per processor, 110 GB of main memory, and Linux kernel version 3.2.0.

The allocators were compiled using their default Makefile (all with compiler optimizations enabled) except ptmalloc2 and tcmalloc which came pre-compiled with Ubuntu LTS 12.04. We obtained ptmalloc2 from the GNU C library version 2.15 and tcmalloc from the Google perftools package version 1.7.

Unless stated otherwise, we use the metrics defined in Section 2.2 and repeated each experiment five times. The graphs show the arithmetic mean and the sample standard deviation. The benchmark duration is set to multiples of maximum liveness where we observed that the relative performance differences between allocators do not change anymore by extending the benchmark duration.

4.1 Allocators

We employ seven state-of-the-art multi-threaded allocators for C/C++ that worked for us out of the box without any modifications. In the following we briefly discuss the key features of these allocators.

The ptmalloc2 allocator by Wolfram Gloger is based on Doug Lea's allocator [14] and shipped as part of the GNU C library (glibc) in most Linux distributions. Objects allocated through ptmalloc2 are 16-byte-aligned and have an 8-byte header. Requests for objects smaller than 64 bytes are served from so-called fast bins, i.e., caching pools of recently freed objects. Objects larger than 512 bytes are managed in a best-fit fashion. The ptmalloc3 allocator is the latest version of Wolfram Gloger's allocator implementation [9]. It uses a POSIX mutex for all public calls to the allocator. The algorithms are also based on Doug Lea's allocator.

The jemalloc allocator [7, 8] written by Jason Evans aims at multicore scalability. It is the default allocator in FreeBSD, NetBSD, and some versions of Mozilla Firefox. The allocator divides the heap into independent sub-heaps called arenas that can be processed in parallel. In addition, each thread maintains a cache that can be accessed without locking. Freed objects are always returned to the arena they were allocated from to control blowup memory fragmentation [5].

A similar approach is taken by the tcmalloc allocator [10] from Google. The allocator serves requests for small objects from thread-local caches. When a request cannot be served, a bunch of objects is fetched from the central heap. Large objects are directly served by the central heap. In contrast to jemalloc, small freed objects are not put in the thread cache of the allocating thread but in the cache of the deallocating thread. When a thread cache exceeds a size of 2MB a garbage collector moves unused objects to the central heap, again to control blowup memory fragmentation.

Hoard by Berger et al. [5] was the first allocator designed for multicore scalability using per-CPU heaps that addressed the blowup fragmentation problem. Objects are allocated in size classes which are organized in so-called superblocks, i.e., contiguous memory allocated from the operating system in multiples of the system page size. Freed objects are returned to the per-CPU heap from which they were allocated. Superblocks that become less utilized than a given empty fraction may be moved to a shared central heap where the available memory can be re-used by another per-CPU heap thus balancing free memory among threads and limiting blowup fragmentation.

The tbb Scalable Allocator [12] by Intel uses thread-local caches and a global free list when a request cannot be served from the object caches. The global free list is protected by fine-grained locks. As with jemalloc, freed objects are returned to the heap they

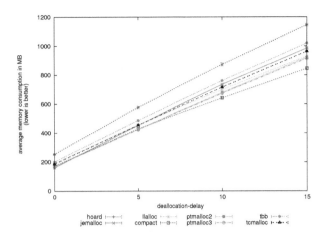

Figure 7: Average memory consumption for an increasing deallocation delay

were allocated from. To reduce synchronization, tbb uses two separate free lists for objects returned by the owner and other threads.

The Lockless Memory Allocator (llalloc) [16] also uses different algorithms for different size classes. Small objects up to 512 bytes are managed by a slab allocator that uses slabs for each size class which are dynamically allocated for each thread. Empty slabs are traded between threads using per-CPU locking. Objects larger than 512 bytes are served by a best-fit allocation strategy which is extended by a per-size object cache that serves objects in LIFO order. Synchronization in llalloc is performed by lock-free queues, one queue per thread. A thread that frees an object allocated by another thread places the object in that thread's queue. Eventually, the allocating thread will empty its queue and reuse the object thereby controlling blowup memory fragmentation.

ACDC itself provides two mutator-aware allocators as baseline, in particular for benchmarking spatial locality and false-sharing performance. The first allocator, called compact, reserves a contiguous area of memory and arranges it as array of objects to store the objects of a lifetime-size-class without any space in between the objects. In list-based lifetime-size-classes the first object is stored at index 0 and the successor of an object stored at index i is located at index $i + 1$. In tree-based lifetime-size-classes the root object resides at position 0 and the left and right child of an object stored at position i is located at index $2i + 1$ and $2i + 2$, respectively. The second allocator, called align, aligns an object to cache line boundaries and adds padding space to occupy the rest of the cache line such that no other object is stored in the same cache line. The align allocator avoids false sharing at the expense of wasted memory and cache space. Both, the compact and the align allocators allocate and deallocate in constant time modulo the underlying allocator. Both are built on top of ptmalloc2 and therefore share its temporal and spatial performance characteristics. We point that out in the relevant parts of the experimental evaluation.

4.2 Capabilities of ACDC: allocation and deallocation time

We measure allocation and deallocation time for an increasing heap size without accessing any objects. The heap size is increased by increasing the deallocation delay without changing any other parameters which may affect allocation and deallocation time, e.g., size, liveness and number of objects. The data in Figure 7 confirms that the deallocation delay does indeed translate nearly linearly into heap size for all allocators. The non-default portion of the ACDC configuration for this experiment is in Table 2.

Parameter	Value
min. size	8 B
max. size	8 KB
deallocation delay	increasing from 0 to 15
time quantum	50 MB
access live objects	FALSE

Table 2: ACDC configuration for the allocation and deallocation time experiment (only non-default values are shown)

Parameter	Value
min. size	increasing from 8 to 1024 B
max. size	2 * min. size
max. liveness	1
time quantum	10 MB
benchmark duration	20
access live objects	FALSE

Table 3: ACDC configuration for the memory consumption experiment (only non-default values are shown)

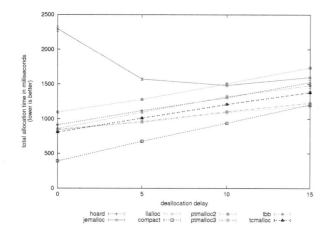

Figure 8: Total allocation time for an increasing deallocation delay

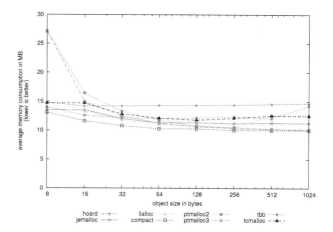

Figure 10: Memory consumption for increasing object sizes. On the x-axis a value for x denotes the range of object sizes from x to $2x$.

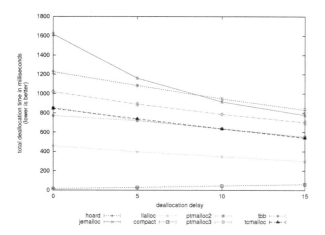

Figure 9: Total deallocation time for an increasing deallocation delay

Figure 8 depicts the total allocation time for an increasing deallocation delay. With the exception of jemalloc, the allocation time of all allocators increases close to linearly with the deallocation delay. However, the slope of the graphs differ by a constant factor where llalloc is less affected by the heap size than the others. The only anomaly in this experiment relative to the other allocators is the behavior of jemalloc.

Figure 9 shows, again for an increasing deallocation delay, the total deallocation time which, unlike the total allocation time, decreases rather than increases. In this case, however, the slope of the graphs is nearly the same for all allocators, again except for jemalloc. We included the compact allocator in this and other experiments below to show experimentally a performance baseline which

may only be reached by mutator-aware allocators. The compact allocator allocates and deallocates whole lifetime-size-classes rather than single objects with a single malloc and free call, respectively.

4.3 Capabilities of ACDC: memory consumption

We are interested in the space overhead introduced by allocators depending on the size of allocated objects. For this purpose, we measure average memory consumption for increasing object sizes (by increasing minimum and maximum sizes in ACDC). Table 3 summarizes the non-default portion of the ACDC configuration for this experiment.

Figure 10 shows the average memory consumption for increasing object sizes. Note that on the x-axis a value for x actually denotes the range of object sizes from x to $2x$. ACDC selects actual sizes randomly from this range. The ptmalloc2 and ptmalloc3 allocators introduce significant space overhead for small objects, possibly caused by the minimum 16-byte alignment. In contrast, both allocators introduce up to 20% less overhead for larger objects than the other allocators in this experiment.

4.4 Capabilities of ACDC: spatial locality

We measure total memory access time for an increasing ratio of list-based rather than tree-based lifetime-size-classes where objects are accessed (and deallocated) increasingly in the order in which they were allocated, i.e., with increasing spatial locality up to sequential locality. The non-default portion of the ACDC configuration for this experiment is in Table 4. The results are shown in Figure 11.

The compact allocator provides the best memory layout in terms of spatial locality because no memory is wasted between objects and the distance between successively accessed objects in memory is minimal. A higher ratio of list-based lifetime-size-classes increases spatial locality even more because the chances for the next

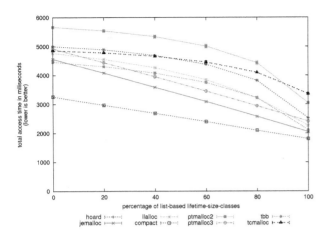

Figure 11: Total memory access time for an increasing ratio of list-based lifetime-size-classes

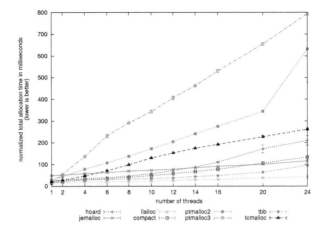

Figure 12: Normalized total allocation time for an increasing number of threads running the thread-local configuration without memory access

Parameter	Value
min. size	16 B
max. size	32 B
time quantum	500 KB
list-based ratio	increasing from 0% to 100%
write access ratio	0%

Table 4: ACDC configuration for the spatial locality experiment (only non-default values are shown)

Parameter	Value
mode	ACDC
number of threads	increasing from 1 to 24
min. size	8 B
max. size	2 KB
min. liveness	1
max. liveness	5
time quantum	1 MB
max. time drift	5
access live objects	FALSE (without memory access) or TRUE (with memory access)
shared objects	FALSE (thread-local configuration) or TRUE (shared-objects configuration)

Table 5: ACDC configuration for all multicore scalability experiments (only non-default values are shown)

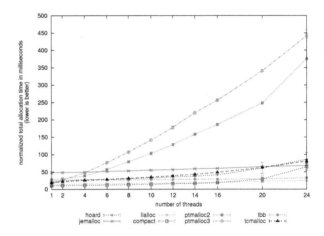

Figure 13: Normalized total allocation time for an increasing number of threads running the thread-local configuration with memory access

object to already reside in the same cache line is higher for compact list-based than for compact tree-based lifetime-size-classes.

For the other allocators, the quality of the memory layout in terms of spatial locality also increases as the access order approaches the allocation order. However, jemaloc, llalloc, and tbb create a memory layout that benefits from spatial locality even more than ptmalloc2 and tcmalloc.

4.5   Capabilities of ACDC: multicore scalability

We are interested in exposing multicore scalability of allocators in terms of allocation and deallocation time as well as memory consumption. We benchmark thread-local and shared-objects configurations with and without accessing objects. The non-default portion

of the ACDC configuration for all four experiments are summarized in Table 5.

Figure 12 depicts the normalized total allocation time for an increasing number of threads in the thread-local configuration without memory access. This configuration puts high pressure on the allocator because ACDC performs no other operations than allocating and deallocating objects. The allocation time increases for all allocators but the slopes differ significantly. The llalloc allocator performs best in this experiment showing nearly perfect scalability (constant normalized allocation time). Also jemalloc scales well, however showing higher absolute allocation time. On the other hand, ptmalloc3 seems to suffer from contention on its locks. The situation with ptmalloc2 is similar, however less dramatic.

Figure 13 shows the data when ACDC performs memory access in between allocation and deallocation which reduces the pressure on the allocators. However, both ptmalloc2 and ptmalloc3 still do not scale but their absolute allocation times are much better, especially with ptmalloc3. The other allocators all scale well. The compact allocator, which is built on top of ptmalloc2, shows for more than 20 threads an increasing allocation time because the

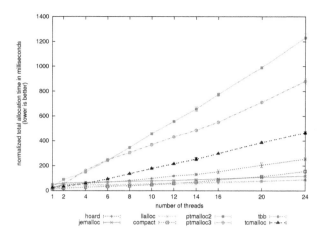

Figure 14: Normalized total allocation time for an increasing number of threads running the shared-objects configuration without memory access

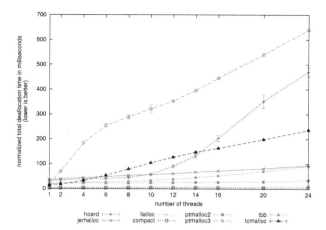

Figure 16: Normalized total deallocation time for an increasing number of threads running the thread-local configuration without memory access

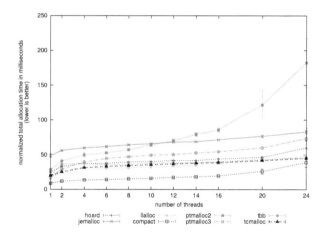

Figure 15: Normalized total allocation time for an increasing number of threads running the shared-objects configuration with memory access

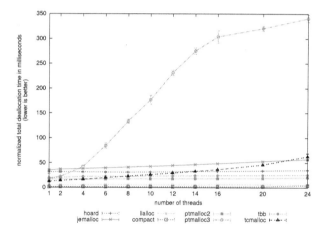

Figure 17: Normalized total deallocation time for an increasing number of threads running the thread-local configuration with memory access

scalability deficiencies of ptmalloc2 dominate the allocation time of the compact allocator.

Figure 14 depicts the data for the shared-objects configuration without memory access. Now, threads have to deallocate objects that were allocated by another thread. The result is higher total allocation time for those allocators that fail to scale in this experiment, namely ptmalloc2 and ptmalloc3. However, now ptmalloc3 performs better than ptmalloc2. The scalable allocators perform similar to the thread-local configuration except tcmalloc which takes about 80% longer to handle allocations in the shared-object configuration than in the thread-local configuration.

When we run ACDC with memory access in the shared-objects configuration the pressure on the allocators drops again. Figure 15 depicts the data for that configuration. Here, the absolute values are much better than in the other three configurations because access to shared objects takes more time than access to unshared objects. This effect decreases the pressure on the allocators even more resulting in less contention and lower allocation times.

The normalized total deallocation time of the thread-local configuration without memory access is shown in Figure 16. In this experiment, llalloc is again the fastest and most scalable alloca-

tor. Note, however, that ptmalloc2 scales nearly perfect in terms of deallocation time. This shows the advantage of ACDC over the benchmarks discussed in Section 3. A benchmark that does not separate allocation and deallocation time is unable to show this phenomenon. The ptmalloc3 allocator does not scale in this experiment and also tcmalloc and Hoard show a significant increase in deallocation time for more than six and ten threads, respectively.

For Figure 17 ACDC again performs memory access in between allocation and deallocation. Reducing the pressure on their deallocation routines, all allocators perform well except ptmalloc3 which, however, produces much better absolute deallocation times than in the experiment without memory access.

Figure 18 depicts the normalized total deallocation time of the shared-objects configuration without memory access. Here, ptmalloc3 and ptmalloc2 show slight scalability deficiencies. However, ptmalloc 3 gives much better absolute values than in the thread-local configuration while ptmalloc2 takes much longer to deallocate shared objects. Still, the overall results are better than for the thread-local configuration.

Adding memory access to the shared-objects configuration yields the normalized total deallocation time shown in Figure 19.

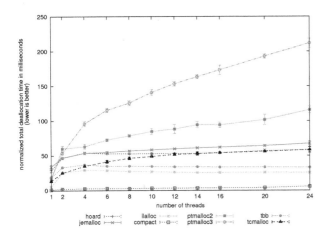

Figure 18: Normalized total deallocation time for an increasing number of threads running the shared-objects configuration without memory access

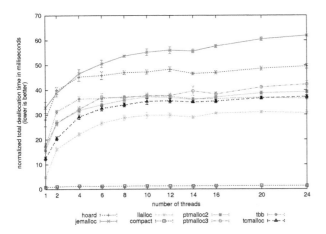

Figure 19: Normalized total deallocation time for an increasing number of threads running the shared-objects configuration with memory access

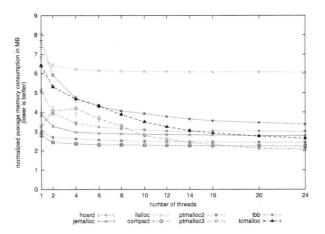

Figure 20: Normalized average memory consumption for an increasing number of threads running the thread-local configuration

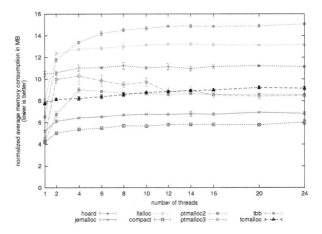

Figure 21: Normalized average memory consumption for an increasing number of threads running the shared-objects configuration

We observe a similar situation as with the allocation time for the shared-objects configuration with memory access. Relaxing the pressure on the deallocation routines results in fast and scalable deallocation of shared objects even for an increasing number of threads.

The normalized average memory consumption of this experiment running the thread-local configuration is presented in Figure 20. The result illustrates the time-space trade-off that the different allocators implement. The llalloc allocator, the fastest and most scalable allocator in this evaluation, shows the highest per-thread memory consumption while ptmalloc2 and ptmalloc3, which did not scale in terms of allocation time, are the most space efficient allocators in this experiment. The tbb, tcmalloc, and jemalloc allocators implement a more balanced trade-off between time and space.

For the shared-objects configuration, Figure 21 shows the normalized average memory consumption. We observe an increasing per-thread memory consumption in this experiment. Deallocating objects that were allocated by a different thread can cause blowup memory fragmentation. This experiment illustrates how effectively the allocators handle this problem. Apparently, none of the allo-

Parameter	Value
mode	false-sharing
number of threads	increasing from 1 to 24
min. size	10 B
max. size	10 B
min. liveness	1
max. liveness	1
benchmark duration	30
time quantum	1 million read and write accesses

Table 6: ACDC configuration for the false-sharing experiment (only non-default values are shown)

cators create unbounded memory consumption. However, the differences in the absolute space demands is significant. The tbb allocator, for example, consumes twice the amount of memory the jemalloc allocator consumes.

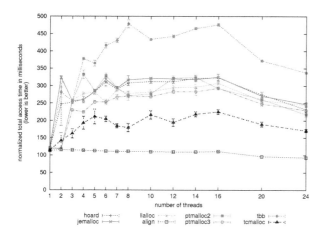

Figure 22: Normalized total access time for an increasing number of threads

4.6 Capabilities of ACDC: false sharing

ACDC allows to run a special mode to expose memory layouts which are prone to false sharing. In this mode one thread allocates as many objects as there are threads, one for each thread including itself. The allocating thread (single producer) passes each object to a different thread (multiple consumers) and then all threads perform a large number of read and write accesses to their object until its lifetime ends. Note that the time quantum in this mode is given in read and write accesses, i.e., after a given number of accesses to the objects the thread clocks advance and a new object is allocated for each thread. Table 6 summarizes the non-default portion of the ACDC configuration for this experiment.

Figure 22 shows the normalized total access time for an increasing number of threads running ACDC in false-sharing mode. The baseline is here the align allocator where each object is allocated in its own cache line avoiding false sharing altogether. For only one thread, of course, there is no false sharing and all allocators yield the same access time. For an increasing number of threads, however, the access time increases up to a factor of five. This experiment in combination with the findings from Figure 11 illustrate yet another time-space trade-off. The allocators which performed best in terms of spacial locality, namely tbb, jemalloc, and llalloc are more prone to introduce false sharing.

5. Conclusion

We have presented ACDC, an open-source benchmark for measuring allocator performance by emulating realistic single- and multi-threaded mutators. We have presented the basic modes of operation of ACDC including allocation and deallocation of objects, emulation of heap access patterns, and sharing objects among multiple threads. In an empirical study involving seven state-of-the-art allocators we showed that ACDC is able to expose differences in their performance in terms of allocation, deallocation, and memory access throughput as well as memory consumption and multicore scalability and we also illustrated the time-space trade-offs implemented by the allocators. As part of future work we plan to extend ACDC for benchmarking managed languages.

Acknowledgments

This work has been supported by the National Research Network RiSE on Rigorous Systems Engineering (Austrian Science Fund S11404-N23). We thank the anonymous referees for their constructive and inspiring comments and suggestions.

References

[1] CITI Projects: Linux scalability, 1999. URL http://www.citi.umich.edu/projects/linux-scalability/.

[2] MicroQuill Inc., 2013. URL http://www.microquill.com/.

[3] D. A. Barrett and B. G. Zorn. Using lifetime predictors to improve memory allocation performance. In *Proceedings of the ACM SIGPLAN 1993 conference on Programming language design and implementation*, PLDI '93, pages 187–196, New York, USA, 1993. ACM.

[4] E. D. Berger. The Hoard Memory Allocator Documentation: Frequently Asked Questions, 2004. URL http://people.cs.umass.edu/~emery/hoard/hoard-documentation.html#IDAOZYP.

[5] E. D. Berger, K. S. McKinley, R. D. Blumofe, and P. R. Wilson. Hoard: A Scalable Memory Allocator for Multithreaded Applications. *SIGPLAN Not.*, 35(11):117–128, Nov. 2000.

[6] J. Bonwick and J. Adams. Magazines and Vmem: Extending the Slab Allocator to Many CPUs and Arbitrary Resources. In *Proceedings of the 2001 USENIX Annual Technical Conference*, 2001.

[7] J. Evans. A Scalable Concurrent malloc(3) Implementation for FreeBSD. In *The Technical BSD Conference*, BSDCan '06, Apr. 2006.

[8] J. Evans. Scalable memory allocation using jemalloc, 2011. URL https://www.facebook.com/notes/facebook-engineering/scalable-memory-allocation-using-jemalloc/480222803919.

[9] W. Gloger. Wolfram Gloger's malloc homepage, 2006. URL http://www.malloc.de/en/.

[10] Google, Inc. Google Performance Tools, 2012. URL http://code.google.com/p/gperftools/wiki/GooglePerformanceTools.

[11] B. Hayes. Using key object opportunism to collect old objects. In *Conference proceedings on Object-oriented programming systems, languages, and applications*, OOPSLA '91, pages 33–46, New York, USA, 1991. ACM.

[12] Intel, Inc. Thread Building Blocks, 2013. URL http://threadingbuildingblocks.org/.

[13] P.-A. Larson and M. Krishnan. Memory allocation for long-running server applications. In *Proceedings of the 1st international symposium on Memory management*, ISMM '98, pages 176–185, New York, USA, 1998. ACM.

[14] D. Lea. A Memory Allocator, 2000. URL http://g.oswego.edu/dl/html/malloc.html.

[15] C. Lever and D. Boreham. malloc() performance in a multithreaded Linux environment. In *Proceedings of the FREENIX Track of the 2000 USENIX Annual Technical Conference*, June 2001.

[16] Lockless, Inc. The Lockless Memory Allocator, 2013. URL http://locklessinc.com/.

[17] M. M. Michael. Scalable lock-free dynamic memory allocation. In *Proceedings of the ACM SIGPLAN 2004 conference on Programming language design and implementation*, PLDI '04, pages 35–46, New York, USA, 2004. ACM.

[18] S. Schneider, C. D. Antonopoulos, and D. S. Nikolopoulos. Scalable locality-conscious multithreaded memory allocation. In *Proceedings of the 5th international symposium on Memory management*, ISMM '06, pages 84–94, New York, USA, 2006. ACM.

[19] Standard Performance Evaluation Corporation. Specjvm2008, 2013. URL http://www.spec.org/jvm2008/.

[20] R. C. Weisner. How Memory Allocation Affects Performance in Multithreaded Programs, 2012. URL http://www.oracle.com/technetwork/articles/servers-storage-dev/mem-alloc-1557798.html.

[21] B. Zorn and D. Grunwald. Empirical measurements of six allocation-intensive C programs. *SIGPLAN Not.*, 27(12):71–80, Dec. 1992.

Precise and Scalable Context-Sensitive Pointer Analysis via Value Flow Graph

Lian Li   Cristina Cifuentes   Nathan Keynes

Oracle Labs, Brisbane, Australia

{lian.li,cristina.cifuentes,nathan.keynes}@oracle.com

Abstract

In this paper, we propose a novel method for context-sensitive pointer analysis using the value flow graph (VFG) formulation. We achieve context-sensitivity by simultaneously applying function cloning and computing context-free language reachability (CFL-reachability) in a novel way. In contrast to existing clone-based and CFL-based approaches, flow-sensitivity is easily integrated in our approach by using a flow-sensitive VFG where each value flow edge is computed in a flow-sensitive manner. We apply context-sensitivity to both local variables and heap objects and propose a new approximation for heap cloning.

We prove that our approach can achieve context-sensitivity without loss of precision, i.e., it is as precise as inlining all function calls. We develop an efficient algorithm and implement a context-, flow-, and field-sensitive pointer analysis with heap cloning support in LLVM. We evaluate the efficiency and precision of our implementation using standard SPEC CPU2006 benchmarks. Our experimental results show that the analysis is much faster than existing approaches, it scales well to large real-world applications, and it enables more effective compiler optimizations.

Categories and Subject Descriptors   F3.2 [*LOGICS AND MEANINGS OF PROGRAMS*]: Semantics of Programming Languages–Program analysis

General Terms   Algorithms, Languages, Performance

Keywords   context-sensitive analysis, flow-sensitive analysis, demand-driven, function summary, CFL-reachability

1. Introduction

Pointer analysis is a fundamental program analysis that statically computes the possible runtime values for pointer variables. It enables a variety of applications, including bug checking [7, 19], program verification [10], code optimization, and memory management for embedded systems [21, 22]. More precise pointer information directly supports more precise analysis tools, and more aggressive optimizations. However, highly precise pointer analysis techniques have previously been considered to be too slow to be usable in practice.

In pointer analysis, heap memory is typically abstracted as a finite set of abstract allocation sites (memory objects), with potential pointer values represented as the set of memory objects that each pointer may point to at runtime, known as the *points-to set*. The precision of pointer analysis can be improved via two major dimensions: *context-sensitivity* and *flow-sensitivity*. Context-sensitive analysis can be applied to both pointer variables or heap objects (aka heap-cloning [26]). It distinguishes the context of a function invocation and prevents information from being erroneously propagated to different call-sites of the same function, thus greatly improving precision.

In context-sensitive analysis, the context of a function invocation is typically distinguished by its *call path*, which is simply the path from the entry function to the invocation site in the call graph. The analysis is said to be precise if it is performed in such a way that all contexts are differentiated, i.e., the full call path (with cycles on the path being discarded) is used to represent a calling context. As the number of contexts (call paths) in a program can be exponential in the call graph size, precise context-sensitive analyses often suffer from scalability problems.

Existing context-sensitive pointer analyses developed to date are either clone-based [4, 36], summary-based [14, 25, 38, 40, 42], or use a context-free language reachability formulation (CFL-based) [32, 39]. Both clone- and CFL-based approaches achieve context-sensitivity at the expense of lack of flow-sensitivity. Recent summary-based approaches [14, 40] successfully scaled context- and flow-sensitive pointer analysis to large applications by computing compact parameterized function summaries. However, compact function summaries also suggest that some useful information may not be preserved in the summary. Hence the computed results may not be general enough to precisely answer various alias queries. For example, it is difficult to precisely answer the query "do the two pointers alias on a particular call path?", if only points-to sets are preserved without extra context information.

In this paper, we propose a novel method for context-sensitive pointer analysis that computes and preserves precise pointer and context information, while scaling to large applications. At its core, we make use of the value flow graph (VFG) formulation [20] where pointer variables and memory objects are represented as nodes in the graph and edges represent dependencies between them. Context-sensitivity is achieved by simultaneously applying function cloning and computing CFL-reachability in a novel way. We address scalability by developing various effective summary-based optimizations, while at the same time preserving all pointer and context information in the compact VFG representation so they can be easily computed on-demand. In contrast to existing clone-based and CFL-based approaches, flow-sensitivity is easily integrated in our approach by using a flow-sensitive VFG where each value flow edge is computed in a flow-sensitive manner [20, 40]. Last but not least, we apply context-sensitivity to both local variables and heap objects and propose a new approximation for heap cloning.

In our approach, context-sensitivity is achieved effectively as follows. We apply function cloning at different call-sites where the local value flows of the callee function (i.e., value flows within the function) may be computed differently. This ensures that all local value flows become context-independent so that each function can be analyzed individually. Our approach avoids the creation of redundant clones, as per existing approaches [4, 36], which clone functions based on each distinct call path to the call-site. With our value flow representation and function cloning, we can achieve context-sensitivity by simply applying CFL-reachability to call-sites, where the call-sites of each pair of call/return edges on a value flow path need to match with each other. This is the well known balanced-parentheses problem in CFL-reachability [29] and it can be computed efficiently with various optimizations developed in this paper. In contrast, existing CFL-based approaches apply CFL-reachability to call-sites and heap accesses at the same time. As a result, it is much more expensive to compute CFL-reachability in those approaches and also much more difficult to develop effective optimization techniques for them.

We prove that our approach can achieve context-sensitivity without loss of precision, i.e., it is as precise as inlining all function calls for recursion-free programs. We implement a context, flow- and field-sensitive analysis in LLVM [16] and evaluate its efficiency and precision using standard CPU2006 benchmarks. Our experimental results suggest that the analysis is much faster than the existing Bootstrapping approach [14], and it enables much more effective compiler optimizations in LLVM. To summarize, this paper makes the following contributions:

- We propose a new method for context-sensitive pointer analysis. The method can be easily extended to achieve flow-sensitivity at the same time. We prove that our approach can effectively achieve context-sensitivity without loss of precision.

- We apply context-sensitivity to both pointer variables and heap objects, and propose a new approximation for heap cloning.

- We develop an efficient algorithm, as well as a set of optimization techniques, to compute flow-sensitive and context-sensitive pointer information efficiently. We implement our algorithm in LLVM and show that our analysis can achieve very high precision and scale to large applications.

The rest of the paper is organized as follows: Section 2 introduces the value flow formulation. Section 3 shows how context-sensitivity can be effectively achieved. We present the algorithm in Section 4 and evaluate our implementation in Section 5. Section 6 reviews related work and Section 7 concludes the paper.

2. The Value Flow Formulation

We describe our formulation of pointer analysis using a small language which captures the important properties of the C language. Functions are constant values defined by the expression $F = func(fp_1...fp_n) \Rightarrow (rp_1...rp_m)\mathcal{S}^*$, where F is the function definition, fp_i are formal parameters, and rp_i are formal return parameters. Note that we have generalized function definitions in C to allow functions with multiple returns. Function calls are represented by the CALL statement $C : (x_1...x_m) = f(ap_1...ap_n)$, where C is the label of the call-site, f is the called value, ap_i are actual parameters and x_i are actual returns.

$$
\begin{aligned}
\mathcal{P} &:= \mathcal{F}* \\
\mathcal{F} &:= F = func(fp_1...fp_n) \Rightarrow (rp_1...rp_m)\mathcal{S}^* \\
\mathcal{S} &:= p_A = \&A & \text{BASE} \\
& \quad\; p = q & \text{ASSIGN} \\
& \quad\; *p = x & \text{STORE} \\
& \quad\; y = *q & \text{LOAD} \\
& \quad\; C : (x_1...x_m) = f(ap_1...ap_n) & \text{CALL}
\end{aligned}
$$

The above set of statements are sufficient for context-sensitive pointer analysis for C. More complicated pointer-manipulating statements can be decomposed into these basic instructions. Nested pointer dereferences are eliminated by introducing auxiliary variables. Allocation of a heap object is modelled by regarding the allocation site as a special memory object.

To support flow-sensitivity, we also need to consider the control flows of the program as in [20]. For clarity, control flow statements are not modeled in our formulation and we explain how to extend our formulation for flow-sensitive analysis in Section 4.1.

2.1 Insensitive Value Flows

In a value flow graph (VFG), values flow along edges between memory objects and pointer variables (represented as nodes). We say that q flows to p, denoted $q \rightarrow p$, if the value of q is assigned to variable p. We say that pointer p points to object A if there exists a value flow path from the object node A to the pointer node p in the VFG, denoted as $A \rightarrow^* p$. The set of objects that p may point to is called the points-to set of p, denoted as $pts(p)$.

Memory objects flow to pointer variables directly via BASE ($p_A = \&A$) instructions, and pointer variables flow to each other either directly, via ASSIGN ($p = q$) instructions, or indirectly, via STORE ($*p = x$) and LOAD ($y = *q$) instructions, as illustrated by the following rules. Without loss of generality, we assume that for each memory object, a unique pointer variable is initialized to take the address of the object and it is accessed via LOAD and STORE instructions to the introduced variable. As such, in a VFG, object nodes are nodes without incoming edges.

$$
\text{BASE } \frac{p_A = \&A}{A \rightarrow p_A} \qquad \text{ASSIGN } \frac{p = q}{q \rightarrow p}
$$

$$
\text{INDIRECT } \frac{\begin{array}{cc} A \rightarrow^* p & A \rightarrow^* q \\ *p = x & y = *q \end{array}}{x \rightarrow y}
$$

The BASE and ASSIGN rules describe the direct value flows for BASE and ASSIGN instructions, respectively. The INDIRECT rule handles pointer dereferences via LOAD and STORE instructions. It states that x can flow to variable y indirectly via pointer dereferences, only if x is stored to a memory object A first (via pointer p) and y is loaded from the same memory object afterwards (via pointer q). Note that the above rules are formulated for insensitive analyses. Next we will show how they are extended for context-sensitivity.

2.2 Context-sensitive Value Flows

We distinguish intra- and inter-procedural value flows for the sake of context-sensitivity.

$$
\text{CALL } \frac{\begin{array}{c} F = func(fp_1...fp_n) \Rightarrow (rp_1...rp_m)\mathcal{S}* \\ F \rightarrow^* f \\ C : (x_1...x_m) = f(ap_1...ap_n) \end{array}}{\wedge_{1 \leq i \leq n} ap_i \xrightarrow{C_{in}} fp_i \qquad \wedge_{1 \leq i \leq m} rp_i \xrightarrow{C_{out}} x_i}
$$

```
List {int val, List *next};
void createList(){
    List *fst=new(List);
    fst->next=NULL;
    List *snd=new(List);
    snd->next=NULL;
C1:List *tmp=movCarCdr(fst,
                       snd);
}

List * movCarCdr(List *dst,
                 List *src){
    List *dcdr=dst->next;
    List *scdr=src->next;
    src->next=dcdr;
    dst->next=src;
    return scdr;
}
```

(a)

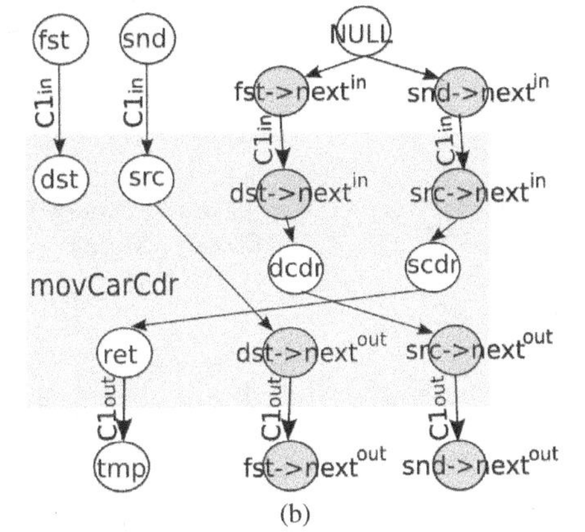

(b)

```
void mangleList(){
    List *fst=new(List);
    List *snd=new(List);
    fst->next=snd;
    snd->next=NULL;
    List *arg=(...)?fst:snd;
C2:List *tmp=movCarCdr(arg,
                       snd);
}
```

(c)

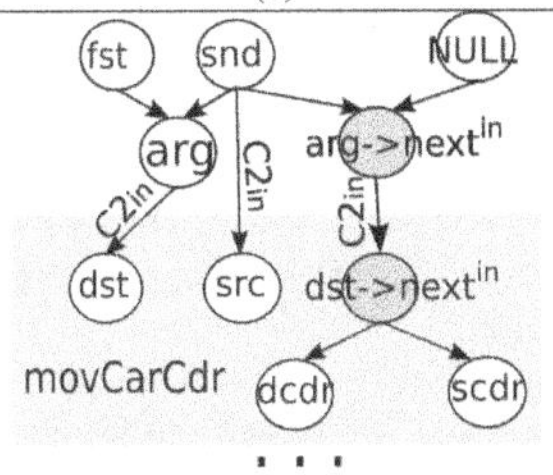

(d)

Figure 1. An Example.

The CALL rule models inter-procedural value flows, i.e., value flows introduced via CALL statements. The notation $ap \xrightarrow{C_{in}} fp$ denotes that ap (actual parameter in the caller function) is assigned to variable fp (formal parameter in the callee function) at call-site C, e.g., parameter passing, and the variable fp is said to be a *function input* of the callee function. Similarly, the edge $rp \xrightarrow{C_{out}} out$ represents value flows from the callee function to the caller at C, e.g., function returns, where variable rp is called a *function output* and out is the returned value at call-site C. In our formulation, a function is allowed to have multiple returns. If the callee function creates a heap object that may escape, the created heap object O_H is regarded as a return of the function. A variable p_H will be introduced at its call-site C in the caller function and we have $O_H \xrightarrow{C_{out}} p_H$. Conceptually, for each global variable, a copy is introduced in every function that may access the variable and there exists inter-procedural flow edges between these introduced copies.

Note that inter-procedural value flows can be introduced not only directly via function parameters or return values, but also indirectly via dereferences of those variables. We use a mechanism similar to [5, 11, 38] for inter-procedural indirect value flows. The idea is to introduce auxiliary variables for pointers that may be dereferenced. Thus inter-procedural indirect value flows are represented explicitly as value flows between introduced auxiliary variables and they can be processed in the same fashion as normal function parameter passing or returns.

We introduce auxiliary variables for a function call as follows:

Rule 1. For function input fp where $ap \xrightarrow{C_{in}} fp$ and $pts(ap) \neq \emptyset$, we introduce auxiliary variables $fp*^{in}$ (as extra formal parameter) and $ap*^{in}$ (as extra actual parameter) where $ap*^{in} = *ap$, $*fp = fp*^{in}$ and $ap*^{in} \xrightarrow{C_{in}} fp*^{in}$. In addition, if fp may be stored in the callee function, we introduce $fp*^{out}$ and $ap*^{out}$ where $fp*^{out} = *fp$, $*ap = ap*^{out}$, and $fp*^{out} \xrightarrow{C_{out}} ap*^{out}$. For a heap object O_H where $O_H \xrightarrow{C_{out}} p_H$, we also introduce $O_H*^{out} \xrightarrow{C_{out}} p_H*^{out}$.

The introduced auxiliary variables are regarded as normal function parameters or return values. For introduced extra formal parameter $fp*^{in}$, we may introduce auxiliary variable $fp *^{in} *^{in}$ for its dereference. The number of auxiliary variables need to be bounded for termination, and we will show how to bound the number without loss of precision in Section 2.3. It is only necessary to introduce auxiliary variables for function inputs (escaping objects) that have been dereferenced. Note that extra LOAD or STORE instructions are introduced for the auxiliary variables. The variables $ap*^{in}$ and $fp*^{in}$ are introduced in such a way that we have $*fp = *ap$ at the entry of the callee function. They represent indirect value flows from the caller function into the callee function. Similarly, after introducing the LOAD and STORE instructions for $fp*^{out}$ and $ap*^{out}$, we have $*ap = *fp$ at the return site to capture side effects of the callee function.

Let us look at the example in Figure 1(a). Function `movCarCdr` removes the head from one linked list (parameter `src`), and insert it into another linked list (parameter `dst`). Function `createList` calls function `movCarCdr` at call-site C_1 with two single nodes. Figure 1(b) gives the VFG (which is computed flow-sensitively) for the example, where the introduced auxiliary variables are highlighted in grey. By introducing $\texttt{fst->next}^{\texttt{in}} \xrightarrow{C_{1in}} \texttt{dst->next}^{\texttt{in}}$, the `NULL` value written to the `next` field of object `fst` can now flow to variables in the callee function `movCarCdr`, e.g., `dcdr`. Similarly, the inter-procedural value flow edge $\texttt{dst->next}^{\texttt{out}} \xrightarrow{C_{1out}} \texttt{fst->next}^{\texttt{out}}$ enables values written to parameter `dst` in the callee function, i.e., parameter variable `src`, flow to its caller function.

Introduction of auxiliary variables enables us to analyze each function individually: for each function input fp, we assume there exists a symbolic object whose address is taken by fp and dereferences of fp are regarded as values stored to or loaded from the symbolic object. This is a key step to performance and scalability.

2.3 Soundness and Precision

For recursive data structures such as linked lists, the number of auxiliary variables that need to be introduced may be infinite. As shown in Figure 2, we introduce an auxiliary variable $\texttt{L->next}^{\texttt{in}}$ as the dereference of formal parameter `L`. Since the introduced auxiliary variable $\texttt{L->next}^{\texttt{in}}$ is also dereferenced in the function, we may introduce another auxiliary variable $\texttt{L->next}^{\texttt{in}}\texttt{->next}^{\texttt{in}}$. The procedure of introducing auxiliary variables is recursive, and the number of introduced auxiliary variables needs to be bounded to guarantee termination.

The approaches in previous works [5, 11, 38] bound the number of auxiliary variables in a similar fashion. The idea is to introduce auxiliary variable for the same object once. For the example in Fig-

```
List {int val, List * next};
void traverse(List * L) {
    List *tmp=L;
    while (tmp) {
        tmp = tmp->next;
        . . .
    }
}
```

Figure 2. An Example with Possible Infinite Auxiliary Variables.

ure 2, L->$next^{in}$->$next^{in}$ will not be introduced if L->$next^{in}$ refer to the same memory object as L. This approach guarantees soundness. However, precision is sacrificed. One of the contributions in this paper is that we highlight the cause of imprecision and propose a solution to address this problem. With our method, both precision and soundness can be guaranteed as shown in the next subsections.

2.3.1 Introducing Auxiliary Variables

Lemma 1. *In a context-sensitive analysis, introducing auxiliary variables as in Rule 1 is both sound and precise: For all pointer variables in the original program, the computed results are the same as in the transformed original program where all function calls are inlined.*

Proof. By introducing auxiliary variables, we have effectively introduced pair of LOAD and STORE instructions into the original program such that $*X = *Y$. This is both sound and precise if we have $pts(Y) \neq \emptyset$ and $pts(X) = pts(Y)$. For $ap \xrightarrow{C_{in}} fp$, in a context-sensitive analysis, $pts(ap) = pts(fp)$ always holds as only variable ap is assigned to fp at call-site C. Hence introducing $*ap = *fp$ and $*fp = *ap$ at call-site C is both sound and safe. A similar proof is applied to escaping heap objects. □

However, imprecision may be introduced when we try to bound the number of introduced variables by merging introduced auxiliary variables for different arguments/parameters together. Previous work universally adopts a similar idea to bound the number of introduced auxiliary variables: only introduce auxiliary variables for the same object once. If an object is pointed to by two different arguments, i.e., aliased arguments, auxiliary variables are only introduced for one of them and indirect value flows via the other argument will be merged if no other object flows to that argument. This approach is sound but may result in spurious value flows.

In Figure 1(c), we modify our example by calling function `movCarCdr` differently. The two arguments alias. The first argument `arg` points to both objects, `fst` and `snd`, and the second argument is `snd`. As a result, auxiliary variable `arg`->$next^{in}$ are only introduced for the first argument `arg`. The resulting VFG is given in Figure 1(d), where there exists a spurious value flow path `snd` $\rightarrow^*$ `scdr`. This happens because in merging auxiliary variables introduced for different parameters, they assume that their aliases also alias with each other. However, alias relation is not transitive. In the example, `fst` $\rightarrow^*$ `dst` and `dst` aliases with `src`, but there is no alias between `fst` and `src`. Hence `snd`, which is stored

into `fst`, cannot flow to `scdr`, which is loaded from `src`. Therefore, we apply the following rule to bound the number of auxiliary variables without loss of precision:

Rule 2. For function input fp_1 where $ap_1 \xrightarrow{C_{in}} fp_1$ and $pts(ap_1) \neq \emptyset$, auxiliary variables will be introduced at call-site C if there exists no function input fp_2 where $ap_2 \xrightarrow{C_{in}} fp_2$ and $pts(ap_2) = pts(ap_1)$. Otherwise, we reuse the auxiliary variables introduced for ap_2 and fp_2.

It may sound expensive as the number of variables introduced can be exponential. The number is bounded to the number of combinations of all objects, i.e., the number of distinct points-to sets. However, if a parameter points to a recursive data structure, very often the parameter and its dereferences (i.e., introduced auxiliary variables) point to the same set of memory objects. As a result, the number of auxiliary variables introduced is small in practice as shown in our experiments over large applications.

Theorem 1. *In a context-sensitive analysis, bounding the number of auxiliary variables using Rule 2 is both sound and precise.*

Proof. In pointer analysis, variables can be safely merged together without loss of precision if and only if they always have the same points-to set. If we have $pts(X) = pts(Y)$, then $pts(*X) = pts(*Y)$ also holds. For $ap_1 \xrightarrow{C_{in}} fp_1$ and $ap_2 \xrightarrow{C_{in}} fp_2$, if $pts(ap_1) = pts(ap_2)$, the auxiliary variables introduced for ap_1 and ap_2 always have the same points-to set and they can be merged together without loss of precision. In a context-sensitive analysis, we also have $pts(fp_1) = pts(ap_1)$ and $pts(fp_2) = pts(ap_2)$ at call-site C, hence we can also merge the auxiliary variables introduced for fp_1 and fp_2 together at C. □

2.3.2 Computing Value Flows

In this section, we show how to extend the INDIRECT rule so that all value flows are computed context-sensitively. Recall that for each function input variable, a symbolic object is introduced whose address is taken by that variable and dereferences of the function input are regarded as LOADs or STOREs to the symbolic object. However, at a call-site, if two input variables of the callee function alias, values stored into one may also flow to values loaded via the other. Hence at a call-site where the actual parameters to function inputs A and B alias, we introduce a new value flow rule:

$$\text{INDIRECT}_{\text{ALIAS}} \quad \frac{\{A, B\}_{\text{ALIAS}} \quad A \rightarrow^* p \quad B \rightarrow^* q}{*p = x \quad y = *q}$$
$$x \rightarrow y$$

The INDIRECT$_{\text{alias}}$ rule guarantees soundness but may lead to spurious value flows. Let us revisit the modified example in Figure 1(c). At call-site C_2, the two parameters `dst` and `src` alias. The introduced auxiliary variable `dst`->$next^{in}$ is regarded as an STORE to `dst`, and `scdr` is loaded from `src`. As a result, there is an spurious value flow edge `dst`->$next^{in}$ $\rightarrow$ `scdr` as well as the spurious value flow path `snd` $\rightarrow^*$ `scdr`.

Hence, we apply the following rule to compute value flows without sacrificing soundness or precision:

Rule 3. Given a STORE $*p = x$ and a LOAD $y = *q$, if x is an introduced auxiliary variable as function input or y is an introduced auxiliary variable as function output, apply the INDIRECT rule. Otherwise, apply the INDIRECT$_{\text{ALIAS}}$ rule.

With the above rule, in the callee function `movCarCdr`, all feasible indirect value flows involve introduced auxiliary variables for parameter `dst` or `src`. As a result, at call-site C_2, the VFG of function `movCarCdr` is computed the same as the one computed at C_1 in Figure 1(b). No spurious value flow is introduced.

Theorem 2. *In a context-sensitive analysis, computing indirect value flows with Rule 3 guarantees soundness and precision.*

Proof. We only prove soundness here and a similar proof can be derived for precision. Given $*p = x$ and $y = *q$, we have $x \to y$ if there exists A such that $A \to^* p$ and $A \to^* q$. The theorem trivially holds if A is in the same function as x and y, or if both p and q alias with the same parameter. Otherwise, assume that $*p = x$ is in *caller* and $y = *q$ in *callee*. There must exist a function input fp such that we have $A \to^* fp$ and $fp \to^* q$. According to Rule 3, there must exist a value flow path from $x \to^* fp*^{in} \to^* y$, where $fp*^{in}$ is the introduced auxiliary variable. Similarly, if $*p = x$ is in *callee* and $y = *q$ in *caller*, there must exist a value flow path $x \to^* fp*^{out} \to^* y$. If x and y are in the same function, then we have two inputs $fp1$ and $fp2$ such that $fp1 \to^* x$, $fp2 \to^* y$, $A \to^* fp1$ and $A \to^* fp2$. Hence $fp1$ and $fp2$ must alias with each other. According to Rule 3, there exists value flow $x \to^* y$. □

3. Context-Sensitivity

Conceptually, our approach to context-sensitivity involves two steps. We transform the program by cloning functions at different call-sites where their local value flows may be computed differently (Rule 3). With this transformation, local value flows of a function become context-independent. Hence each function can be analyzed individually. In the second step, we apply context-matching to inter-procedural value flow paths. For a feasible value flow path, the call-site of each pair of call and return edges on the path need to match with each other. This ensures that pointer values computed in one call-site cannot erroneously propagate to other call-sites of the same function. The two steps together guarantee context-sensitivity.

In practice, the above two steps are inter-dependent and need to be performed together. We need context-sensitive pointer information to effectively determine when function cloning needs to be applied, which in turn is required to compute such information.

3.1 Function Cloning

We clone functions at call-sites where their local value flows may be computed differently. As such, all local value flows become context-independent. In contrast, existing cloning-based approaches [4, 36] create a function clone at each distinct call path. Our approach avoids explicitly representing the exponentially large number of call paths in a program and only a small number of function clones are created as shown in our experiments in Section 5.

As discussed in Section 2.3, local value flows of a function may be computed differently given different input values.

Theorem 3. *The local value flows of a function are the same at different call-sites if 1) the set of introduced input variables are identical, 2) aliases between function inputs (represented as alias sets) are the same, and 3) for input variables which are function pointers, their points-to sets are the same.*

Proof. The first two conditions guarantee that local indirect value flows within the function are computed exactly the same, according to the INDIRECT and INDIRECT$_{ALIAS}$ value flow rules (Rule 3). The third condition ensures that all CALL statements in the function also behave the same, i.e., same value flows introduced via CALL statements. Since local direct value flows introduced via BASE and ASSIGN statements always exist regardless of the call-sites. The local value flows of the function will be computed the same. □

As for our example in Figure 1(a) and Figure 1(c), the function `movCarCdr` is called at two different locations, C_1 in

`createList`, and C_2 in `mangleList`. Since the function inputs alias differently at C_1 and C_2, a function clone $\widehat{\texttt{movCarCdr}}$ is created at C_2 where its local value flows are computed with the given alias set $\{\texttt{dst}, \texttt{src}, \texttt{dst->next}^{in}\}$. For this example, the value flows of $\widehat{\texttt{movCarCdr}}$ happen to be identical to that of `movCarCdr` in Figure 1(b).

Various summary-based approaches [11, 25, 38, 40] use methods similar to ours to differentiate calling contexts. In contrast to our approach, those approaches compute parameterized summaries for each function, which are then instantiated at their call-sites to create the summaries for their callers. Compact function summaries are key to performance. However, it also suggests that some useful information may not be preserved in the summary and the computed result, may not preserve enough context information to precisely answer queries such as "do the two variables alias on a particular call path?". In addition, it is very difficult to compute a full compact function summary, especially when flow-sensitivity is needed. One solution is to use partial summary functions [38]. We bring this idea one step further by cloning the function instead of generating partial summaries. This enables us to compute precise pointer information efficiently without loss of generality.

3.2 Context Matching

By explicitly representing indirect value flows in the VFG and with our function cloning, context-sensitive pointer analysis can be simplified to a well known balanced-parentheses problem in CFL-reachability [29]. The CFL-reachability formulation is an extended graph reachability problem: graph edges are annotated with labels and two nodes in the graph are connected only if there exists a path such that the concatenation of the labels on the edges of the path is acceptable in a defined context-free language. We apply CFL-reachability to the VFG with a simple language for context matching [29], where the call-site C of each pair of inter-procedural value flow edges, $\xrightarrow{C_{in}}$ and $\xrightarrow{C_{out}}$, need to match with each other.

One advantage of the CFL-reachability formulation is that context (i.e., call path) and pointer information are implicitly encoded in a compact graph representation and they can be computed on-demand. Existing CFL-based context-sensitive pointer analyses [32, 39] define a language using a grammar to model both function calls and memory accesses at the same time. They can be very efficient for some applications where we only need to compute pointer information for a small subset of variables. However, if we need the precise pointer information for all variables, CFL-based pointer analysis is generally more expensive as it has $O(L^3 N^3)$ complexity [29], where L is the size of the grammar and N is the size of the graph.

Optimizations. We improve performance by computing CFL-reachability only for feasible inter-procedural value flow paths. In addition, since all local value flows become context-independent with our function cloning, we can develop effective optimizations to further improve its performance. Note that those optimizations are not applicable to existing CFL-based pointer analyses.

- We summarize the local value flow path $x \to^* y$ as a value flow edge while all other nodes on the path can be discarded. This greatly reduces the number of nodes visited during context matching, without loss of precision. Note that the summarized value flows from function inputs to outputs are effectively transfer functions as in summary-based approaches.

- We represent pointer values with respect to the values of function inputs, i.e., the points-to set of a variable is the set of function inputs it aliases. This greatly improves performance and reduces memory footprint. We compute full points-to sets for function pointers only, while the full points-to sets for other variables can be computed on-demand as in other demand-driven pointer analyses [32, 41].

- We memoise matching inter-procedural value flow paths. Specifically, for a matching value flow path $ap \xrightarrow{C_{in}} fp \rightarrow^* ret \xrightarrow{C_{out}} out$, a local value flow edge $ap \rightarrow out$ will be introduced (in the caller function) as a summary of the path. This enables further optimization opportunities.

It can be proved that the above two steps together guarantee context-sensitivity: for recursion free programs, the analysis is as precise as inlining all function calls. For recursive programs, precise context-sensitive analysis is undecidable. Similar to [32, 36], we handle recursion by regarding function calls and returns within a recursive cycle as gotos. During the analysis, when recursion is detected, inter-procedural value flows within the recursive cycle are treated as intra-procedural value flows and the value flows of all functions in the cycle are computed together insensitively.

3.3 Heap Cloning

Recall that if a heap object O_H in the callee function escapes, a variable p_H is introduced at its call-site C in the caller function and we have $O_H \xrightarrow{C_{out}} p_H$. With heap cloning, for $O_H \xrightarrow{C_{1out}} p'_H$ and $O_H \xrightarrow{C_{2out}} p''_H$, two distinct heap objects will be introduced as the copy of O_H at the two different call-sites C_1 and C_2, respectively. As a result, heap objects created at different call-sites are distinguished. In contrast, the edge $O_H \xrightarrow{C_{out}} p_H$ is simply regarded as a local value flow edge if heap cloning is not supported. Previous works [17, 26] show that heap cloning can significantly improve precision.

```
char * sm_rpool_allocblock_x(rpool, size){
    p = sm_malloc(sizeof(SM_POOLHDR_T)+size);
    rpool->sm_pool = p;
    return p+sizeof(SM_POOLHDR_T);
}
void * sm_rpool_malloc_x(rpool, size){
O¹: if (...) return sm_malloc(...);
O²: if (...) return sm_rpool_allocblock_x(...);
O³: return sm_rpool_allocblock_x(...);
}
HDR * allocheader(...){
C₁:    h=sm_rpool_malloc_x(rp, sizeof(HDR));
C₂:    ... = sm_rpool_malloc_x(rp,sizeof(HDR));
    ...
}
```

Figure 3. Code snippet from sendmail 8.17.

However, algorithms with heap cloning often suffer from scalability problems as the number of heap objects grows exponentially [17, 31, 32]. Existing analyses trade precision for scalability in various ways. The most common approach is the K-limiting approach [8, 31], which restricts the depth of the call paths to K, and call paths deeper than K are not distinguished. In practice, K is often set to a small number (2 or 3) for scalability. However, many applications, such as sendmail 8.17 in Figure 3, use 5 levels of wrapper functions (some are not shown in Figure 3) to support their customized memory allocation schemes. It is not practical to set K to such a large number. The authors in [17] propose an alternative solution which merges heap objects with equivalent structures to avoid creating too many heap objects. Their approach can distinguish full acyclic call paths and is very fast. However, it is based on a unification-based approximation [33] to merge as many objects as possible. Compared to inclusion-based analysis, unification-based analysis is much less precise.

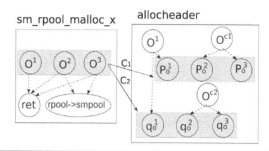

Figure 4. Heap cloning for sendmail 8.17 with one cloned object per call-site. Solid edge represent inter-procedural value flows.

We propose a different tradeoff for heap cloning. Similar to [17], we merge the clones for distinct objects O_{H_1} and O_{H_2} together if they *escape in the exact same way*, i.e., clones of O_{H_1} and O_{H_2} can be merged together if for any flow path $O_{H_1} \rightarrow^* ret$ where ret is a function output, we have $O_{H_2} \rightarrow^* ret$. This is both sound and precise as the merged objects are always pointed to by the same set of pointers. As in our example Figure 3, the three objects O^1, O^2 and O^3 in function sm_rpool_malloc_x may escape. As a result, in Figure 4, at C_1, three pointer variables P_{O1}, P_{O2} and P_{O3} are introduced where $O^1 \xrightarrow{C_{1out}} P_{O1}$, $O^2 \xrightarrow{C_{1out}} P_{O2}$, and $O^3 \xrightarrow{C_{1out}} P_{O3}$. Since the two objects O^2 and O^3 escape in the same way, only one clone O^{C_1} is created for them at C_1.

Instead of bounding the depth of the call paths, we limit the number of objects to be cloned at each call-site. As in Figure 4, the number of clones is limited to one per call-site. Hence we do not create clones for O^1. This approximation works well in practice as many applications use deeply-nested wrapper functions on top of the C malloc function to create one or two objects. Some functions may potentially create many heap objects. However, very often only a few of them are created at runtime. Hence many of the created objects escape in the exact same way and their clones can be merged together. In addition, if an object escapes in a very complicated way then it is very hard to be analyzed precisely. In that case, heap cloning will not be very helpful in improving analysis precision.

4. The Algorithm

In our algorithm VF-PTRANALYSIS (Algorithm 1), the two interleaving steps for context-sensitivity are performed together. We start our analysis with only direct value flows. Since all local value flows are context-independent, we compute a local VFG for each individual function. During the analysis, new value flows will be introduced and new functions may be cloned. In the end, the algorithm terminates when all local value flows for all functions are computed.

In Line 2, the procedural INITIALIZE is called to initialize all direct value flow edges. The while loop in Lines 3 - 10 performs the analysis. The local VFG of a given function is computed in COMPUTEVFG (Line 5) , where function clones may be created and added to $funcSet$. For each function f, we maintain two sets of memory objects, $f.directSet$ and $f.indSet$ for those objects in f whose direct and indirect value flows need to be computed, respectively.

Next, context matching is effectively applied at every call-site to f by calling the procedure CONTEXTMATCHING (Lines 6 - 10). Heap objects escaping from f will be cloned and new local value flows will be introduced in the caller function for matching inter-procedural value flow paths. As a result, the caller function needs

Algorithm 1 Context-sensitive pointer analysis

Let $funcSet$ be the set of all functions
Let $f.directSet$ include all objects of f and $f.indSet$ be $\emptyset$
Let $st(x), ld(x)$ be two empty sets for each variable x
1: **procedure** VF-PTRANALYSIS
2:     INITIALIZE()
3:     **while** $funcSet \neq \emptyset$ **do**
4:       Select f, and remove it from $funcSet$
5:       COMPUTEVFG(f)
6:       **for** each call-site C where f is a target **do**
7:         Let $caller$ be the caller function
8:         CONTEXTMATCHING($caller$, f, C)
9:       **end for**
10:    **end while**
11: **end procedure**
12: **procedure** INITIALIZE
13:    **for** each function $f \in funcSet$ **do**
14:      **for** each BASE instruction $p_A = \&A$ in f **do**
15:        Add edge $A \rightarrow p_A$
16:      **end for**
17:      **for** each ASSIGN instruction $p = q$ in f **do**
18:        Add edge $p \rightarrow q$
19:      **end for**
20:      **for** each STORE instruction $*p = x$ in f **do**
21:        $st(p) := st(p) \bigcup \{x\}$
22:      **end for**
23:      **for** each LOAD instruction $x = *p$ in f **do**
24:        $ld(p) := ld(p) \bigcup \{x\}$
25:      **end for**
26:      **for** each call-site C in f **do**
27:        Add value flow $ap \xrightarrow{C_{in}} fp$ for parameter passing
28:        Add value flow $ret \xrightarrow{C_{out}} out$ for the callee's return value
29:      **end for**
30:    **end for**
31: **end procedure**

Algorithm 2 Compute Local Value Flows of a Function

1: **procedure** COMPUTEVFG(f)
2:    **while** $\{f.directSet \bigcup f.indSet\} \neq \emptyset$ **do**
3:      TRAVERSEVFG(f)
4:      Let C be a call-site in f and $callee$ be the callee function
5:      **if** input values of $callee$ changed as Theorem 3 **then**
6:        CLONEFUNC(f, $callee$, C)
7:      **end if**
8:      UPDATEVFG(f)
9:    **end while**
10: **end procedure**
11: **procedure** TRAVERSEVFG(f)
12:    **while** $f.directSet \neq \emptyset$ **do**
13:      Select O, and remove it from $f.directSet$
14:      Let $\mathcal{V}$ be the set of variables in f newly reachable from O
15:      **for** each variable v in $\mathcal{V}$ **do**
16:        $pts(v) := pts(v) \bigcup \{O\}$
17:        $st(O) := st(O) \bigcup st(v)$
18:        $ld(O) := ld(O) \bigcup ld(v)$
19:        **if** $\{st(v) \bigcup ld(v)\} \neq \emptyset$ **then**
20:          $f.indSet := f.indSet \bigcup \{O\}$
21:        **end if**
22:      **end for**
23:    **end while**
24: **end procedure**
25: **procedure** UPDATEVFG(f)
26:    **while** $f.indSet \neq \emptyset$ **do**
27:      Select O, and remove it from $f.indSet$
28:      $stset := st(O)$
29:      $ldset := ld(O)$
30:      **if** O is function input which aliases with another input O_a **then**
31:        $stset := stset \bigcup st(O_a)$
32:        $ldset := stset \bigcup ld(O_a)$
33:      **end if**
34:      **for** each variable $p \in stset$ **do**
35:        **for** each variable $q \in ldset$ **do**
36:          **if** indirect value flow exists as in Rule 3 **then**
            // Reachability analysis can be applied to compute
            // value flows flow-sensitively
37:            ADDEDGE(f, $p \rightarrow q$)
38:          **end if**
39:        **end for**
40:      **end for**
41:    **end while**
42: **end procedure**
43: **procedure** ADDEDGE(f, $p \rightarrow q$)
44:    Add $p \rightarrow q$ to the local VFG of f
45:    $f.directSet := f.directSet \bigcup pts(p)$
46: **end procedure**

to be re-analyzed. Since the algorithm always introduces new edges into the value flow graph, it is guaranteed to terminate.

4.1 Computing Local Value Flows

In Algorithm 2, the procedure COMPUTEVFG computes local value flows for each function f individually. In Line 3, local value flows of f are computed in procedure TRAVERSEVFG by traversing its local VFG. In Lines 4 - 7, we check at every call-site in f whether input values of the callee function have changed or not, and function cloning is performed accordingly (Line 6). The local VFG of f is then updated by introducing indirect value flows of each object, i.e., flows from variables stored into an object to those loaded from it (Line 8). As a result, the value flows of some memory objects need to be updated. The algorithm stops at a fixed point where the local VFG is complete and no more indirect value flows can be introduced.

In procedure TRAVERSEVFG, only local flow edges in f are followed during the traversal. The points-to sets of all visited pointer variables are updated (Line 16). For efficiently computing indirect value flows, we also keep track of the set of variables stored into an object and the set of variables loaded from it (Lines 17 and 18). In Lines 19 - 21, those objects whose indirect value flows need to be computed are included in $f.indSet$.

The procedure UPDATEVFG updates the local VFG with new indirect flow edges. Indirect value flows are computed according to the rule in Rule 3 (Lines 28 - 40). When the local VFG is updated with new value flow edge $p \rightarrow q$, as shown in ADDEDGE, the value flows of all memory objects that are pointed-to by p need to be updated (Line 45).

Flow-sensitivity. Note that in our approach, flow-sensitivity can be easily achieved by adopting the method proposed in [20] with small extensions. We compute a flow-sensitive local VFG for each function where each value flow is computed flow-sensitively. Direct value flows can be trivially computed in a flow-sensitive manner after translating the program into static single assignment form (SSA). For indirect value flows, each STORE and LOAD instruction in the original program is represented as a distinct node in the VFG and a sparse data-flow analysis is employed to check whether a STORE can reach a LOAD in the control flow graph without being *killed* by another STORE.

It is said that a STORE $*p = x$ to object O can *kill* all previous values stored to O if O represents a singleton address and the dereferenced pointer p points to object O only. This is also referred to as *strong update*. Hence for the sake of flow-sensitivity, we extend the rule in Theorem 3 where *must aliases* and *may aliases* between function inputs are differentiated and we also check whether a function input can be strongly updated in the callee function or not. To the best of our knowledge, flow-sensitivity is not supported in existing CFL-based or cloning-based pointer analyses.

4.2 Function Cloning

Algorithm 3 Function Cloning

Let $\widehat{X}$ denote the clone of X
1: **procedure** CLONEFUNC($caller, callee, C$)
2:     Let fp be a function input and $ap \xrightarrow{C_{in}} fp$
3:     Let ret be a function output and $ret \xrightarrow{C_{out}} out$
4:     **if** $\nexists \widehat{callee}$ with the same input values as at C **then**
5:         $funcSet := funcSet \bigcup \{\widehat{callee}\}$
6:         Duplicate the VFG of $callee$ to that of $\widehat{callee}$
7:         **if** auxiliary variables need to be introduced for $\widehat{fp}$ **then**
8:             Add $ap*^{in} \xrightarrow{C_{in}} \widehat{fp*}^{in}, fp*^{out} \xrightarrow{C_{out}} \widehat{ap*}^{out}$ as in Rule 1
9:             $caller.indSet := caller.indSet \bigcup pts(ap)$
10:            $\widehat{callee}.indSet := \widehat{callee}.indSet \bigcup \{\widehat{fp}\}$
11:         **else if** Aliases of $\widehat{fp}$ changed **then**
12:            $\widehat{callee}.indSet := \widehat{callee}.indSet \bigcup \{\widehat{fp}\}$
13:         **end if**
14:     **else**
15:         **if** $\exists \widehat{fp*}^{in}, \widehat{fp*}^{out}$ and $\nexists fp*^{in}, fp*^{out}$ **then**
16:            Add $ap*^{in} \xrightarrow{C_{in}} \widehat{fp*}^{in}, \widehat{fp*}^{out} \xrightarrow{C_{out}} ap*^{out}$
17:            $caller.indSet := caller.indSet \bigcup pts(ap)$
18:         **else if** $\exists \widehat{fp} \to^* \widehat{ret}$ and $\nexists fp \to^* ret$ **then**
19:            ADDEDGE($caller, ap \to out$)
20:         **end if**
21:     **end if**
22:     Remove $ap \xrightarrow{C_{in}} fp$ and add $ap \xrightarrow{C_{in}} \widehat{fp}$
23:     Remove $ret \xrightarrow{C_{out}} out$ and add $\widehat{ret} \xrightarrow{C_{out}} out$
24: **end procedure**

Property 1. *All local value flows of function callee are included in its clone $\widehat{callee}$.*

By construction, Property 1 is enforced when a function is cloned. This is both precise and safe as at a call-site, input values to the callee function may change only if 1) new auxiliary variables need to be introduced, or 2) there are new aliases between function inputs, or 3) there are extra targets for a function pointer. In all three cases, previously computed value flows still exist.

As shown in CLONEFUNC in Algorithm 3, we duplicate all previously computed value flows to the local VFG of the cloned function (Lines 5 and 6). As such, the function clone does not need to be analyzed from scratch. In Line 8, auxiliary variables are introduced as in Rule 1: the auxiliary variables for input variable $fp1$ will be merged into those of $fp2$ if we have $ap1 \xrightarrow{C_{in}} fp1$, $ap2 \xrightarrow{C_{in}} fp2$ and $pts(ap1) = pts(ap2)$. During the analysis, if $pts(ap1) = pts(ap2)$ no longer holds, a copy of the initially merged node will be introduced as the auxiliary variables for $fp1$. This is always safe and precise.

In Lines 9 - 13, the $indSet$ for both the caller function and the function clone are modified so that their local VFGs can be effectively updated. Note that if there already exists a clone of the callee function with same input values, we can reuse the existing clone as the call target instead of creating a new one. The local VFG of the caller function needs to be updated accordingly (Lines 15 - 20). In Lines 22 and 23, we change the target of the call by redirecting all previous inter-procedural value flows to the cloned function. Because of Property 1, this is always safe and precise.

Algorithm 4 Context matching

1: **procedure** CONTEXTMATCHING($caller, callee, C$)
2:     Let $O \to^* ret$ be a newly introduced flow path in $callee$ where O is an object that can return and ret is function output
3:     **if** O is function input **then**
4:         Let $ap \xrightarrow{C_{in}} O \to^* ret \xrightarrow{C_{out}} out$ be a flow path
5:         ADDEDGE($caller, ap \to out$)
6:         $funcSet := funcSet \bigcup \{caller\}$
7:     **else if** O is heap object **then**
8:         HEAPCLONE($caller, callee, C, O \to^* ret$)
9:         $funcSet := funcSet \bigcup \{caller\}$
10:     **end if**
11: **end procedure**
12: **procedure** HEAPCLONE($caller, callee, C, O_H \to^* ret$)
13:     **if** $\nexists O_H \xrightarrow{C_{out}} p_H$ **then**
        // Create new copy for O_H in $caller$
14:         Add p_H at C and $O_H \xrightarrow{C_{out}} p_H$
15:         Let $\widehat{O_H}$ be the copy for O_H at C, as described in Section 3.3
16:         ADDEDGE($caller, \widehat{O_H} \to p_H$)
17:         Add $O_H*^{out} \xrightarrow{C_{out}} p_H*^{out}$ as described in Rule 1
18:     **else if** O_H, O_X were cloned together but escape differently **then**
        // Split the merged clones in $caller$
19:         Remove edge from the old clone $\widehat{O_X} \to p_H$
20:         Let $\widehat{O_H}$ be the new copy for O_H, as described in Section 3.3
21:         ADDEDGE($caller, \widehat{O_H} \to p_H$)
22:     **end if**
23:     Let $ret \xrightarrow{C_{out}} out$ be the inter-procedural flow edge
24:     ADDEDGE($caller, p_H \to out$)
25: **end procedure**

4.3 Context Matching

In Algorithm 4, we apply context-matching in such a way that CFL-reachability is computed for matching inter-procedural value flow paths only. The observation is that new matching inter-procedural paths only exist if there exists a new value flow path from function inputs to function outputs (Line 2 in CONTEXTMATCHING). Matching inter-procedural value flow paths are then memoized and summarized as local value flows of the caller function (Lines 4 - 6). In Line 8, the procedure HEAPCLONE is called for heap objects escaping from the callee function. In both cases, new local value flow edges are introduced in the caller function hence the caller function is included in $funcSet$ for further updating (Lines 6 and 9).

In HEAPCLONE, for heap object O_H escaping from f, a heap object $\widehat{O_H}$ will be introduced as its copy in the caller function (Lines 15 and 20). As described in Section 3.3, objects escaping in the same way are cloned together, hence the same object may be used as copies of different objects at the same call-site. Similar to how we handle auxiliary variables, if two objects O_H, O_X, whose clones were merged together, now escape differently, their merged copies need to be separated. As shown in Lines 18 - 22, we split merged clones by introducing a new copy $\widehat{O_H}$ and replacing the flow edge $\widehat{O_X} \to p_H$ with a new edge $\widehat{O_H} \to p_H$ (Lines 21 - 23). This amounts to creating a copy of the initially merged node, which is always safe and precise.

5. Implementation and Experimental Results

We have implemented our context- and flow-sensitive points-to analysis in LLVM [16]. The analysis is also field-sensitive [27] in that for objects with struct types, pointers that point to distinct offsets of the same object are not regarded as aliases. In this section we evaluate the efficiency of our implementation in terms of runtime and memory consumption, against standard benchmarks used in the

Benchmark	NC-LOC C/C++	Bitcode Files	# Functions			# Pointers				Points-to Set	
			Original	Cloned	Total	Original	With Copies	Auxiliary	Total	Average	Max
sendmail 8.17	115.6K	17.9MB	1,340	201	1,541	103,517	285,935	381,168	667,103	1.25	77
httpd 2.0.63	177.8K	9.1MB	992	1	993	41,966	42,099	29,177	71,276	1.04	8
400.perlbench	126.3K	20.0MB	1,865	185	2,050	177,264	403,876	516,486	920,272	2.10	83
401.bzip2	5.7K	807KB	100	0	100	5,567	5,567	1,955	7,522	1.02	2
403.gcc	234.3K	50.6MB	5,577	1,514	7,091	432,651	975,295	1,610,456	2,585,751	4.14	249
429.mcf	1.6K	578KB	24	2	26	1,261	1,493	1,165	2,658	1.42	8
445.gobmk	157.6K	11.4MB	2,679	238	2,917	81,770	115,779	145,389	261,168	1.02	5
456.hmmer	20.7K	4.8MB	538	27	565	26,398	33,983	20,047	54,030	1.13	5
458.sjeng	10.5K	1.4MB	144	0	14	5,303	5,303	1,023	6,326	1.01	5
462.libquantum	2.6K	610KB	115	0	115	2,095	2,095	1,936	4,031	1.00	2
464.h264ref	36.1K	5.4MB	590	181	771	59,729	217,962	219,491	437,453	1.03	4
471.omnetpp	20.0K	19.6MB	2,887	38	2,925	53,294	60,004	211,706	271,710	1.13	88
473.astar	4.3K	836KB	167	3	170	3,042	3,172	2,910	6,082	1.02	4

Table 1. Summary and Statistics of the benchmark data. The analysis is performed without heap cloning.

points-to analysis literature, as well as its precision, by integration into an existing compiler.

5.1 Benchmarks

Table 1 shows summary information for the benchmarks used in this evaluation. For each benchmark, we list its version number, the number of non-commented lines of C/C++ code (NC-LOC) as reported by the SLOCCount [37] tool, and the size of the bit-code files generated by the LLVM (version 3.1) front-end. The two benchmarks sendmail 8.17 and httpd 2.0.63 were selected in order to compare our analysis with the Bootstrapping approach proposed by Kahlon [14]. Bootstrapping is a state-of-the-art flow- and context-sensitive pointer analysis; these two benchmarks are the largest applications used in Kahlon's experiments. The other benchmarks include all integer benchmarks from CPU2006, except for 483.xalancbmk, which we have not been able to successfully compile with LLVM-3.1.

Our approach to context-sensitivity, together with the various summary-based optimizations, is key to the scalability of our analysis. As shown in Table 1 (Columns 4 - 6), the number of functions that are cloned in our analysis is small. For all benchmarks, the number of function clones is less than or close to 30% of the number of functions in the original program, and it is less than 10% for 10 out of 13 benchmarks.

Columns 7 - 10 give the number of pointer variables in the original program, as well as the total number of pointer variables after the analysis, where copies of original program variables and auxiliary variables have been introduced. In our implementation, we introduce a copy for each global variable that is accessed in a function (including those indirectly accessed in its callees). As a result, for some benchmarks, e.g., sendmail 8.17, 400.perlbench, 403.gcc, and 464.h264ref, the number of pointer variables more than doubled after introducing these copies (Column 8). Column 9 and 10 present the number of introduced auxiliary variables, and the total number of pointers after the analysis. For 9 out of 13 benchmarks, the number of pointer variables increases by 20% to 100% after the analysis. For the four benchmarks listed above, the total number of pointer variables after the analysis becomes 6 to 8 times larger. This may sound expensive. However, it enables us to analyze each function individually. In all those benchmarks, the average number of pointers in each function is much smaller than the program size hence our analysis can be efficiently performed. The last two columns present the average and largest size of the points-to set, respectively. Since we compactly represent pointer values with respect to function inputs, the average size of the points-to set is very small. This is key to scalability and also explains the small memory footprint of our analysis as shown in Table 3.

5.2 Runtime and Memory Consumption Evaluation

Benchmark	Bootstrapping [14]		Our Approach	
	Time	Mem	Time	Mem
httpd 2.0.63	161s	161MB	2.4s	195MB
sendmail 8.17	939s	939MB	137s	1,346MB

Table 2. Comparison against Bootstrapping [14]. The results of Boot-strapping are directly taken from the paper, where Kahlon conducted his experiments on a slower machine (Intel Pentium4 3.2GHz with 2GB of memory). This is the closest comparison we can make.

We conducted our evaluation on an Intel XeonE5432 3.0GHz processor with 24GB of memory. Table 2 compares our analysis against Bootstrapping. Both analyses are context- and flow-sensitive. Since no precision data is reported in Kahlon's paper, we can only compare the performance. In this experiment, we disabled heap cloning in our analysis and restricted our memory usage to 2GB for a fair comparison. For the two benchmarks, on a slightly faster machine, our analysis is 60× and 7× faster, respectively. It does require more memory to preserve all value flow information computed during the analysis, so that we can precisely answer various alias queries from different client applications.

Table 3 shows the results of our analysis, with different heap cloning strategies, as described in Section 3.3. We evaluate four different heap cloning strategies; namely, no-cloning, 2-level cloning, 2-limiting cloning, and full cloning. The 2-level cloning strategy limits the length of call paths to two, where the call-site and the object creation site, together, are used to distinguish a heap object. In 2-limiting cloning, the number of objects created at each call-site is restricted to two. We use a simple heuristic to choose objects to be cloned: objects that directly return are chosen first, followed by those that escape to input parameters and returns. We clone objects that escape to global variables last.

Recall that we clone two objects together if they escape in the same way. Hence in Table 3, we present the total number of clones (#Clones), together with the number of clones that have been merged (#Merges). We also show the runtime and memory consumption under each strategy. Some benchmarks are processed too quickly for memory consumption to be precisely measured. Hence, for those benchmarks, the memory consumption is not given.

As shown in Table 3, for 10 out 13 benchmarks, full heap cloning support can be achieved with relatively small performance loss. Merging cloned objects is very effective for the two benchmarks, 445.gobmk and 462.libquantum, where 25,827 out of 38,643 cloned objects, and 3,909 out of 4,226 cloned ob-

Benchmark	No-Cloning		2-Level Cloning		2-Limiting Cloning		Full-Cloning	
	#Objs	Time:Mem	#Clones:#Merges	Time:Mem	#Clones:#Merges	Time:Mem	#Clones:#Merges	Time:Mem
sendmail 8.17	14	137s:1.35GB	14,033:4,644	1,523s:1.94GB	27,506:6,983	374s:1.73GB	–:–	–:–
httpd 2.0.63	4	2.4s:195MB	2:1	2.4s:195MB	2:1	2.4s:195MB	2:1	2.4s:195MB
400.perlbench	8	522s:2.61GB	9,332:494	981s:3.13GB	11,068:719	859s:3.27GB	–:–	–:–
401.bzip2	5	68ms:–	24:0	73ms:–	30:0	90ms:-	44:0	85ms:–
403.gcc	9	1,097s:6.3GB	–:–	–:–	–:–	–:–	–:–	–:–
429.mcf	4	25ms:–	6:0	24ms:–	6:0	24ms:-	6:0	27ms:–
445.gobmk	22	120s:696MB	1,795:153	131s:754MB	3,623:420	136s:837MB	38,643:25,827	150s:966MB
456.hmmer	45	585ms:–	1,058:74	618ms:–	1,375:139	600ms:–	5,605:1,951	1.1s:–
458.sjeng	10	111ms:–	38:0	113ms:–	33:0	112ms:–	38:0	120ms:–
462.libquantum	19	59ms:-	480:163	79ms:–	480:183	74ms:–	4,226:3,909	141ms:–
464.h264ref	169	4.2s:327MB	2,009:0	4.7s:345MB	994:0	4.3s:330MB	20,324:1,260	20.3s:455MB
471.omnetpp	211	21.1s:1.09GB	9,850:1,345	103s:1.20GB	11,580:1,803	115s:1.20GB	14,003:2,064	136s:1.27GB
473.astar	32	101ms:–	207:10	119ms:–	199:11	103ms:–	390:126	129ms:–

Table 3. Runtime (minutes:seconds) and memory performance of our analysis using different heap cloning strategies. #Clones is the number of objects that have been cloned, and #Merges is the number of merged object clones.

jects, can be merged together under the full-cloning strategy, respectively. However, for the three benchmarks sendmail 8.17, 400.perlbench, and 403.gcc, it becomes expensive to compute value flows for each cloned heap object and the analysis cannot finish in 4 hours when full cloning is enabled. In 403.gcc, there are several very large functions and any heap cloning strategy will result in tens of thousands of heap objects being created in those functions. As a result, it can only be analyzed without heap cloning support.

Next we compare the two different heap cloning approximations for the two benchmarks sendmail 8.17 and 400.perlbench. For sendmail 8.17, 2-level cloning is 4× slower than 2-limiting cloning, while the number of clones being introduced is actually much smaller. The reason is that with 2-level cloning, the average points-to set size increases to 3.22, compared to 1.97 in 2-limiting cloning. Hence more value flows need to be computed. It seems that for this benchmark, the analysis result is more precise with 2-level cloning: there are 147 functions being cloned, compared to 193 in 2-limiting cloning, suggesting less aliases. However, for 400.perlbench, there are 153 function clones with 2-level cloning, compared to 95 with 2-limiting cloning. In general, it is difficult to tell which approximation is more precise but the 2-limiting approximation scales better.

5.3 Precision Evaluation

Benchmark	Number of LICMs		
	BasicAA	DSA	Ours
400.perlbench	3,567	461	4,273
401.bzip2	899	108	3,023
403.gcc	18,750	1,243	24,320
429.mcf	165	4	221
445.gobmk	8,863	845	10,754
456.hmmer	5,868	429	10,013
458.sjeng	960	416	1,124
462.libquantum	1,090	232	1,156
464.h264ref	13,938	1,749	37,574
471.omnetpp	1,936	880	2,008
473.astar	904	542	962

Table 4. Number of instructions hoisted out of loop with different alias analysis, the larger the better. Our analysis is performed without heap cloning.

We evaluate the precision of our analysis using a classic compiler optimization as the client application: loop invariant code mo-

tion (LICM). Table 4 compares our analysis with two alias analyses in LLVM, the default alias analysis (BasicAA), and the data structure alias analysis (DSA) [17]. BasicAA is a simple intraprocedural alias analysis, and DSA is a context-sensitive, unification based alias analysis with full heap cloning support. As shown in the table, with our analysis, the optimization becomes much more effective: for 401.bzip2, the number of instructions being hoisted out of loops is 3,023, compared to 899 with BasicAA, and 108 with DSA.

For this optimization, heap cloning makes little differences in our experiments. This is because pointers referring to the same heap object are conservatively regarded as may aliases, since one heap object may potentially represent multiple objects created at runtime. However, the optimization requires precise must alias information to be effective and there is little difference whether we distinguish distinct heap objects or not. This also explains why BasicAA also outperforms DSA. BasicAA implements quite a few effective checks to compute must and may alias information by examining the local use-def chain of an instruction. While in DSA, such information is computed based on a graph node representation with all aliased pointers being unified. As a result, only a small number of must aliases can be identified. Overall, our analysis can significantly improve the effectiveness of this optimization.

6. Related Work

There are many variations of pointer analysis that make different trade-offs between precision and run time, including a number of analyses that are both context- and flow-sensitive.

Precise pointer analysis. Earlier work on flow- and context-sensitive (FSCS) pointer analysis has shown to scale up to thousands of LOC [5, 11, 15, 38]. Great progress has been made recently. Zhu [42] proposes a FSCS pointer analysis using symbolic summary functions. The approach scales to 200 KLOC of C code. In [14], a summary-based approach is also used to scale FSCS pointer analysis. To further improve the performance, the author bootstraps the more precise and costly FSCS pointer analysis by using cheaper and less precise analyses to partition programs into small sections that can be analyzed independently. The algorithm scales up to 128 KLOC of C code. The bootstrapping idea is further extended in [40], where the authors partition the program variables into different points-to levels using an insensitive analysis. FSCS pointer analysis is then applied by processing variables level by level, from the highest to the lowest. The analyzed results of higher level variables can be used in computing the context- and flow-sensitive pointer information for variables in the lower level. This is the first FSCS analysis that scales to large applications with millions of LOC. The analysis is not fully field-sensitive as struct field accesses are differentiated by scalarization, which cannot be applied to structs whose addresses escape. More importantly, the above approaches do not support heap cloning, which is very important for analysis precision and often a large overhead to performance [17, 26]. To the best of our knowledge, our analysis is the first FSCS analysis that supports heap cloning and scales to large applications.

Context-sensitivity. Many pointer analysis algorithms focus on context-sensitivity only [4, 17, 25, 32, 36, 39, 43]. The approaches in [4, 31] trade off precision for scalability using a *k-limited* representation which restricts the length of call paths to a small fixed number k. This leads to a different yet interesting research question: how to effectively distinguish contexts without representing the full call path? For object-oriented languages, some smart heuristics (e.g., *object sensitivity* [24] and *type sensitivity* [31]) have been developed to effectively differentiate contexts. It is reported that with those heuristics, the loss of precision is insignificant. Alternatively, as in [17, 25, 32, 36, 43], the context can be precisely represented using the full call path (with cycles on the path being discarded). This guarantees precision, making scalability the main challenge.

Most precise pointer analyses developed to date [25, 40, 43] are summary-based. They develop different algorithms to generate function summaries and context-sensitivity is efficiently achieved by applying these function summaries at their corresponding callsites. On the other hand, the authors in [4, 36] use a clone-based approach which differentiates calling contexts at distinct call paths. Binary-decision diagrams (BDDs) are used to compactly represent the exponentially large number of contexts. The algorithms in [23, 30, 32, 39] formulate context-sensitive pointer analysis as a CFL-reachability problem, where a context-free language is defined to simultaneously model heap accesses and function calls. The authors develop a refinement-based algorithm for scalability: imprecise results with approximation are computed first, which can be refined on queries for more precise results. Our approach to context-sensitivity differs from previous work in that we apply function cloning and CFL-reachability analysis together for context-sensitivity, and compute various summaries for efficiency.

The use of BDDs [1] has been adopted in many pointer analysis algorithms, especially the context-sensitive ones [4, 36, 40, 43]. It attempts to solve the problem of the large amount of data in context-sensitive analysis by representing redundancy efficiently. Our approach to this problem is to use context abstraction for equivalent contexts on distinct call paths and we represent pointer information with respect to the inputs of the context.

Heap-cloning. A number of context-sensitive pointer analyses use a context-sensitive heap abstraction [4, 17, 25, 32, 35, 39]. This abstraction is also referred to as object-sensitivity for object-oriented languages [31]. Those approaches trade precision for scalability in different ways: Lattner et al. [17] use a unification based approximation, the authors in [32, 39] employ a refinement-based approach, Sui et al. [35] use a demand-drive approach based on alias queries from compiler optimizations, and the most common method is to limit the depth of the call paths as in [4, 31]. In this work, we propose an alternative approximation to efficiently support heap cloning by limiting the number of objects that can be cloned at a call-site.

Flow-sensitivity. Flow-sensitive pointer analysis has attracted much attention recently [12, 13, 18, 20]. One of the key insights is to use a sparse representation, such as SSA, so that the def-use information of pointers can be efficiently propagated on the CFG. For example, the approach adopted in this paper [20] di-

rectly represents pointer def-use information as flow edges so that flow-sensitive pointer analysis can be performed efficiently.

Value flow. Value flow analysis computes which program variables hold which values of interest and it has been studied in many different areas, including compiler optimizations [2, 3], error detection [6, 34], software validation [9], and symbolic evaluation [28]. Existing value flow analyses rely on external points-to analysis to handle memory dependencies with aliases. Our approach can be used in existing value flow analyses to make them more effective.

7. Conclusion

In this paper, we present a novel method for context-sensitive analysis using the value flow graph formulation that scales well to large applications. We highlight the cause of imprecision in previous approaches and propose a solution to address this problem. We prove that our method is as precise as inlining all function calls and we show that unlike existing clone-based or CFL-based approaches, flow-sensitivity can be easily integrated in our approach. By applying context sensitivity to both, local variables and heap objects, we propose a new approximation for heap cloning.

We develop an efficient context-, flow-, and field-sensitive pointer analysis and implement it in a production compiler: LLVM. Experimental results using the SPEC CPU benchmarks and other real-world code-bases show that our analysis is much faster than existing approaches, and that its precision can significantly improve the effectiveness of existing compiler optimizations such as loop invariant code motion.

References

[1] M. Berndl, O. Lhoták, F. Qian, L. Hendren, and N. Umanee. Points-to analysis using BDDs. In *Proceedings of the ACM SIGPLAN 2003 conference on Programming language design and implementation*, PLDI '03, pages 103–114. ACM, 2003.

[2] R. Bodik. *Path-sensitive, value-flow optimizations of programs*. PhD thesis, University of Pittsburgh, 1999.

[3] R. Bodik and S. Anik. Path-sensitive value-flow analysis. In *Proceedings of the 25th ACM SIGPLAN-SIGACT symposium on Principles of programming languages*, POPL '98, pages 237–251. ACM, 1998.

[4] M. Bravenboer and Y. Smaragdakis. Strictly declarative specification of sophisticated points-to analyses. In *Proceeding of the 24th ACM SIGPLAN conference on Object oriented programming systems languages and applications*, OOPSLA '09, pages 243–262. ACM, 2009.

[5] R. Chatterjee, B. G. Ryder, and W. A. Landi. Relevant context inference. In *Proceedings of the 26th ACM SIGPLAN-SIGACT symposium on Principles of programming languages*, POPL '99, pages 133–146. ACM, 1999.

[6] S. Cherem, L. Princehouse, and R. Rugina. Practical memory leak detection using guarded value-flow analysis. In *Proceedings of the 2007 ACM SIGPLAN conference on Programming language design and implementation*, PLDI '07, pages 480–491. ACM, 2007.

[7] C. Cifuentes, N. Keynes, L. Li, N. Hawes, M. Valdiviezo, A. Browne, J. Zimmermann, A. Craik, D. Teoh, and C. Hoermann. Static deep error checking in large system applications using parfait. In *Proceedings of the 19th ACM SIGSOFT symposium and the 13th European conference on Foundations of software engineering*, ESEC/FSE '11, pages 432–435, New York, NY, USA, 2011. ACM.

[8] A. Deutsch. Interprocedural may-alias analysis for pointers: beyond K-limiting. In *Proceedings of the ACM SIGPLAN 1994 conference on Programming language design and implementation*, PLDI '94, pages 230–241. ACM, 1994.

[9] N. Dor, S. Adams, M. Das, and Z. Yang. Software validation via scalable path-sensitive value flow analysis. In *Proceedings of the 2004 ACM SIGSOFT international symposium on Software testing and analysis*, ISSTA '04, pages 12–22. ACM, 2004.

[10] V. D'silva, D. Kroening, and G. Weissenbacher. A survey of automated techniques for formal software verification. *Computer-Aided Design of Integrated Circuits and Systems, IEEE Transactions on*, 27(7):1165–1178, 2008.

[11] M. Emami, R. Ghiya, and L. J. Hendren. Context-sensitive interprocedural points-to analysis in the presence of function pointers. In *Proceedings of the ACM SIGPLAN 1994 conference on Programming language design and implementation*, PLDI '94, pages 242–256. ACM, 1994.

[12] B. Hardekopf and C. Lin. Semi-sparse flow-sensitive pointer analysis. In *Proceedings of the 36th annual ACM SIGPLAN-SIGACT symposium on Principles of programming languages*, POPL '09, pages 226–238. ACM, 2009.

[13] B. C. Hardekopf. *Pointer analysis: building a foundation for effective program analysis*. PhD thesis, University of Texas at Austin, 2009.

[14] V. Kahlon. Bootstrapping: a technique for scalable flow and context-sensitive pointer alias analysis. In *Proceedings of the 2008 ACM SIGPLAN conference on Programming language design and implementation*, PLDI '08, pages 249–259. ACM, 2008.

[15] W. Landi and B. G. Ryder. A safe approximate algorithm for interprocedural aliasing. In *Proceedings of the ACM SIGPLAN 1992 conference on Programming language design and implementation*, PLDI '92, pages 235–248. ACM, 1992.

[16] C. Lattner and V. Adve. LLVM: A compilation framework for lifelong program analysis & transformation. In *Proceedings of the international symposium on Code generation and optimization: feedback-directed and runtime optimization*, CGO '04, pages 75–, Washington, DC, USA, 2004. IEEE Computer Society.

[17] C. Lattner, A. Lenharth, and V. Adve. Making context-sensitive points-to analysis with heap cloning practical for the real world. In *Proceedings of the 2007 ACM SIGPLAN conference on Programming language design and implementation*, PLDI '07, pages 278–289. ACM, 2007.

[18] O. Lhoták and K.-C. A. Chung. Points-to analysis with efficient strong updates. In *Proceedings of the 38th annual ACM SIGPLAN-SIGACT symposium on Principles of programming languages*, POPL '11, pages 3–16. ACM, 2011.

[19] L. Li, C. Cifuentes, and N. Keynes. Practical and effective symbolic analysis for buffer overflow detection. In *Proceedings of the eighteenth ACM SIGSOFT international symposium on Foundations of software engineering*, FSE '10, pages 317–326. ACM, 2010.

[20] L. Li, C. Cifuentes, and N. Keynes. Boosting the performance of flow-sensitive points-to analysis using value flow. In *Proceedings of the 19th ACM SIGSOFT symposium and the 13th European conference on Foundations of software engineering*, ESEC/FSE '11, pages 343–353. ACM, 2011.

[21] L. Li, H. Feng, and J. Xue. Compiler-directed scratchpad memory management via graph coloring. *ACM Transactions on Architecture Code Optimization*, 6(3):9:1–9:17, Oct. 2009.

[22] L. Li, J. Xue, and J. Knoop. Scratchpad memory allocation for data aggregates via interval coloring in superperfect graphs. *ACM Transactions on Embedded Computing Systems*, 10(2):28:1–28:42, Jan. 2011.

[23] Y. Lu, L. Shang, X. Xie, and J. Xue. An incremental points-to analysis with CFL-reachability. In R. Jhala and K. Bosschere, editors, *Compiler Construction*, volume 7791 of *Lecture Notes in Computer Science*, pages 61–81. Springer Berlin Heidelberg, 2013.

[24] A. Milanova, A. Rountev, and B. G. Ryder. Parameterized object sensitivity for points-to analysis for Java. *ACM Transaction on Software Engineering Methodolology*, 14(1):1–41, Jan. 2005.

[25] E. M. Nystrom, H. S. Kim, and W. M. Hwu. Bottom-up and top-down context-sensitive summary-based pointer analysis. In *SAS'04*, pages 165–180, 2004.

[26] E. M. Nystrom, H. S. Kim, and W. M. Hwu. Importance of heap specialization in pointer analysis. In *Proceedings of the 5th ACM SIGPLAN-SIGSOFT workshop on Program analysis for software tools and engineering*, PASTE '04, pages 43–48. ACM, 2004.

[27] D. J. Pearce, P. H. Kelly, and C. Hankin. Efficient field-sensitive pointer analysis of C. *ACM Transactions on Programming Languages and Systems*, 30(1), Nov. 2007.

[28] J. H. Reif and H. R. Lewis. Symbolic evaluation and the global value graph. In *Proceedings of the 4th ACM SIGACT-SIGPLAN symposium on Principles of programming languages*, POPL '77, pages 104–118. ACM, 1977.

[29] T. Reps. Program analysis via graph reachability. In *Proceedings of the 1997 international symposium on Logic programming*, ILPS '97, pages 5–19. MIT Press, 1997.

[30] L. Shang, X. Xie, and J. Xue. On-demand dynamic summary-based points-to analysis. In *Proceedings of the Tenth International Symposium on Code Generation and Optimization*, CGO '12, pages 264–274, New York, NY, USA, 2012. ACM.

[31] Y. Smaragdakis, M. Bravenboer, and O. Lhoták. Pick your contexts well: understanding object-sensitivity. In *Proceedings of the 38th annual ACM SIGPLAN-SIGACT symposium on Principles of programming languages*, POPL '11, pages 17–30. ACM, 2011.

[32] M. Sridharan and R. Bodík. Refinement-based context-sensitive points-to analysis for Java. In *Proceedings of the 2006 ACM SIGPLAN conference on Programming language design and implementation*, PLDI '06, pages 387–400. ACM, 2006.

[33] B. Steensgaard. Points-to analysis in almost linear time. In *Proceedings of the 23rd ACM SIGPLAN-SIGACT symposium on Principles of programming languages*, POPL '96, pages 32–41. ACM, 1996.

[34] Y. Sui, D. Ye, and J. Xue. Static memory leak detection using full-sparse value-flow analysis. In *Proceedings of the 2012 International Symposium on Software Testing and Analysis*, ISSTA '12, pages 254–264, New York, NY, USA, 2012. ACM.

[35] Y. Sui, L. Yue, and J. Xue. Query-directed adaptive heap cloning for optimizing compilers. In *Proceedings of the 2013 International Symposium on Code Generation and Optmization*, CGO '13, New York, NY, USA, 2013. ACM.

[36] J. Whaley and M. S. Lam. Cloning-based context-sensitive pointer alias analysis using binary decision diagrams. In *Proceedings of the ACM SIGPLAN 2004 conference on Programming language design and implementation*, PLDI '04, pages 131–144. ACM, 2004.

[37] D. A. Wheeler. SLOC Count User Guide. http://www.dwheeler.com/sloccount/. Last accessed: 11 Nov 2012.

[38] R. P. Wilson and M. S. Lam. Efficient context-sensitive pointer analysis for C programs. In *Proceedings of the ACM SIGPLAN 1995 conference on Programming language design and implementation*, PLDI '95, pages 1–12. ACM, 1995.

[39] G. Xu, A. Rountev, and M. Sridharan. Scaling CFL-reachability-based points-to analysis using context-sensitive must-not-alias analysis. In *Proceedings of the 23rd European Conference on ECOOP 2009 — Object-Oriented Programming*, Genoa, pages 98–122. Springer-Verlag, 2009.

[40] H. Yu, J. Xue, W. Huo, X. Feng, and Z. Zhang. Level by level: making flow- and context-sensitive pointer analysis scalable for millions of lines of code. In *Proceedings of the 8th annual IEEE/ACM international symposium on Code generation and optimization*, CGO '10, pages 218–229. ACM, 2010.

[41] X. Zheng and R. Rugina. Demand-driven alias analysis for C. In *Proceedings of the 35th annual ACM SIGPLAN-SIGACT symposium on Principles of programming languages*, POPL '08, pages 197–208. ACM, 2008.

[42] J. Zhu. Towards scalable flow and context sensitive pointer analysis. In *Proceedings of the 42nd annual Design Automation Conference*, DAC '05, pages 831–836. ACM, 2005.

[43] J. Zhu and S. Calman. Symbolic pointer analysis revisited. In *Proceedings of the ACM SIGPLAN 2004 conference on Programming language design and implementation*, PLDI '04, pages 145–157. ACM, 2004.

Analyzing Memory Ownership Patterns in C Libraries *

Tristan Ravitch

Department of Computer Sciences
University of Wisconsin–Madison
travitch@cs.wisc.edu

Ben Liblit

Department of Computer Sciences
University of Wisconsin–Madison
liblit@cs.wisc.edu

Abstract

Programs written in multiple languages are known as *polyglot programs*. In part due to the proliferation of new and productive high-level programming languages, these programs are becoming more common in environments that must interoperate with existing systems. Polyglot programs must manage resource lifetimes across language boundaries. Resource lifetime management bugs can lead to leaks and crashes, which are more difficult to debug in polyglot programs than monoglot programs.

We present analyses to automatically infer the ownership semantics of C libraries. The results of these analyses can be used to generate bindings to C libraries that intelligently manage resources, to check the correctness of polyglot programs, and to document the interfaces of C libraries. While these analyses are unsound and incomplete, we demonstrate that they significantly reduce the manual annotation burden for a suite of fifteen open source libraries.

Categories and Subject Descriptors D.2.11 [*Software Engineering*]: Software Architectures—Languages; D.2.12 [*Software Engineering*]: Interoperability; D.2.13 [*Software Engineering*]: Reusable Software—Reusable libraries; D.3.2 [*Programming Languages*]: Language Classifications—C, Python; D.3.3 [*Programming Languages*]: Language Constructs and Features—Dynamic storage management, Procedures, functions, and subroutines; D.3.4 [*Programming Languages*]: Processors—Code generation, Memory management; E.1 [*Data Structures*]: Arrays, Records; F.3.2 [*Logics and Meanings of Programs*]: Semantics of Programming Languages—Program analysis

Keywords resource lifetime management; memory allocation; allocators; finalizers; ownership transfer; escape analysis; sharing; reference counting; foreign function interfaces (FFIs); bindings; libraries; dataflow analysis; interprocedural static program analysis; polyglot programming; interoperability

* Supported in part by DoE contract DE-SC0002153, LLNL contract B580360, NSF grants CCF-0953478 and CCF-1217582, and a grant from the Wisconsin Alumni Research Foundation. Opinions, findings, conclusions, or recommendations expressed herein are those of the authors and do not necessarily reflect the views of NSF or other institutions.

```
1  char *strdup(const char *s);
2  char *asctime(const struct tm *tm);
```

Figure 1. C function signatures

1. Introduction

High-level programming languages have been gaining acceptance in many application domains where unsafe low-level languages like C and C++ were once the only option. For example, Python and JavaScript have a significant presence in the desktop application space. Additionally, Python has gained acceptance in the scientific computing community [14]. Unfortunately, these high-level languages do not exist in a vacuum. They depend on code written in unsafe lower-level languages for, among other reasons, performance and interoperability. Some performance-sensitive pieces of code simply cannot be rewritten in the desired high-level language. In other cases, it is possible but not economically feasible to rewrite working and tested code, so the original implementation must be used from the high-level language.

Production-quality high-level languages support calling functions from libraries written in other languages through foreign function interfaces (FFIs). High-level language programs using FFIs execute code from more than one language, making them *polyglot programs*. A critical challenge in writing correct polyglot programs lies in managing the flow of resources across language boundaries. Programs lacking a precise cross-language ownership semantics are vulnerable to resource leaks, threatening reliability. Unclear ownership semantics can also lead to crashes induced by use-after-free or double-free errors. Both of these types of errors are more difficult to debug in polyglot programs, as common debugging tools target programs written in a single language.

Most low-level languages like C do not provide any means for describing, much less checking, object ownership semantics. Instead, this critical information must be conveyed through documentation or recovered through static analysis. Library interfaces defined in C typically refer to dynamically-allocated resources by their address (a pointer). Unfortunately one cannot simply call free on all pointers obtained from a low-level language to release the associated resources, or *finalize* them. This approach fails because, while C functions expose most resources through pointers, they use pointers for many other purposes as well.

Consider the two C function declarations in figure 1. Each returns a **char***. The value returned by strdup must be freed to prevent memory leaks, but freeing the value returned by asctime will cause a crash. The caller owns the result of strdup but not the result of asctime. Furthermore, some dynamically-allocated resources may require specialized finalizer functions instead of generic free. Consider fopen and fclose: calling free on the result of fopen is a partial resource leak. Thus, functions returning managed resources must be identified along with their associated resource finalizers.

```
1    typedef struct pvl_elem_t {
2      void *data;
3      struct pvl_elem_t *next;
4    } pvl_elem;
5
6    typedef struct pvl_list_t {
7      pvl_elem *head;
8    } pvl_list;
9
10   typedef struct icalcomponent {
11     pvl_list *components;
12     struct icalcomponent* parent;
13   } icalcomponent;
14
15   void pvl_push(pvl_list *lst, void *d) {
16     pvl_elem *e = calloc(1, sizeof(pvl_elem));
17     e→next = lst→head;
18     lst→head = e;
19     e→data = d;
20   }
21
22   void* pvl_pop(pvl_list *lst) {
23     if(lst→head == NULL) return NULL;
24     list_elem *e = lst→head;
25     void *ret = e→data;
26     lst→head = e→next;
27     free(e);
28     return ret;
29   }
```

Figure 2. Definitions for figure 3

```
1    struct icalcomponent* icalcomponent_new() {
2      icalcomponent* comp = malloc(sizeof(icalcomponent));
3
4      if (!comp) return NULL;
5
6      comp→components = newlist();
7      comp→parent = NULL;
8
9      return comp;
10   }
11
12   void icalcomponent_free(icalcomponent* c) {
13     icalcomponent* comp;
14
15     if (!c) return;
16
17     while ((comp=pvl_pop(c→components)) != NULL) {
18       icalcomponent_remove_component(c,comp);
19       icalcomponent_free(comp);
20     }
21
22     pvl_free(c→components);
23     free(c);
24   }
25
26   void icalcomponent_remove_component(
27     icalcomponent *component, icalcomponent *child);
28
29   void icalcomponent_add_component(icalcomponent *c,
30     icalcomponent *child) {
31     pvl_push(c→components, child);
32   }
33
34   void icalcomponent_set_parent(icalcomponnent *c,
35     icalcomponent* parent) {
36     c→parent = parent;
37   }
```

Figure 3. Example from ical

Resource management semantics are unclear in C even without the additional complexities of polyglot programming.

We describe our ownership model for C resources and present algorithms to infer the ownership semantics of C libraries. These semantics are presented to users and tools through *inferred annotations* on library functions. While these analyses are unsound and incomplete, they are nonetheless useful. As discussed in section 8, our algorithms significantly reduce the *manual* annotation burden required to create library bindings. With review by a programmer familiar with the library being analyzed, these inferred annotations are sufficient to generate idiomatic FFI library bindings for high-level languages. The resulting bindings will be idiomatic in that they *automatically* manage the flow of resources between languages and clean them up when they become garbage. They also serve as an aid in program understanding and can augment documentation. Our primary contributions over prior work are: (1) two methods for identifying the ownership transfers of objects in C libraries (sections 4 and 5), (2) a method for inferring contracts that must be obeyed for function pointers (section 6), and (3) an algorithm for identifying reference-counted resources (section 7).

2. Resource Ownership Model

We adopt the ownership model of Heine and Lam [6] whereby each object is pointed to by exactly one owning reference. The object must eventually either be *finalized* through the owning reference, or ownership must be transferred to another owning reference. When a pointer is finalized, the resources held by the object it points to are safely released. Non-owning references to any object can be created at any time and are valid until the object is finalized. In the Heine and Lam model, pointer-typed members of C++ objects are either always owning references or are never owning references (at public

interface boundaries). We extend this model to pointer-typed fields of some C structures for all functions.

2.1 Memory Ownership in C

A memory allocator is an abstraction over the most prevalent resource in most programs: dynamically allocated memory. The standard C library's allocator and finalizer functions are malloc and free, respectively. When the memory allocator owns a piece of memory (i.e., the memory is unallocated), it is an error for any other part of the program to use it. When the allocator function is called, it completely transfers ownership of the memory to the caller via the returned owning reference.

Complex resources may own other resources through owned pointer fields. Finalizers for these complex resources must finalize their owned resources to obey the ownership model and to avoid leaks, as in figures 2 and 3. The icalcomponent type is a resource allocated with icalcomponent_new. It owns a component list, along with each of the components in the list of children. The finalizer for this type, icalcomponent_free, finalizes the list of children as well as the child components before finalizing the component itself with a call to free on line 23.

Ownership extends beyond just allocators and finalizers. For example, the function icalcomponent_remove_component removes a child component from a component without finalizing it.

```
1  with pinned(r):
2      # allow r to escape into a global
3      stash_in_global(r)
4
5      # drop explicit reference to r, but is still pinned
6      del r
7
8      # r is pinned, so safe to access via stashed global
9      use_stashed_global()
```

Figure 4. Pinning Python objects with a context manager

After a call to this function, the component no longer owns the child and ownership is implicitly transferred to the caller. Note that simply reading a child component from a component does not transfer ownership because the component will still finalize all of its children when it is itself finalized. Similarly, components do not own the component referenced by their parent field because that field is not finalized in the component finalizer. Our analysis does not automatically recognize this type of ownership transfer. It is relatively rare in real code, and would require expensive shape analysis [18].

2.2 Ownership in High-Level Languages

When a C allocator is called from a high-level language, the high-level language run-time system assumes exclusive ownership of the allocated resource by wrapping it in a special object. All references to the C resource in the high-level language are mediated through this wrapper object, which is managed by the high-level language memory manager (i.e., garbage collector). Since the wrapper object is a normal high-level language object, the memory manager knows when it is unreferenced and safe to finalize. The wrapper object uses memory manager hooks to *automatically* invoke the appropriate finalizer for the C resource when doing so is safe. In contrast, there is no such system in C unless it is implemented manually, such as through reference counting.

Of course, to be of any use these resources must be passed back to low-level code, in which operations on them are written. For a low-level language resource r owned exclusively by a high-level language run-time, assume that it is passed to a low-level language function f: $f(\ldots, r, \ldots)$. For each such call, one of the following must hold:

1. f assumes ownership of r. The high-level language must relinquish ownership of r by disabling any garbage collector hooks that would have run a finalizer on r.

2. f creates only transient references to r, all of which are destroyed when f returns. The high-level language still owns r and need take no further actions.

3. f creates a non-transient non-owning reference n to r. The high-level language run-time system still owns r and does not need to take any further actions. However, the programmer passing r to f must ensure that the lifetime of r exceeds that of n.

4. r does not obey our ownership model, but is instead reference-counted. In this case, as long as the reference manipulation functions are known, the object can safely be passed between languages.

5. r does not obey our ownership model and its resources cannot be automatically managed by the high-level language.

Cases one, two, and four can be fully automated and are ideal for robust language interoperability. The third case requires the high-level language caller of f to understand the semantics of the called function and its effect on the lifetime of r. Note that this semantic knowledge is required of any caller of f, even in C. While the lifetime management of r in the third case cannot be

fully automated, a high-level language library binding could provide programmers with tools to make such lifetime management simpler. For example, a Python library binding could provide a resource manager to pin objects to keep them alive within a lexical scope, as in figure 4. In this example, assume that stash_in_global(r) lets r escape into a global location managed by the library. If use_stashed_global accesses r through that global location, then r must still be live when use_stashed_global is called. The pinned resource manager retains a reference to its argument for the lexical scope of the **with** statement.

3. Allocators and Finalizers

Prior work in automating language interoperability by Ravitch et al. [16] presented algorithms for identifying the functions comprising memory allocators. We characterize the memory allocators identified by this work as *derived allocators* because they are built on top of lower-level allocators, with the standard allocator malloc as the ultimate base.

This prior work identifies a function as an allocator if it always returns the result of a base allocator (such as malloc) and gives up ownership of the allocation or returns NULL (to report failure). This is a *must* analysis: it identifies functions that must return a new resource. A must analysis is appropriate here because it can only miss allocator functions. At worst this can cause a leak (or require explicit resource-release calls). By contrast, over-approximating the set of allocators could lead to crashes. In figure 3, icalcomponent_new is an allocator because it returns NULL on line 4 and the result of a call to malloc on line 9.

The corresponding finalizer for an allocator f is a function that takes an argument that is the same type as the return value of f and, on every path, that argument is NULL or is finalized. Ravitch et al. under-approximate the set of finalizers with dataflow analysis. The example in figure 3 shows a finalizer: icalcomponent_free. On one path (at line 15), the argument c is NULL and on the other path it is finalized (at line 23).

A key feature of derived allocators is that they obtain a resource from a lower-level allocator and completely transfer ownership of it to their caller. While most allocation functions in libraries are derived allocators, some libraries define custom memory allocators based on pools, arenas, or some other abstraction. We require manual annotations to identify these custom low-level allocators. This burden is low because few libraries define their own allocators. Additionally, a manual annotation for the allocator and its associated finalizer of a custom allocator allows the analysis to identify many derived allocators.

In principle, shape analysis could identify even these custom allocators. We do not attempt this due to the scarcity of custom allocators and the relative expense of the required analysis.

4. Recognizing Ownership Transfer

As discussed in section 2.2, knowledge of the ownership model of a resource allows a high-level language library binding to automatically manage its lifetime. A key aspect of the ownership model is recognizing which library functions transfer ownership of resources; this allows the high-level language run-time system to assume responsibility for managing library resources safely. Prior work by Ravitch et al. [16] used an escape analysis to conservatively identify library functions that take ownership away from the caller. Intuitively, when a library function causes a pointer provided by the high-level language caller to escape, the lifetime of the pointed-to object becomes unknown and the high-level language run-time system can never safely finalize it.

Certainly if a parameter does not escape, then its ownership is not transferred. Escaping allows transfer, but does not necessarily lead to transfer in all cases. For example, common container-like data structures in C (e.g., lists, trees, or hash tables) typically store pointers to data objects. Clearly, storing an object in one of these containers allows it to escape. However, most of these containers do not take ownership of their elements: the caller must still manage their memory. Ma and Foster [10] note that ownership transfer in library interfaces is relatively rare; we note that escaping parameters are anything but rare. We therefore suggest that escape analysis is distinct from ownership transfer analysis. In this section, we present a transfer analysis to more accurately identify ownership transfers in C library functions. We revisit escape analysis in section 5.

The essence of our ownership transfer analysis follows from our resource ownership model in section 2. We consider a structure field to be owned if that field will be finalized within the context of a finalizer function. Thus, ownership of an object is transferred from a caller when another object assumes responsibility for finalizing it (i.e., it is stored into a field that will be finalized). Fields finalized in other contexts are sometimes used to store temporary allocations, but these fields are not guaranteed to be finalized with the rest of the object and are managed separately. The analysis proceeds in two phases. First it identifies all of the *owned fields* in a library. Then it identifies all of the function parameters that may be stored into an owned field. We describe fields in terms of *symbolic access paths*. Note that we assume that any given field is either always owned or never owned. We do not attempt to reason about fields that are only owned sometimes. Furthermore, we assume that, if one element held in a container-like field (i.e., an array or linked data structure) is owned, all elements in that field are owned.

4.1 Symbolic Access Paths

This analysis is based on symbolic access paths [2, 7]; we follow the formulation of Matosevic and Abdelrahman [11]. An *access path* describes a memory location accessible from a base value by a (possibly empty) sequence of path components. While we will only discuss field accesses in this paper, pointer dereferences, array accesses, and union accesses are also valid path components. We treat all array elements in a single array as identical; a more precise analysis could differentiate between them. This treatment of field accesses is unsound when pointers to **struct** types are cast to unrelated types [15], which could cause the analysis to identify invalid ownership transfers.

Let $ap(v)$ represent the access path for a source expression v. For example, the assignment on line 18 of figure 3 assigns a value to lst→head. The corresponding access path $ap(\text{lst→head})$ is the pair $(\text{lst}, \langle \text{head} \rangle)$. In this pair, lst is the base value and $\langle \text{head} \rangle$ is a sequence of one field access to reach the affected memory location. We sometimes refer to locations abstractly in terms of a base type rather than a base value. Here, lst has type pvl_list, so the abstract access path for this field access is $(\text{pvl\_list}, \langle \text{head} \rangle)$.

Following Matosevic and Abdelrahman, we construct symbolic access paths by traversing the call graph bottom-up, with strongly-connected components being iteratively re-analyzed until a fixed-point is reached. We will assume that functions are normalized such that the return value is the first parameter in the list of formal parameters (always indexed as zero). Functions return values by writing to their return parameter. Void functions have a placeholder in argument zero. For each library analyzed, we construct two maps, each keyed by function and formal parameter number:

- Let f be a function and i be the zero-based index of a parameter to that function. Then *finalizePaths*$[f, i]$ is a set of access paths that function f finalizes in its ith parameter.

- Let f be a function and i be the zero-based index of a parameter to that function. Then *writePaths*$[f, i]$ is a set of triples of the form (p, j, q) where function f reads the value at access path q

of its jth parameter and ultimately stores this value into access path p of its ith parameter.

Let $argno(v)$ return the index of formal parameter v in the formal parameter list of the enclosing function. Let $base(p)$ return the base of access path p and $components(p)$ return the path components of p. The access path extend operation $p_1 \oplus p_2$ extends p_1 by p_2 in the natural way; the resulting path has the same base value as p_1 and the path components of p_2 appended to those of p_1. The set-valued operation $nr(p)$ returns the singleton set containing p if each path component in $components(p)$ is unique within p; otherwise, it returns the empty set. Likewise, $nr((p, j, q))$ returns a singleton set containing a triple if neither p nor q has repeated path components. This condition excludes cyclic paths that could grow indefinitely; such paths are common in the presence of inductive data structures.

Our handling and representation of cyclic access paths differs from Matosevic and Abdelrahman [11]. They represent paths using a regular expression-like language with repetition operators. Our analysis does not require information about cycles in paths, so we use the simpler representation discussed above; this requires the no-repetition condition (through the $nr()$ operator) to prevent cyclic paths from growing without bound. This less expressive treatment of paths is a potential source of unsoundness, though it has not been a problem in practice.

We analyze code represented as LLVM bitcode: three-address code in static single assignment (SSA) form [8]. Two types of statements add elements to *finalizePaths* or *writePaths*: function calls and store instructions. This analysis is flow-insensitive and paths are created or extended for any relevant store or function call that *may* be executed. We consider function calls first. Suppose function f contains a function call of the form g(value). Let $p = ap(value)$ be the access path of *value*. If g is a finalizer and $base(p)$ is among the formal parameters of f, then:

$$finalizePaths[f, argno(base(p))] \cup= nr(p)$$

Now consider a store of the form *location = value in function f. Let $lp = ap(location)$ and $p = ap(value)$. If both $base(lp)$ and $base(p)$ are among the formal parameters of f, then:

$$writePaths[f, argno(base(lp))] \cup= nr((lp, argno(base(p)), p))$$

Calls to non-finalizer functions generate new paths by extending access paths in *finalizePaths* and *writePaths*. At a high level, paths are extended by mapping access paths in callees to the arguments of their callers. For each call callee(..., a, ...) in function f where a is the ith argument to *callee* and $p \in finalizePaths[callee, i]$, let $pext = ap(a) \oplus p$. If $base(pext)$ is a formal parameter of f, then:

$$finalizePaths[f, argno(base(pext))] \cup= nr(pext)$$

For each call callee(..., a, ..., b, ...) in function f where a and b are the ith and j^{th} arguments to *callee*, respectively, and $(p, j, q) \in writePaths[callee, i]$, let $qext = ap(b) \oplus q$ and $pext = ap(a) \oplus p$. Let $qextB = base(qext)$ and $pextB = base(pext)$. If both $qextB$ and $pextB$ are formal parameters of f, then:

$$writePaths[f, argno(pextB)] \cup= nr((pext, argno(qextB), qext))$$

Lastly, assume a function f calls v = g(..., a, ...); and then later calls h(..., v, ...); where h finalizes v and a is the jth argument to g. Further assume that $(p, j, q) \in writePaths[g, 0]$ and that $base(ap(a))$ is a formal parameter of f with index i. p is a degenerate access path with no components because it is the return value of g. Let $qext = ap(a) \oplus q$, the path of $base(ap(a))$ that is finalized by h. Then:

$$finalizePaths[f, i] \cup= nr(qext)$$

In each of these cases, we use local points-to information (the PT-relation from Matosevic and Abdelrahman [11]) to produce maximal access paths. For the pvl_push function in figure 2, the analysis can only conclude that d is written to the path (e, ⟨data⟩) without local points-to information. Since e is not a formal parameter of pvl_push, this fact is not recorded in *writePaths*. With local points-to information, the analysis can construct the maximal path (lst, ⟨head,data⟩). The base of this maximal path is lst, which is a formal parameter of pvl_push. Thus, *writePaths* can be updated to reflect the write of d to this path.

4.2 Identifying Owned Fields

After all of the symbolic access paths in a library are constructed, we next identify the owned fields in the library. According to our resource ownership model from section 2, owned fields of a type are those fields that will be finalized when an object of that type is finalized. Our analysis determines this by analyzing the finalized access paths of each function: if a field of the argument of a finalizer function is finalized, that field is owned. That is, if some function f is a finalizer for its ith formal parameter, all of the fields in *finalizePaths*$[f, i]$ are owned fields.

In figure 3, the function icalcomponent_free is a finalizer because the c parameter (of type icalcomponent*) is finalized (or NULL) on every path. The pvl_free and icalcomponent_free functions are finalizers as well (implementations not shown). We see that icalcomponent_free passes the return value of pvl_pop to a finalizer. pvl_pop returns the data from the head of its list argument through the access path (lst, ⟨head,data⟩). Thus, the value passed to the finalizer is (icalcomponent, ⟨components,head,data⟩); we conclude that this field of icalcomponent is owned.

4.3 Transferred Ownership

The key insight of the ownership transfer analysis is that ownership of any function argument stored into an owned field is transferred from the caller. Assume a function f has formal parameters a and b at positions i and j in the formal parameter list respectively. If $(p, j, q) \in$ *writePaths*$[f, i]$ where $ap(b)$ is q (q is the degenerate access path of just the formal parameter b) and the last component of p is an owned field, as per section 4.2, then f transfers ownership of b to a.

Returning to figure 3, the function pvl_push stores its d argument into a field of lst, which is summarized by the access path (lst, ⟨head,data⟩). icalcomponent_add_component calls pvl_push with a field of c, components, as an argument, extending the write access path to (c, ⟨components,head,data⟩). The first phase of the analysis identified the last component of this path as an owned field, and thus the c argument of icalcomponent_add_component assumes ownership of child. Note that icalcomponent_set_parent does not assume ownership of its parent parameter: the corresponding field is never finalized, and is thus not owned.

Our access path construction proceeds backwards from an address across pointer dereferences, field accesses, union accesses, and array accesses. We stop the construction at SSA ϕ-nodes to avoid a potential exponential explosion of generated access paths. While this is unsound, we have not observed any missed ownership transfers in practice.

5. An Improved Escape Analysis

While the results of the transfer analysis are essential to minimize the effort of generating language bindings that automate resource management, an escape analysis still provides important information. If a pointer to an object escapes, but ownership of that object is not transferred, we still learn information about the lifetime of that object. While we cannot always automatically manage this lifetime, the user can at least be informed that some scope management is

required. Helper functions could be used to pin objects with scoped lifetimes to keep them from being collected while references exist in a C library that are not visible to the garbage collector. While prior work has described an escape analysis for this purpose, we present a more precise analysis that eliminates many of the false positives of prior work.

We describe a bottom-up summary-based flow-insensitive escape analysis with limited field and context sensitivity for C. This analysis is a form of stack escape analysis [3, 21], rather than a thread escape analysis [19]. Our analysis is based on a *value flow escape graph*, which is a value flow graph [9] with extra annotations. Our analysis is most similar to that of Whaley and Rinard [21], though ours is flow-insensitive and requires only a single graph per function. Like Whaley and Rinard [21], we analyze functions independently of their callers. We require this because callers may be written in another language and unavailable at analysis time. Furthermore, we trade precision for speed and simpler handling of callees. Instead of unifying the points-to escape graph of each callee into the graph of the caller at call sites, we use summary information to mark only the escaping parameters as escaping. This allows for more compact representations of callees at the cost of some of the precision of graph unification. We conservatively assume that values passed to callees with no summaries do escape. The value flow graph does not allow us to answer points-to queries, which we do not require, but it can be constructed in a single pass, unlike the points-to escape graph.

Our value flow graph has two types of nodes: *location nodes* and *sink nodes*. An edge $a \rightarrow b$ denotes that values flow from a to b. A value escapes if there is a path from it to a sink. The analysis is conservative and identifies values that *may* escape. This approximation is appropriate in that false positives (values incorrectly identified as escaping) lead to leaks, not crashes.

Sink nodes are created for (1) **return** statements in functions that return aggregate or pointer values and (2) stores to global variables, arguments, the return values of callees, and access paths thereof. A sink is also created for each escaping actual argument of a callee. The following statements induce edges in the value flow graph:

- $*a = b$ adds $b \rightarrow a$ or $b_p \rightarrow a$

  Assignments cause the source operand to flow to the destination operand. The edge $b_p \rightarrow a$ is added if the right-hand side of the assignment is a field reference with concrete access path $(b, \langle p \rangle)$; if there is no field access, the simpler form $b \rightarrow a$ is added.

- **return** a adds $a \rightarrow sink_{ret}$

  The returned value flows to the special return sink node.

For example, the function CaseWalkerInit in figure 5 has the value-flow escape graph shown in figure 6. We represent location nodes as circles and sinks as rectangles. The argument src is represented by its location node, which flows into a field of the w argument. src escapes because there is a path from it to a sink.

Function calls of the form f(a1, a2, ..., aN) act as a sequence of assignments $*f_1 = a1, *f_2 = a2, ..., *f_N = aN$ where f_i is the node representing the ith formal argument of f. If f_i allows its argument to escape, then f_i is a sink node. Local value v escapes from f if $v \rightarrow^* s$ for some $s \in sinkNodes$; that is if any sink node s is reachable from v. If v does not escape according to this query, then field p of v escapes from f if, $v_p \rightarrow^* s$ for some $s \in sinkNodes$.

To introduce a limited form of context sensitivity, we make special note of arguments that escape into fields of other arguments. Assume there is a function call f(a, b) where the first argument of f escapes into the second argument. We add an edge $a \rightarrow b$ in all callers of f to model the effects of f on the value flow escape graph of the caller. For example, the CmpIgnoreCase function in

```
1    void CaseWalkerInit(const char *src, CaseWalker *w) {
2       w→src = src;
3       w→read = 0;
4    }
5
6    int CmpIgnoreCase(const char *s1, const char *s2) {
7       CaseWalker w1, w2;
8       Char8 c1, c2;
9
10      if (s1 == s2) return 0;
11
12      CaseWalkerInit(s1, &w1);
13      CaseWalkerInit(s2, &w2);
14
15      for (;;) {
16         c1 = CaseWalkerNext(&w1);
17         c2 = CaseWalkerNext(&w2);
18         if (!c1 || (c1 != c2)) break;
19      }
20      return (int)c1 -(int)c2;
21   }
```

Figure 5. Examples of escaping pointers from fontconfig library

Figure 6. Value flow escape graph for CaseWalkerInit in figure 5

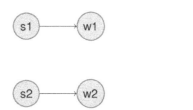

Figure 7. Value flow escape graph for CmpIgnoreCase in figure 5

```
1    typedef struct XML_ParserStruct {
2       const char *m_encoding;
3       XML_MemSuite m_mem;
4    } *XML_Parser;
5
6    XML_Parser parserCreate(const char *encodingName)
7    {
8       XML_Parser parser;
9       parser = malloc(sizeof(struct XML_ParserStruct));
10      if (parser != NULL) {
11         parser→m_encoding = encodingName;
12         parser→m_mem.malloc_fcn = malloc;
13         parser→m_mem.realloc_fcn = realloc;
14         parser→m_mem.free_fcn = free;
15      }
16
17      return parser;
18   }
19
20   DTD* dtdCreate(const XML_MemSuite *ms) {
21      DTD *p = ms→malloc_fcn(sizeof(DTD));
22      if (p == NULL) return p;
23
24      p→scaffLevel = 0;
25      p→scaffSize = 0;
26      p→scaffCount = 0;
27      p→contentStringLen = 0;
28      return p;
29   }
```

Figure 8. Contracts in expat library

- many indirect function calls are made through function pointers stored in object fields, particularly in the case where they are used to implement polymorphic behavior; and

- libraries initialize many of these fields with default functions defined in the same library.

While callers can technically store the address of any function in one of these function pointers, the library-provided initializers clearly indicate what semantics the library expects the call targets to obey. Violating those semantics is possible, but risks undefined behavior. Library-provided function pointer initializers effectively induce *contracts* on internally-initialized function pointers. The library obeys these contracts, and inferences based on them hold as long as client code obeys them as well. Recognizing these contracts and incorporating them into the analyses discussed in sections 3 to 7 improves precision.

Consider the example in figure 8. When parser objects are created in parserCreate, the malloc_fcn field of their XML_MemSuite is initialized with a pointer to the standard malloc function on line 12. While this does not mean that every malloc_fcn field will refer to malloc, it strongly suggests that the library expects the target to be an allocator. Since we consider the assignment on line 12 to create a contract on the malloc_fcn field, we conclude that dtdCreate is an allocator because of the call-under-contract on line 21.

figure 5 calls CaseWalkerInit, which we already established allows its src argument to escape into w. Thus, the value flow escape graph of CmpIgnoreCase, shown in figure 7, has edges from s1 to w1 and s2 and w2. Since w1 and w2 are local variables that do not otherwise escape, we are able to conclude that s1 and s2 do not escape, despite being passed as arguments that could escape if considered only in isolation.

Field sensitivity prevents a single escaping field from causing all other fields of the same object to also escape. We take a field-based approach to field sensitivity that is unsound when pointers to **struct** types are cast to structurally unrelated types [15] as in section 4.1. This unsoundness could make us label an escaping pointer as non-escaping. It could be made sound by having any casts to structurally unrelated types cause all affected fields to escape. We have not done this because such casts are rare in practice and have not yet caused problems.

6. Indirect Calls as Contracts

While analyzing library code, indirect calls (calls through function pointers) pose a problem. Libraries typically have many entry points and context of the call is unavailable. While some indirect call targets can be resolved, most cannot. Thus, whenever one of our analyses encounters an indirect call, it seems that we must conservatively assume that any function at all could be called. Instead of accepting this often overly-conservative conclusion, we note that:

7. Safely Sharing Ownership

Most resources in our model must be exclusively owned in order for them to be automatically managed by a high-level language run-time system. However, we support shared ownership for reference-counted resources. Moreover, ownership can be safely shared between a low-level language and a high-level language run-time system, provided the high-level language run-time safely manipu-

```
1    typedef struct {
2        int refcount;
3        Connection *connection;
4    } PendingCall;
5
6    PendingCall* pending_call_ref(PendingCall *pending) {
7        ++pending→refcount;
8        return pending;
9    }
10
11   void pending_call_unref(PendingCall *pending) {
12       --pending→refcount;
13       if (pending→refcount) return;
14
15       Connection *c = pending→connection;
16       free(pending);
17       connection_unref(c);
18   }
```

Figure 9. Reference counting in dbus-1 library

lates the reference count. When the high-level language acquires shared ownership of a resource, it must increment its reference count. When the high-level language is ready to relinquish ownership of the resource, it must decrement the reference count instead of calling a finalizer on it. If the high-level language finalizes the resource directly, later accesses through outstanding shared references in library code could lead to a crash. Note that shared resources may safely escape into library code (c.f. section 5) because the reference counts mediate their lifetimes.

7.1 Identifying Reference Increment and Decrement Functions

We describe an analysis to identify, for a library with reference-counted resources:

- the set of types that must be reference-counted (to know when references must be managed) and

- the functions to increment and decrement references (*IncRef* and *DecRef*, respectively) for each type (to correctly manipulate the reference counts).

We begin by identifying the *DecRef* function of a resource. Fundamentally, *DecRef*:

- takes a pointer to a resource as an argument,

- decrements an integer field of the resource, and

- if the reference count becomes zero, calls a finalizer on the argument.

A common variant of *DecRef* calls the finalizer directly without decrementing the reference count if there is only a single reference to the resource. Another interesting variant, such as from gobject-2.0, has multiple reference count decrement attempts; these arise because gobject-2.0 supports finalizers that can add references to objects that are in the process of being finalized. Instead of precisely modeling every possible variant of reference counting, we employ an over-approximation that is unsound and incomplete, but nonetheless effective.

Without loss of generality, assume that *DecRef* functions take only single argument: a pointer to a resource. First, identify all *conditional finalizers* in the library. These are functions that finalize their argument on some, but not all, paths. Building on the results of the finalizer analysis described in section 3, this is a linear scan of the instructions in each function. A conditional finalizer is a

function that calls at least one finalizer on its argument but is not itself a finalizer. (If it were a finalizer, it would call a finalizer on *all* paths.)

Consider the example in figure 9, which is adapted from code in the dbus-1 library simplified for exposition. Following the algorithm, we note that pending_call_unref takes a single pointer-typed argument. It passes this argument to finalizer free on line 16. However, pending_call_unref may also return early on line 13. Therefore, pending_call_unref is not itself a finalizer, but it is a conditional finalizer.

For each conditional finalizer cf with argument a, cf is a *DecRef* function with access path $(a, \langle p \rangle)$ if it decrements an integer field of a via a sequence of field accesses p. We do not require that cf always decrement the reference count because some variants skip it under certain circumstances; this is a potential source of imprecision. For example, the conditional finalizer pending_call_unref in figure 9 always decrements the refcount field of its pending argument on line line 12. Therefore, pending_call_unref is a *DecRef* function with access path (pending, ⟨refcount⟩).

For each *DecRef* function and its associated access path $(a, \langle p \rangle)$, the corresponding *IncRef* function is the one that takes a single argument of the same type as a, the root of the access path, and always increments the location in the resource described by p. If there is more than one *IncRef* function for a given *DecRef* function, we do not associate them and an annotation would be required to match the desired pairs. If more than one *DecRef* function could manage a given type, a consumer of the analysis results would need an annotation to prefer one. Returning to figure 9, we find that pending_call_ref always increments the refcount field of its one argument. Therefore, pending_call_ref is the *IncRef* function corresponding to pending_call_unref.

Note that we assume that libraries correctly manage reference counts internally. We make no attempt to verify this assumption, for which other analyses already exist [4].

7.2 Identifying Reference-Counted Types

So far we have identified the *IncRef* and *DecRef* functions that manipulate reference counts. We must also determine the set of types whose reference counts are managed by these functions. Clearly, this set includes the common argument type between *IncRef* and *DecRef*. Polymorphic reference counting functions, however, manage multiple types. One way to identify the set of managed types is to note that any polymorphic *DecRef* function needs some way to perform type-specific finalization when the reference count reaches zero. The types handled by these type-specific finalization functions are the types managed by the *IncRef* and *DecRef* pair.

More formally, let c be a function that has already been identified as a *DecRef* function for some type. Identify all indirect function callees in c to which c passes its argument. For each such callee f, let τ_f be the set of types to which f casts its argument. The set of types managed by c is the type of the argument of c unioned with $\bigcup_f \tau_f$.

The example in figure 10 is simplified from the open-source library glib-2.0. Our analysis recognizes g_object_unref as a *DecRef* function because of the decrements of the ref_count field on lines 6 and 9 and the call to finalizer g_type_free_instance on line 13. Next, we identify the targets of indirect calls in g_object_unref. The only indirect call appears on line 12. As initialized in g_emblem_class_init, the only known target is g_emblem_finalize. Thus, g_object_unref and g_object_ref are the *DecRef* and *IncRef* functions for GObject and GEmblem. As in this example, the indirect callees of *DecRef* often represent *finalizers* for resource-specific data members.

This algorithm assumes that *DecRef* functions operate on structural subtypes of the input value. An alternative approach is to

```
1   void g_object_unref(GObject *object) {
2     gint oref;
3
4     oref = g_atomic_int_get(&object→ref_count);
5     if (oref > 1) {
6       g_atomic_int_add(&object→ref_count, −1);
7     }
8     else {
9       oref = g_atomic_int_add(&object→ref_count, −1);
10
11      if (oref == 1) {
12        object→klass→finalize(object);
13        g_type_free_instance(object);
14      }
15    }
16  }
17
18  void g_emblem_class_init(GEmblemClass *klass) {
19    klass→finalize = g_emblem_finalize;
20  }
21
22  void g_emblem_finalize(GObject *object) {
23    GEmblem *emblem = (GEmblem*)object;
24    g_object_unref(emblem→icon);
25  }
```

Figure 10. Managed types example from glib-2.0 library

Table 1. Number of inferred transfer and escape annotations

Library Analyzed		Transferred Parameters			
Name	Functions	Transfer	Contract	Indirect	Direct
archive	267	9	33	18	47
freenect	61	2	0	5	13
fuse	188	4	5	106	28
glpk	1072	0	67	54	149
gsl	3910	39	68	21	88
ical	1045	10	0	7	142

directly exploit the structural subtyping relationship and consider all structural subtypes of the input to *DecRef* as being managed. We compare these two approaches in section 8.2.

7.3 Interprocedural Reference Count Manipulation

Not all functions directly increment and decrement references. Many use auxiliary functions, particularly those that rely on atomic increments and decrements. We employ a simple analysis to summarize the effects that functions have on the integer fields of their pointer-typed arguments. This analysis also tracks these effects for arguments of type **int*** to accommodate reference counting functions that pass the address of their reference count field instead of the object containing it.

7.4 Benefits of Automation

For users unfamiliar with a library, the inferred annotations document that reference counts must be maintained. More importantly, automatically finding the vast majority of reference-counted types decreases a potentially large annotation burden.

8. Evaluation

We have applied the analyses described in sections 3 to 6 to a suite of fifteen open-source libraries. The libraries range in size from a few functions and a few hundred lines of code up to several thousand functions with hundreds of thousands of lines of code.

We evaluate the effectiveness of the ownership transfer analysis and the reference counting analysis separately. For the most part, libraries using a reference counting discipline do not require the results of the ownership transfer analysis because ownership is explicitly shared through the reference counts. Thus, the results of the ownership transfer analysis are typically not necessary to generate library bindings for reference-counted libraries.

8.1 Transfer Analysis

This section evaluates the effectiveness of the ownership transfer analysis, with a particular focus on the reduction in manual annota-

tion burden compared to relying solely on the results of an escape analysis. Table 1 shows the number of inferred annotations for six libraries of various sizes. The transfer analysis was designed based on archive and ical. The remaining libraries can be considered as the test set. The second column in the table notes the number of functions in each library. The "Transfer" column reports the number of function parameters that our analysis has identified as transferring ownership from the caller. The rest of the columns break down the results of our escape analysis.

We partition escaping parameters into three categories: contract escapes, indirect escapes, and direct escapes. *Contract escapes* are parameters that escape through calls to function pointers where some targets are known, and all of those targets agree that the parameter does not escape. We refer to these parameters as contract escapes because they only escape if the contract on the function pointer they are passed to is violated, i.e., only if the assumptions of section 6 do not apply. *Indirect escapes* are parameters that are passed as arguments to calls through function pointers for which no targets can be identified. However, it is rare in practice for parameters to truly escape through function pointers because that would make the code difficult to reason about. If a consumer of these analysis results can make this assumption, the distinction can make a significant difference. For example, the fuse client library has many more indirect escapes than direct escapes. *Direct escapes* in table 1 are the remaining escaping parameters: simple escapes, such as to global variables, that are not due to calls through function pointers.

While contract escapes are clearly not expected to escape by the library, by virtue of library-provided initializers, they offer more information still. Each indirect function call that induces contract escapes imposes a contract on the function pointer that is dereferenced for that call. We can say that any function that could be pointed to by that function pointer should obey the contract that its arguments not escape. Contract escapes are most prevalent in libraries with polymorphic behavior, as can be seen in archive. In this library, polymorphism is implemented through function pointers stored in each object. These function pointer fields are initialized with functions defined in the library when objects are created, allowing us to infer the corresponding contracts as suggested in section 6. It is important to note that we do not consider an argument to an indirect function call to be a contract escape if we merely know some of the targets of the call. We only label it as a contract escape if all known call targets agree that the parameter does not escape.

Each *transfer* annotation has an accompanying *direct escape* annotation. If the results of the ownership transfer analysis, rather than the escape analysis, are used to automate resource management, then the difference between the "Direct" and "Transfer" columns in table 1 is the number of manual annotations saved by the ownership transfer analysis. Without the ownership transfer analysis, each extra escape annotation introduces a memory leak that must be plugged with a manual annotation. This difference is striking in glpk and ical: the ownership transfer analysis saves over 100 manual annotations in each. Further, glpk does not seem to ever transfer ownership. However, as discussed in section 5, the escape annotations are still useful as object lifetime documentation to the user.

Note that the transfer analysis requires an accurate view of the finalizer functions in a given library. The finalizer analysis is beyond the scope of this paper, and the one used for this evaluation was not able to identify all of the finalizers in the libraries used for this evaluation. To compensate, we manually annotated four missed finalizers in ical and two in glpk. The finalizers in archive, freenect, and fuse were automatically identified. We have not exhaustively inspected the results for glpk or gsl and some finalizers may have been missed in those libraries; if so, our ownership transfer analysis would identify *more* transferred parameters if the missed finalizers were manually annotated. We note that manually annotating finalizers is significantly easier than manually examining possible ownership transfers because finalizers tend to follow uniform naming conventions.

In the remainder of this subsection, we provide a more detailed analysis of the results for three of the libraries in our evaluation. These three libraries were chosen because they have interesting ownership transfer properties while being small enough to thoroughly evaluate by hand.

8.1.1 ical

The ical library provides a representation of calendar data. It has many functions, but only a few actually transfer ownership of objects. The primary data structures in this library form a tree; when an item is added to a tree representing some calendar event, that tree assumes ownership of the new item.

The two analyses agree that 10 parameters induce ownership transfers. The escape analysis flags over 100 extra parameters, however. Some of these non-transferred escapes can be explained by the presence of a container API that does not own its elements: adding an item to the container causes an escape but the container does not own anything except its own internal structures. Many of the remaining discrepancies arise from parent pointers. When one item is inserted as the child of another in a tree, the parent field of the newly inserted item is updated to point to its new parent element. This causes the child to escape into the parent and the parent to escape into the child. Similarly, many functions cause one or more of their parameters to escape into themselves. These self-escapes could potentially be special-cased when generating library bindings.

One function with an escape annotation but no transfer annotation was particularly interesting. This function adds an attachment to another object; however, attachments are the one resource in ical that are reference-counted. Since attachments are reference-counted, they do not have a finalizer function that our analysis could automatically identify. Adding a manual annotation to the unref function for attachments causes the analysis to correctly identify the ownership transfer in question. This suggests that it may be prudent to consider unref functions for reference-counted resources as finalizers for the purposes of the ownership transfer analysis.

8.1.2 freenect

This library provides a driver and userspace control for Kinect hardware. Our analysis infers ownership transfer of two parameters in two different functions, freenect_init and fnusb_init. Both of these inferences are incorrect. The root cause is fnusb_init, which freenect_init calls. The parameter in question is an optional libusb_context. If the caller provides a context, the library keeps a reference to it but does not assume ownership. However, if the caller does not provide a context, fnusb_init allocates its own context over which it does assume ownership. This ownership is recorded with a flag alongside the reference to the libusb_context. This violates one of the assumptions of our ownership transfer analysis: that fields are either always owned or never owned. This particular field is sometimes owned. While these inferred transfer annotations are not correct, the analysis still relieves the user of having to provide

eleven annotations to compensate for the overzealous escape analysis. The transfer analysis also reduced the amount of code that must be inspected manually to two functions.

We could adapt our analysis to make special note of fields that are only sometimes finalized. Perhaps we could restrict it to fields that are finalized only based on some flag. These conditionally-owned fields could be reported in diagnostics and in generated documentation; with this extra information, users could decide on the correct ownership semantics for their case. Although adding to the manual inspection burden for users is undesirable, our analysis can show users exactly where the ambiguity arises, limiting the scope of the inspection to just unusual finalizers, rather than potentially every function in the library.

8.1.3 fuse

The fuse library is the userspace component of the Filesystem in Userspace project for some *NIX systems. This library has only a handful of ownership transfers; three of the four are transfers of a single type. In these cases, fuse_session objects assume ownership of communication channels through constructors and an explicit fuse_session_add_chan function.

The fourth ownership transferring function, fuse_session_new, is more interesting. It creates a new fuse_session with two parameters: a **void**∗ for arbitrary user-provided data and a **struct** with metadata. Among the metadata is an optional function to finalize the user-provided data, which the finalizer for fuse_session objects invokes if it is present.

This function exhibits an unforeseen interaction with our assumption that fields will either always be owned or never owned: the user has control over the ownership of a field, and our analysis finds evidence within the library being analyzed that the field may be owned. This case suggests that our restriction, as well as our notion of finalizers, could benefit from more nuance. In this case, we see that a field is conditionally finalized based on a value provided by the user, whereas the example in freenect made its decision to finalize or not based on a field set by the library. While the correctness of the transfer annotation in the case of this user data parameter to fuse_session_new may depend on the preferences of the library user, the transfer analysis still saves a user from having to provide at least 24 annotations to prevent leaks due to the escape analysis. Furthermore, the user need only examine the four annotations inferred by the transfer analysis. In reading the documentation on how to call fuse_session_new, the meaning of the transfer annotation on the user data parameter would become clear.

One might be tempted to generate library bindings that never transfer ownership of user data pointers to a C library. This example shows that such special treatment for even this extremely common C idiom is not completely safe. In most cases user data is not owned, but when it is the type system bears no indication one way or another.

Most of the escaping parameters whose ownership is not transferred are other user data pointers. There are also a few instances of self-escaping parameters as in ical. A third class of escapes are due to an imprecision in the escape analysis that could be fixed. The fuse library uses non-escaping heap allocations; parameters stored into these heap allocations are reported as escaping because our escape analysis does not take advantage of the fact that pointers returned by allocators like malloc are not aliased by anything. This could be fixed by treating heap-allocated locals in the same way that we treat non-escaping stack-allocated locals.

8.2 Reference Counting Analysis

Table 2 summarizes the results of our reference counting analysis. This analysis was designed based on the dbus-1, exif, gobject-2.0, and gio-2.0 libraries. For each library, we report (1) the number of functions in the library, (2) the number of functions that are

Table 2. Number of inferred reference counting annotations. "Ref/ Unref" refers to the number of inferred *IncRef* and *DecRef* function pairs, rather than single functions.

Library Analyzed		Reference Counting		
Name	Functions	Allocators	Finalizers	Ref/Unref
cairo	379	2	2	4
dbus-1	804	36	8	11
exif	142	16	5	7
fontconfig	196	51	8	3
freetype	289	9	6	3
gio-2.0	1772	58	11	9
glib-2.0	1529	228	39	16
gobject-2.0	394	15	3	1
soup-2.4	530	46	6	3

```
1  void exif_mem_free(ExifMem *mem, void *d)
2  {
3    if (!mem) return;
4    if (mem→free_func) {
5      mem→free_func(d);
6      return;
7    }
8  }
```

Figure 11. Finalizer from exif library

allocators, (3) the number of functions that are finalizers, and (4) the number of *IncRef* and *DecRef* function pairs. As with our ownership transfer analysis, the reference counting analysis requires an accurate view of the allocators and finalizers present in each library. The dbus-1 library required two manual annotations, exif required four, gobject required one, and glib required seven in order for all of the allocators and finalizers to be recognized. Some of these libraries use custom memory allocators, while others have finalizers that do not quite match the notion of a finalizer that our tools use because they include extra not-NULL checks. Figure 11 shows an example. On line 4, this finalizer checks that a function pointer that it calls is not-NULL. Extending the allocator and finalizer identification analyses is beyond the scope of this work.

This analysis is useful in several ways. First, it alerts users that their library uses reference counting. Our experiments revealed reference-counted types in libraries where we did not expect them, including ical and libusb. Reference counting is not the primary resource management discipline in either library, but is still important yet not apparent from a visual scan. More importantly, even in cases where reference counting is the primary resource management discipline, our reference counting analysis identifies both polymorphic *IncRef*/*DecRef* functions and the types they operate on. For example, in dbus-1 we recognize dbus_auth_unref and dbus_auth_ref as polymorphic managers of reference counts for three related types: DBusAuthClient, DBusAuthServer, and DBusAuth.

The gio-2.0 library highlights the importance of the reference counting analysis in the presence of polymorphic reference counters. While gio-2.0 has 9 *IncRef*/*DecRef* pairs that are identified by the analysis, it defines a further 138 types that are managed by the g_object_unref and g_object_ref functions defined in the gobject-2.0 library. Note that the 9 types with their own reference counting functions *cannot* be managed with the generic gobject-2.0 reference counting functions, though nothing in the names of the types reveals this. Section 7.2 describes two algorithms for recognizing which types are managed by polymorphic reference counting functions. The first relies on the presence of type-specific finalizers and the second relies only on structural subtyping. The second algorithm

has been more reliable in practice, identifying 23 types as managed by the gobject-2.0 reference counting functions that were missed by the first algorithm. The first algorithm misses these types because they have no type-specific resources that need to be finalized, and so do not define a finalizer. However, they are still structural subtypes of GObject, so the second algorithm recognizes them.

9. Related Work

The C/C++ leak detector of Heine and Lam [6] is very similar in spirit to our work. They present an inference algorithm based on inequality constraints to assign an owner to each object in a program. Our algorithms work on partial programs (libraries) and are formulated in terms of symbolic access paths. Our major contributions beyond their work are to (1) recognize ownership semantics for C objects with a generalized notion of allocators and finalizers (instead of C++) and (2) incorporate shared ownership via reference counting and inferred contracts on function pointers used in library code. Rayside and Mendel [17] take a more dynamic approach with ownership profiling; they report detailed hierarchical ownership information that is more precise than what we can achieve statically. Negara et al. [13] describe an inference algorithm based on liveness analysis for identifying ownership transfer semantics in message passing applications. In cases where ownership can be proved to transfer to another process via message passing, the copy of the message can be skipped and the receiving process can assume ownership of the message directly. Boyapati et al. [1] address ownership at the type level with work on ownership types. Müller and Rudich [12] extend Universe Types to support ownership transfer. Their notion of temporary aliases correspond closely to our transient references. In effect, we infer ownership types for C. Focusing specifically on memory, Wegiel and Krintz [20] discuss methods for sharing heap-allocated objects between different managed run-time environments. They do not need to establish an owner for each heap object because the run-time environments are able to cooperate and safely share objects. Since one of our run-time systems is C, which has no facilities for such object sharing, we must infer ownership.

As discussed in section 7, we do not verify the correctness of reference count handling in the libraries we analyze. Emmi et al. [4] present an analysis to perform this complex verification building on the Blast model checker. Our work is complementary in that Emmi et al. require manual specification of the set of reference-counted types, which could be automated with our analysis.

10. Conclusion

We have described an ownership model for C resources to make sharing resources between languages in polyglot programs safer. Documenting the ownership properties of even moderately large programs by hand is difficult and labor-intensive. We have described the allocator and finalizer analyses of Ravitch et al. in terms of our ownership model. We have discussed the difficulty in relying only on an escape analysis to model the ownership of objects in C libraries: many manual annotations are required to compensate for the prevalence of escaping function parameters when true ownership transfer is rare. We addressed this difficulty by describing a new ownership transfer analysis based on our ownership model. We also argue that the results of an escape analysis are still useful for understanding the semantics of libraries. We presented a scalable and composable escape analysis to further reduce the number of false positive escape annotations. We have described trade-offs for this escape analysis in context and field sensitivity that are suitable for analyzing an important class of incomplete program: library code. We have also presented an analysis to automatically identify reference-counted types and their associated reference count management functions.

Our algorithms automatically infer hundreds of annotations describing the resource ownership semantics of fifteen significant open source libraries, significantly reducing the manual annotation burden for those wishing to generate library bindings. While these inferred annotations clearly have applications to polyglot programming, they are also useful for understanding and documenting the behavior of complex C libraries.

References

[1] C. Boyapati, B. Liskov, and L. Shrira. Ownership types for object encapsulation. In A. Aiken and G. Morrisett, editors, *POPL*, pages 213–223. ACM, 2003. ISBN 1-58113-628-5.

[2] B.-C. Cheng and W. W. Hwu. Modular interprocedural pointer analysis using access paths: design, implementation, and evaluation. In M. S. Lam, editor, *PLDI*, pages 57–69. ACM, 2000. ISBN 1-58113-199-2.

[3] J.-D. Choi, M. Gupta, M. J. Serrano, V. C. Sreedhar, and S. P. Midkiff. Stack allocation and synchronization optimizations for Java using escape analysis. *ACM Trans. Program. Lang. Syst.*, 25(6):876–910, 2003.

[4] M. Emmi, R. Jhala, E. Kohler, and R. Majumdar. Verifying reference counting implementations. In S. Kowalewski and A. Philippou, editors, *TACAS*, volume 5505 of *Lecture Notes in Computer Science*, pages 352–367. Springer, 2009. ISBN 978-3-642-00767-5.

[5] R. P. Gabriel, D. F. Bacon, C. V. Lopes, and G. L. S. Jr., editors. *Proceedings of the 22nd Annual ACM SIGPLAN Conference on Object-Oriented Programming, Systems, Languages, and Applications, OOPSLA 2007, October 21-25, 2007, Montreal, Quebec, Canada*, 2007. ACM. ISBN 978-1-59593-786-5.

[6] D. L. Heine and M. S. Lam. A practical flow-sensitive and context-sensitive C and C++ memory leak detector. In *PLDI*, pages 168–181. ACM, 2003. ISBN 1-58113-662-5.

[7] U. P. Khedker, A. Sanyal, and A. Karkare. Heap reference analysis using access graphs. *ACM Trans. Program. Lang. Syst.*, 30(1), 2007.

[8] C. Lattner and V. S. Adve. LLVM: A compilation framework for lifelong program analysis & transformation. In *CGO*, pages 75–88. IEEE Computer Society, 2004. ISBN 0-7695-2102-9.

[9] L. Li, C. Cifuentes, and N. Keynes. Boosting the performance of flow-sensitive points-to analysis using value flow. In T. Gyimóthy and

[10] K.-K. Ma and J. S. Foster. Inferring aliasing and encapsulation properties for Java. In Gabriel et al. [5], pages 423–440. ISBN 978-1-59593-786-5.

[11] I. Matosevic and T. S. Abdelrahman. Efficient bottom-up heap analysis for symbolic path-based data access summaries. In C. Eidt, A. M. Holler, U. Srinivasan, and S. P. Amarasinghe, editors, *CGO*, pages 252–263. ACM, 2012. ISBN 978-1-4503-1206-6.

[12] P. Müller and A. Rudich. Ownership transfer in universe types. In Gabriel et al. [5], pages 461–478. ISBN 978-1-59593-786-5.

[13] S. Negara, R. K. Karmani, and G. A. Agha. Inferring ownership transfer for efficient message passing. In C. Cascaval and P.-C. Yew, editors, *PPOPP*, pages 81–90. ACM, 2011. ISBN 978-1-4503-0119-0.

[14] T. E. Oliphant. Python for scientific computing. *Computing in Science and Engineering*, 9(3):10–20, 2007.

[15] D. J. Pearce, P. H. J. Kelly, and C. Hankin. Efficient field-sensitive pointer analysis of c. *ACM Trans. Program. Lang. Syst.*, 30(1), 2007.

[16] T. Ravitch, S. Jackson, E. Aderhold, and B. Liblit. Automatic Generation of Library Bindings using Static Analysis. In M. Hind and A. Diwan, editors, *PLDI*, pages 352–362. ACM, 2009. ISBN 978-1-60558-392-1.

[17] D. Rayside and L. Mendel. Object ownership profiling: a technique for finding and fixing memory leaks. In R. E. K. Stirewalt, A. Egyed, and B. Fischer, editors, *ASE*, pages 194–203. ACM, 2007. ISBN 978-1-59593-882-4.

[18] S. Sagiv, T. W. Reps, and R. Wilhelm. Parametric shape analysis via 3-valued logic. *ACM Trans. Program. Lang. Syst.*, 24(3):217–298, 2002.

[19] A. Salcianu and M. C. Rinard. Pointer and escape analysis for multithreaded programs. In M. T. Heath and A. Lumsdaine, editors, *PPOPP*, pages 12–23. ACM, 2001. ISBN 1-58113-346-4.

[20] M. Wegiel and C. Krintz. Cross-language, Type-safe, and Transparent Object Sharing for co-Located Managed Runtimes. In W. R. Cook, S. Clarke, and M. C. Rinard, editors, *OOPSLA*, pages 223–240. ACM, 2010. ISBN 978-1-4503-0203-6.

[21] J. Whaley and M. C. Rinard. Compositional pointer and escape analysis for Java programs. In B. Hailpern, L. M. Northrop, and A. M. Berman, editors, *OOPSLA*, pages 187–206. ACM, 1999. ISBN 1-58113-238-7.

[9] (continued) A. Zeller, editors, *SIGSOFT FSE*, pages 343–353. ACM, 2011. ISBN 978-1-4503-0443-6.

Elephant Tracks: Portable Production
of Complete and Precise GC Traces

Nathan P. Ricci

Tufts University

nricci01@cs.tufts.edu

Samuel Z. Guyer

Tufts University

sguyer@cs.tufts.edu

J. Eliot B. Moss

University of Massachusetts Amherst

moss@cs.umass.edu

Categories and Subject Descriptors D.3.4 [*Programming Languages*]: Processors—Memory Management–(garbage collection); C.4 [*Performance of Systems*]: [measurement techniques]

General Terms Languages, Measurement

Keywords Traces; garbage collection; Merlin algorithm; Java

Abstract

We present *Elephant Tracks* (ET), a dynamic program analysis tool for Java that produces detailed traces of garbage collection-related events, including object allocations, object deaths, and pointer updates. Like prior work, our tracing tool is based on the Merlin algorithm [6, 7], but offers several substantial new capabilities. First, it is much more precise than previous tools: it traces method entries and exits and measures time in terms of them, allowing it to place events precisely in the context of the program structure. Second, it is implemented using a combination of JVM Tool Interface (JVMTI) [13] callbacks and bytecode rewriting, and works with any standard JVM. Finally, it produces complete traces, including weak references, events from the Java Native Interface and `sun.misc.Unsafe`, and VM start up objects. In this paper we also explore the general design space of tracing tools, and carefully define the execution model that the traces represent.

1. Introduction

Garbage collection tracing tools have been instrumental in the development of new garbage collection algorithms. A GC tracing tool produces an accurate trace of all the dynamic program events that are relevant to memory management, including allocations, pointer updates, and object deaths. We can quickly test a new GC algorithm by building a simulator that reads the GC trace, instead of developing a full GC implementation in a real virtual machine, which is a considerable undertaking.

One of the widely used GC tracing tools for Java, GCTrace, is available as a component of the JikesRVM Java virtual machine [2]. That tool, like ours, is based on the Merlin algorithm [6, 7], but suffers from several limitations. First, the implementation is integrated directly into the garbage collector. Due to the ongoing evolution of the JikesRVM Memory Management Toolkit, it no longer functions with recent versions of JikesRVM, and older versions will not

run modern Java software. Second, GCTrace measures time only in terms of bytes allocated, a fine metric for GC simulation, but not useful for program analysis since it cannot readily be tied back to points in the program. Third, allocation time is not very precise for events other than allocation: many pointer updates and object deaths can occur at various points in between two allocations. Finally, the existing tool does not support a number of features found in real programs, including weak references and multithreading.

In this paper we present *Elephant Tracks*, a new GC tracing tool that is precise, informative, and can run on top of any standard JVM. Our goal is not simply to address the limitations of prior work, but to provide new capabilities that allow our tool to support a wider variety of program analysis and run-time systems research. Our implementation uses a combination of bytecode instrumentation and JVMTI (JVM Tool Interface) callbacks to construct a shadow heap on which it runs the Merlin algorithm to compute idealized object death times. Its attributes include:

Precise: Trace time is configurable and can be made arbitrarily precise. We currently measure time in terms of method calls (i.e., the clock ticks at every method entry and exit), which are *much* more frequent than allocations.[1]

Complete: The implementation properly handles all relevant events, including difficult cases, such as weak references, the Java Native Interface, `sun.misc.Unsafe`, and JVM start up objects.

Informative: Traces include much more than just GC-related events. We emit a record for every method call and return, allowing us to tie memory behavior back to the program structure. In fact, we can reconstruct the complete dynamic calling context for any time step. We also record information about threads and exceptions, and, optionally, counts of heap reads and writes and number of bytecodes executed.

Well-defined: We carefully define the trace execution model, which embodies a number of subtle design issues that affect the meaning of the traces. These include trace time, the definition of object lifetime, and the ordering of events in multithreaded programs. In this paper we explore these issues in detail and justify our choices.

Portable: Elephant Tracks is implemented as a JVMTI agent that runs on any compliant Java virtual machine.

Fast: OK, not fast, but faster. Elephant Tracks includes performance tuning and optimizations to reduce overhead, which is critical for larger, long-running programs.

In the following sections we explore the design space of GC tracing tools, and explain the choices made for Elephant Tracks. We

---

[1] This includes constructor calls, thus tightly bounding most allocations as well.

discuss the technical challenges of building such a tool using the JVMTI interface, which does not provide direct access to the JVM's representation of Java Objects, or to the garbage collector. We also discuss the handling of weak references. This proved difficult because the JVM is able to side-step some of our instrumentation techniques in this case. Finally, we present some results, including overhead measurements, as well as new insights about the benchmarks gleaned from our precise traces.

2. Background and related work

In this section we describe the general garbage collection tracing problem and existing solutions, and motivate the need for a new trace generator.

2.1 Garbage collection tracing

A GC trace is a record of the sequence of memory management events that occur during a program's execution. The events of interest may vary depending on the intended use of the trace, but typically include object allocation, object reclamation, and mutations in the heap. Many of these events are straightforward to capture, such as object allocation, since they are explicitly invoked in the code.[2] We can instrument those operations directly to emit a trace record with the relevant information.

The central challenge in GC tracing is determining object death times. An obvious solution is to emit an object death record when the garbage collector actually reclaims each object. This approach is easy to implement using JVMTI, but is unappealing for at least two reasons. First, the particular timing of these events is collector-specific—we would be measuring a property of the GC algorithm used during trace generation, rather than a fundamental property of the program. Second, the resulting information is very imprecise. Most garbage collectors run infrequently, reclaiming large numbers of objects long after they are no longer needed by the program. As a consequence, object deaths appear far removed from the program events that actually cause them. This makes the traces poorly suited to evaluating new GC algorithms, as the Merlin work showed [7].

2.1.1 Idealized death times

Our goal is to generate traces with idealized death records. That is, each object death appears in the trace at the earliest time at which the object *could be* reclaimed. An idealized trace captures the behavior of a program independent of any particular GC algorithm, with object death events appearing close to the program actions that cause them. The exact nature of this problem depends on how we define "the earliest time". For example, we could compute death times based on object *liveness*: an object is dead immediately after its last use. While interesting as a lower bound, this level of precision is potentially expensive to compute and cannot be exploited by any real memory manager. Therefore, we adopt the definition used in garbage collection and in prior work on tracing: an object is dead when it is no longer *reachable* from the roots (local and global variables) directly or indirectly through any sequence of pointers. This choice still leaves many subtle issues, however, including the granularity of trace time and the liveness of root variables, which are discussed in more detail in Section 3.

A naive algorithm for computing idealized death times is to run the garbage collector much more frequently. For example, we could produce a very precise trace by invoking the collector at every program point where an object could become dead. Not surprisingly, this approach is totally impractical.

---

[2] This is more subtle than you might think. In Java, the virtual machine may allocate application-visible objects as side-effects of other actions, such as class loading, and native libraries can also do so. Similar remarks apply to pointer updates.

2.1.2 The Merlin algorithm

The Merlin algorithm, introduced by Hertz et al. [6], solves this problem by using timestamps to *infer* the idealized death times of objects when they are reclaimed at regularly scheduled garbage collections. During normal execution the algorithm timestamps objects whenever they lose an incoming pointer. At any point in time an object's timestamp represents the last time it was *directly* observed to be reachable. When the collector reclaims an object, however, its timestamp is not necessarily its death time. In many cases an object becomes unreachable *indirectly*, when an object that points to it becomes unreachable. In this case we need to determine which event occurred later: the direct loss of an incoming pointer (the timestamp), or the indirect loss of reachability (the death times of the referring objects). So, the idealized death time of an object ($T_d(o)$) is computed from its timestamp ($T_s(o)$) and the death times of any objects that point to it:

$$T_d(o) = Max(T_s(o), \{T_d(p), \forall p : p \to o\})$$

This insight leads to a practical approach for GC tracing that is also at the heart of the system we present in this paper:

- During normal execution:
  - Record ordinary events in the trace as they occur (e.g., object allocations and pointer updates).
  - Timestamp objects whenever they might become directly unreachable (i.e., when they lose an incoming pointer).
- At GC time:
  - Compute idealized death times using the formula above (implemented roughly as a depth-first search on the graph of dead objects, pushing computed death times across the pointers).
  - Generate a death event record for each reclaimed object and insert it in the proper place in the trace.
  - Flush records to disk, and continue ...

An important implication of the Merlin algorithm is that it requires a notion of *trace time* for use in the timestamps. In fact, all trace records need timestamps because the object death records are generated out of order—we discover the true death times of objects only at GC time, which is typically much later. The model of trace time (in particular, its granularity) has a profound impact on the implementation of the trace generator and the precision of the traces it generates.

2.2 Why a new trace generator?

The first realization of Merlin took the form of a customized garbage collector called GCTrace, implemented in JikesRVM. The main advantage of this approach is that the implementation can be integrated directly into the virtual machine code. The compiler can be modified to add instrumentation to object allocations and pointer updates, and the garbage collector can be modified to perform the extra death time computation. While GCTrace has proved to be a valuable tool, it has a number of serious limitations, several of which are a consequence of its dependence on JikesRVM:

Imprecise: GCTrace uses *allocation time* for its traces: the trace time clock "ticks" at each object allocation. As a result, object deaths and other events that occur in between allocations cannot be ordered or precisely localized at any finer granularity.

Divorced from program structure: A related problem is that allocation time does not correspond to anything static in the program itself, so figuring out where events occur relative to the code is very difficult (e.g., "In which method did the death of object 739229 occur?").

Incomplete: GCTrace ignores a number of difficult corner cases, including multithreading, JNI, and the various forms of weak references.

Java-in-Java: Because JikesRVM is implemented in Java, great pains must be taken not to include VM events and objects in the trace. Furthermore, parts of the algorithm, such as sorting death records, are extremely painful to implement because they must run inside the garbage collector and therefore cannot allocate any ordinary data structures themselves.

Performance: While all trace generators are likely to be slow, GC-Trace is particularly slow for several reasons. First, it performs local variable timestamping using an expensive stack walk at every time step (every allocation). Second, it works only with the non-optimizing compiler. Third, it supports only a simple whole-heap garbage collector.

Application limitations: While in principle any Java application runs under any JVM, in practice there are variations. JikesRVM, which is maintained by volunteers, tends to lag commercial implementations to some extent, so there are applications of interest that run on commercial JVMs but not on JikesRVM.

Bit rot: MMTk (the memory management toolkit used in JikesRVM) has undergone a number of radical refactorings, often leaving the GCTrace implementation out of date.

2.3 Related work

There is a huge body of work on tracing programs to produce a record of various run-time events. The work most closely related to ours is the original GCTrace implementation of the Merlin algorithm [7], which is discussed in detail throughout this paper. Foucar reimplemented GCTrace using a shadow heap implemented in C++, like Elephant Tracks, but otherwise preserving the execution model and dependence on JikesRVM [4].

Another potential approach is to use non-deferred reference counting, which reclaims objects as soon as their reference counts becomes zero. Like reference counting collection, however, this approach cannot directly detect the death of cycles of objects, and would require frequent tracing collections to achieve high precision.

Two prior papers explore the relationship between liveness and reachability for garbage collection. Agesen et al. [1] examine the effects of applying different levels of liveness analysis to the GC root set (variables on the stack). They found that on average the differences were small, but on occasion static liveness analysis would improve collection efficiency noticeably. This result suggests that our dynamic liveness model is reasonable for most purposes, but could be improved (see later discussion). Hirzel et al. [8] additionally consider the difference between reachability from live roots and true liveness of objects. They also find that schemes based on liveness of variables have little impact on reachability. True object liveness, however, is significantly different. Elephant Tracks currently cannot compute equivalent information, since it does not record reads from objects, but there is no fundamental impediment to adding this feature.

GC traces have been used to drive empirical studies of heap behavior, especially those examining the distribution and predictability of the lifetimes of objects [10, 11]. At a coarse level, allocation time and method time do not produce dramatically different lifetime distributions. For analyses that are sensitive to program structure, however, small differences in allocation time can span many methods. In addition, allocation time is not stable across runs of a program under different inputs.

Jones and Ryder [11] offered perhaps the most well-known study of object demographics. They showed that the calling context of object allocation correlates well with lifetime. They could not determine, however, whether the calling context of object *death* correlates with lifetime, which might be a more useful fact for further improving garbage collection.

Inoue et al. [10] look at what information is needed to precisely predict the lifetime of an object at its allocation point. They define a *fully precise* predictor as one that is accurate to within a single unit of time. By using allocation time, however, they significantly reduce the coverage and accuracy of their predictors. The lifetime of an object in allocation time is much less stable than the calling context of its death, since the latter is directly related to its cause of death, while the former includes many irrelevant events (i.e., unrelated allocations). This instability is particularly acute across runs of a program with different inputs.

Compile-time GC [5] and connectivity-based garbage collection [9] are two examples of techniques where knowing the program location at which an object dies is crucial. Such techniques are often evaluated using trace-driven simulation before embarking on a full implementation. Using Elephant Tracks traces would yield a more accurate assessment of their potential.

Lambert et al. present a system for performing platform-independent JVM timing [12]. Although similar in spirit to our JVM-independent execution model, the focus of this work is on developing a model of code execution, rather than heap memory behavior.

Uhlig and Mudge [14] present a survey of memory tracing techniques. While their focus is on tracing memory accesses for architecture and system research, they enumerate a set of features they consider desirable for tracing systems in general: completeness (all relevant events are recorded), detail (events are associated with program-level information), low distortion (tracing does not change the program's behavior), and portability. Elephant Tracks achieves many of these goals, although it significantly distorts actual running time, however, which is why we use a separate notion of time.

3. Elephant Tracks Design

Our goals in designing a new trace generator are to address the limitations of prior systems and to add new functionality to support new kinds of program analysis and memory management research. The central features of this design are (1) the kinds of program events recorded in a trace, and (2) the accuracy of this information with respect to some model of program execution. In this section we present the design of Elephant Tracks, and we discuss our choices in the context of the general GC tracing design space. In Section 4 we describe how this design is implemented.

3.1 Kinds of trace records

A minimal GC trace consists of just a sequence of object allocations and object deaths, labeled with the trace time and thread ID of each event. Without more information, though, such a trace has limited utility. In practice we add trace records for other kinds of relevant events to provide context for program analysis and to enable more kinds of trace-based simulations. For garbage collection research, for example, it is useful to add trace records for pointer updates in the heap, allowing a simulator to maintain an accurate heap model. Elephant Tracks can be configured to produce different kinds of trace records. We currently support the following kinds of records:

- Object allocations and object deaths (with idealized death times computed using the Merlin algorithm).

- Pointer updates in the heap: These records include the source and target objects, as well as the object field or array index being updated. We also include updates of static fields.

- Method entry and exit: These records allow trace times to be mapped to specific methods, and even more precisely, to specific calling contexts.

- Exceptions: We augment method entry and exit to indicate when an exception is thrown, the sequence of method calls (if any) that are terminated early because of the exception, and the entry to a handler for the exception. The main purpose of these events is to provide accurate information about method execution context.

- (Optional) Heap read/write counts: Each time the clock ticks or a basic block ends, we generate a counts record that summarizes the number of heap reads and writes (of pointers and non-pointers), and the number of bytecodes executed, since the last counts record. Note, however, that multiple counts records can occur between clock ticks, and they cannot be ordered with respect to object deaths in the same tick.

Separately from the trace, Elephant Tracks also emits information about each class loaded, each field declared in the class, each method declared in the class, and each allocation site in each method. This information is referred to by the trace, e.g., the trace will mention a unique allocation site number, which can be found in the side description file.

We currently do not generate trace records for object timestamps or for general memory accesses (including stack reads and writes). This information would enable an even wider range of applications, such as cache simulations. These events are extremely frequent, however, and would result in overwhelmingly large traces. In addition, instrumenting every single variable access would be technically challenging—bytecode rewriting might not be the best approach for this level of detail.

3.2 Execution model

Ideally, we would like to generate perfect traces, in which every event is recorded with a perfectly accurate and precise time. But this goal raises a critical question: accurate with respect to *what*? That is, what is the *execution model* that we want the trace to represent? Elephant Tracks, like other trace generators, relies on a host virtual machine to execute the target program. It runs alongside the VM, recording relevant events. The problem is that the timing of some events is highly VM dependent—directly recording these events as they occur produces a trace that has the VM's execution model "baked in." Instead, we want to generate traces that have their own well-defined, less VM-specific, execution model. The possible models range widely, with some elements closer to the VM (essentially profiling the VM), and other elements more abstract, capturing an idealized execution of the program.

The main components of a GC tracing execution model are (1) the definition of object lifetime (in particular, when are objects considered dead), and (2) the definition of trace time (i.e., when does the trace time clock "tick" and with what frequency). The overall goal of the Elephant Tracks execution model is to define these components in such a way that events can be localized precisely within the structure of the code. The model is idealized for object lifetimes, but resorts to VM timing in cases where an idealized model is not possible, such as the interleaving of concurrent threads and the clearing of weak references.

3.2.1 Defining object lifetime

Object lifetimes are delineated by allocation and death events. Most object allocations are explicit in the program, so simply recording them as they occur produces a VM-independent trace. We have found, however, that there are several other sources of allocations, including VM internal allocations (e.g., `String` constants in class files and `Class` objects themselves), objects allocated by the VM before it can even turn instrumentation on, and objects allocated by JNI calls. We capture all of these, but cannot associate them with a usual allocation site in the application, and for those allocated very early in the run, we cannot provide relative time or context of allocation.

For object deaths, however, an explicit goal of GC tracing is to compute idealized death times. Both Elephant Tracks and GCTrace adopt the standard GC definition: an object is dead when it is no longer reachable from the roots (local and global variables). Even within this seemingly narrow definition, however, there are a range of possible models. To see why, consider the program events that can cause an object to become unreachable:

- The program overwrites a pointer in the heap (`putfield`, etc.)
- The program overwrites a static (global) reference (`putstatic`)
- A local reference variable goes out of scope
- The program changes the value of a local reference variable
- A weak reference is cleared by the garbage collector

While the first two (heap and global writes) are straightforward to instrument, local variables and weak references are more difficult to pin down. Furthermore, there are roots inside the VM that we cannot observe and that the VM does not necessarily inform us about when they change. Fortunately these are mostly "immortal" references, such as to class objects, or relate to constants constructed from class files (these may come and go).

Local variables

Tracing local variables presents many design choices and challenges. The key question is: at what point is a local pointer variable dead, and therefore no longer keeping the target object alive? At one end of the spectrum we could consider local variables live throughout the method invocation with which they are associated. In practice, however, most virtual machines apply some form of static liveness analysis to compute more precise lifetimes. The virtual machine uses this information to construct GC maps, which tell the garbage collector which variables to consider as GC roots at a given point in the method.

GCTrace uses the GC maps in JikesRVM to determine which variables are live. The advantage of this approach is that it is straightforward to implement. The downside is that the timing of the object death records depends on the specific liveness analysis algorithm and choice of GC points made in JikesRVM.

Elephant Tracks currently uses a form of dynamic liveness to determine the lifetimes of local variables. This choice reflects implementation decisions (described in more detail below). A variable is considered dead after its last dynamic use. We define a *use* as one of the following: (1) a direct dereference (access to an object or array), (2) a type test, such as `instanceof`, (3) obtaining an array's length, (4) use as a receiver of a dynamic method dispatch, or (5) a reference test, such as `ifnull`.

Dynamic liveness, however, is more precise than static liveness analysis, primarily because it is not conservative about liveness on different execution paths. The resulting traces show some object death times earlier than any real garbage collector could achieve. For example, a reference variable that is passed through a series of methods, but never used, is considered dead in all the methods. As partial compensation we consider a variable live if it is passed to a method call as a parameter, or returned.

In the future, we plan to add one or more reference implementations of static liveness analysis that allows us to control the model of variable lifetimes more precisely, and thus model more closely what idealized optimizing and non-optimizing compilers might do. For example, an idealized non-optimizing compiler would keep a variable live as long as its type, as computed according to the JVM specification, is a pointer type. On the other hand, an idealized optimizing compiler would apply a backwards data flow analysis to determine a static estimate of liveness. However, real compilers may transform code in various ways, such as inlining methods and duplicating tails to form superblocks. While we admit that such transformations occasionally affect liveness for some objects, at the same time we contend that the vast majority of cases will be approximated well, for purposes of evaluating GC algorithms, by a suitable idealized model. Elephant Tracks is a good foundation from which to explore questions like this.

Weak references

Weak references present an interesting challenge. In principle, the garbage collector can choose to clear weak references at any time (or not at all) once an object is no longer strongly reachable. In practice, they will only be cleared when the collector is actually run. Further, soft references are cleared "at the discretion" of the collector, in response to memory pressure. Phantom references are similarly affected by the timing of collector runs by the host VM. For a trace, though, this leaves no obvious idealized model of when to clear a weak reference. Both Elephant Tracks and GCTrace opt to record these events when the VM chooses to perform them. Given that programs can perceive and respond to the collector's decision, there is no good alternative to this approach.

3.2.2 Trace time

For Merlin-based tracing we need a notion of trace time, so that object death records, which are generated only at GC time, can be inserted in their proper place in the trace. The choice of trace time has a profound affect on the implementation of the tool and on the resulting traces.

Real time is a bad choice, since it is dependent on many factors, including the virtual machine, the operating system, and the hardware. In addition, tracing tends to slow programs down significantly, so the real times are likely to be significantly different from uninstrumented runs. Real time is also, in some sense, too precise: we do not want the trace to reflect the time it takes to actually perform a timestamp or record a trace record.

The solution is to express time in terms of some program-level event: each time the event is encountered we tick the trace clock. In this way, time depends only on a property of the program, not on the VM or underlying machine. This model breaks time into discrete steps, each of which represents a small region of program execution.

The choice of which event(s) to use for the clock affects the granularity of time, which ultimately determines the precision of the trace, since trace records labeled with the same time cannot be ordered or localized within the region covered by that time step. The trade-off is that more fine-grained notions of time are more difficult to implement correctly, since we need to place the instrumentation more precisely to make sure that every event is labeled with the correct time. They may also incur more overhead.

Allocation time vs method time

GCTrace measures time in terms of the number of bytes allocated since the program started (called *allocation time*). At each allocation, time advances by the number of bytes allocated. Allocation time is good for basic GC research, since the traces are precise enough to drive simulations of experimental GC algorithms. Allocation time is fairly coarse, however, and a single time step can cover a large region of the code spanning multiple method calls. Answering questions like "What caused this object to die?" is not possible.

Elephant Tracks measures time in terms of the number of method entries and exits executed (which we call *method time*). For most programs method time is much more precise than allocation time because method calls occur around 10 times more frequently than allocations, depending on the program (we present measurements in Section 5). Method time is almost a strict superset of allocation time, since every allocation of a scalar object also calls at least one constructor. The exception is array allocations, but in our experience these are not frequent enough to change the results significantly. Also, if a constructor receives as an *argument* (not the receiver) a new object, there can be two allocations without an intervening constructor call. Again, this is not common.

The ideal notion of time is probably something like "bytecodes executed", since a single bytecode is the finest grain event that is still VM-independent. A reasonable alternative might be to tick the clock at both method call/return *and* object allocations. As we discuss further in Section 4, ticking the clock more frequently necessitates more object timestamping operations, and thus increases overhead (and can risk expanding methods such that they exceed the maximum allowed method size of 65,535 bytes).

While it may seem that the heap read/write counts records that we make available as an option allow one to use "bytecodes executed" as a measure of time, the counts records do not "tick" the clock, in part for the reasons just mentioned. Further, using them as the clock may make the idealized model too "tight," allowing little re-ordering of the kind typically done by optimizing compilers.

3.2.3 Concurrency

Most modern software uses concurrency in some form, which raises the question of how to order trace events that occur in different threads. We adopt a straightforward approach in which time is global, but trace records include both the time[3] and the ID of the thread in which the event occurred. In the current implementation, however, timestamps on objects do not include the thread ID, so object deaths cannot necessarily be assigned to particular threads.

One problem with this approach is that the resulting traces encode the scheduling decisions of the VM and operating system. Furthermore, trace instrumentation perturbs program execution significantly, resulting in schedules that could be quite different from the uninstrumented programs. While interesting, this problem is difficult to address without controlling the scheduler directly—for example, by replaying a schedule from a real run. One potential solution is to represent time using vector clocks, which would encode only the necessary timing dependences between threads. However, this would still suffer from particularity of orders of interactions. We hope to investigate alternative designs in the future.

4. Implementation

Elephant Tracks is implemented as a Java *agent* that uses the Java Virtual Machine Tool Interface (JVMTI). The primary components of a system using ET are: the JVM itself, including its JVMTI and JNI support; the application; the Elephant Tracks agent; the `ElephantTracks` Java class file, which connects bytecode instrumentation to the agent via Java Native Interface (JNI) calls; and the instrumenter, which rewrites the bytecode of classes as they are loaded.

4.1 Timestamping strategy

For Merlin to produce precise death times, the timestamp on an object must always be the time at which the object last lost an incoming reference. This invariant is easy to maintain for heap and

---

[3] We do not actually output the time value, but it can be derived by knowing which events "tick" the clock.

static references, since we can directly instrument these operations, timestamping the old target before allowing the store to proceed. For stack references, however, there is no explicit operation denoting the end of a variable's scope. There are essentially two strategies for solving this problem: (1) timestamp all live variables at every time step, or (2) timestamp each variable exactly when its lifetime ends. (Recall that we define a *variable* as being live only up to its last actual use.)

GCTrace uses strategy (1), which has the advantage that it is straightforward to implement: at each tick of the clock, walk the stack and timestamp each object referred to by a live variable. This strategy, however, creates a trade-off between performance and precision. Walking the stack is a starkly expensive operation, so it cannot be performed frequently, limiting the granularity of the clock. The problem is particularly acute when using allocation time, since a single time step can span multiple methods, requiring a full walk of the call stack at every tick. We believe that stack walking also inhibits code optimizations (or forces de-optimization), further slowing execution. Furthermore, as mentioned in Section 3 it relies on the VM's GC maps to define variable liveness.

Elephant Tracks uses strategy (2). This approach requires more instrumentation to timestamp a variable's referent whenever the variable is used. It has several advantages, though. The most important is that it works correctly for any granularity of time. In addition, it gives the trace generator explicit control over the model of variable liveness. Finally, it is amenable to an instrumentation-time optimization (described below) that eliminates redundant timestamping operations.

4.2 The instrumenter

The instrumenter is ordinary Java code and is written using the ASM bytecode rewriting tool [3]. The current version of ET is written to use ASM 3.3.1. In order to avoid possible tangle between instrumenter code and the application, we run the instrumenter in a separate operating system process, connected with the agent via pipes in both directions. The agent uses the JVMTI `ClassFileLoadHook` callback, which causes the JVM to present to the agent each class that the JVM wants to load, and to give the agent the opportunity to substitute other bytecode for what the JVM presents. The ET agent sends the bytecode to the instrumenter, which sends back an instrumented class file.

The instrumenter assigns a unique number to each class, each field, each method, and each allocation site (for both scalars and arrays) in each method, writing them to what we call the *names* file. The instrumenter also sends the class and field information to the agent. (At present the agent has no need to maintain tables for the other information, so it is not sent.)

4.2.1 Ordinary instrumentation

We defer to Section 4.2.2 some special cases, and describe now the usual instrumentation added by the ET instrumenter. We organize the description by feature.

Method entry and exit: On entry, and just before a return, we insert a call noting the id of the method and the receiver (for instance methods). In a constructor we cannot actually pass the receiver (it's not initialized yet), so we pass `null` and the agent uses a JNI `GetLocalObject` call to retrieve the receiver from the stack frame.

Exception throw: At an `athrow` bytecode we insert a call that passes the exception object, the method id, and the receiver (for instance methods). The same special handling of the receiver in constructors happens here, too.

Exception exit: To detect exceptional exit of a method, we wrap each method's original bytecode with a catch-anything excep-

tion handler, which makes a call indicating the same information as for a throw, and then re-throws the exception.

Exception handle: At the start of each exception handler we insert a call that notes the same information as for a throw.

Scalar object allocations: The basic idea is to insert, after the `new` bytecode, a call that indicates the new object, its class, and the allocation site number. However, we cannot pass the new object directly since it is uninitialized. Further, it is on the JVM stack, not in a local variable, so the JNI `GetLocalObject` function will not work. Our solution is to add one extra local variable to any method that allocates a scalar. We `dup` the new object reference and `astore` it to the extra local. In the call to the agent we indicate which local variable the agent should examine to obtain the object reference. Strictly speaking, we do not need to pass the class, since the agent can figure it out; we may remove that in the future.

Array allocations: New arrays start life fully initialized, so we simply pass them in a call to the agent, along with the allocation site number. For `multianewarray` we call an out-of-line instrumentation routine that informs the agent of each of the whole collection of new arrays that are created. This could also be done in the agent, if desired.

Pointer updates: For `putfield` of a reference and for `aastore` we insert, before the bytecode, a call that notes the object being changed, the object reference being stored, and the field (or index, for an array) being updated. Java allows `putfield` on uninitialized objects (mostly so that an instance of an inner class can have its pointer to its "containing" outer class instance installed, *before* invoking the inner class constructor). In that case we use the same technique as for scalar allocations to indicate to the agent the object being updated.

Uses of objects: As mentioned in Section 3, ET timestamps objects when they are used. We mentioned there the cases in which that happens. We simply insert a call, passing the object to be timestamped. On method entry we timestamp all pointer arguments, including the receiver. (In constructors we make a slightly different call since we cannot pass the receiver; the agent fetches it out of the frame.) For efficiency on method entry, we have timestamp calls that take 2, 3, 4, or 5 objects to stamp.

Counts: As an extension controlled by a command line flag, the instrumenter will also track the number of heap read and writes, the number of heap reads and writes of reference values, and the number of bytecodes executed, and insert calls reporting these just before each action that advances the timestamp clock, and just before control flow branch and merge points.

We further include a simple kind of optimization to reduce the number of timestamp calls. We track which variables (locals and stack) have been timestamped since the last tick or the last bytecode frame object. (Frames occur at control flow merge points, and detail the types of the local and stack variables at that point.) We avoid timestamping an object twice in the same tick. This optimization requires tracking object references as bytecodes move them around, but is straightforward. The optimization is effective, and we found it necessary in order to avoid having some methods increase in size so much, because of added instrumentation, that they overflow the maximum allowed method size.

4.2.2 Instrumentation special cases

We now detail various special cases (beyond access to uninitialized new objects, mentioned in the previous section).

Native methods: In order to indicated when a native method is called and returns, we change its name, prepending `$$ET$$`, and insert a non-native method that calls the native method. We instrument the non-native method essentially as usual. A number of native methods require special treatment, however:

getStackClass: This method of `java.lang.Class`, and several similar methods, include an argument specifying the number of stack frames to go up to look for some information. To wrap these native methods, the ET non-native wrapper adds one to the number of frames before calling the native. This properly adjusts for the extra level of call that the wrapper adds.

getClassContext: This method of the IBM J9 `ClassLoader` probes a specific number of frames up the stack, so wrapping it disturbs the result. With regret, we do not wrap it. (We contend that native methods subject to this problem should be redesigned, like `getStackClass` described above, so that they can be wrapped.) A number of other methods exhibit essentially the same problem.

Several native methods of class `Object`: Specifically, `getClass`, `notify`, `notifyAll`, and `wait` do not operate correctly if wrapped, so we omit them.

initReferenceImpl: This method of class `Reference` initializes the `referent` field of a weak reference object. We instrument it specially so that the agent can observe the update to the field, which otherwise would be hidden to ET.

Several methods of `sun.misc.Unsafe`: for `allocateInstance` we note the allocation; for a successful `compareAndSwapObject` we note the pointer update, as we do for `putObject`, `putObject-Volatile`, and `putObjectOrdered`. All of these updating operations work in terms of the offset of a field or array element into the object, a fact not readily available to the agent. Therefore we instrument `objectFieldOffset`, `staticFieldBase`, `staticFieldOffset`, `arrayBaseOffset`, and `arrayBase-Scale` to inform the agent of the base or offset information they return, so that the agent can map the offsets and bases back to fields and array elements.

System.arraycopy: We instrument this specially so that the agent can note all the resulting updates to arrays of objects. The agent does the actual work *and* notes the effects, taking care to deal correctly with situations that will throw an exception, etc.

Class `Object`: We instrument `Object.<init>` to report the newly initialized object. Sometimes this is the first time we see an object, e.g., for some objects created via JNI calls. We carefully *avoid* instrumenting `Object.finalize` since having any bytecode in that method will cause every object to be scheduled for finalization (which breaks JVMs). Any `finalize` method in another class *is* instrumented, so finalizations are visible in the trace.

Timestamping new objects: Trying to obtain a reference to and timestamp a new object in `Object.<init>` or `Thread.<init>` fails, but the object will be reported soon anyway, so skipping the timestamp operation is not harmful.

4.3 The agent

The agent performs these functions to support ET's goals:

- Sends classes to the instrumenter and returns instrumented classes to the JVM.

- Notes several actions of the JVM and responds appropriately. These include: changes in the JVMTI phase of execution (VMStart, VMInit, and VMDeath); GarbageCollectionFinish, which triggers a scan (described further below) to see if any weak references have been cleared; and VMObjectAlloc, to detect objects allocated directly by the VM.

- Intercepts various JNI calls so that it can emit suitable trace records, specifically, AllocObject, ThrowNew, and the var-

ious NewObject and NewString calls, to note the new object; and SetObjectField, SetStaticObjectField, and SetObjectArrayElement to note reference updates.

- Handles the various instrumentation calls from the Elephant-Tracks class and (generally) creates a trace record, inserting it into a buffer.

- Maintains a model of the heap graph. Each node represents an object and each directed edge a pointer. The model also includes static variables, but does not (cannot) include various VM internal roots, and as previously described, we do not model stack roots directly, but employ timestamping to determine liveness from thread stacks.

- To help maintain the heap graph model, and to identify objects in trace records, the agent uses the JVMTI object tagging facility to associate a unique serial number with each object, as early as possible after the object is created.

- Maintains a table of object liveness timestamps, and the timestamp "tick" clock.

- Maintains a data structure describing weak objects and their referents. Whenever the JVM runs its garbage collector, after collection completes the agent notifies a separate agent thread to check each weak object to see if its referent has been cleared. This thread will timestamp the now-unreachable referent with the current time, giving a good-faith estimate as to when it died.

Trace outputting proceeds in cycles. This is because determining which objects have died, propagating timestamps, and inserting death records at the right place in the trace, is a periodic activity, done in batches. When the agent is notified that the JVM is entering the JVMTI Live phase, the agent iterates over the initial heap and creates an object allocation record for each object and a pointer update record for each non-null instance and static field. When the agent is notified that the JVM is entering the JVMTI Dead phase (JVM shutdown), it closes out the current buffer of trace records.

In between, during the Live phase, whenever the trace buffer fills with records, the agent:

1. Forces a garbage collection and then iterates over the remaining heap. This allows the agent to detect which objects have been reclaimed since the trace buffer was last emptied.

2. Applies the Merlin algorithm to compute object death times (really "last time alive" times).

3. Checks weak objects to see if their referent as been cleared. The VM does not inform the agent directly about this, but since we note referent field initialization, we know about weak objects and their referent targets. The tables the agent maintains for these are carefully designed not to keep the objects live (we use JNI weak references).

4. Adds death records to the trace buffer, properly timestamped.

5. Sorts the records using a stable sort, and outputs them.

The last step, sorting and outputting, we observed to consume about half the time of creating a trace and so we developed a parallel version. We report performance results in Section 5.

4.4 Properties of our implementation approach

Our implementation strategy has many advantages and few drawbacks. Its advantages include:

- It works with commercial JVMs (in principle with any JVM supporting JVMTI) and can run any application. Of course timing-dependent applications may misbehave as with any tool that slows execution, etc. This prevents several DaCapo benchmarks from completing successfully.

- The run-time is implemented in C++, with all of its data structures outside of the JVM. This makes it easier to insure that ET data structures and actions are not inappropriately entwined with the application and JVM.

- The instrumenter is in a separate process, insuring it does not become tangled with the application and allowing it to run on a different model JVM, if that is convenient. Our reliance on ASM is not problematic because ASM is widely used, actively maintained, and part of the infrastructure of at least one major commercial JVM (Oracle's HotSpot).

- We capture even some very tricky cases, including weak references, field updates via `sun.misc.Unsafe`, reflective object creation, updates, and method calls, VM internal allocations, relevant JNI calls made by the VM or other native libraries, and `System.arraycopy`.

Drawbacks of ET as it stands are mostly ones that similar tools are likely to share:

- A few methods cannot be instrumented, since doing so breaks the JVM.

- Relative timing and thread interactions are affected, which may change application behavior.

- Weak reference clearing is dependent on the vagaries of the JVM.

- Precision in determining object deaths, and the general wealth of information in the traces, come at a cost: the execution dilation factor is on the order of hundreds (see Section 5 for performance results).

- The resulting system is not as simple as we would like. There are places with somewhat tricky synchronization and more data structures and mappings than we would like, but it is not easy to deal with features such as weak references and `sun.misc.Unsafe`.

- We rely heavily on correctness and completeness of JVMTI and JNI support. One implication is that, at present, JikesRVM cannot support ET. Also, we have discovered previously unreported JVM bugs, such as failure of one JVM to present for rewriting *every* class it loads, which implies that a handful of classes go uninstrumented. (That bug is being fixed, but it appears we later found a similar case whose fix will take longer.)

4.5 Some future directions

We have in mind a few things to work on in the future. One is to devote additional effort to streamlining common cases to improve ET's performance further. For example, at object allocations we do not need to pass the name of the class of the object in the instrumentation call at all, and we would save effort (and bytes in the trace) if we output the instrumenter's number for the class rather than the class name. Perhaps of more significance, we want to tune the data structures that are accessed concurrently, and in particular the locking protocols. We wish to explore different models of local variable and stack liveness, approaching more closely what bytecode interpreters and JIT compilers are likely to do. The time required to rewrite bytecodes in the instrumenter is generally quite small compared with ET's overall running time, so performing data flow analyses, etc., will not itself create bottlenecks. A semantic extension we want to explore is moving ET from being a *GC tracing* tool to being (also) a *memory tracing* tool, outputting traces that include all heap accesses. This might be useful for modeling cache and memory system behavior (neglecting the stack). It might be tricky to accomplish this without causing method size to increase so much that methods exceed the JVM specification limit of 64K bytes.

5. Results

5.1 Performance

In this section we present results from running Elephant Tracks on the DaCapo Benchmarks, in order to give a sense of its performance and the properties of the resulting traces. (Unfortunately, it fails to run `tradebeans` and `tradesoap`, perhaps because of internal timeouts.)

In Table 1 we present the run-time overhead of our tool under several configurations:

In the No Callback configuration, all of our bytecode instrumentation was injected, but callbacks into the JVMTI agent were disabled (resulting in an empty trace). Additionally, the No Callback configuration enables only the absolute minimum number of JVMTI features necessary to instrument classes. This represents a practical lower bound on the overhead of instrumenting class files and executing the instrumented bytecode, without the overhead of calling into the JVMTI agent, processing the events, or producing a trace record.

The Serial ET configuration periodically pauses to generate death records, put them in order, and output them to the trace file. In contrast, the Parallel ET configuration spawns a separate thread to do this work. This generally results in better performance and fewer pauses in the traced application, but may be of no benefit if the machine lacks sufficient resources to execute this thread in parallel with the application.

With a geometric mean of about 250, the overall dilation factor of Elephant Tracks is within a factor of two of the published dilation factors of GCTrace [6, 7], while providing much more information.

The dilation factors of the different benchmarks are not uniform. This diversity cannot be explained only by the differences in amount of instrumentation, since there is no simple linear relationship between the No Callback configuration and the other configurations. Similarly, it could not be explained by a simple linear model relating number of calls into the JVMTI agent and/or average heap size of the benchmark being traced (at least, no model we were able to discover). Therefore, we theorize that it relates to complex interactions between our instrumentation, Java optimizations, and/or the implementation details of the JVMTI interface.

5.2 Trace analysis

Table 2 shows the composition of the traces by event type (percentage of the trace accounted for by each type). Method entry and exit events outnumber the others significantly, which is why method time is so much more precise than allocation time. In fact, on average there are 70 method entry/exit events between any two allocations. In other words, a single tick of the *allocation* clock can span dozens of methods, making it difficult to localize object death events within the code. A single tick of the *method time* clock occasionally contains an allocation, and depending on where the starting and ending method events are found, we might not be able to tell if a death event occurred before or after the allocation. In a few cases, a single unit of method time might contain two or more allocations.

In order to demonstrate the value of these more precise traces, we present a few simple trace analysis examples. First, a simple escape analysis is easy to perform with ET traces. We process a trace, and upon encountering a record of object allocation, note the context in which it occurred. Then, if the death event for that same object is encountered before the associated method return, we know the object has not escaped. Conversely, if we do not find the death record before this point, the object has escaped. Note that this does not necessarily mean that there is any static analysis that could have determined in advance that the object would or would not have escaped. The results of this escape analysis are reported

Benchmark	No Callback Dilation	Serial ET Dilation	Parallel ET Dilation
avrora-default	1.6	436.5	291.1
avrora-large	0.9	553.9	436.1
avrora-small	1.7	354.0	227.3
batik-default	3.7	152.5	102.6
batik-large	3.0	124.6	84.1
batik-small	2.9	58.3	41.9
eclipse-default	18.0	310.5	2110.5
eclipse-large	19.3	498.6	1603.6
eclipse-small	50.5	47.6	4297.5
fop-default	2.6	181.2	130.2
fop-small	2.8	42.0	30.7
h2-default	4.4	3137.3	3245.8
h2-large	4.3	2652.7	3583.1
h2-small	3.1	1272.9	1038.7
h2-tiny	3.9	947.5	754.7
jython-default	2.0	342.2	235.0
jython-large	2.5	949.4	774.9
jython-small	1.6	93.1	71.5
luindex-default	1.7	88.4	71.6
luindex-small	1.6	5.8	4.4
lusearch-default	2.7	385.7	304.3
lusearch-large	2.8	451.8	327.9
lusearch-small	2.9	112.5	85.7
pmd-default	2.0	276.1	134.6
pmd-large	2.4	549.1	230.2
pmd-small	1.8	7.4	5.6
sunflow-default	5.9	1830.1	1457.8
sunflow-large	6.4	2073.2	1583.3
sunflow-small	6.9	598.1	481.2
tomcat-default	1.8	100.3	72.3
tomcat-large	1.7	240.0	175.4
tomcat-small	1.8	48.4	38.4
xalan-default	3.0	482.0	372.5
xalan-large	3.7	922.6	715.4
xalan-small	2.8	114.8	95.5
geometric mean	3.2	257.7	245.8

Table 1. Run-time overhead for Elephant Tracks on the DaCapo benchmark suite

Benchmark	Method	Alloc + Death	Catch + Throw	Pointer Update
avrora-default	97.97	0.30	0.00	1.74
avrora-large	95.17	0.24	0.00	4.59
avrora-small	97.85	0.30	0.00	1.85
batik-default	92.01	1.70	0.00	6.29
batik-large	92.34	1.77	0.00	5.89
batik-small	92.55	2.55	0.00	4.89
eclipse-default	88.65	4.29	0.00	7.06
eclipse-large	90.24	3.23	0.00	6.52
eclipse-small	93.67	3.27	0.01	3.05
fop-default	90.30	4.63	0.00	5.07
fop-small	89.83	4.21	0.00	5.95
h2-default	94.23	2.86	0.00	2.90
h2-large	94.92	2.02	0.00	3.06
h2-small	94.05	3.04	0.00	2.91
h2-tiny	93.98	3.11	0.00	2.91
jython-default	91.64	3.08	0.02	5.26
jython-large	91.74	2.79	0.01	5.46
jython-small	97.36	1.11	0.00	1.53
luindex-default	96.37	0.28	0.00	3.36
luindex-small	94.91	1.36	0.00	3.72
lusearch-default	91.70	2.73	0.05	5.52
lusearch-large	91.70	2.72	0.05	5.52
lusearch-small	91.77	2.74	0.05	5.43
pmd-default	87.31	3.86	0.10	8.73
pmd-large	87.04	4.27	0.09	8.60
pmd-small	92.54	3.48	0.01	3.97
sunflow-default	94.84	3.00	0.00	2.16
sunflow-large	94.83	3.00	0.00	2.17
sunflow-small	94.90	2.96	0.00	2.14
tomcat-default	89.92	5.92	0.02	4.14
tomcat-large	90.47	6.33	0.01	3.19
tomcat-small	89.00	5.28	0.03	5.70
xalan-default	94.10	1.54	0.00	4.37
xalan-large	94.11	1.52	0.00	4.37
xalan-small	93.99	1.65	0.00	4.36
mean	92.74	2.85	0.01	4.40

Table 2. Percentage of each record type in traces of the DaCapo benchmark suite

in Table 3, where we see that in most benchmarks a majority of objects escape their allocating context.

Second, previous work has shown that the allocation site plus some calling context is a good basis for predicting object lifetime (measured in bytes of allocation) [11]. Since Elephant Tracks' traces can also provide the calling context of an object's death, it is possible to consider whether the allocation context is also a predictor of *death context*.

As a preliminary investigation, we performed the following analysis. Each object's allocation is recorded with a triple, consisting of the allocation site, the allocating method, and the caller of the allocating method (this gives us a partial calling context). Next, the analysis finds the top ten allocation contexts (based on number of objects allocated). For each object allocated in these contexts, it determines the object's partial death context (there is no *site* for a death event, so we consider only the method in which it died, and the calling method). Finally, the analysis finds, for each allocation context, the most common death context for objects with that allocation context. In Table 4 we report the average percentage of objects allocated in the top ten contexts that die in the plurality context.

This initial work suggests that the death context of an object may be a stable and predictable feature. However, additional refine-

ment will be required to further illuminate the relationship between an object's allocation context and its death context, as well as to determine if this relationship can be exploited for any optimization.

6. Conclusions

We have presented Elephant Tracks, a tool for efficiently generating program traces including accurate object death records. Unlike previous tools, Elephant Tracks traces allow recorded events to be placed in the context of the methods of the program being traced. It also works independently of any particular choice of the JVM to which it attaches. These two features will allow the prototyping of new GC algorithms and new kinds of program analysis, and let the tool keep up with changes in the JVM and class libraries. Elephant Tracks offers performance comparable to similar previous tools but a wealth more information and covers many more of the tricky and corner cases of Java and Java virtual machines.

Acknowledgments

This material is based upon work supported by the National Science Foundation under Grants CCF-1018038 (Guyer and Ricci) and CNS-1162246 (Moss).

Benchmark	% Escaping	Benchmark	% Escaping
avrora-default	83.53	luindex-default	54.14
avrora-large	79.39	luindex-small	46.25
avrora-small	87.41	lusearch-default	39.98
batik-default	63.79	lusearch-large	40.00
batik-large	62.97	lusearch-small	40.02
batik-small	62.22	pmd-default	53.68
eclipse-default	32.32	pmd-large	52.66
eclipse-large	41.97	pmd-small	51.78
eclipse-small	26.85	sunflow-default	68.63
fop-default	55.25	sunflow-large	68.49
fop-small	65.06	sunflow-small	68.38
h2-default	58.03	tomcat-default	25.44
h2-large	58.24	tomcat-large	21.87
h2-small	58.00	tomcat-small	32.44
h2-tiny	57.82	xalan-default	54.99
jython-default	42.13	xalan-large	55.16
jython-large	42.95	xalan-small	53.59
jython-small	68.02		

Table 3. Percentage of objects escaping their allocating context in the DaCapo benchmark suite

Benchmark	Mean %	Benchmark	Mean %
avrora-default	41.22	luindex-small	76.57
avrora-large	44.38	lusearch-default	83.39
avrora-small	30.06	lusearch-large	79.63
batik-default	63.05	lusearch-small	83.37
batik-large	59.64	pmd-default	47.82
batik-small	75.08	pmd-large	34.98
fop-default	81.24	pmd-small	57.70
fop-small	64.54	sunflow-default	86.12
h2-default	86.37	sunflow-large	80.12
h2-large	88.09	sunflow-small	89.54
h2-small	86.78	tomcat-default	75.80
jython-default	68.79	tomcat-large	72.15
jython-large	74.03	tomcat-small	79.32
jython-small	74.15	xalan-default	71.48
luindex-default	78.45	xalan-large	71.55

Table 4. Mean percentage of objects that are born in the same context and die in the same context (over top 10 allocation contexts).

References

[1] Ole Agesen, David Detlefs, and J. Eliot B. Moss. Garbage collection and local variable type-precision and liveness in Java virtual machines. In *PLDI*, pages 269–279, 1998.

[2] Bowen Alpern, Steve Augart, Stephen M. Blackburn, Maria A. Butrico, Anthony Cocchi, Perry Cheng, Julian Dolby, Stephen J. Fink, David Grove, Michael Hind, Kathryn S. McKinley, Mark F. Mergen, J. Eliot B. Moss, Ton Anh Ngo, Vivek Sarkar, and Martin Trapp. The Jikes Research Virtual Machine project: Building an open-source research community. *IBM Systems Journal*, 44(2): 399–418, 2005.

[3] Eric Bruneton, Romain Langlet, and Thierry Coupaye. ASM: A code manipulation tool to implement adaptable systems. In *Adaptable and Extensible Component Systems*, Grenoble, France, November 2002. 12 pages.

[4] James Foucar. *A Platform for Research into Object-Level Trace Generation*. PhD thesis, The University of New Mexico, 2006.

[5] Samuel Z. Guyer, Kathryn S. McKinley, and Daniel Frampton. Free-Me: A static analysis for automatic individual object reclamation. *ACM SIGPLAN Notices*, 41(6):364–375, 2006.

[6] Matthew Hertz, Stephen M. Blackburn, J. Eliot B. Moss, Kathryn S. McKinley, and Darko Stefanović. Error-free garbage collection traces: How to cheat and not get caught. *SIGMETRICS Perform. Eval. Rev.*, 30:140–151, June 2002. ISSN 0163-5999. doi: http://doi.acm.org/10.1145/511399.511352. URL http://doi.acm.org/10.1145/511399.511352.

[7] Matthew Hertz, Stephen M. Blackburn, J. Eliot B. Moss, Kathryn S. McKinley, and Darko Stefanovic. Generating object lifetime traces with Merlin. *ACM Transactions on Programming Languages and Systems*, 28(3):476–516, 2006.

[8] Martin Hirzel, Amer Diwan, and Johannes Henkel. On the usefulness of type and liveness accuracy for garbage collection and leak detection. *ACM Transactions on Programming Languages and Systems (TOPLAS)*, 24(6):593–624, 2002.

[9] Martin Hirzel, Amer Diwan, and Matthew Hertz. Connectivity-based garbage collection. In *ACM SIGPLAN Conference on Object-Oriented Programming, Systems, Languages, and Applications*, pages 359–373, 2003. ISBN 1-58113-712-5.

[10] Hajime Inoue, Darko Stefanović, and Stephanie Forrest. On the prediction of Java object lifetimes. *IEEE Transactions on Computers*, 55(7):880–892, 2006.

[11] Richard E. Jones and Chris Ryder. A study of Java object demographics. In *Proceedings of the 7th International Symposium on Memory Management*, pages 121–130. ACM, 2008.

[12] Jonathan M. Lambert and James F. Power. Platform independent timing of Java virtual machine bytecode instructions. *Electronic Notes in Theoretical Computer Science*, 220(3):97–113, 2008.

[13] Sun Microsystems. JVM Tool Interface, 2004. http://java.sun.com/javase/6/docs/platform/jvmti/jvmti.html.

[14] Richard A. Uhlig and Trevor N. Mudge. Trace-driven memory simulation: A survey. *ACM Computing Surveys (CSUR)*, 29(2): 128–170, 1997.

A Bloat-Aware Design for Big Data Applications

Yingyi Bu   Vinayak Borkar   Guoqing Xu   Michael J. Carey

Department of Computer Science, University of California, Irvine

{yingyib,vborkar,guoqingx, mjcarey}@ics.uci.edu

Abstract

Over the past decade, the increasing demands on data-driven business intelligence have led to the proliferation of large-scale, data-intensive applications that often have huge amounts of data (often at terabyte or petabyte scale) to process. An object-oriented programming language such as Java is often the developer's choice for implementing such applications, primarily due to its quick development cycle and rich community resource. While the use of such languages makes programming easier, significant performance problems can often be seen — the combination of the inefficiencies inherent in a managed run-time system and the impact of the huge amount of data to be processed in the limited memory space often leads to memory bloat and performance degradation at a surprisingly early stage.

This paper proposes a bloat-aware design paradigm towards the development of efficient and scalable Big Data applications in object-oriented GC enabled languages. To motivate this work, we first perform a study on the impact of several typical memory bloat patterns. These patterns are summarized from the user complaints on the mailing lists of two widely-used open-source Big Data applications. Next, we discuss our design paradigm to eliminate bloat. Using examples and real-world experience, we demonstrate that programming under this paradigm does not incur significant programming burden. We have implemented a few common data processing tasks both using this design and using the conventional object-oriented design. Our experimental results show that this new design paradigm is extremely effective in improving performance — even for the moderate-size data sets processed, we have observed 2.5×+ performance gains, and the improvement grows substantially with the size of the data set.

Categories and Subject Descriptors   D.3.4 [*Programming Languages*]: Processors—Memory management, optimization, runtime environment;   H.4 [*Information Systems Applications*]: Miscellaneous

General Terms   Languages, Design, Performance

Keywords   Big Data Applications, Memory Bloat, Design

1. Introduction

Modern computing has entered the era of Big Data. The massive amounts of information available on the Internet enable com-

ISMM'13,   June 20–21, 2013, Seattle, Washington, USA.
Copyright © 2013 ACM 978-1-4503-2100-6/13/06. . . $15.00

puter scientists, physicists, economists, mathematicians, political scientists, bio-informaticists, sociologists, and many others to discover interesting properties about people, things, and their interactions. Analyzing information from Twitter, Google, Facebook, Wikipedia, or the Human Genome Project requires the development of scalable platforms that can quickly process massive-scale data. Such frameworks often utilize large numbers of machines in a cluster or in the cloud to process data in a parallel manner. Typical data-processing frameworks include data-flow and message passing runtime systems. A data-flow system (such as MapReduce [19], Hadoop [10], Hyracks [16], Spark [49], or Storm [40]) uses distributed file system to store data and computes results by pushing data through a processing pipeline, while a message passing system (such as Pregel [29] or Giraph [9]) often loads one partition of data per processing unit (machine, process, or thread) and sends/receives messages among different units to perform computations. High-level languages (such as Hive [11], Pig [34], FlumeJava [18], or AsterixDB [14]) are designed to describe data processing at a more abstract level.

An object-oriented programming language such as Java is often the developer's choice for implementing data-processing frameworks. In fact, the Java community has already been the home of many data-intensive computing infrastructures, such as Hadoop [10], Hyracks [16], Storm [40], and Giraph [9]. Spark [49] is written in Scala, but it relies on a Java Virtual Machine (JVM) to execute. Despite the many development benefits provided by Java, these applications commonly suffer from severe memory bloat—a situation where large amounts of memory are used to store information not strictly necessary for the execution—that can lead to significant performance degradation and reduced scalability.

Bloat in such applications stems primarily from a combination of the inefficient memory usage inherent in the run time of a managed language as well as the processing of huge volumes of data that can exacerbate the already-existing inefficiencies by orders of magnitude. As such, Big Data applications are much more vulnerable to runtime bloat than regular Java applications. As an interesting reference point, our experience shows that the latest (Indigo) release of the Eclipse framework with 16 large Java projects loaded can successfully run (without any noticeable lag) on a 2GB heap; however, a moderate-size application on Giraph [9] with 1GB input data can easily run out of memory on a 12 GB heap. Due to the increasing popularity of Big Data applications in modern computing, it is important to understand why these applications are so vulnerable, how they are affected by runtime bloat, and what changes should be made to the existing design and implementation principles in order to make them scalable.

In this paper, we describe a study of memory bloat using two real-world Big Data applications: Hive [11] and Giraph [9], where Hive is a large-scale data warehouse software (Apache top-level project, powering Facebook's data analytics) built on top of Hadoop and Giraph is an Apache open-source graph analytics framework initiated by Yahoo!. Our study shows that *freely creat-*

ing objects (as encouraged by object-orientation) is the root cause of the performance bottleneck that prevents these applications from scaling up to large data sets.

To gain a deep understanding of the bottleneck and how to effectively optimize it away, we break down the problem of excessive object creation into two different aspects, (1) what is the space overhead if all data items are represented by Java objects? and (2) given all these objects, what is the memory management (i.e., GC) costs in a typical Big Data application? These two questions are related, respectively, to the spatial impact and the temporal impact that object creation can have on performance and scalability.

On the one hand, each Java object has a fixed-size header space to store its type and the information necessary for garbage collection. What constitutes the space overhead is not just object headers; the other major component is from the pervasive use of object-oriented data structures that commonly have multiple layers of delegations. Such delegation patterns, while simplifying development tasks, can easily lead to wasteful memory space that stores *pointers* to form data structures, rather than *the actual data* needed for the forward execution. Based on a study reported in [32], the fraction of the actual data in an IBM application is only 13% of the total used space. This impact can be significantly magnified in a Big Data application that contains a huge number of (relatively small) data item objects. For such small objects, the space overhead cannot be easily amortized by the actual data content. The problem of inefficient memory usage becomes increasingly painful for highly-parallel data-processing systems because each thread consumes excessive memory resource, leading to increased I/O costs and reduced concurrency.

On the other hand, a typical tracing garbage collection (GC) algorithm periodically traverses the entire live object graph to identify and reclaim unreachable objects. For non-allocation-intensive applications, efficient garbage collection algorithms such as a generational GC can quickly mark reachable objects and reclaim memory from dead objects, causing negligible interruptions from the main execution threads. However, once the heap grows to be large (e.g., a few dozens of GBs) and most objects in the heap are live, a single GC call can become exceedingly longer. In addition, because the amount of used memory in a Big Data application is often close to the heap size, GC can be frequently triggered and would eventually become the major bottleneck that prevents the main threads from making satisfactory progress. We observe that in most Big Data applications, a huge number of objects (representing data to be processed in the same batch) often have the same lifetime, and hence it is highly unnecessary for the GC to traverse each individual object every time to determine whether or not it is reachable.

Switch back to an unmanaged language? Switching back to an unmanaged language such as C++ appears to be a reasonable choice. However, our experience with many Big Data applications (such as Hive, Pig, Jaql, Giraph, or Mahout) suggests that a Big Data application often exhibits clear distinction between a *control path* and a *data path*. The control path organizes tasks into the pipeline and performs optimizations while the data path represents and manipulates data. For example, in a typical Big Data application that runs on a shared-nothing cluster, there is often a driver at the client side that controls the data flow and there are multiple run-time data operators executing data processing algorithms on each machine. The execution of the driver in the control path does not touch any actual data. Only the execution of the data operators in the data path manipulates data items. While the data path creates most of the run-time objects, its development often takes a very small amount of coding effort, primarily because data processing algorithms (e.g., joining, grouping, sorting, etc.) can be easily shared and reused across applications.

One study we have performed on seven open-source Big Data applications shows that the data flow path takes an overage 36.8% of the lines of source code but creates more than 90% of the objects during execution. Details of this study can be found in Section 4.3. Following the conventional object-oriented design for the control path is often unharmful; *it is the data path that needs a non-conventional design and an extremely careful implementation.* As the control path takes the majority of the development work, it is unnecessary to force developers to switch to an unmanaged language for the whole application where they have to face the (old) problems of low productivity, less community resource, manual memory management, and error-prone implementations.

Although the inefficient use of memory in an object-oriented language is a known problem and has been studied before (e.g., in [32]), there does not exist any systematic analysis of its impact on Big Data applications. In this paper, we study this impact both analytically and empirically. We argue that the designers of a Big Data application should strictly follow the following principle: *the number of data objects in the system has to be bounded and cannot grow proportionally with the size of the data to be processed.* To achieve this, we propose a new design paradigm that advocates to merge small objects in the storage and access the merged objects using data processors. The idea is inspired from old memory management technique called *page-based record management*, which has been used widely to build database systems. We adopt the proposed design paradigm in our "build-from-scratch" general-purpose Big Data processing framework (called Hyracks) at the application (Java) level, without requiring the modification of the JVM or the Java compiler. We demonstrate, using both examples and experience, that writing programs using the proposed design paradigm does not create much burden for developers.

We have implemented several common data processing tasks by following both this new design paradigm and the conventional object-oriented design principle. Our experimental results demonstrate that the implementations following the new design can scale to much larger data sizes than those following the conventional design. We believe that this new design paradigm is valuable in guiding the future implementations of Big Data applications using managed object-oriented languages. The observations made in this paper strongly call for novel optimization techniques targeting Big Data applications. For example, optimizer designers can develop automated compiler and/or runtime system support (e.g., within a JVM) to remove the identified inefficiency patterns in order to promote the use of object-oriented languages in developing Big Data applications. Furthermore, future development of benchmark suites should consider the inclusion of such applications to measure JVM performance.

Contributions of this paper include:

- an analytical study on the memory usage of common Big Data processing tasks such as the graph link analysis and the relational join. We find that the excessive creation of objects to represent and process data items is the bottleneck that prevents Big Data applications from scaling up to large datasets (Section 2);

- a bloat-aware design paradigm for the development of highly-efficient Big Data applications; instead of building a new memory system to solve the memory issues from scratch, we propose two application-level optimizations, including (1) merging (inlining) a chunk of small data item objects with the same lifetime into few large objects (e.g., few byte arrays) and (2) manipulating data by directly accessing merged objects (i.e., at the binary level), in order to mitigate the observed memory bloat patterns (Section 3);

- a set of experimental results (Section 5) that demonstrate significant memory and time savings using the design. We report our experience of programming for real-world data-processing tasks in the Hyracks platform (Section 4). We compare the performance of several Big Data applications with and without using the proposed design; the experimental results show that our optimizations are extremely effective (Section 5).

2. Memory Analysis of Big Data Applications

In this section, we study two popular data-intensive applications, Giraph [9] and Hive [11], to investigate the impact of creating of Java objects to represent and process data on performance and scalability. Our analysis drills down to two fundamental problems, one in space and one in time: (1) large space consumed by object headers and object references, leading to low packing factor of the memory, and (2) massive amounts of objects and references, leading to poor GC performance. We analyze these two problems using examples from Giraph and Hive, respectively.

2.1 Low Packing Factor

In the Java runtime, each object requires a header space for type and memory management purposes. An additional space is needed by an array to store its length. For instance, in the Oracle 64-bit HotSpot JVM, the header spaces for a regular object and for an array take 8 and 12 bytes, respectively. In a typical Big Data application, the heap often contains many small objects (such as `Integers` representing record IDs), in which the overhead incurred by headers cannot be easily amortized by the actual data content. Space inefficiencies are exacerbated by the pervasive utilization of object-oriented data structures. These data structures often use multiple-level of delegations to achieve their functionality, leading to large space storing *pointers* instead of the actual data. In order to measure the space inefficiencies introduced by the use of objects, we employ a metric called *packing factor*, which is defined as the maximal amount of actual data that be accommodated into a fixed amount of memory. While a similar analysis [32] has been conducted to understand the health of Java collections, our analysis is specific to Big Data applications where a huge amount of data flow through a fixed amount memory in a batch-by-batch manner.

To analyze the packing factor for the heap of a typical Big Data application, we use the PageRank algorithm [35] (i.e., an application built on top of Giraph [9]) as a running example. PageRank is a link analysis algorithm that assigns weights (ranks) to each vertex in a graph by iteratively computing the weight of each vertex based on the weight of its inbound neighbors. This algorithm is widely used to rank web pages in search engines.

We ran PageRank on different open-source Big Data computing systems, including Giraph [9], Spark [49], and Mahout [12], using a 6-rack, 180-machine research cluster. Each machine has 2 quad-core Intel Xeon E5420 processors and 16GB RAM. We used a 70GB web graph dataset that has a total of $1,413,511,393$ vertices. We found none of the three systems could successfully process this dataset. They all crashed with `java.lang.OutOfMemoryError`, even though the data partitioned for each machine (i.e., less than 500MB) should easily fit into its physical memory.

We found that many real-world developers experienced similar problems. For example, we saw a number of complaints on `OutOfMemoryError` from Giraph's user mailing list, and there were 13 bloat-related threads on Giraph's mailing list during the past 8 months[1]. In order to locate the bottleneck, we perform a quantitative analysis using PageRank. Giraph contains an example

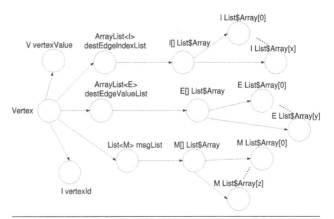

Figure 1. Giraph object subgraph rooted at a vertex.

Class	#Objects	Header (b)	Pointer (b)
Vertex	1	8	40
List	3	24	24
List$Array	3	36	$8(m+n)$
LongWritable	$m+1$	$8m+8$	0
DoubleWritable	$n+1$	$8n+8$	0
Total	$m+n+9$	$8(m+n)+84$	$8(m+n)+64$

Table 1. Numbers of objects per vertex and their space overhead (in bytes) in PageRank in the Sun 64-bit Hopspot JVM.

implementation of the PageRank algorithm. Part of its data representation implementation[2] is shown below.

```
public abstract class EdgeListVertex<
        I extends WritableComparable,
        V extends Writable,
        E extends Writable, M extends Writable>
        extends MutableVertex<I, V, E, M> {
    private I vertexId = null;

    private V vertexValue = null;

    /** indices of its outgoing edges */
    private List<I> destEdgeIndexList;

    /** values of its outgoing edges */
    private List<E> destEdgeValueList;

    /** incoming messages from
        the previous iteration */
    private List<M> msgList;
    ......

    /** return the edge indices starting from 0 */
    public List<I> getEdegeIndexes(){
        ...
    }
}
```

Graphs handled in Giraph are labeled (i.e., both their vertices and edges are annotated with values) and their edges are directional. Class `EdgeListVertex` represents a graph vertex. Among its fields, `vertexId` and `vertexValue` store the ID and the value of the vertex, respectively. Field `destEdgeIndexList` and `destEdgeValueList` reference, respectively, a list of IDs and a list of values of its outgoing edges. `msgList` contains incoming messages sent to the vertex from the previous iteration. Figure 1 visualizes the Java object subgraph rooted at an `EdgeListVertex` object.

In Giraph's PageRank implementation, the concrete types for I, V, E, and M are `LongWritable`, `DoubleWritable`,

---

[1] http://mail-archives.apache.org/mod_mbox/giraph-user/

[2] in revision 1232166.

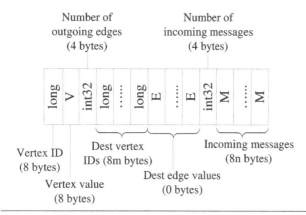

Figure 2. The compact layout of a vertex.

`FloatWritable`, and `DoubleWritable`, respectively. Each edge in the graph is equi-weighted, and thus the list referenced by `destEdgeValueList` is always empty. Assume that each vertex has an average of m outgoing edges and n incoming messages. Table 1 shows the memory consumption statistics of a vertex data structure in the Oracle 64-bit HotSpot JVM. Each row in the table reports a class name, the number of its objects needed in this representation, the number of bytes used by the headers of these objects, and the number of bytes used by the reference-typed fields in these objects. It is easy to calculate that the space overhead for each vertex in the current implementation is $16(m+n)+148$ (i.e., the sum of the header size and pointer size in Table 1).

On the contrary, Figure 2 shows an ideal memory layout that stores only the *necessary* information for each vertex (without using objects). In this case, the representation of a vertex requires $m+1$ long values (for vertex IDs), n double values (for messages), and two 32-bit int values (for specifying the number of outgoing edges and the number of messages, respectively), which consume a total of $8(m+n+1)+16 = 8(m+n)+24$ bytes of memory. This memory consumption is even less than half of the space used for object headers and pointers in the object-based representation. Clearly, the space overhead of the object-based representation is greater than 200%.

2.2 Large Volumes of Objects and References

In a JVM, the GC threads periodically iterate all live objects in the heap to identify and reclaim dead objects. Suppose the number of live objects is n and the total number of edges in the object graph is e, the asymptotic computational complexity of a tracing garbage collection algorithm is $O(n + e)$. For a typical Big Data application, its object graph consists of a great number of isolated object subgraphs, each of which represents either a data item or a data structure created for processing items. As such, there often exists an extremely large number of in-memory data objects, and both n and e can be orders of magnitude larger than those of a regular Java application.

We use an exception example from Hive's user mailing list to analyze the problem. This exception was found in a discussion thread named "how to deal with Java heap space errors"[3]:

```
FATAL org.apache.hadoop.mapred.TaskTracker:
  Error running child : java.lang.OutOfMemoryError:
  Java heap space
    org.apache.hadoop.io.Text.setCapacity(Text.java:240)
  at org.apache.hadoop.io.Text.set(Text.java:204)
  at org.apache.hadoop.io.Text.set(Text.java:194)
  at org.apache.hadoop.io.Text.<init>(Text.java:86)
```

---

[3] http://mail-archives.apache.org/mod_mbox/hive-user/201107.mbox/

```
......
  at org.apache.hadoop.hive.ql.exec.persistence.Row
    Container.next(RowContainer.java:263)
  org.apache.hadoop.hive.ql.exec.persistence.Row
    Container.next(RowContainer.java:74)
  at org.apache.hadoop.hive.ql.exec.CommonJoinOperator.
    checkAndGenObject(CommonJoinOperator.java:823)
  at org.apache.hadoop.hive.ql.exec.JoinOperator.
    endGroup(JoinOperator.java:263)
  at org.apache.hadoop.hive.ql.exec.ExecReducer.
    reduce(ExecReducer.java:198)
......
  at org.apache.hadoop.hive.ql.exec.persistence.Row
    Container.nextBlock(RowContainer.java:397)
  at org.apache.hadoop.mapred.Child.main(Child.java:170)
```

We inspected the source code of Hive and found that the top method `Text.setCapacity()` in the stack trace is not the cause of the problem. In Hive's join implementation, its `JoinOperator` holds all the `Row` objects from one of the input branches in the `RowContainer`. In cases where a large number of `Row` objects is stored in the `RowContainer`, a single GC run can become very expensive. For the reported stack trace, the total size of the `Row` objects exceeds the heap upper bound, which causes the `OutOfMemory` error.

Even in cases where no `OutOfMemory` error is triggered, the large number of `Row` objects can still cause severe performance degradation. Suppose the number of `Row` objects in the `RowContainer` is n. Hence, the GC time for traversing the internal structure of the `RowContainer` object is at least $O(n)$. For Hive, n grows proportionally with the size of the input data, which can easily drive up the GC overhead substantially. The following is an example obtained from a user report at StackOverflow[4]. Although this problem has a different manifestation, the root cause is the same.

"I have a Hive query which is selecting about 30 columns and around 400,000 records and inserting them into another table. I have one join in my SQL clause, which is just an inner join. The query fails because of a Java GC overhead limit exceeded."

In fact, complaints about large GC overhead can be commonly seen on either Hive's mailing list or the StackOverflow website. What makes the problem even worse is that there is not much that can be done from the developer's side to optimize the application, because the inefficiencies are inherent in the design of Hive. All the data processing-related interfaces in Hive require the use of Java objects to represent data items. To manipulate data contained in `Row`, for example, we have to wrap it into a `Row` object, as designated by the interfaces. If we wish to completely solve this performance problem, we would have to re-design and re-implement all the related interfaces from scratch, a task that any user could not afford to do. This example motivates us to look for solutions at the design level, so that we would not be limited by the many (conventional) object-oriented guidelines and principles.

3. The Bloat-Aware Design Paradigm

The fundamental reason for the performance problems discussed in Section 2 is that the two Big Data applications were designed and implemented the same way as regular object-oriented applications: *everything is object*. Objects are used to represent both *data processors* and *data items* to be processed. While creating objects to represent data processors may not have significant impact on performance, the use of objects to represent data items creates a big scalability bottleneck that prevents the application from processing large data sets. Since a typical Big Data application does similar data processing tasks repeatedly, a group of related data items of-

---

[4] http://stackoverflow.com/questions/11387543/performance-tuning-a-hive-query.

ten has similar liveness behaviors. They can be easily managed together in large chunks of buffers, so that the GC does not have to traverse each individual object to test its reachability. For instance, all vertex objects in the Giraph example have the same lifetimes; so do `Row` objects in the Hive example. A natural idea is to allocate them in the same memory region, which is reclaimed as a whole if the contained data items are no longer needed.

Based on this observation, we propose a bloat-aware design paradigm for developing highly efficient Big Data applications. This paradigm includes the following two important components: (1) merging and organizing related small data record objects into few large objects (e.g., byte buffers) instead of representing them explicitly as one-object-per-record, and (2) manipulating data by directly accessing buffers (e.g., at the byte chunk level as opposed to the object level). The central goal of this design paradigm is to bound the number of objects in the application, instead of making it grow proportionally with the cardinality of the input data. It is important to note that these guidelines should be considered explicitly at the early design stage of a Big Data processing system, so that the resulting APIs and implementations would comply with the principles. We have built our own Big Data processing framework Hyracks from the scratch by strictly following this design paradigm. We will use Hyracks a running example to illustrate these design principles.

3.1 Data Storage Design: Merging Small Objects

As described in Section 2, storing data in Java objects adds much overhead in terms of both memory consumption as well as CPU cycles. As such, we propose to store a group of data items together in *Java memory pages*. Unlike a system-level memory page, which deals with virtual memory, a Java memory page is a fixed-length contiguous block of memory in the (managed) Java heap. For simplicity of presentation, we will use "page" to refer to "Java memory page" in the rest of the paper. In Hyracks, each page is represented by an object of type `java.nio.ByteBuffer`. Arranging records into pages can reduce the number of objects created in the system from the total number of data items to the number of pages. Hence, the packing factor in such a system can be much closer to that in the ideal representation where data are explicitly laid out in memory and no bookkeeping information needs to be stored. Note that grouping data items into a binary page is just one of many ways to merge small objects; other merging (inlining) approaches may also be considered in the future to achieve the same goal.

Multiple ways exist to put records into a page. The Hyracks system takes an approach called "slot-based record management" [36] used widely in the existing DBMS implementations. To illustrate, consider again the PageRank algorithm. Figure 3 shows how 4 vertices are stored in a page. It is easy to see that each vertex is stored in its compact layout (as in Figure 2) and we use 4 slots (each takes 4 bytes) at the end of the page to store the start offset of each vertex. These offsets will be used to quickly locate data items and support *variable-length* records. Note that the format of data records is invisible to developers, so that they could still focus on high-level data management tasks. Because pages are of fixed size, there is often a small *residual space* that is wasted and cannot be used to store any vertex. To understand the packing factor for this design, we assume each page holds p records on average, and the residual space has r bytes. The overhead for this representation of a vertex includes three parts: the offset slot (4 bytes), the amortized residual space (i.e., r/p), and the amortized overhead of the page object itself (i.e., `java.nio.ByteBuffer`). The page object has an 8-byte header space (in the Oracle 64-bit HotSpot JVM) and a reference (8 bytes) to an internal byte array whose header takes 12

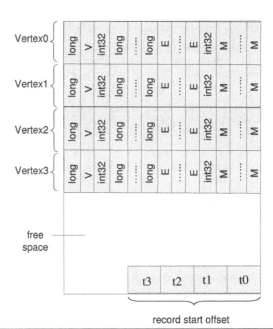

Figure 3. Vertices aligning in a page (slots at the end of the page are to support variable-sized vertices).

bytes. This makes the amortized overhead of the page object $28/p$. Combining this overhead with the result from Section 2.1, we need a total of $(8m + 8n) + 24 + 4 + \frac{r+28}{p}$ bytes to represent a vertex, where $(8m + 8n) + 24$ bytes are used to store the necessary data and $4 + \frac{r+28}{p}$ is the overhead. Because r is the size of the residual space, we have:

$$r \leq 8m + 8n + 24$$

and thus the space overhead of a vertex is bounded by $4 + \frac{8m+8n+52}{p}$. In Hyracks, we use 32KB (as recommended by literature [23]) as the size of a page, and p ranges from 100 to 200 (as seen in experiments with real-world data). To calculate the largest possible overhead, consider the worst case where the residual space has the same size as a vertex. The size of a vertex is thus between $(32768 - 200 * 4)/(200 + 1)$=159 bytes and $(32768 - 100 * 4)/(100 + 1)$=320 bytes. Because the residual space is as large as a vertex, we have $159 \leq r \leq 320$. This leaves the space overhead of a vertex in the range between 4 bytes (because at least 4 bytes are required for the offset slot) and $(4 + (320 + 28)/100)$=7 bytes. Hence, the overall overhead is only $2 - 4\%$ of the actual data size, much less than the 200% overhead of object-based representation (as described in Section 2.1).

3.2 Data Processor Design: Access Buffers

To support programming with the proposed buffer-based memory management, we propose an *accessor-based* programming pattern. Instead of creating a heap data structure to contain data items and represent their logical relationships, we propose to define an accessor structure that consists of multiple accessors, each to access a different type of data. As such, we need only a very number of accessor structures to process all data, leading to significantly reduced heap objects. In this subsection, we discuss a transformation that can transform regular data structure classes into their corresponding accessor classes. We will also describe the execution model using a few examples.

3.2.1 Design Transformations

For each data item class D in a regular object-oriented design, we transform D into an accessor class D_a. Whether a class is a data item class can be specified by the developer. The steps that this transformation includes are as follows.

- *S1*: for each data item field f of type F in D, we add a field f_a of type F_a into D_a, where F_a is the accessor class of F. For each non-data-item field f' in D, we copy it directly into D_a.

- *S2*: add a public method `set(byte[] data, int start, int length)` into D_a. The goal of this method is to bind the accessor to a specific byte region where the data items of type D are located. The method can be implemented either by doing *eager materialization*, which recursively binds the binary regions for all its member accessors, or by doing *lazy materialization*, which defers such bindings to the point where the member accessors are actually needed.

- *S3*: for each method M in D, we first create a method M_a which duplicates M in D_a. Next, M_a's signature is modified in a way so that all data-item-type parameters are changed to use their corresponding data accessor types. A parameter accessor provides a way for accessing and manipulating the bound data items in the provided byte regions.

Note that transforming a regular object-oriented design into the above design should be done at the early development stage of a Big Data application in order to avoid the potential development overhead of re-designing after the implementation. Future work will develop compiler support that can automatically transform designs to make them compatible with our memory system.

3.2.2 Execution Model

At run time, we form a set of *accessor graphs*, and each accessor graph processes a batch of top-level records. Each node in the graph is an accessor object for a field and each edge represents a "member field" relationship. An accessor graph has the same skeleton as its corresponding heap data structure but does not store any data internally. We let pages flow through the accessor graphs, where a accessor binds to and processes a data item record one-at-a-time. For each thread in the program, the number of accessor graphs needed is equal to the number of data structure types in the program, which is statically bounded. Different instances of a data structure can be processed by the same accessor graph.

If one uses eager materialization in the accessor implementation, the number of accessor objects that need to be created during a data processing task is equal to the total number of nodes in all the accessor graphs. If lazy materialization is chosen to implement accessors, the number of created accessor objects can be significantly reduced, because a member accessor can often be reused for accessing several different data times of the same type. In some cases, additional accessor objects are needed for methods that operate on multiple data items of the same type. For example, a `compare` method defined in a data item class compares two argument data items, and hence, in order to the transformed version of the method would need two accessor objects at run time to perform the comparison. Despite these different ways of implementing accessors, the number of accessor objects needed is always bounded at compile time and does not grow proportionally with the cardinality the dataset.

3.2.3 A Running Example

Following the three steps, we manually transform the vertex example in Section 2.1 into the following form.

```
public abstract class EdgeListVertexAccessor<
      /** by S1: */
```

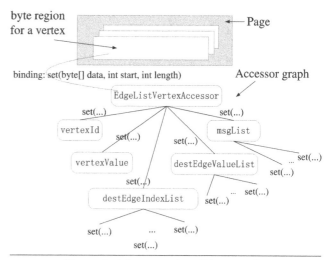

Figure 4. A heap snapshot of the example.

```
   I extends WritableComparableAccessor,
   V extends WritableAccessor,
   E extends WritableAccessor,
   M extends WritableAccessor>
     extends MutableVertexAccessor<I, V, E, M> {
private I vertexId = null;

private V vertexValue = null;

/** by S1: indices of its outgoing edges */
private ListAccessor<I> destEdgeIndexList = new
                       ArrayListAccessor<I>();

/** by S1: values of its outgoing edges */
private ListAccessor<E> destEdgeValueList = new
                       ArrayListAccessor<E>();

/** by S1: incoming messages from
    the previous iteration */
private ListAccessor<M> msgList = new
                       ArrayListAccessor<M>();
......

/** by S2:
 * binds the accessor to a binary region
 * of a vertex
 */
public void set(byte[] data, int start, int length){
    /* This may in turn call the set method
       of its member objects. */
       ......
}

/** by S3:  replacing the return type*/
public ListAccessor<I> getEdegeIndexes(){
    ...
}
}
```

In the above code snippet, we highlight the modified code and add the transformation steps as the comments. Figure 4 shows a heap snapshot of the running example. The actual data are laid out in pages while an accessor graph is used to process all the vertices, each-at-a-time. For each vertex, the `set` method binds the accessor graph to its byte region.

4. Programming Experience

The bloat-aware design paradigm separates the *logical* data access and the *physical* data storage to achieve both compact in-memory data layout and efficient memory management. However, it appears that programming with binary data is a daunting task that creates much burden for the developers. To help reduce the burden, we have developed a comprehensive data management library in Hyracks. In this section, we describe case studies and report our own experience with three real-world projects to show the development effort under this design.

4.1 Case Study 1: Quick Sort

In this case study, we compare the major parts of two implementations of quick sort, one in Hyracks manipulating binary data using our library, and the other manipulating objects using the standard Java library (e.g., `Collections.sort()`). The code shown below is the method `siftDown`, which is the core component of the quick sort algorithm. We first show its implementation in JDK.

```
private static void siftDown(Accessor acc,
                  int start, int end) {
  for (int parent = start ; parent < end ; ) {
    int child1 = start + (parent - start) * 2 + 1;
    int child2 = child1 + 1;
    int child = (child2 > end) ? child1
                    : (acc.compare(child1, child2)
                  < 0) ? child2 : child1;
    if (child > end)
        break;
    if (acc.compare(parent, child) < 0)
        acc.swap(parent, child);
    parent = child;
  }
}
```

The corresponding implementation using our library is a segment in the `sort` method, shown as follows:

```
private void sort(int[] tPointers, int offset, int length){
  ......
  while(true){
    ......
    while (c >= b) {
        int cmp = compare(tPointers, c, mi, mj, mv);
        if (cmp < 0) {
          break;
        }
        if (cmp == 0) {
          swap(tPointers, c, d--);
        }
        --c;
    }
    if (b > c)
        break;
    swap(tPointers, b++, c--);
  }
  ......
}
```

The `compare` method eventually calls a user-defined comparator implementation in which two accessors are bound to the two input byte regions once-at-a-time for the actual comparison. The following code snippet is an example comparator implementation.

```
public class StudentBinaryComparator implements
                  IBinaryComparator{
  private StudentAccessor acc1 =
          StudentAccessor.getAvailableAccessor();
  private StudentAccessor acc2 =
          StudentAccessor.getAvailableAccessor();

  public int compare(byte[] data1, int start1, int len1,
      byte[] data2, int start2, int len2){
    acc1.set(data1, start1, len1);
    acc2.set(data2, start2, len2);
    return acc1.compare(acc2);
  }
}
```

Method `getAvailableAccessor` can be implemented in different ways, depending on the materialization mode. For example, it can directly return a new `StudentAccessor` object or use an object pool to cache and reuse old objects. As one can tell, the data access code paths in both implementation are well encapsulated with libraries, which allows application developers to focus on the business logic (when to call `compare` and `swap`) rather than writing code to access data. As such, the two different implementations have comparable numbers of lines of code.

4.2 Case Study 2: Print Records

The second case study is to use a certain format to print data records from a byte array. A typical Java implementation is as follows.

```
private void printData(byte[] data) {
  Reader input = new BufferedReader(new InputStreamReader(
          new DataInputStream(new ByteArrayInputStream(
          data))));
  String line = null;
  while((line = input.readLine())!= null){
    String[] fields = line.split(',');
    //print the record
    ......
  }
  input.close();
}
```

The above implementation reads `String` objects from the input, splits them into fields, and prints them out. In this implementation, the number of created `String` objects is proportional to the cardinality of records multiplied by the number of fields per record. The following code snippet is our printer implementation using the bloat-aware design paradigm.

```
private void printData(byte[] data) {
  PageAccessor pageAcc =
      PageAccessor.getAvailableAccessor(data);
  RecordPrintingAccessor recordAcc =
      RecordPrintingAccessor.getAvailableAccessor();
  while(pageAcc.nextRecord()){
    //print the record in the set call
    recordAcc.set(toBinaryRegion(pageAcc));
  }
}
```

In our implementation, we build one accessor graph for printing, let binary data flow through the accessor graph, and print every record by traversing the accessor graph and calling the `set` method on each accessor. It is easy to see that the number of created objects is bounded by the number of nodes of the accessor graph while the programming effort is not significantly increased.

4.3 Big Data Projects using the Bloat-Aware Design

The proposed design paradigm has already been used in six Java-based open-source Big Data processing systems, listed as follows:

- Hyracks [4] is a data parallel platform that runs data-intensive jobs on a cluster of shared-nothing machines. It executes jobs in the form of directed acyclic graphs that consist of user-defined data processing operators and data redistribution connectors.

- Algebricks [1] is a generalized, extensible, data model-agnostic, and language-independent algebra/optimization layer which is intended to facilitate the implementation of new high-level languages that process Big Data in parallel.

- AsterixDB [2] is a semi-structured parallel Big Data management system, which is built on-top-of Algebricks and Hyracks.

- VXQuery [6] is data-parallel XQuery processing engine on top of Algebricks and Hyracks as well.

- Pregelix [5] is Big Giraph analytics platform that supports the bulk-synchronous vertex-oriented programming model [29]. It internally uses Hyracks as the run-time execution engine.

- Hivesterix [3] is a SQL-like layer on top of Algebricks and Hyracks; it reuses the modules of the grammar and first-order run-time functions from HiveQL [11].

In these six projects, the proposed bloat-aware design paradigm is used in the data processing code paths (e.g., the runtime data processing operators such as join, group-by, and sort, as well as the user-defined runtime functions such as plus, minus, sum, and count) while the control code paths (e.g., the runtime control events, the query language parser, the algebra rewriting/optimization, and the job generation module) still use the traditional object-oriented design. Note that for Big Data applications, usually the control path is well isolated from the data path changes (e.g., data format changes) because they execute on different machines — the control path is on the master (controller) machines while the data path is on the slave machines.

We show a comparison of the lines-of-code (LOC) of the control paths and the data paths in those projects, as listed in Table 2. On average, the data path takes about 36.84% of the code base, which is much smaller than the size of the control path. Based on the feedback from the development teams, programming and debugging the data processing components consumes approximately 2× as much time as doing that with the traditional object-orientated design. However, overall, since the data processing components take only 36.84% of the total development effort, the actual development overhead should be much smaller than 2×.

4.4 Future Work

The major limitation of the proposed technique is that it requires developers to manipulate low-level, binary representation of data, leading to increased difficulty in programming and debugging. We are in the process of adding another-level-of-indirection to address this issue— we are developing annotation and compiler support to allow for the declarative specifications of data structures. The resulting system will allow developers to annotate data item classes and provide relational specifications. The compiler will automatically generate code that uses the Hyracks library from the user specifications. We hope this system will enable developers to develop high-performance Big Data applications with a low human effort.

5. Performance Evaluation

This section presents a set of experiments focusing on performance comparisons between implementations with and without the proposed design paradigm. All experiments were conducted on a cluster of 10 IBM research machines. Each machine has a 4-core Intel Xeon 2.27 GHz processor, 12GB RAM, and 4 300GB 10,000 rpm SATA disk drives, and runs CentOS 5.5 and Java HotSpot(TM) 64-bit server VM (build17.0-b16, mixed node). JVM command line option "-Xmx10g" was used for all our experiments. We use a parallel generational GC in HotSpot, which combines parallel Scavenge (i.e., copying) for the young generation and parallel Mark-Sweep-Compact for the old generation. We collected the application running times and the JVM heap usage statistics in all the 10 machines. Their average is reported in this section. The rest of this section presents experimental studies of our design paradigm on the overall scalability (Section 5.1), the packing factors (Section 5.2), and the GC costs (Section 5.3).

5.1 Effectiveness On Overall Scalability: Using PageRank

The Pregelix [5] system mentioned in Section 4 supports nearly the same user interfaces and functionalities as Giraph, but uses the bloat-aware design paradigm. Internally, Pregelix employs a Hyracks runtime dataflow pipeline that contains several data processing operators (i.e., sort, group-by and join) and connectors (i.e.,

m-to-n hash partitioning merging connector) to execute graph processing jobs. Pregelix supports out-of-core computations, as it uses disk-based operators (e.g., external sort, external group-by, and index outer join) in the dataflow to deal with large amounts of data that cannot be accommodated in the main memory. In Pregelix, both the data storage storage design and data processor design are enabled: it stores all data in pages but employs accessors during data processing. The code shown in Section 3.2 is exactly what we used to process vertices.

In order to quantify the potential efficiency gains, we compared the performance of PageRank between Pregelix and Giraph. The goal of this experiment is not to understand the out-of-core performance, but rather to investigate the impact of memory bloat. Therefore, the PageRank algorithm was performed on a subset of Yahoo!'s publicly available AltaVista Web Page Hyperlink Connectivity Graph dataset [48], a snapshot of the World Wide Web from 2002. The subset consists of a total of $561, 365, 953$ vertices, each of which represents a web page. The size of the decompressed data is 27.8GB, which, if distributed appropriately, should easily fit into the memory of the 10 machines (e.g., 2.78GB for each machine). Each record in the dataset consists of a source vertex identifier and an array of destination vertex identifiers forming the links among different webpages in the graph.

In the experiment, we also ran PageRank with two smaller (1/100 and 1/10 of the original) datasets to obtain the scale-up trend. Figure 5 (a), (b), and (c) show, respectively, the overall execution times for the processing of the three datasets, their GC times, and their heap usages. It is easy to see that the total GC time for each dataset is less than 3% of the overall execution time. The JVM heap size is obtained by measuring the overall JVM memory consumption from the operating system. In general, it is slightly larger than the raw data size for each machine (i.e., 2.78GB). This is because extra memory is needed to (1) store object metadata (as we still have objects) and (2) sort and group messages. We also ran the Giraph PageRank implementation on the same three input datasets, but could not succeed for any of the datasets. Giraph crashed with `java.lang.OutOfMemoryError` in all the cases. We confirmed from the Giraph developers that the crash was because of the skewness (e.g., www.yahoo.com has a huge number of inbound links and messages) in the Yahoo! AltaVista Web Page Hyperlink Connectivity Graph dataset, combined with the object-based data representation.

5.2 Effectiveness On Packing Factor: Using External Sort

As the second experiment, we compared the performance of two implementations of the standard external sort algorithm [36] on Hyracks. One uses Java objects to represent data records, while the other employs Java memory pages. The goal here is to understand the impact of the low packing factor of the object-based data representation on performance as well as the benefit of the bloat-aware design paradigm.

In the Java object-based implementation, the operator takes deserialized records (i.e., in objects) as input and puts them into a list. Once the number of buffered records exceeds a user-defined threshold, method `sort` is invoked on the list and then the sorted list is dumped to a run file. The processing of the incoming data results in a number of run files. Next, the merge phase starts. This phase reads and merges run files using a priority queue to produce output records. During the merge phase, run files are read into the main memory one-block(32KB)-at-a-time. If the number of files is too large and one pass can not merge all of them, multiple merge passes need be performed.

In the page-based implementation, we never load records from pages into objects. Therefore, the page-based storage removes the header/pointer overhead and improves the packing factor. We im-

Project	Overall #LOC	Control #LOC	Data #LOC	Data #LOC Percentage
Hyracks	125930	71227	54803	43.52%
Algebricks	40116	36033	4083	10.17%
AsterixDB	140013	93071	46942	33.53%
VXQuery	45416	19224	26192	57.67%
Pregelix	18411	11958	6453	35.05%
Hivesterix	18503	13910	4593	33.01%
Overall	**388389**	**245323**	**143066**	**36.84%**

Table 2. The line-of-code statistics of Big Data projects which uses the bloat-aware design.

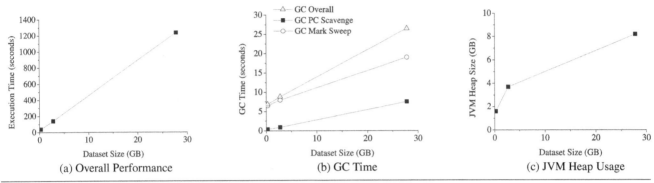

(a) Overall Performance   (b) GC Time   (c) JVM Heap Usage

Figure 5. PageRank Performance on Pregelix.

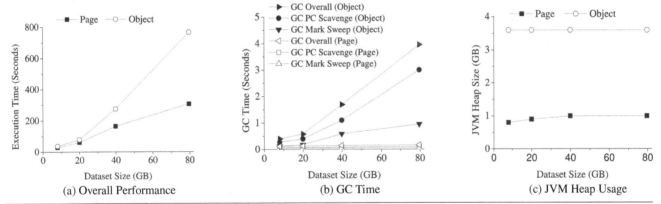

(a) Overall Performance   (b) GC Time   (c) JVM Heap Usage

Figure 6. ExternalSort Performance.

plemented a quick sort algorithm to sort in-memory records at the binary level. In this experiment, we used the TPC-H[5] lineitem table as the input data, where each record represents an item in a transaction order. We generated TPC-H data at $10\times$, $25\times$, $50\times$ and $100\times$ scales, which correspond to 7.96GB, 19.9GB, 39.8GB and 79.6GB line-item tables, respectively. Each dataset was partitioned among the 10 nodes in a round-robin manner. Particularly, it was divided into 40 partitions, one partition per disk drive (recall that each machine has 4 disk drives).

The task was executed as follows: we created a total of 40 concurrent sorters across the cluster, each of which reads a partition of data locally, sorted them, and wrote the sorted data back to the disk. In this experiment, the page-based implementation used a 32MB sort buffer. The object-based implementation used 5000 the maximal number of in-memory records. The results of two

different external sort implementations are plotted in Figure 6. The run-time statistics include the overall execution time (Figure 6 (a)), the GC overhead (Figure 6 (b)), and the JVM heap usage (Figure 6 (c)). Note that the Scavenge and Mark-Sweep lines show the GC costs for the young generation and the old generation, respectively. Because sorting a single memory buffer (either 32MB pages or 5000 records) is fast, most data objects are *short-lived and small*, and their lifetimes are usually limited within the iterations where they are created. They rarely get copied into old generations and thus the nursery scans dominate the GC effort.

From Figure 6 (a), it is clear to see that as the size of dataset increases, the page-based implementation scales much better (e.g., $2.5\times$ faster on 79.6GB input) than the object-based implementation, and the improvement factor keeps increasing with the increase of the dataset size. The following two factors may contribute to this improvement: (1) due to the low packing factor, the object-

[5] The standard data warehousing benchmark, http://www.tpc.org/tpch/

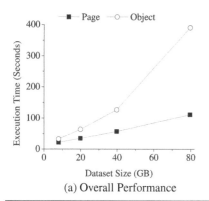 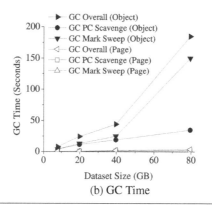 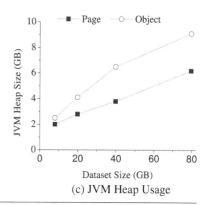

(a) Overall Performance (b) GC Time (c) JVM Heap Usage

Figure 7. Hash-based Grouping Performance.

based implementation often has more merge passes (hence more I/O) than the page-based implementation, and (2) the use of objects to represent data items leads to increased JVM heap size and hence the operating system has less memory for the file system cache. For example, in the case where the size of the input data is 79.6GB, the page-based implementation has only one merge pass while the object-based one has two merge passes. The page-based implementation also has much less GC time than the object-based implementation (Figure 6 (b)). Figure 6 (c) shows that the amount of memory required by the object-based implementation is almost 4× larger than that of the page-based implementation, even though the former holds much less actual data in memory (i.e., reflected by the need of an additional merge phase).

5.3 Effectiveness On GC Costs: Using Hash-Based Grouping

The goal of the experiment described in this subsection is to understand the GC overhead in the presence of large volumes of objects and references. The input data and scales for this experiment are the same as those in Section 5.2. For comparison, we implemented a logical SQL query by hand-coding the physical execution plan and runtime operators, in order to count how many items there are in each order:

```
SELECT l_orderkey, COUNT(*) AS items
FROM lineitem
GROUP BY l_orderkey;
```

We created two different implementations of the underlying hash-based grouping as Hyracks operators. They were exactly the same except that one of them used the object-based hash table (e.g., `java.util.Hashtable`) for grouping and the other used a page-based hash table implementation (e.g., all the intermediate states along with the grouping keys were stored in pages). The hash table size (number of buckets) was 10,485,767 for this experiment, because larger hash tables are often encouraged in Big Data applications to reduce collisions.

The Hyracks job of this task had four operators along the pipeline: a file scan operator (FS), a hash grouping operator (G1), another hash grouping operator (G2), and a file write operator (FW). In the job, FS was locally connected to G1, and then the output of G1 was hash partitioned and fed to G2 (using a m-to-n hash partitioning connector). Finally, G2 was locally connected to FW. Each operator had 40 clones across the cluster, one per partition. Note that G1 was used to group data locally and compress the data in order for it to be sent to the network. G2 performed the final grouping and aggregation.

Figure 7 shows the performance of the two different hash-based grouping implementations over the four input datasets. The

measurements include the overall performance (Figure 7 (a)), the GC time (Figure 7 (b)), and the JVM heap size (Figure 7(c)). From Figure 7(a), one can see that the implementation with the page-based hash table scales much better to the size of data than the other one: in the case where the size of input data is 79.6GB, the former is already 3.5× faster than the latter and the improvement factor keeps growing. In Figure 7 (b), we can clearly see that the use of the object-based hash table makes the GC costs go up to 47% of the overall execution time while the page-based hash table does not add much overhead (<3% of the overall execution time). A similar observation can be made on the memory consumption: Figure 7 (c) shows that the object-based implementation leads to much larger memory consumption than the page-based one.

Summary Our experimental results clearly demonstrate that, for many data-processing tasks, the bloat-aware design paradigm can lead to far better performance. The source code of all the experiments can be found at: http://code.google.com/p/hyracks.

6. Related Work

There exists a large body of work on efficient memory management techniques and data processing algorithms. This section discusses only those that are most closely related to the proposed work. These techniques are classified into three categories: data-processing infrastructures implemented in managed languages, software bloat analysis, and region-based memory management systems.

Java-based data-processing infrastructures Telegraph [37] is a data management system implemented in Java. It uses native byte arrays to store data and has its own memory manager for object allocation, deallocation, and memory de-fragmentation. However, because it is built on top of native memory, developers lose various benefits of a managed language and have to worry about low-level memory correctness issues such as dangling pointers, buffer overflow, and memory leaks. Our approach overcomes the problem by building applications on top of the Java managed memory, providing high efficiency and yet retaining most of the benefits provided by a managed runtime.

Hadoop [10] is a widely-used open-source MapReduce implementation. Although it provides a certain level of object reuse for sorting algorithms, its (major) map and reduce interfaces are object-based. The user has to create a great number of objects to implement a new algorithm on top of Hadoop. For example, the reduce-side join implementation in Hive [11] uses a Java `HashMap` in the reduce function to hold the inner branch records, which is very likely to suffer from the same performance problem (i.e., high GC costs) as discussed in Section 2.

Other data-processing infrastructures such as Spark [49] and Storm [40] also make heavy use of Java objects in both their core data-processing modules and their application programming interfaces, and thus they are vulnerable to memory bloat as reported in this paper.

Software bloat analysis Software bloat analysis [8, 30–33, 38, 41–47] attempts to find, remove, and prevent performance problems due to inefficiencies in the code execution and the use of memory. Prior work [32, 33] proposes metrics to provide performance assessment of use of data structures. Their observation that a large portion of the heap is not used to store data is also confirmed in our study. In addition to measure memory usage, our work proposes optimizations specifically targeting the problems we found and our experimental results show that these optimizations are very effective.

Work by Dufour *et al.* [20] uses a blended escape analysis to characterize and find excessive use of temporary data structures. By approximating object lifetimes, the analysis has been shown to be useful in classifying the usage of newly created objects in the problematic areas. Shankar *et al.* propose Jolt [38], an approach that makes aggressive method inlining decisions based on the identification of regions that make extensive use of temporary objects. Work by Xu *et al.* [43] detects memory bloat by profiling copy activities, and their later work [42] looks for high-cost-low-benefit data structures to detect execution bloat. Our work is the first attempt to analyze bloat under the context of Big Data applications and perform effective optimizations to remove bloat.

Region-based memory management Region-based memory management was first used in the implementations of functional languages [7, 39] such as Standard ML [25], and then was extended to Prolog [28], C [21, 22, 24, 26], and real-time Java [13, 17, 27]. More recently, some mark-region hybrid methods such as Immix [15] combine tracing GC with regions to improve GC performance for Java. Our work uses a region-based approach to manage pages, but in a different context — the emerging Big Data applications. Data are stored in pages in the binary form leading to both increased packing factor and decreased memory management cost.

Value types Expanded types in Eiffel and value types in C# are used to declare data with simple structures. However, these types cannot solve the entire bloat problem. In these languages, objects still need to be used to represent data with complicated structures, such as hash maps or lists. The scalability issues that we found in Big Data applications are primarily due to inefficiencies inherent in the object-oriented system design, rather than problems with any specific implementation of a managed language.

7. Conclusion

This paper presents a bloat-aware design paradigm for Java-based Big Data applications. The study starts with a quantitative analysis of memory bloat using real-world examples, in order for us to understand the impact of excessive object creation on the memory consumption and GC costs. To alleviate this negative influence, we propose a bloat-aware design paradigm, including: merging small objects and accessing data at the binary level. We have performed an extensive set of experiments, and the experimental results have demonstrated that implementations following the design paradigm have much better performance and scalability than the applications that use regular Java objects. The design paradigm can be applied to other managed languages such as C# as well. We believe that the results of this work demonstrate the viability of implementing efficient Big Data applications in a managed, object-oriented language, and open up possibilities for the programming language and systems community to develop novel optimizations targeting data-intensive computing.

Acknowledgements

We thank anonymous reviewers for their thorough comments. Our Big Data projects using the bloat-aware design are supported by NSF IIS awards 0910989, 0910859, 0910820, and 0844574, a grant from the UC Discovery program, a matching donation from eBay, and generous industrial gifts from Google, HTC, Microsoft and Oracle Labs.

References

[1] Algebricks. https://code.google.com/p/hyracks/source/browse/#git%2Ffullstack%2Falgebricks.

[2] AsterixDB. https://code.google.com/p/asterixdb/wiki/AsterixAlphaRelease.

[3] Hivesterix. http://hyracks.org/projects/hivesterix/.

[4] Hyracks: A data parallel platform. http://code.google.com/p/hyracks/.

[5] Pregelix. http://hyracks.org/projects/pregelix/.

[6] VXQuery. http://incubator.apache.org/vxquery/.

[7] A. Aiken, M. Fähndrich, and R. Levien. Better static memory management: improving region-based analysis of higher-order languages. In *ACM SIGPLAN Conference on Programming Language Design and Implementation (PLDI)*, pages 174–185, 1995.

[8] E. Altman, M. Arnold, S. Fink, and N. Mitchell. Performance analysis of idle programs. In *ACM SIGPLAN International Conference on Object-Oriented Programming, Systems, Languages, and Applications (OOPSLA)*, pages 739–753, 2010.

[9] Giraph: Open-source implementation of Pregel. http://incubator.apache.org/giraph/.

[10] Hadoop: Open-source implementation of MapReduce. http://hadoop.apache.org.

[11] The Hive Project. http://hive.apache.org/.

[12] The Mahout Project. http://mahout.apache.org/.

[13] W. S. Beebee and M. C. Rinard. An implementation of scoped memory for real-time java. In *International Conference on Embedded Software (EMSOFT)*, pages 289–305, 2001.

[14] A. Behm, V. R. Borkar, M. J. Carey, R. Grover, C. Li, N. Onose, R. Vernica, A. Deutsch, Y. Papakonstantinou, and V. J. Tsotras. AS-TERIX: towards a scalable, semistructured data platform for evolving-world models. *Distrib. Parallel Databases*, 29:185–216, June 2011.

[15] S. M. Blackburn and K. S. McKinley. Immix: a mark-region garbage collector with space efficiency, fast collection, and mutator performance. In *ACM SIGPLAN Conference on Programming Language Design and Implementation (PLDI)*, pages 22–32, 2008.

[16] V. R. Borkar, M. J. Carey, R. Grover, N. Onose, and R. Vernica. Hyracks: A flexible and extensible foundation for data-intensive computing. In *International Conference on Data Engineering (ICDE)*, pages 1151–1162, 2011.

[17] C. Boyapati, A. Salcianu, W. Beebee, Jr., and M. Rinard. Ownership types for safe region-based memory management in real-time java. In *ACM SIGPLAN Conference on Programming Language Design and Implementation (PLDI)*, pages 324–337, 2003.

[18] C. Chambers, A. Raniwala, F. Perry, S. Adams, R. R. Henry, R. Bradshaw, and N. Weizenbaum. Flumejava: easy, efficient data-parallel pipelines. In *ACM SIGPLAN Conference on Programming Language Design and Implementation (PLDI)*, pages 363–375, 2010.

[19] J. Dean and S. Ghemawat. MapReduce: Simplified data processing on large clusters. In *USENIX Symposium on Operating Systems Design and Implementation (OSDI)*, pages 137–150, 2004.

[20] B. Dufour, B. G. Ryder, and G. Sevitsky. A scalable technique for characterizing the usage of temporaries in framework-intensive Java applications. In *ACM SIGSOFT International Symposium on the Foundations of Software Engineering (FSE)*, pages 59–70, 2008.

[21] D. Gay and A. Aiken. Memory management with explicit regions. In *ACM SIGPLAN Conference on Programming Language Design and Implementation (PLDI)*, pages 313–323, 1998.

[22] D. Gay and A. Aiken. Language support for regions. In *ACM SIG-PLAN Conference on Programming Language Design and Implementation (PLDI)*, pages 70–80, 2001.

[23] G. Graefe. Query evaluation techniques for large databases. *ACM Comput. Surv.*, 25(2):73–170, 1993.

[24] D. Grossman, G. Morrisett, T. Jim, M. Hicks, Y. Wang, and J. Cheney. Region-based memory management in cyclone. In *ACM SIGPLAN Conference on Programming Language Design and Implementation (PLDI)*, pages 282–293, 2002.

[25] N. Hallenberg, M. Elsman, and M. Tofte. Combining region inference and garbage collection. In *ACM SIGPLAN Conference on Programming Language Design and Implementation (PLDI)*, pages 141–152, 2002.

[26] M. Hicks, G. Morrisett, D. Grossman, and T. Jim. Experience with safe manual memory-management in cyclone. In *International Symposium on Memory Management (ISMM)*, pages 73–84, 2004.

[27] S. Kowshik, D. Dhurjati, and V. Adve. Ensuring code safety without runtime checks for real-time control systems. In *International Conference on Architecture and Synthesis for Embedded Systems (CASES)*, pages 288–297, 2002.

[28] H. Makholm. A region-based memory manager for prolog. In *International Symposium on Memory Management (ISMM)*, pages 25–34, 2000.

[29] G. Malewicz, M. H. Austern, A. J. C. Bik, J. C. Dehnert, I. Horn, N. Leiser, and G. Czajkowski. Pregel: a system for large-scale graph processing. In *ACM SIGMOD International Conference on Management of Data (SIGMOD)*, pages 135–146, 2010.

[30] N. Mitchell, E. Schonberg, and G. Sevitsky. Making sense of large heaps. In *European Conference on Object-Oriented Programming (ECOOP)*, pages 77–97, 2009.

[31] N. Mitchell, E. Schonberg, and G. Sevitsky. Four trends leading to Java runtime bloat. *IEEE Software*, 27(1):56–63, 2010.

[32] N. Mitchell and G. Sevitsky. The causes of bloat, the limits of health. In *ACM SIGPLAN International Conference on Object-Oriented Programming, Systems, Languages, and Applications (OOPSLA)*, pages 245–260, 2007.

[33] N. Mitchell, G. Sevitsky, and H. Srinivasan. Modeling runtime behavior in framework-based applications. In *European Conference on Object-Oriented Programming (ECOOP)*, pages 429–451, 2006.

[34] C. Olston, B. Reed, U. Srivastava, R. Kumar, and A. Tomkins. Pig Latin: a not-so-foreign language for data processing. In *ACM SIGMOD International Conference on Management of Data (SIGMOD)*, pages 1099–1110, 2008.

[35] L. Page, S. Brin, R. Motwani, and T. Winograd. The pagerank citation ranking: Bringing order to the web. Technical Report 1999-66, Stanford InfoLab, November 1999.

[36] R. Ramakrishnan and J. Gehrke. *Database Management Systems (3. ed.)*. McGraw-Hill, 2003.

[37] M. A. Shah, S. Madden, M. J. Franklin, and J. M. Hellerstein. Java support for data-intensive systems: Experiences building the telegraph dataflow system. *SIGMOD Record*, 30(4):103–114, 2001.

[38] A. Shankar, M. Arnold, and R. Bodik. JOLT: Lightweight dynamic analysis and removal of object churn. In *ACM SIGPLAN International Conference on Object-Oriented Programming, Systems, Languages, and Applications (OOPSLA)*, pages 127–142, 2008.

[39] M. Tofte and J.-P. Talpin. Implementation of the typed call-by-value lamda-calculus using a stack of regions. In *ACM SIGPLAN-SIGACT Symposium on Principles of Programming Languages (POPL)*, pages 188–201, 1994.

[40] Storm: dstributed and fault-tolerant realtime computation. https://github.com/nathanmarz/storm.

[41] G. Xu. Finding reusable data structures. In *ACM SIGPLAN International Conference on Object-Oriented Programming, Systems, Languages, and Applications (OOPSLA)*, pages 1017–1034, 2012.

[42] G. Xu, M. Arnold, N. Mitchell, A. Rountev, E. Schonberg, and G. Sevitsky. Finding low-utility data structures. In *ACM SIGPLAN Conference on Programming Language Design and Implementation (PLDI)*, pages 174–186, 2010.

[43] G. Xu, M. Arnold, N. Mitchell, A. Rountev, and G. Sevitsky. Go with the flow: Profiling copies to find runtime bloat. In *ACM SIGPLAN Conference on Programming Language Design and Implementation (PLDI)*, pages 419–430, 2009.

[44] G. Xu, N. Mitchell, M. Arnold, A. Rountev, and G. Sevitsky. Software bloat analysis: Finding, removing, and preventing performance problems in modern large-scale object-oriented applications. In *FSE/SDP Working Conference on the Future of Software Engineering Research (FoSER)*, pages 421–426, 2010.

[45] G. Xu and A. Rountev. Precise memory leak detection for Java software using container profiling. In *International Conference on Software Engineering (ICSE)*, pages 151–160, 2008.

[46] G. Xu and A. Rountev. Detecting inefficiently-used containers to avoid bloat. In *ACM SIGPLAN Conference on Programming Language Design and Implementation (PLDI)*, pages 160–173, 2010.

[47] G. Xu, D. Yan, and A. Rountev. Static detection of loop-invariant data structures. In *European Conference on Object-Oriented Programming (ECOOP)*, pages 738–763, 2012.

[48] Yahoo! Webscope Program. http://webscope.sandbox.yahoo.com/.

[49] M. Zaharia, M. Chowdhury, M. J. Franklin, S. Shenker, and I. Stoica. Spark: cluster computing with working sets. USENIX Workshop on Hot Topics in Cloud Computing, page 10, Berkeley, CA, USA, 2010.

Author Index

www.ingramcontent.com/pod-product-compliance
Lightning Source LLC
LaVergne TN
LVHW060143070326
832902LV00018B/2933

9 781450 321006